PRIVATE CRIMINAL JUSTICE

The United States is in the midst of a significant reevaluation of its criminal justice system, with increasing calls for reforming or defunding the police and efforts to curb mass incarceration. But focusing on the public criminal justice system paints an incomplete picture of how we address criminal activity. In *Private Criminal Justice*, Ric Simmons shows how significant amounts of criminal activity are detected by private police and how many disputes are settled not in public courts, but through informal agreements between the victim and the accused or through adjudicative procedures run by private institutions. In this timely and eye-opening book, Simmons examines the vast, diverse, and underappreciated private criminal justice system, suggesting reforms that can make these private responses fairer and revealing lessons that the private criminal justice system can teach reformers of the public criminal justice system.

Ric Simmons is the Jacob E. Davis and Jacob E. Davis II Chair in Law and the Associate Dean for Faculty and Intellectual Life at The Ohio State University Moritz College of Law. He is the author of *Smart Surveillance: How to Interpret the Fourth Amendment in the Twenty-First Century* (2019) and the coauthor of four textbooks on criminal procedure and evidence.

Private Criminal Justice

HOW PRIVATE PARTIES ARE ENFORCING CRIMINAL LAW AND TRANSFORMING OUR JUSTICE SYSTEM

RIC SIMMONS

The Ohio State University

Shaftesbury Road, Cambridge CB2 8EA, United Kingdom

One Liberty Plaza, 20th Floor, New York, NY 10006, USA

477 Williamstown Road, Port Melbourne, VIC 3207, Australia

314–321, 3rd Floor, Plot 3, Splendor Forum, Jasola District Centre, New Delhi – 110025, India

103 Penang Road, #05–06/07, Visioncrest Commercial, Singapore 238467

Cambridge University Press is part of Cambridge University Press & Assessment, a department of the University of Cambridge.

We share the University's mission to contribute to society through the pursuit of education, learning and research at the highest international levels of excellence.

www.cambridge.org
Information on this title: www.cambridge.org/9781009347174

DOI: 10.1017/9781009347181

© Ric Simmons 2024

This publication is in copyright. Subject to statutory exception and to the provisions of relevant collective licensing agreements, no reproduction of any part may take place without the written permission of Cambridge University Press & Assessment.

First published 2024

A catalogue record for this publication is available from the British Library

Library of Congress Cataloging-in-Publication Data
NAMES: Simmons, Ric, author.
TITLE: Private criminal justice : how private parties are enforcing criminal law and transforming our justice / Ric Simmons, Ohio State University.
DESCRIPTION: Cambridge, United Kingdom ; New York, NY : Cambridge University Press, 2024. | Includes bibliographical references and index.
IDENTIFIERS: LCCN 2023015889 (print) | LCCN 2023015890 (ebook) | ISBN 9781009347174 (hardback) | ISBN 9781009347136 (paperback) | ISBN 9781009347181 (ebook)
SUBJECTS: LCSH: Criminal justice, Administration of – United States. | Police, Private – Legal status, laws, etc. – United States. | Dispute resolution (Law) – United States. | Alternatives to imprisonment – United States. | Alternative convictions – United States.
CLASSIFICATION: LCC KF9223 .S556 2024 (print) | LCC KF9223 (ebook) | DDC 345.73/05–dc23/eng/20230712
LC record available at https://lccn.loc.gov/2023015889
LC ebook record available at https://lccn.loc.gov/2023015890

ISBN 978-1-009-34717-4 Hardback
ISBN 978-1-009-34713-6 Paperback

Cambridge University Press & Assessment has no responsibility for the persistence or accuracy of URLs for external or third-party internet websites referred to in this publication and does not guarantee that any content on such websites is, or will remain, accurate or appropriate.

Contents

Acknowledgments		*page* vi
	Introduction: The Rise of Private Criminal Justice	1
1	Criminal Justice without the State	9
2	A Brief History of Crime	29
3	Public Failings, Private Opportunities	40
4	Private Law Enforcement	54
5	Private Criminal Settlements as Plea Bargains	73
6	Private Criminal Settlements as Blackmail	101
7	Private Adjudications	117
8	Private Dispositions	134
9	Regulating Private Criminal Justice	156
10	The Verdict on Private Criminal Justice	170
Notes		194
Index		244

Acknowledgments

For their feedback on earlier incarnations of this work, I would like to thank Erin C. Blondel, John Braithwaite, Sarah Cole, Elizabeth Joh, Brenner Fissell, Michael Gentithes, Joe Kennedy, Guha Krishnamurthi, Michael J. Zydney Mannheimer, Alice Ristroph, and David Sklansky. I am indebted to my many wonderful Ohio State colleagues who participated in numerous faculty workshops for different parts of this book. I also received helpful feedback from the faculty of Salmon P. Chase College of Law at Northern Kentucky University and from participants in the CrimFest conference in the summer of 2021 and the summer of 2022. I would like to extend further thanks to Jessica Ackerman, Courtney Cook, Shawn Davisson, Leah Finley, Doug Hattaway, Chloe Palmer, and Brian Stewart for their research assistance. I especially want to thank my research assistant Nathan Rhodes for his extremely helpful contributions in pulling this book together. Above all, and as always, I give my thanks to Angie Lloyd for her constant support and invaluable feedback.

Portions of the following articles appear in a substantially reworked form in this book: *Legal Vigilantes*, AMERICAN CRIMINAL LAW REVIEW (forthcoming 2024); *Constitutional Double Standards: The Unintended Consequences of Reducing Police Presence*, 91 GEORGE WASHINGTON LAW REVIEW (2023); *Private Plea Bargains*, 89 NORTH CAROLINA LAW REVIEW 1125 (2011); and *Private Criminal Justice*, 42 WAKE FOREST LAW REVIEW 911 (2007).

Introduction: The Rise of Private Criminal Justice

Every year, over twenty-seven million crimes are committed in the United States, including nearly four million violent crimes. In many of these cases, the victim or another witness reports the crime to the police, thereby initiating a case in the public criminal justice system. However, this course of action is an *atypical* response to criminal activity. Surveys of crime victims show that over half of violent crimes, and about two-thirds of all property crimes, are never reported to the police. This translates to over eighteen million crimes annually that never enter the public criminal justice system.[1] Since that number only counts crimes with identifiable victims, such as assault and theft, it does not include most "victimless" crimes, such as narcotic sales, drug or firearm possession, prostitution, driving while intoxicated, and vandalism against state property. As there are no reporting statistics for these crimes, it is likely that many millions of them are witnessed by private individuals but not reported to the police. This raises a critically important question: When witnesses do not report crimes to the police, what actions do they take?

Many times the answer is: nothing. The witness or victim may not know the identity of the perpetrator. In other cases, the perpetrator is a friend or a family member, and the victim wishes to forgive and forget. Or perhaps the perpetrator is able to intimidate or otherwise persuade the witness not to report the crime. Or perhaps the injury – whether to person or property – is so slight that it is simply easier for the witness to move on rather than take any action (especially if the witness was not a victim of the crime).[2] Any of these reasons could result in a witness taking no action in response to criminal activity.

However, many non-reporting witnesses and victims do take some action.[3] Instead of calling the police, these individuals pursue private justice, whether by making a deal with the perpetrator to obtain something of value, bringing the case to a private adjudicative body, or taking direct action against the perpetrator themselves. These private responses are so common that it is fair to say that they – not the process and punishment imposed by the state – constitute our society's primary response to criminal activity. However, little is known about these private responses.

They are often conducted in secret and they are regulated lightly, if at all, by a patchwork of rules and norms.

The vast private criminal justice system begins at the law enforcement stage. Private security officers outnumber public police officers by nearly a two to one margin.[4] They conduct residential security patrols; monitor shoppers in department stores; safeguard warehouses; patrol college campuses and shopping malls; and guard factories, casinos, office parks, schools, and parking lots. Companies maintain internal security personnel to monitor their workers, investigate employee theft, and detect customer fraud. The rise of the internet has created an entirely new branch of the private security industry, as companies, governments, and nonprofit organizations hire specialists to ensure that their presence on the web is secure.[5] Beyond this diverse army of paid private security are reserves of volunteers who form neighborhood watch groups or safety patrols, like the Guardian Angels in New York City or the Minutemen Project along the southern border.

When these private police or volunteers apprehend a suspect, they have no duty to refer them to a state prosecutor. Private police serve the interests of their clients – private companies or homeowners' associations – which, for a variety of reasons, often have no interest in traditional prosecution and prefer a private alternative response. Volunteers who engage in private law enforcement respond to criminal activity in ways that are based on their own interest and values, which often does not include contacting the authorities. And these formal private organizations are not the only on-ramp to the private criminal justice system: As noted above, other private individuals may see criminal activity and decide that the optimal response to the crime – whether it is vigilante justice, public shaming, or simply threatening to call the police if the alleged perpetrator does not take some remedial action – is preferable to involving the authorities.

Private responses often involve a sophisticated procedure for dealing with suspected criminals. For example, many universities and professional associations operate private tribunals, with their own versions of due process. Other private parties contract with third party companies to deal with alleged criminals. For many years, major retail stores in the United States, including Walmart and Bloomingdale's, maintained a contract with the Corrective Education Company (CEC), a private corporation. When store security caught a suspected shoplifter, the store gave the alleged perpetrator a choice: either the store would call the police or the shoplifter could enroll in one of the CEC's "restorative justice programs" at the cost of $400–$500 in "tuition."[6] The vast majority of those who were apprehended chose to pay the money rather than enter the public criminal justice system.

Other private entities and individuals operate similarly, but on a smaller scale. In some communities, local neighborhood boards seek to rehabilitate those suspected of committing crimes in their neighborhood; in other communities, neighborhood watch officers record the license plate numbers of individuals who come to their street to buy drugs and then send the buyers letters threatening to call the police if they return to the neighborhood. After a company detective identifies financial malfeasance by an employee, the business might choose to quietly fire the perpetrator rather than contact the authorities. A wife who suffers from abuse could threaten to leave her husband and take the children with her unless he stops drinking. Some individuals or groups act as vigilantes, imposing their own punishment upon those whom they believe have committed a crime. All of these are examples of private responses to criminal behavior – methods of resolving the criminal dispute without involving the public criminal justice system. In these and many other contexts, the response to criminal activity is kept completely private; there are no police, no prosecutors, no courts, and no jails involved.

Most Americans are familiar with the basic processes of our public criminal justice system. The process always starts with the enforcement stage: Police officers patrol neighborhoods, investigate crime, and make arrests. Next comes the adjudication stage, in which prosecutors file charges and argue cases to judges and juries, defense attorneys represent their clients, and judges oversee hearings and trials. The final step is the disposition stage: After a trial verdict or a plea bargain, a judge will impose a sentence, such as a fine, probation, or incarceration.

Enforcement, adjudication, and disposition are the component parts of any criminal justice system. The goals of the public criminal justice system underpin these components and determine when the state decides to bring its unique coercive power against its own citizens. Criminal justice systems exist for both a moral and a practical purpose. Morally, the state attempts to punish individuals who violate society's shared values and restores the dignity of the victim of the crime. Practically, the state tries to prevent future crimes – by deterring future criminal conduct, incarcerating the most dangerous individuals to incapacitate them, or (less often) rehabilitating them so that they no longer engage in criminal activity.

Conventional wisdom holds that the state is an essential party to the criminal justice system because only the state can define what conduct is criminal, and the state's monopoly on the legitimate use of force means that only state actors should apprehend lawbreakers, coerce them into standing trial, and impose punishment. Meanwhile, the same conventional wisdom states that the goals of the criminal justice system – punishment for moral wrongs and preventing future harms – are primarily the concerns of the state, and it is inappropriate and even dangerous for private parties to take matters into their own hands. When private parties try to enforce criminal laws, they are labelled as vigilantes pursuing vengeance, and their actions in responding to crime are often considered crimes in themselves.

However, it is increasingly clear that this conventional wisdom is wrong. The public criminal justice system that every American knows about is only a part of the story – and perhaps not even the most important part. While most policymakers and criminal law scholars focus on the public criminal justice system, a large proportion of our society's response to criminal activity is occurring outside the public sphere. As the earlier examples show, these responses go far beyond vigilante actions.

They include sophisticated adjudicative procedures, formal agreements, and informal understandings, as well as threats, promises, and rehabilitative efforts. The actors who make up the private criminal justice system are sprawling and diverse: They include sizeable entities such as major universities, retail stores, and large corporations, as well as smaller companies and even individuals who detect criminal activity and decide to deal with the suspected perpetrator on their own rather than call the police. This parallel criminal justice system – the private criminal justice system – has become the primary way that our society responds to criminal activity. Thus, we cannot truly understand our country's criminal justice policy without acknowledging and understanding the private criminal justice system.

Most Americans are at least vaguely aware of some aspects of the private criminal justice system. In fact, both victims and the general public often expect private institutions to resolve criminal cases and are highly critical when they perceive that private institutions fail to reach a just disposition. When a professional athlete is accused of domestic violence, society looks to the professional sports organization rather than the state to impose a suitable punishment. When a sexual assault allegedly occurs on a college campus, the victim often turns to university disciplinary proceedings rather than to the criminal courts to resolve the case. However, the private criminal justice system extends beyond these well-known examples. Most people do not realize the degree to which private entities have taken over our criminal justice system and the implications that this has on our criminal justice policy. This book seeks to uncover the surprising breadth and scale of the private criminal justice system and describe its various incarnations, from individual agreements between victims and perpetrators to entire industries that have developed around adjudicating criminal disputes.

In addition to describing the private criminal justice system, this book has two other goals. The first is to examine why the private system has become so prevalent. There are many reasons why private parties might decide to bypass the police, prosecutors, courts, and jails of the traditional public criminal justice system, such as streamlined procedures and dispositions that are tailored to the needs of the victims. Structural reasons have also contributed to this shift. A growing number of people are dissatisfied with both the means and the ends of the public criminal justice system. In 1999, 75 percent of Americans stated they were in favor of "totally revamping the way the criminal justice system works."[7] If anything, that number has increased in subsequent decades: A 2021 Gallup Poll found that only 20 percent of Americans have "a great deal" or "quite a lot" of confidence in the criminal justice system, ranking the institution below public schools, banks, and organized labor – the only institutions it beat were big business, television news, and Congress.[8] Many communities of color do not trust the police to treat them fairly, and calls to reduce police footprints or even to abolish the police reached a peak during the summer of 2020. Many public courthouses are associated with assembly-line justice, overworked public defenders, overzealous prosecutors, and the widespread substitution of plea bargains for trials.

At the back end of the system, we seem to have given up on rehabilitation altogether, and mass incarceration imposes an enormous economic, social, and personal cost on society, a cost that – like every other aspect of the public criminal justice system – disproportionately affects minority populations.

Perhaps most significantly, victims are rarely satisfied with how they are treated or with the outcomes of their criminal cases. Studies show that involvement with the criminal justice system can exacerbate the harm of the initial crime, and that the system does not meet the needs of victims.[9] Victims' rights groups have worked over the last forty years to pass legislation that gives victims the right to be notified and heard at various points in the criminal proceedings. However, such efforts are limited by the very nature of the public criminal justice system, which is designed to meet the needs of the state, using the victim as a means to that end. As the United States Supreme Court held in the 1970s, "a private citizen lacks a judicially cognizable interest in the prosecution or non-prosecution of another,"[10] such that, in most cases, a victim has no formal legal status beyond that of a witness.[11] In contrast, the private criminal justice system gives the victim agency in both its process and its result.

This is not to say that the public criminal justice system is irrelevant to these private resolutions. Many of the private responses take place "in the shadow of the law." Often, the victim and the alleged perpetrator know that their choice is to either resolve the dispute among themselves or take the case to the police. The threat of the public criminal justice system can persuade suspects to accept a punishment at the hands of the private entity. In addition, the procedures used by private entities are often judged by whether they are as robust as those used by criminal courts. Thus, the outcomes and processes of the public criminal justice system have a significant effect on the outcomes and processes of the various aspects of the private criminal justice system.

But, make no mistake, the methods, goals, and ultimate effects of the private criminal justice system are distinct from those of its public counterpart. In fact, some versions of the private criminal justice system operate not in the shadow of the public system, but rather in parallel with it. Private organizations occasionally institute their own proceedings and impose their own punishments, regardless of whether the public system is involved. Compared with its public counterpart, the private criminal justice system is far more likely to detect criminal activity; it imposes more lenient punishments; and it operates more efficiently. At the same time, the private criminal justice system is less concerned with individual rights and due process; it often involves massive power imbalances; and it is much less transparent.

This leads to the final goal of the book: to evaluate the social desirability of the private criminal justice system. When private entities respond to criminal conduct, are they only serving their own interests or are they also serving the public interest? Is the private criminal justice system something that we should support and encourage, or something that should be limited and discouraged? In many contexts, relying on private individuals to set our criminal justice policy leads to undesirable results. However, in evaluating the system as a whole, we should compare the procedures and the outcomes of the private system not to some utopian ideal, but to the alternatives offered by the public system. In the end, I will argue that, contrary to popular wisdom, the private criminal justice system is a positive development that can fill the gaps in our public criminal justice system and help lower the crime rate while addressing problems of mass incarceration. The private criminal justice system can facilitate a process I call "soft decriminalization," in which many activities that are now considered criminal – and that usually result in incarceration – are deterred by various private entities, and punished through a variety of non-carceral means. Private entities can also be more effective than their public counterparts in detecting crime, and can do so with fewer resources – and certainly with fewer state resources – leading to greater deterrence and, potentially, lower crime rates overall. Finally, the private criminal justice system can help reform the traditional public system, making it more responsive to the needs of the people it is serving.

Before moving forward, it is important to distinguish between the *private criminal justice system* and the *privatization* of the public criminal justice system. The former occurs whenever private parties respond to criminal activity on their own, without direction from the state. The latter, which is beyond the scope of this book, involves agencies in the public criminal justice system contracting private companies to carry out certain jobs. Many aspects of the post-conviction phase in the public criminal justice system are contracted out to private parties: Approximately 8 percent of prisoners in this country are serving time in a privately run correctional facility.[12] Private organizations also manage some of the treatment, counseling, and rehabilitation programs to which many convicted criminals are sentenced or referred.[13] Public police sometimes pay private companies or individuals to engage in investigations or conduct forensic work. However, this type of "contracting out" does not in itself represent any significant change in criminal justice policy.[14]

Privatization of criminal justice services carries its own costs and benefits,[15] but ultimately a state agency controls the provision of services, which means a prison guard or law enforcement officer is subject to the same rules and restrictions under the law whether hired directly by a state agency or by a company that is in turn hired by a state agency. More importantly, the goals and policies of the police force or prison institution will ultimately be set by the state agency in charge, regardless of whether the services are managed and coordinated by a private corporation.[16]

For example, when Wackenhut Services runs a juvenile detention facility for the federal government, it decides how to design the prison, how many employees to hire, how much to pay them, and what kind of training to give them. However, Wackenhut's treatment of the prisoners must still abide by the statutory and constitutional regulations set out for prison management. There may be abuses, but these abuses are the responsibility of the state entity that hired the private company.

They occur either because the state entity failed to set out the appropriate standards in the contractual arrangement or because it failed to appropriately monitor the actions of the private company for the duration of the contract. In other words, the failure of a state-contracted private corrections company to provide appropriate care for prisoners is doctrinally no different from the failure of a public civil servant (such as a warden of a public prison) to provide appropriate care. The purpose of the private prison's actions is identical to the purpose of the state agency that hired it – or, more accurately, it aligns with the incentives that the state agency put into the contract: To punish the prisoners in accordance with the sentence that the state courts have found to be appropriate.[17]

In contrast, in the private criminal justice system, a private citizen or private entity sets the rules, the goals, and the policies for the provision of the criminal justice services. The rules may be similar to those that regulate the public criminal justice system, but often they are not. Likewise, as noted above, the goals of the parties in the private criminal justice system may coincide with the goals of the public system, but sometimes the two will diverge.

Thus, when Macy's hires guards to watch for shoplifters inside its stores, or a neighborhood watch association hires a security company to patrol its streets, the private entities' undertakings are not bound by any of the constitutional restrictions that impede public entities: They can search a suspect without probable cause or consent, for example, and they can elicit confessions without concern for Miranda rights. Of course, these private law enforcement entities are still bound by the same laws that apply to any other private citizen, so these private actors may not commit a crime or a tort (e.g., assault or kidnapping) against the suspect. However, many states give private citizens significant powers to apprehend suspected criminals, and the professional private law enforcers are well aware of their rights and entitlements under the law. Most importantly, the goals of private law enforcers are the goals of the private entity that hired them – which, as we have seen, may or may not be consistent with the goals of the public criminal justice system.

With that clarification aside, we can begin our examination and evaluation of the private criminal justice system. Chapter 1 addresses how we define crime and establish the appropriate response to criminal activity. Chapters 2 and 3 provide a brief review of how the criminal justice system has evolved into its modern incarnation, including a description of the shortcomings of the modern public criminal justice system that encourage victims and defendants to opt out of the public system and seek resolutions in the private sphere.

The core of the book, in Chapters 4–8, discusses the development and efficacy of the private criminal justice system. Chapter 4 addresses the law enforcement stage of the system, which includes not just the enormous and growing army of private police that enforces the criminal law in our country, but also the rise of neighborhood watch groups and new technologies that allow private individuals to engage in law enforcement activities. The next three chapters examine the adjudicative stage by exploring how private parties resolve criminal disputes either through settlements (Chapters 5 and 6) or through various forms of adjudication, such as the disciplinary procedures of a university or a professional licensing organization (Chapter 7). Chapter 8 describes the consequences and punishments that criminals face in the private criminal justice system, from the often extra-legal punishments meted out by traditional vigilantes to the more subtle responses from employers, companies, and other private individuals.

Finally, Chapter 9 sets out some proposals for regulating the private criminal justice system and Chapter 10 evaluates the overall costs and benefits of private criminal justice.

The discussions in this book are particularly timely today because society is undergoing a significant reevaluation of our criminal justice system. Cities across the country are reconsidering how to fund, train, and regulate the public police. Dozens of prosecutors throughout the country have been elected on progressive platforms, promising to focus on defendants' rights and to reduce the footprint of the criminal justice system. There is even a rare bipartisan consensus that too many people are being incarcerated in our jails and prisons. However, any national dialogue on reforming our criminal justice system is incomplete without a thorough understanding of the private criminal justice system, since it processes more criminals than its public counterpart. The experimentation and innovation in the private criminal justice system can teach us valuable lessons about how – and how not – to reform our public system. Finally, reformers should be aware that, if they succeed in reducing the size of the public criminal justice system – by reducing police funding, electing prosecutors who bring fewer cases, shortening the length of sentencing, or a combination of these approaches – the inevitable and perhaps unintended result will be an increase in the size of the private criminal justice system. Private parties will move in to fill the gaps created by the retreating public criminal justice system. Therefore, it is imperative that we understand the mechanisms at work when private parties respond to criminal actions.

Our first step is to answer some fundamental questions. What is the purpose of a criminal justice system? How do we distinguish criminal activity from other socially undesirable activity? Can you even have a criminal justice system without the participation of the state? The next chapter will discuss these questions.

1

Criminal Justice without the State

The title of this book will strike many readers as an oxymoron: How can criminal justice be private? Most people believe that the state is an essential part of the criminal justice system. This belief is often based on one of three assumptions.

The first assumption is that only the state can delineate exactly which acts constitute a crime. BLACK'S LAW DICTIONARY defines "crime" as "[a] positive or negative act in violation of penal law."[1] In other words, governments define criminal behavior by passing laws that tell us what actions constitute a crime; thus, the argument goes, without the state we would have no way of distinguishing criminal behavior (such as rape, theft, and assault) from any other kind of socially undesirable behavior (such as lying, carelessly damaging property, or breaking a promise).

The second assumption involves the purpose of the criminal justice system. Our legal system is divided into two types of law. Civil law comprises issues such as property disputes, personal injury, and breach of contract, in which one private party sues another, claiming that the other party harmed them in some way. The alleged injury is specific and personal, so we expect the private parties to enforce their own rights in court without needing the state to intervene on one side or the other. In a criminal case, on the other hand, the perpetrator has allegedly committed a wrong not just against one person but against society at large. The social contract has been broken; the community as a whole has suffered and it will continue to suffer until the perpetrator is brought to justice. Under this theory, criminal law acts as a tool of "collective condemnation" of the actor and, more specifically, of the act that has been committed.[2] As the legal theorist Henry M. Hart put it: "What distinguishes a criminal from a civil sanction and all that distinguishes it ... is the judgment of community condemnation which accompanies and justifies its imposition."[3] By extension, if the state is not a party to a dispute, even if the dispute arose from criminal conduct, the dispute is not part of the criminal justice system.

The third assumption involves the methods that are used in the criminal justice system. Coercion and even violence are sometimes necessary to apprehend suspected criminals, and these tools are usually used to punish criminals after they have been found guilty. Within the last 150 years, the United States (as well as most

Western industrialized states) has achieved a monopoly on the legitimate use of force, whether for policing, punishment for criminal activity, or military action. Since the state enjoys a legal monopoly on using force, this theory contends that only the state can lawfully use coercion to apprehend and punish criminals.[4]

Given that the state defines crime, and that it is the only entity with the legitimacy and the means to respond to criminal activity, how can we have a private system of criminal justice? The simplest answer to this question, and one that describes a good number of private responses to criminal activity, is to see the private realm of criminal justice as a supplement to the public criminal justice system. Private police merely enforce the laws set out by the state, and when private parties resolve their criminal disputes, the perpetrators agree to the deal only because they face greater coercive punishment from the state if they refuse. In this view, the private criminal justice system acts like a parasite of the public criminal justice system – the state defines the crimes, the state ensures that the consequences of committing a crime are commensurate with the harm the crime has done to society, and the state provides a coercive club that can be threatened against those who commit crimes. Private actors then leverage the infrastructure created by the state to supplement the public criminal justice system with additional enforcement and punishment.

The parasite theory has some truth to it, as we will see in future chapters, but it overstates the dependency that the private criminal justice system has on its public counterpart. In fact, a significant portion of the private criminal justice system is not dependent on the threats of the public system; rather, it exists in parallel to the public system. Its sanctions can also have a greater impact on the defendant and on society as a whole than the punishments imposed by the public criminal system. As we will see in the next chapter, this is not a historical anomaly; for most of the past 1,000 years, the link between crime control and the state has been relatively weak, with private parties playing a dominant role a majority of that time. The state has rarely been the sole – or even the primary – enforcer and punisher of criminal activity. As noted in later chapters, modern criminal activity is more likely to be detected and resolved by private parties than government actors, and private methods of resolving criminal disputes are becoming increasingly commonplace.

In order to truly appreciate the extent and nature of the private criminal justice system, we need to question the assumptions surrounding the link between the state and crime. First, do we need the state to define what is criminal? In the narrowest sense, an act is technically criminal only because the state has passed a law that deems it so, but this ends up being a very cramped definition of the term. BLACK'S LAW DICTIONARY provides a further definition of a "crime" as "any act done in violation of those duties which an individual owes to the community."[5] As I note later in this chapter, there are many sources other than the penal law that we use to distinguish criminal actions from other kinds of wrongful conduct, ranging from "natural law" to cultural norms to our own innate genetic predisposition about right and wrong. Indeed, philosophers for centuries have debated whether crimes are a construct of the state or represent a more fundamental breach of community duty that exists outside the state.

Second, do we need the state to be involved in a criminal case in order to fulfill the purpose of the criminal justice system? To some people, this assumption is impossible to refute. If one defines criminal justice as a process in which the state is a party, then there is by definition no way to have a private criminal justice system.[6] But this too is a rather limited (and, as we will see, historically inaccurate) definition of criminal justice. A more appropriate definition might be that a criminal justice system is one that responds to, processes, and resolves criminal disputes – and such a system may or may not involve the state. If an individual steals a shirt from a department store and is apprehended, the activity is criminal regardless of whether the thief is apprehended by a police officer or a private security officer. Similarly, if a person hits another person in the face while waiting in line at Disneyland and is arrested by a park security guard, the act of violence is still a criminal action, despite the fact that no state official is involved in the case. Any of the individuals involved – the victim, the guard, or (theoretically) the defendant – could report the incident to the public police or the local prosecutor and the state would become involved. However, if all three parties agree to resolve the dispute in some alternative way, the private resolution could end the matter altogether. Whether we call that process a private criminal adjudication or a private adjudication that avoids public criminal charges from being filed is really only a matter of terminology. Either way, a crime was committed and the matter was resolved without recourse to the public criminal justice system.

It is true that the fundamental nature of criminal conduct is that it harms society as a whole, rather than a specific individual or group. But it does not follow that the state must be involved in resolving the criminal dispute in order to further the goals of the criminal justice system. Some private entities respond to criminal actions in ways that protect their microcosm of society, such as when neighborhood community boards adjudicate a vandalism case or universities pass judgment on a student who committed sexual assault against another student. The sanctions handed out by these organizations are not necessarily meant to make the victim whole, but rather to further the interests of their community. Other private entities, such as retail stores that punish shoplifters or gated communities that eject trespassers, are acting in their own narrow private interest but may still be furthering societal goals.

Third, is state involvement in the criminal justice system necessary because force, violence, and incarceration are required aspects of the criminal justice system? This is the easiest assumption to dispute, at least in principle. Many individuals accused of criminal activity will submit to adjudication and punishment without force, and there is no particular reason that the resolution to a criminal dispute needs to involve violence or incarceration. Indeed, many minor crimes are resolved in the public criminal justice system without resorting to incarceration.[7] In practice, the small but growing movement toward the private resolution of criminal law cases has shown that these resolutions need not involve the use of force or incarceration against the accused. Some advocates of reform movements such as restorative justice believe that traditional coercive punishments are almost never appropriate for criminal defendants, regardless of the severity of the crime.[8]

Even when force is occasionally required to resolve a criminal dispute, we will see that there are many examples of private parties resorting to force or threats of force to respond to criminal actions – sometimes with the blessing of the state and sometimes without it. As discussed in Chapter 4, all states allow private citizens to make arrests, which could involve detention through force, and some states have supplemented these rights with greater powers to use reasonable force to retrieve stolen property. Chapter 8 discusses the quasi-legal use of force by vigilantes, such as George Zimmerman and Kyle Rittenhouse, who are often able to successfully claim self-defense, even when using deadly force.

We now turn to a more robust examination – and dismantling – of the three assumptions that underlie the thesis that the state must be a participant in the criminal justice system. In doing so we will answer three fundamental questions. First, what makes an act "criminal?" Second, what is the purpose behind creating criminal prohibitions? Finally, what is the proper response to criminal activity?

WHAT ACTIONS SHOULD BE CONSIDERED "CRIMINAL"?

A casual observer of criminal law may conclude that what societies classify as criminal conduct does not remain constant over time. In ancient times, crime was primarily defined by religious authorities, and criminal punishments were imposed only in response to actions that were perceived to harm the community or the religion. The most commonly punished crimes for early societies were treason, witchcraft, sacrilege, incest or other sex offenses, poisoning, and breaches of hunting rules.[9] Some societies had their own particular additions to this list; for example, in the Aztec civilization, it was a capital crime to cut down a living tree or for a commoner to wear cotton clothing. In contrast, wrongs committed by one person against another were generally not the concern of the state; the victims and perpetrators of such crimes were expected to "fight it out themselves" or reach some resolution on their own.[10] It was not until much later that the state became involved in resolving disputes between private individuals.

Even in our own country, we have seen dramatic examples of the evolution of penal codes in just the past 100 years: At the beginning of the twentieth century, adultery and fornication were punished as crimes,[11] while selling and possessing cocaine and morphine were perfectly legal activities.[12] In short, what is defined as a crime differs across cultures depending on the moral beliefs, political structures, and economic needs of the society.

Given the apparently wide divergence in what is defined as a crime, it is tempting to think of crime as purely a state-created concept: a list of rules set out by the government that, while not entirely arbitrary, vary considerably over time and across jurisdictions. Thus, one might conclude that the only way to know if a certain act is criminal is to consult the most recent iteration of the state's penal code. This perspective is an example of the "positivist" theory of law, which argues that law is distinct from morality. Positivists claim that the law is exclusively defined as what legislatures say it is; thus, under their theory, the definition of a crime is nothing more or less than what legislatures say constitutes a crime. This conception of crime as a government construct can be traced back at least as far as the writings of Thomas Hobbes, who argued that in a state of nature, where no law or government exists, there is no conception of a "crime," since the only imperative is self-preservation.[13]

But a more in-depth examination reveals a different picture. In actuality, our sense of what constitutes criminal behavior comes from social norms rather than originating with the state. Additionally, while the number and breadth of crimes have changed over the centuries, the fundamental principles of what constitutes criminal conduct has remained remarkably consistent.

Most definitions of crime begin with the basic distinction between "malum in se" crimes and "malum prohibitum" crimes. Malum in se, meaning "evil in itself," refers to actions that are inherently wrong and violate the natural law, such as murder, rape, and theft. Malum prohibitum, meaning "evil because prohibited," refers to actions that are criminal only because a law or rule states that the action is criminal. Malum prohibitum crimes generally are not immoral actions (beyond the fact that a knowing violation of a criminal statute might be considered immoral); they tend to be public welfare offenses or actions that do not directly harm others. They also tend to have minimal punishments and are often indistinguishable from violations of civil law.

Malum prohibitum laws vary widely and can even be somewhat arbitrary (such as the law that states you must drive on the right side of the road rather than on the left). But the natural law underpinning malum in se crimes is, at least in theory, universal and immutable. In practice, of course, humans' interpretations of natural law vary widely, leading to variations over time and across cultures. But, in the roots of the Anglo-American criminal justice system, "natural law" was derived from religious principles, specifically Christian principles. Indeed, natural law is most often associated with Saint Thomas Aquinas, who wrote that natural law consists of pursuing the good and avoiding evil, and that each of us has the inherent ability to discover natural law by learning what is good and evil.[14] The religious foundation of our criminal justice system was dominant for the first half of our country's existence: Crime was seen as a sin and a criminal had broken not just human law but also God's law.

The religious underpinnings of natural law do not hold up well in our modern, multicultural, and more secular Western society. The United States, like most modern Western countries, no longer formally acknowledges a divine source for our criminal code. Also, the criminal prohibitions listed by Aquinas – which include lying, adultery, sodomy, and blasphemy – have not aged well. Many modern-day Americans do not have an innate sense that the latter two are wrong or evil, and even though most may agree that lying and adultery are inherently wrong, most would not support enforcing that belief with criminal sanctions. But even if we no longer create new criminal laws based on our interpretations of God's will, natural law theory has heavily influenced our criminal code for centuries, and we can still see aspects of natural law and religious (predominantly Christian) principles in our current criminal prohibitions. Echoes of Christian morality are reflected in many modern so-called crimes against morality, such as gambling, prostitution, and drug use.

Secular philosophers have also argued for a "natural law" that exists independently of the laws of the state. John Locke, one of the preeminent Western political philosophers, wrote that every individual was endowed with certain natural rights, so that even in the state of nature there was a law that "obliges every one ... that all being equal and independent, no one ought to harm another in his life, health, liberty or possessions."[15] When an individual in the state of nature violates your rights, you are entitled to punish the offender, since there "is no reason to suppose, that he, who would take away my liberty, would not, when he had me in his power, take away everything else ... and therefore it is lawful for me to treat him as one who has put himself into a state of war with me."[16] A government's power to punish criminal activity, therefore, is a redistribution of the power that all individuals possessed in the state of nature. Thus, according to Locke, crime is not a state construct but rather a codification of existing principles and duties that existed long before the state came into existence. (Even Hobbes, who argued that there was no "crime" without a state, agreed that there could be violations of "moral virtue" in the state of nature.[17])

In the late nineteenth century, the United States began to secularize its criminal law system. Social scientists replaced the pastors and priests in determining what should be criminalized and how to deal with criminals. Criminal propensity was seen as a disease, not a sin, and psychiatrists and criminologists sought to rehabilitate criminals rather than simply punish them. Instead of killing, exiling, or shaming criminals, this new generation of experts decided to subject criminals to a strict regimen of hard work and discipline in new buildings known as "correctional institutions" or "reformatories" – the first modern prisons.[18] As one law professor noted, "[a]lmost all the characteristic innovations in criminal justice [from this time period] are reflections of the rehabilitative ideal: the juvenile court, the indeterminate sentence, systems of probation and parole, the youth authority, and the promise (if not the reality) of therapeutic programs in prisons, juvenile institutions, and mental hospitals."[19] Through the first two-thirds of the twentieth century, these scientific reformers reimagined the causes and consequences of crime, focusing on social, cultural, and psychological factors.[20] In 1949, the United States Supreme Court stated that "[r]eformation and rehabilitation of offenders have become important goals of criminal jurisprudence"[21] and, as late as 1971, a national report on the criminal justice system stated that "the treatment approach receives nearly unanimous support from those working in the field of criminal justice."[22]

Another aspect of the rise of this scientific approach to crime was to move from a system of common law crimes, which are defined by judges in court opinions, to codified crimes, which are specifically described in criminal statutes. By the end of the Second World War, there was enough momentum for this codification project that criminal law experts began an ambitious project to propose a common substantive criminal law for the United States. After years of work, they succeeded, producing what has been termed "the most consequential criminal law code in the history of Anglo-American law"[23] – the Model Penal Code. This document set out proposed statutes for all major crimes, and thirty-four states used its principles to codify or recodify their criminal codes. The primary benefit of the Model Penal Code was its "principled pragmatism" – it confined itself to crimes that "would be intolerable in any society," and it defined those crimes with logic and precision.[24] Its drafting – and subsequent influence on state penal codes throughout the country – represented the zenith of the influence of experts in criminal law theory.

However, almost as soon as the criminal law experts had reached this apotheosis, another factor began growing in influence on our criminal code, an influence that continues to dominate today: politics. Beginning in the 1960s, average citizens were no longer content to leave criminal law policy questions to the "experts"; they wanted their own say in what conduct should be criminalized and the severity of the sanctions imposed. The primary driver of this shift was the increased crime rate: In 1960, the FBI reported just over two million "index" crimes (defined as the most fundamentally basic crimes, such as murder, rape, and larceny) across the country; by 1972, the number was nearly six million.[25] The 1960s were also a time of great social upheaval, with massive numbers of peaceful civil rights and anti-war protests, combined with violent riots and political assassinations in many cities, all of which contributed to a pervading sense of lawlessness.

As a result, voter interest in criminal law policy skyrocketed. Very few people were concerned about crime in the 1950s,[26] and during the 1960 presidential campaign crime control was not raised as an issue by either candidate.[27] But, by 1965, Lyndon Johnson had declared a "war on crime"[28] and, in 1968, it became one of the centerpieces of the Nixon presidential campaign.[29] Since then, crime has remained a significant political issue on nearly every level.

Thus, for the past fifty years, criminal justice policy has primarily been driven by cultural norms as expressed through interest groups and politicians – from the draconian sentences for drug crimes in the 1970s and 1980s, to the "three strikes" laws in the 1990s, to the sexual registration laws in the late 1990s and early 2000s. Candidates and parties began to compete to demonstrate who could be the toughest on crime.[30] Once in office, legislators "reclaimed the power to punish that they had previously delegated to [the] experts,"[31] thereby beginning a spectacular increase in both the number of crimes and the severity of punishments for those crimes. On the federal level, the number of crimes nearly doubled between 1970 and 2000;[32] a similar increase during this period occurred on the state level.[33] Strict sentencing regimes, including mandatory minimum sentences, were also enacted.[34]

Populism has driven our response to criminal activity for half a century, and populism, at least in this context, is retributive, punitive, and motivated by fear. For most of this period, politicians of both parties have competed to see who could be tougher on crime, and any sign of mercy or attempts at rehabilitation were portrayed as weak. Then, in the mid-2010s, populist preferences began to shift in a number of cities, giving rise to a new political movement known as "progressive prosecutors." These new prosecutors, who took over county offices in Philadelphia, Chicago, Los Angeles, St. Louis, Brooklyn, and dozens of other cities, vowed to decrease mass incarceration by seeking less punitive sentences and more diversion programs, especially for nonviolent crimes.[35] Although these prosecutors are taking an approach that represents a dramatic shift in the way criminals are treated, their rise confirms the modern power of social norms and political power in defining criminal justice policy.

One lesson from this history of criminalization is that our current era, in which lengthy state-imposed incarceration is still the default response to criminal activity, is a historical anomaly – and, indeed, the rapid spread of progressive prosecution is evidence that it may be coming to an end. However, the progressive prosecution movement is still in in its infancy; in the meantime, a primary reason that most people today automatically link crime to the state is because of the massive prison industrial complex that still exists, and which has created the highest rate of incarceration in the Western world.[36] The statistics are simultaneously familiar and shocking: The population of our jails and prisons has grown from under 200,000 in 1970[37] to 1.9 million in 2022, while the total population of the United States grew by only 60 percent during that time period.[38] Meanwhile, government expenditures on correctional facilities outpaced inflation, increasing from 47 billion dollars to 57 billion dollars in real terms.[39] For most of the country's history, however, the prison footprint was much smaller. As we will see in the following chapters, one of the effects of the growing private criminal justice system will be to shrink this carceral footprint, as private entities – which are unable to wield the coercive power of the state – find other ways to respond to criminal activity.

Another lesson of this history is that the very method of defining criminal behavior has evolved, and most of the methods that we have used over time are only tangentially related to the state. The modern conception of crime is derived from many different sources: In the religious era, "natural law" and supposedly universal moral truths formed the foundation of early criminal prohibitions; in the scientific area, the more practical utilitarian concerns of the sociologists and criminologists shaped our penal codes; and, in the modern political era, social norms and political advocacy groups create new crimes and occasionally abolish old ones. As it turns out, this modern era has led to a virtual explosion of criminalization, as legislatures across the country continue to add laws to their penal code.

This recent over-criminalization belies the simplistic claim that we can rely on government penal codes to define which actions are considered criminal. In the past fifty years, political considerations have motivated legislatures to pass more and more criminal prohibitions, increasing the state and federal penal codes. A recent study by The Heritage Foundation found that, as of 2019, the federal government had created nearly 5,200 separate crimes. The Heritage Foundation report noted that "there is no single place where any citizen can go to learn" what is criminalized under federal law and, even worse, many of the crimes "are so vague that ... no reasonable person could understand what they mean." The Heritage Foundation also calculated that the number of federal code sections that create at least one crime has increased by 36 percent since 1994, which was as far back as the analysis went.[40] As might be expected in a penal code that includes over 5,000 crimes, there was a good amount of overlap among the criminal prohibitions, as well as many obscure crimes of which almost no American citizen is aware. For example, it is a federal crime to modify the weather without notifying the secretary of commerce, to write a check for less than one dollar, and to enter the Library of Congress with "offensive personal hygiene."[41] A significant number of these 5,000 crimes are what are known as strict liability crimes, which means that a person can be found guilty of committing the crime even if they had no idea that their actions were against the law.[42]

Over-criminalization in the federal penal code is only the tip of the iceberg. The Heritage Foundation report acknowledged that its study did not include any of the thousands of crimes that can be found in the Code of Federal Regulations, which consists of 175,000 pages in 236 different volumes. In addition to federal crimes, each of the fifty states has its own penal code, each containing thousands more crimes. In order to understand what counts as "criminal conduct" in this country, it would be exceedingly unhelpful to page through these tens of thousands of separate laws criminalizing behavior. So, how do we actually know what behavior is considered "criminal?"

Given that our current set of criminal laws springs from a variety of sources, that each state (as well as the federal government) has created its own unique penal code, and that the number of different crimes has been growing exponentially in the political era, you might be tempted to conclude that there is no general consensus of what constitutes a crime. However, a close look at how the criminal justice system operates reveals that exactly the opposite is the case: Even with all of this diversity, there is a surprising consistency in what is treated as a crime on a practical level. Of all state felony convictions, 85 percent are for a small handful of categories of crimes – drug transactions, larceny, burglary, fraud, weapons offenses, and violent crimes.[43] The story for less severe crimes is the same. Although every state's penal code lists several hundred crimes that are classified as misdemeanors[44] and over thirteen million misdemeanor cases are filed each year,[45] most misdemeanor convictions are based on a narrow category of crimes: drug possession, petty larceny, simple assault, and driving under the influence.[46]

Professor Robert Leider of George Mason University explains this consistency by arguing that criminal law is defined by conventions, not by statute. He rejects the argument that our criminal law is defined by the statutes passed by legislatures. Legislatures have passed so many criminal prohibitions, and have defined them so broadly, that a foreign visitor to our country could not possibly know what actions are prohibited by reading state penal codes. As he notes, "if one peruses the statute books, one can find many [outdated] crimes and trivial offenses."[47] As another scholar has noted: "changes in criminal liability rules do not necessarily mean changes in the scope or nature of behavior the system punishes. In a system structured as ours is, the law on the street may remain unchanged even as the law on the books changes dramatically."[48] Some scholars have argued that over-criminalization in the penal codes has simply enabled prosecutors to decide which crimes to enforce; these scholars conclude that prosecutors, not legislatures, are the public officials who truly get to determine which acts are criminal.[49] However, in truth, prosecutors are constrained by community norms – norms that are set by judges, politicians, and most of all by the public at large. These norms – or "legal conventions," as Professor Leider calls them – determine what should and should not be treated as a crime. They limit prosecutorial discretion and force prosecutors to focus on the acts that the public believes should be prioritized. This explains the extraordinary homogeneity across jurisdictions of the crimes that are actually prosecuted, even though there are literally thousands of different crimes on the books and tens of thousands of prosecutors enforcing them around the country.[50]

There are many examples of cultural norms and legal conventions trumping the written law set out by legislatures. Dozens of states keep outdated laws on the books that criminalize crimes such as adultery and fornication,[51] as well as lesser crimes prohibiting swearing and engaging in various activities on Sundays.[52] Although the legislature has passed laws deeming these actions to be criminal, and has never repealed those laws, no prosecutor would ever charge these crimes today because to do so would contradict cultural norms.[53] Another example, from the malum prohibitum category, is traffic offenses. Everybody knows that the true speed limit on a road is not the actual posted speed limit; as Professor Leider notes: "[t]he real norms for traffic speed are not found in statutory law or regulations. ... No individual or government body having authority has promulgated them, and no court has recognized them .... Despite this, these traffic customs are public, well-known, and respected as norms by both law enforcers and citizens."[54]

Of course, as Professor Leider concedes, traffic offenses are relatively trivial crimes. However, the cultural norms that define criminal activity are even more powerful for more serious crimes, which we saw in the rise of populist thirst for incarceration starting in the 1960s, when people demanded – and legislators and prosecutors delivered – longer sentences, particularly for low-level drug crimes.

We now see it acting in the other direction, as the overly punitive policies of prosecutors have begun to outpace the cultural norms of their constituents, giving rise to the progressive prosecution movement. The success of this new prosecutorial ideology is itself proof of the predominance of cultural norms – the laws on the books that allow for years or even decades of prison for drug crimes are no longer acceptable to the general public.

However, this new brand of prosecutor knew the limits of their power – they had to keep prosecuting violent actions, for example, because these are universally considered to be criminal activities. And when progressive prosecutors try to push too far past legal norms, public pressure often pulls them back in range with what is acceptable to their community. For example, when progressive Alvin Bragg took office as the New York County district attorney in January 2022, one of his first actions was to issue a memo to all of his prosecutors telling them to avoid seeking jail time for many types of felonies, including robbery, burglary, and gun possession, and to never charge certain categories of crime, including resisting arrest.[55] The community backlash was immediate and severe, as police officers, other public officials, and small business owners criticized his new policies and warned of their potential effect on crime rates. Within a month, Bragg had essentially reversed many of the positions in the memo, allowing prosecutors to seek jail time for robberies and gun possession and asserting that his prosecutors would charge anyone who attempted to harm a police officer. He also clarified that the other policies in the memo were merely recommendations and that individual prosecutors were free to use their own judgment and experience in deciding how to proceed with their cases.[56] As one former prosecutor noted: "Progressive criminal justice reform has to find a balance. Old-school law enforcement went too far in one direction, but lessons we're learning in some big cities suggest that others may have gone too far in the other direction."[57]

Numerous studies have confirmed the universality of what constitutes criminal behavior. In 1960, sociologists surveyed 575 individuals and asked them to rate the relative severity of fifty-one criminal actions. They found "pervasive social agreement" among the group, with no differences based on personal characteristics.[58] Since then, versions of this experiment have been replicated countless times, each with hundreds or thousands of subjects from a wide variety of demographic groups, and the results are always the same.[59] In one of the more recent studies, from 2007, participants were given twenty-four cards, each with a specific fact pattern describing a potentially criminal scenario. The scenarios covered various actions, including theft, destruction of property, assault, robbery, rape, and murder, as well as a variety of potentially mitigating factors, such as self-defense, provocation, and mental illness. Overall, the fact patterns represented approximately 95 percent of the offenses committed in the United States. Participants were asked to rank all twenty-four scenarios in order of severity of the offense committed. The level of agreement was dramatic – out of all of the possible deviations from the rank order, the participants only deviated 4 percent of the time.[60] These studies were replicated on an international level, in countries such as Ireland, the United Kingdom, Taiwan, India, Indonesia, Iran, and Italy, and all cases found a worldwide consensus about what should be criminalized and the relative scale of punishments that each crime deserved.[61]

In other words, our principles of criminal law come from legal conventions, which in turn come from universal cultural norms. And where do these cultural norms come from? Studies show that we internalize most of them at a very young age. Echoing Locke, Professor Paul Robinson of the University of Pennsylvania Law School argues that "certain principles of criminal law are innate to humans," since "intuitions about injury, theft, and fairness are among the first principles of justice understood by young children."[62] Professor Robinson points to studies that show that very young children have a sense of moral imperatives even in the absence of official rules – for example, preschoolers would still say it was wrong to hit another child or to steal their property even if there were no rules against it.[63] This set of moral imperatives might have evolved from the need to create a consistent set of rules against aggression and theft beginning in the earliest of human societies, or it may have even more ancient roots – primates and other animals have been known to punish those who act in ways that are contrary to the overall well-being of the group.[64]

This does not mean that our definition of crime remains constant. Although there are certain categories of actions – such as violence, theft, and destruction of property – that will almost always be considered criminal, what we define as crime on the margins evolves as society changes. However, this evolution is driven by societal factors, not by the state; in fact, the state tends to be a lagging indicator of what society identifies as criminal conduct. We have already discussed the dozens of laws criminalizing acts that remain on the books that have long since fallen into disuse. Likewise, legislatures can pass laws that lie dormant until advocacy groups and public opinion transform them into actions that actually face a criminal sanction. For example, states began criminalizing driving under the influence in 1910, but it was not seriously enforced until the 1980s, after a public awareness campaign by Mothers Against Drunk Driving (MADD) that increased the penalties and pressured police and prosecutors to take the crime seriously.[65] At the same time, MADD influenced the federal government and states to criminalize the consumption of alcohol by anyone under the age of 21, leading to the creation of new crimes as cultural attitudes about drinking began to shift.[66]

Similarly, a man assaulting his wife was not considered a crime for the first 100 years of our nation's history.[67] Eventually, in response to the first feminist movement around the turn of the twentieth century, every state had outlawed domestic violence by 1920. Even then, however, police would usually just intervene to "de-escalate" the situation but make no arrests, since they considered spousal abuse to be a "family matter" that was outside the purview of the state. It was not until the next wave of the feminist movement in the 1970s and 1980s that the criminal justice system began to take these crimes seriously, with mandatory arrest policies and increased punishment for offenders.[68]

In evaluating how individuals resolve disputes, we frequently overestimate the influence of the formal law and underestimate the influence of social norms. In 1981, Professor Robert Ellickson of Stanford Law School conducted field research to study how individuals dealt with each other in a jurisdiction where "legal rights vary from one place to the next." He traveled to Shasta County, a rural region in California just south of the Oregon border, where cattle ranchers had to contend with two different complex legal regimes governing the rules that applied to cattle trespass, depending on the location of the land where the trespass occurred. He was curious as to how well the ranchers knew the law, and how they navigated its complexities. What he learned was that the formal law bore little relevance to how the ranchers resolved their disputes; residents "frequently appl[ied] informal norms of neighborliness to resolve disputes even when they knew that their norms were inconsistent with the law."[69] The experience led him to write a seminal book, ORDER WITHOUT LAW, that uses game theory and examples from history to show that the formal law is only one of a number of different influences on a person's behavior. Other influences include the person's own ethics, society's norms, and the organizational rules of nongovernment institutions.[70]

Professor Ellickson points out that, the parable of the LORD OF THE FLIES notwithstanding, people have a tendency to follow norms even in the absence of any legal authority. He describes the "virtually Hobbesian environment" that existed in the mid-1800s on the Overland Trail from Missouri to the west: "the situation on the trail was nearly anarchic; the identity of the national sovereign over much of the territory was disputed, and no law-enforcement agents were in the area." Nonetheless, when individuals lacked necessary goods or equipment, "they felt constrained to buy, not to take, what they needed from others."[71] Indeed, even when legal authority is present, there are many close-knit communities that prefer to resolve disputes among themselves rather than involve the state. Ellickson gives the example of lobstermen in Maine. When they learn that another lobsterman has stolen their traps, they consistently resort to self-help rather than calling the authorities: "Any fisherman who goes to the police about trap cutting not only looks ineffectual and ridiculous but is also somewhat of a threat. When a man's traps are missing, taking the law into his own hands is not only more effective but also maintains his standing among fellow fisherman."[72] We will further explore how closed communities respond to criminal behavior in their own unique ways in Chapter 7.

In short, the state's role in deciding what behavior should be treated as criminal is far smaller than it first appears. Religion, shifting social and political norms, and even evolutionary biology play varying roles in what de facto is considered a crime. As we will see in future chapters, this decoupling of crime from the state opens up possibilities for non-state actors to enforce, adjudicate, and punish crime all without recourse to the government.

WHY DO WE MAKE AND ENFORCE CRIMINAL LAWS?

Once a society has agreed on which acts should be criminal, we must answer the next question: What is the purpose of enforcing the criminal law? What are we trying to accomplish by apprehending, adjudicating, and then imposing some type of sentence on those who commit crimes? There are two primary answers to these questions. The first, most closely associated with the theory of retributivism, is that we enforce the criminal law in order to punish those who deserve to be punished. In this view, moral culpability is not only a necessary condition for the state to impose punishment, but it also creates a *duty* for the state to impose punishment. When an individual commits a crime, the action creates a moral imbalance in the universe and the only way to rebalance the scales is to impose a sanction on the criminal. Retributivism is essentially backward-looking and reactive; it is not concerned with whether the punishment will have any positive (or negative) effect on the criminal or on society in general.

The alternative answer to this question, associated with the theory of utilitarianism, is that we enforce the criminal law in order to prevent future crimes from occurring. Under this theory, punishment is a means to an end, not a moral imperative – by punishing a criminal, we deter them from committing a crime in the future (what is known as "specific deterrence"), and the visibility of the punishment also deters others from committing crimes in the future (which is referred to as "general deterrence"). Also, unlike retributivists, utilitarians do not believe that imposing suffering in order to deter future conduct is the only appropriate response to crime. Utilitarians acknowledge that certain kinds of punishment – locking people up, killing them, or sending them into exile – can not only deter but also have the additional benefit of incapacitating dangerous individuals so that they cannot commit future crimes. However, utilitarian theory also supports rehabilitation, which is the opposite of punishment – providing the criminal with job training, anger management counseling, or a drug treatment program so that they are less likely to commit crimes in the future.[73] This is a forward-thinking, proactive ideology; it is not concerned with whether the criminal deserves the punishment.[74]

These two purposes, of course, are not always mutually exclusive. If we respond to crime with a punitive sanction – such as a fine or incarceration – we are using methods that are supported by both retributivists and utilitarians. The punishment is causing the criminal to suffer for their immoral action and also deterring them (and others who are aware of the punishment) from committing crimes in the future. However, these two different purposes often lead in different directions. Perhaps the most effective way to prevent a criminal from committing a future crime is to rehabilitate them, for example by providing them with drug treatment to prevent narcotics possession, anger management programs to prevent assaults, or job training to prevent thefts. A pure utilitarian would run the numbers and compare the recidivism rate for those who receive rehabilitation with the rate for those who receive jail time and would generally choose the option that minimized the chance that the perpetrator would re-offend.[75] A pure retributivist would recoil at the idea of providing the criminal with benefits; the only appropriate response to their crime would be to impose suffering on them. On the other hand, if it was assumed that there was a high incidence of a certain type of crime in a jurisdiction, and police were ineffective at catching the perpetrators, perhaps because of a lack of resources or because the crime was difficult to investigate, a utilitarian might correctly determine that the most effective way to deter future incidents of that crime would be to make a number of high-profile arrests for the crime and impose severe and very visible punishments. In doing so, the utilitarian would not care much if those arrested and punished were in fact guilty of the crime, as long as the general population believed they were guilty – so a utilitarian would find the standard of proof being lowered to be acceptable to convict those who were accused. A utilitarian would even agree to frame innocent people in order to publicly punish them, as long as the frame up was convincing to others. A retributivist would never agree to these compromises, since it would be immoral to punish a person unless their guilt could be proven with near certainty.

The retributivist/utilitarian divide also explains why our country remains divided about the death penalty. As of 2021, 60 percent of Americans supported the death penalty for convicted murderers, while 39 percent were opposed to it. When those who support the punishment are asked why, only half of them argue that it deters crime, while 90 percent of them say that it is "morally justified" to execute a murderer.[76] Thus, when death penalty abolitionists bring forward multiple studies showing that the death penalty does nothing to deter crime, and that it is extremely expensive to administer, they are unable to persuade most death penalty proponents because they are presenting utilitarian arguments to retributivists.

In one sense, whether we seek retribution or pursue a utilitarian solution may be related to the first question in this chapter: Why have we criminalized the conduct in the first place? If we see the criminal law as an extension of the natural law, that is, as essentially a codified code of immoral actions, the retributivist philosophy becomes much more appealing. If we see criminal law as a means to an end, a tool to ensure society functions smoothly, then we may gravitate toward the utilitarian view. It is no surprise, therefore, that during the religious era, we sought retribution through punishment and during the scientific era, we sought prevention through rehabilitation and deterrence. The current populist era is harder to classify – certainly many recent changes to the criminal justice system seem retributivist, with longer and harsher sentences and the abandonment of rehabilitation. However, recently, utilitarian arguments have been gaining headway, such as the successful push to decriminalize marijuana, the increased interest in treatment for those addicted to drugs,[77] and the reimagining of ways to achieve public safety that is presented by the Black Lives Matter movement.

Of course, very few of us are "pure retributivists" or "pure utilitarians." Many of us believe that it is morally appropriate to punish wrongdoers and are eager to deter crime in any way that is proven to be effective. The level of retributivism and utilitarianism that we apply may depend on the crime being prosecuted. When a person is caught using drugs, we may not feel any moral imperative to punish and instead may seek ways to discourage them or prevent others from committing the same crime. When a person is caught sexually assaulting someone, we may want to see them pay for their actions, without caring too much about the effect the punishment has on their future conduct. Our goals may also change depending on the identity of the perpetrator; we may feel less retribution toward an eighteen-year-old who has never been in trouble before and more toward a thirty-year-old repeat offender.

What does all of this have to do with the private criminal justice system? Quite a bit, as it turns out. The private criminal justice system can be very effective at achieving utilitarian goals, and not as effective at achieving retribution. Private systems of criminal justice, as we will see, are far more likely to detect criminal activity and are far less likely to impose severe punishments. Studies have shown that the amount of deterrence achieved is much more dependent on the chances of getting caught than on the severity of the punishment. Furthermore, the private parties who make decisions are usually (although not always) seeking to prevent future harm rather than to punish past harm. Harsh punishments – the kind that retributivists often believe are necessary to restore moral balance to the universe – are more limited in the private criminal justice system than in the public one.

This discussion naturally leads to the final question of the chapter: What is the appropriate response to criminal activity? As we have already discussed, the answer to this question depends quite a bit on our answers to the previous two questions.

HOW SHOULD WE RESPOND TO CRIMINAL ACTIVITY?

Once we have defined what is considered criminal, what should be the proper response to criminal activity? As we have already seen, the answer to this question depends on the purpose of criminal law. A pure utilitarian would want a highly visible punishment that is severe enough to deter not only the perpetrator from committing the crime again but also other would-be perpetrators from committing that crime. A utilitarian would also want a relatively inexpensive punishment, since they seek to expend the fewest resources necessary to achieve the goal. A pure retributivist would not care about visibility, deterrence, or cost, as long as the severity of the punishment matched the moral transgression of the wrongdoer. Thus, the high cost of our current system of mass incarceration matters little to retributivists, as long as those who are in prison deserve their punishment; likewise, the fact that modern prisons do little to rehabilitate their inmates is irrelevant in their view.

Like the definition of substantive crime itself, our responses to criminal activity vary across time and across various cultures. In ancient times, corporal punishment was the primary, if not exclusive, form of punishment, up to and including capital punishment. The CODE OF HAMMURABI, published around 1750 BC in Babylon, famously proclaimed the lex talionis: A criminal who causes a person to lose an eye will have his own eye removed as punishment.[78] The same principle is found in the OLD TESTAMENT: "And thine eye shall not pity; but life shall go for life, eye for eye, tooth for tooth, hand for hand, foot for foot."[79] This principle carried over to Greek and Roman times. In Rome, punishment was imposed by the head of the household and "[d]eath [was] the usual penalty" to be carried out "by hanging, crucifixion, decapitation, hurling from the Tarpian Rock, being thrown to wild beasts, or it seems almost any other way the ingenuity of the punisher may devise."[80] For less serious crimes, the sanction would be a less severe physical punishment, although one that was still brutal to modern sensibilities, such as flogging or the loss of a limb.

The severity of criminal punishments persisted through to the Middle Ages, but in England it was ultimately mitigated by the "benefit of clergy." This was a legal loophole that began as a way to shield religious figures from the royal courts but later expanded to a way to mitigate the harshness of the medieval punishments to large portions of the general population. By the 14th century, any defendant who could read from the Bible would be given the benefit of the clergy, and instead of being put to death, the lucky literate criminal would only receive penance and often a branding of the thumbs.

The emphasis on corporal punishment was imported to the New World, and up until the mid-eighteenth century the primary punishments for crime in the colonies were physical or financial. Many of the original colonies were founded by religious communities, and their theocratic roots were reflected in their criminal codes – for example, the Plymouth colony in Massachusetts adapted its penal code directly from the "life shall go for life" passages found in the book of Deuteronomy.[81] Jails in the North American colonies and the early United States were used primarily as holding areas for those awaiting trial or punishment, or as locations to confine debtors. This began to change in the late eighteenth century, when social reformers began to argue that death and physical violence were not appropriate state sanctions for an enlightened republic. These reformers believed that criminals should be rehabilitated rather than physically punished, and they successfully lobbied for terms of imprisonment in institutions where solitude, hard work, discipline, and a structured routine could reform them into law-abiding citizens. These new institutions were called penitentiaries (since they were meant to be a place for penitents) and were later known as correctional facilities or reformatories – all names that reflect the rehabilitative goals of those who created them. In the United States, this movement was spearheaded by the Quakers, and the first penitentiaries sprang up in New England at the end of the eighteenth century.[82] As might be expected, these experiments utterly failed – a regimen of incarceration and discipline did nothing to reduce recidivism rates, and prison conditions quickly deteriorated, leading to overcrowding, frequent instances of prison violence, and rampant disease inside the penitentiaries. Subsequent reform attempts over the next

100 years did little to improve conditions in the long run, but states kept building prisons, and by the twentieth century, incarceration had become the primary response to criminal activity.

It is against this backdrop that the phenomenon of mass incarceration began to take root. Within a thirty-five year period starting in the 1970s, the number of prison inmates in our country increased fivefold, so that we now incarcerate about one out of every 250 Americans.[83] Many factors explain this dramatic increase, including a higher number of arrests for drug crimes, more mandatory minimum sentences, and prosecutors exercising their discretion to charge more cases as felonies rather than misdemeanors.[84] However, the driving force behind all of these factors was the populist push for the country to be tougher on crime – both for utilitarian reasons (to lower the crime rate through deterrence and incapacitation) and retributive reasons (to inflict punishment on those who broke the social contract).

Crime rates have certainly decreased since the 1980s, and many Americans seem to agree that violent offenders deserve to suffer for their crimes, but the general consensus among experts is that current levels of incarceration cannot be justified under utilitarian or retributive arguments.[85] Empirical evidence shows that the vast majority of crimes are committed by individuals under the age of forty, so keeping people in prison for years or decades beyond that age does almost nothing from an incapacitation standpoint.[86] Yet one in seven prisoners in the United States – over 200,000 people – are serving sentences of fifty years or more, while 46 percent of prisoners – over 600,000 people – are over the age of forty.[87] Likewise, repeated studies have shown that the level of deterrence increases dramatically with the chance of getting caught, but increasing the severity of the sentence after a certain point has little to no effect on deterrence.[88] In fact, criminologists have found that longer sentences often increase recidivism rates, probably because the longer people spend in prison, the more difficult it becomes to find gainful employment and otherwise adjust to a law-abiding life outside prison.[89] And, as far as retribution is concerned, there is growing evidence that Americans are losing their affinity for long prison sentences, even for more serious crimes, as evidenced both by the election of progressive prosecutors across the country and more broadly in a series of polls that show substantial majorities supporting lowering sentences.[90] Americans appear to be turning against the system of mass incarceration we have constructed, because we feel less punitive toward criminals, are beginning to realize the vast economic and social cost of prison, or are recognizing the dramatically diminishing marginal returns for incapacitation and deterrence for longer sentences, or because of the extraordinary racial inequities inherent in the prison system.

There is one other factor that looms large in society's response to crime, which is the stigma and shame that is traditionally attached to those who engage in criminal activity. As noted early in this chapter, under classical criminal law theory, this stigma was created quite intentionally; it is one of the characteristics that distinguishes criminal conduct from other illegal activities, such as breaching a contract or causing an accident while driving negligently. It is also one of the responses – along with incarceration – that the private criminal justice system cannot really provide, since the stigma of a criminal conviction must be imposed by a state actor in order to officially condemn the conduct and bring the community's formal approbation. This stigma serves to set criminal conduct apart from other types of conduct, but it is also meant to act as an additional deterrent to criminal behavior. A would-be criminal knows that if they commit a crime, they will not only be punished but also be labeled a "criminal" or "felon" for the rest of their lives.

This stigma has existed for centuries but, in recent decades, the public criminal justice system has formalized stigma in a number of ways. Some judges become creative with their sentencing and impose a "shaming" punishment rather than a traditional punishment, such as requiring the criminal to wear a T-shirt or a sandwich board proclaiming their crime, sometimes while standing outside the establishment where they were caught stealing.[91] Some legislatures have created special shaming punishments for certain crimes, such as requiring those who were convicted of drunk driving to obtain a different color license plate that indicates their crime. However, the primary way that criminal stigmas have been formalized is through the many collateral consequences that are attached to criminal convictions. Individuals who have been convicted of a crime may not be able to vote, own a gun, obtain a professional license, or obtain housing or certain government benefits, along with many other potential restrictions. Employers routinely deny jobs to applicants with criminal records, even if the past criminal activity has nothing to do with the job. And individuals who are convicted of sex crimes have to place their name on a registry that is open to the public and easily searchable online.

However, like the movement against mass incarceration, there is a growing sense that the stigma attached to criminal conduct imposes more costs than benefits. Over thirty states and 150 cities have adopted hiring practices that prohibit state agencies from considering or even inquiring into a job applicant's criminal history; fifteen of these states bar most private employers from doing so.[92] The Collateral Consequences Resource Center (CCRC), an advocacy group that lobbies for reducing collateral consequences of convictions, reported in 2022 that "[s]ubstantial progress has been made in a number of states, and in the Nation as a whole, toward devising and implementing an effective and functional system for relieving collateral consequences." The CCRC notes that there is now a "bipartisan public commitment to a reintegration agenda" driving this change, based primarily on economic motivations to get more workers into the workforce.[93]

CONCLUSION

The answer to the question "Can you have a criminal justice system without the state?" depends on what you want out of a criminal justice system. We have seen that the public, state-controlled criminal justice system defines crimes through the legislative process, seeks to deter crime and punish criminals, and relies heavily on incarceration to achieve these goals. However, we have also seen that legislation is not the only way to define crime, and that the current state focus on incarceration is more of a historical accident than the product of a serious study of how best to achieve the goals of deterrence and punishment. In fact, our concept of what is criminal is usually set by cultural norms, and due to the past few decades of over-criminalization, the official penal codes are not particularly good guides for what we in fact treat as criminal activity. When we consider the goals of the criminal justice system, we learn that the state is uniquely empowered to further the retributive goal by imposing punishment for the sake of punishment, usually by incarcerating wrongdoers and branding them with the stigma of being criminals. However, there are signs that private entities and individuals may be able to contribute – perhaps substantially – to deterring crime. Of course, the agents in the private criminal justice system are, by definition, acting to further their own interest, and the degree to which these interests coincide – or conflict – with society's interest in deterrence will be a continuing theme throughout the rest of the book.

The purpose of this chapter was twofold: first, to think more broadly about what we mean when we talk about a system of criminal justice and, second, to thereby challenge the conventional wisdom about how a criminal justice system should operate. The textbook version of the criminal justice system – in which legislatures define crimes, police arrest perpetrators, courts adjudicate their cases, and those who are deemed guilty are confined in prison – is not the only way that society defines and responds to criminal activity. In future chapters, we will examine the various ways in which the modern-day private criminal justice system can and does accomplish some of the same goals as the public system by enforcing the criminal law and adjudicating criminal disputes.

As it turns out, relying on private parties and institutions to run the criminal justice system is not a new idea – in fact, for most of history, private actors bore the primary responsibility in responding to criminal activity, particularly for the policing function. In the next chapter, we will briefly review the history of the criminal justice system to see how the participation of private individuals has waxed and waned throughout the years.

2

A Brief History of Crime

THE BIRTH OF "CRIMES AGAINST THE STATE"

The very idea of defining certain conduct as "criminal" first arose approximately 1,000 years ago. Before that, the distinction between private harms and public harms that today serves as the foundation of criminal law did not exist. The eleventh century nation-state had virtually nothing to do with maintaining law and order – or much of anything else, for that matter. Kings did little except tax their citizens and wage war against each other, and became interested in law enforcement only when it became apparent that the criminal law could be another source of state funding.[1] In England, for example, King Henry I declared in 1116 that certain intentional torts – such as arson, robbery, and murder – would henceforth be considered crimes.[2] Henry II took the next step and "replaced the private, decentralized civil law with a public, centralized, and politicized criminal law," which created the first criminal code in Britain.[3] Thus, instead of the perpetrator being subject to a civil suit in which he would be liable to the victim for damages, the perpetrator's property would be forfeited to the state. In addition to providing more revenue for the king, the criminalization of intentional torts was meant to cut down on instances of private retribution by the victim, a process that came to be seen as less legitimate than state action.[4]

However, even though the concept of a "crime against the state" was slowly coming into existence, the responsibility for maintaining order in society fell to private individuals, with very little state intervention. In early Britain, adult males banded together into groups called "tithings," headed by a tithingman, who provided collective security for the community. If a member of the tithing committed a crime, the other members of the tithing had the responsibility of apprehending him and bringing him to a larger group called a hundred, which would conduct a trial. By the twelfth century, the position of tithingman had merged with the Norman position of a constable, who was a royal officer charged with maintaining order. The constable had broad duties beyond law enforcement; according to one source, his job was to "punish mothers bearing bastards, whip vagabonds, force the unwilling to work, uphold apprenticeship statutes, confine begging to the licensed, restrain lunatics and detain the suspicious."[5] The constable was also in charge of collecting taxes for the area. Aside from this public officer with his broad mandate, the primary responsibility for apprehending and even prosecuting the criminals remained a private responsibility for many centuries.

PRIVATE LAW ENFORCEMENT

In 1285, the Statute of Winchester assigned to the hundreds the responsibility of catching the perpetrators of any thefts that occurred – and, if they failed to do so, they were financially liable for the amount that was stolen. The statute also stated that every community had to appoint night watchmen on a rotating basis. These watchmen were ordinary citizens who were not paid for their service. Their job was to guard or patrol the community; if any trouble occurred, they were meant to raise a "hue and cry," at which point all citizens were required to assist in the arrest.[6] The watchmen did little besides "keeping an eye out for trouble, raising an alarm when it was spotted, and perhaps deterring some of it by mere presence."[7] However, as the centuries progressed and society stratified, the mechanism of rotating through every male citizen began to show strains. Those with any amount of wealth would hire others to take over their shifts, and ultimately the only people who took on the jobs were people who had no other employment options.[8] Thus, the watchmen often ended up being incompetent and poorly trained – in the words of one historian, they were "unarmed, untrained, under-supervised, often unwilling, and frequently drunk."[9] The ineptitude of this semipublic police force led wealthier individuals to hire their own private guards, or to form private police units to patrol their neighborhoods,[10] while the government was forced to offer large rewards for apprehending criminals. This in turn created a cottage industry of professional informers or "thief-takers" who earned their money either by tracking down criminals and claiming the reward or by simply fencing the stolen goods from the thief and then turning it over to the rightful owner for a higher price.[11]

Early American towns and cities inherited this model, as Boston, New York, and other cities in the colonies copied the watchman system. Thus, law enforcement in early America was almost exclusively a private affair; although the state conscripted private citizens into watchmen duties, the responsibility of actually apprehending criminals and bringing them to justice fell to the citizens themselves. For the first seventy years of our country's history, watchmen were the primary, if not the only, type of law enforcement in the United States. The only public law enforcement officers were the United States Marshals, who worked for the federal courts and whose primary responsibilities were to serve warrants and run federal courthouses, and their local counterparts, the county sheriffs, who performed the same function on the local level.

In 1838, Boston became the first city in the United States to hire paid police officers; seven years later, New York established a professional police department, modeled on the paramilitary structure of the London Metropolitan Police founded in 1829.¹² Other major cities followed suit, with Cincinnati, Philadelphia, Chicago, and Baltimore all establishing their own police departments by the 1850s. The leaders of these cities believed that an organized police force was necessary to combat the unique problems of growing urban areas, namely increased crimes such as prostitution and burglary, mounting tensions arising from income inequality, and cultural clashes in the wake of a massive amount of immigration from Ireland and Germany.¹³ Initially the police were concerned with both deterring crime and "controlling" the lower economic classes to ensure that they did not threaten social stability; police handed out food to paupers and provided temporary lodging for the homeless. During certain periods, the number of homeless for whom they provided lodgings outnumbered the total number of arrests they made.¹⁴

In the American south, the origin story of the police is quite different. Most southern states organized "slave patrols" in the eighteenth century to hunt for escaped enslaved people, as well as to put down uprisings and discipline enslaved persons for violating rules. After the Civil War, these organizations evolved into police forces, which spent a substantial amount of resources enforcing Jim Crow laws and other segregationist policies.¹⁵

Even as police forces began to spread throughout urban areas and on the east coast, private law enforcement remained dominant in the rest of the country throughout the nineteenth century. As Professor Seth Stoughton of the University of South Carolina writes: "[D]espite the rise of the police department in its modern incarnation, it would be a mistake to think that law enforcement was exclusively or even primarily a governmental responsibility. Municipal police agencies with limited jurisdiction were simply unable to accommodate large-scale commercial entities operating on an interstate or national scale, such as railroads, banks, and mining companies."¹⁶ The new police departments were understaffed and often corrupt, and law enforcement officers were scarce or nonexistent in the territories west of the Ohio River. Large corporations therefore hired their own "company police" to protect their interests, while large private police forces provided patrol and investigative services to the growing nation.¹⁷

The most well known of these private forces was the Pinkerton Northwest Police Agency. William A. Pinkerton was a former deputy sheriff and United States mail agent before he began his own detective agency in Chicago in 1855. Pinkerton saw the need for a national private security company after consulting with the owners of various Midwestern railroads, who were suffering from frequent robberies that local law enforcement departments, with their jurisdictionally limited boundaries, could not address. Pinkerton's organization was paid $10,000 a year to provide protection for the railroads and provided valuable and necessary security in areas of the country that were all but devoid of public police. The agency got its biggest publicity boost when it was contracted to deliver Abraham Lincoln from Illinois to Washington, DC, after the newly elected President had received an assassination threat. According to legend, the agent who accompanied Lincoln to the capitol on the train did not sleep throughout the entire journey, giving birth to the logo of the Pinkerton Agency: a watchful eye next to the slogan "We Never Sleep."[18] To this day, private detectives are known as "private eyes" as a result. The Pinkerton Agency's reputation was later tarnished as its mission evolved into protecting industrial assets, which involved infiltrating coal and iron unions and breaking strikes (often with extreme violence), but, for a number of decades, its detectives were considered the gold standard of law enforcement.[19]

The Pinkerton Agency was only one of hundreds of private organizations that enforced the criminal law in the late nineteenth century – there were also various cattlemen's associations, bounty hunters, and vigilantes who filled the gaps left by weak or nonexistent law enforcement in the western states and territories. As we will see in Chapter 4, this pattern has repeated itself in modern-day society: When public law enforcement is insufficient – or appears to be insufficient – private security companies step in to fill the vacuum and provide their own security, whether in the form of security guards in retail stores or private police for gated communities, for example.

As the twentieth century progressed and public police supplanted private security across the country, police forces spread beyond major urban areas as smaller communities, states, and even the federal government began to develop their own police departments.[20] These departments increased in size and professionalism, which led to a shift in public attitudes toward the concept of public police forces. When these public forces were first introduced, they were met with great resistance from the general population, especially in the United States. However, eventually, public sentiment switched, as the increasing use of "private armies" to protect the interests of the railroads and other industrial-age giants led to a backlash against private police forces. This political fallout and the increasing professionalization of police departments led to a widespread belief that policing was a public function, to be controlled and overseen by the government.[21] As we will see in Chapter 4, this belief is still prevalent today; even though private police have once again grown to outnumber their public counterparts, they are perceived as less legitimate and less trustworthy than public police officers.

However, even as private security companies became less socially acceptable as the primary provider of law enforcement services, private volunteer groups continued to form when public law enforcement failed to meet community expectations. Chapter 4 examines a number of these volunteer groups that are still operating, such as the Guardian Angels in urban areas, neighborhood watch associations in cities and suburbs, and the Minutemen on the United States–Mexico border. For now, it will be useful to highlight a couple of historical examples of private volunteer groups from the 1960s and 1970s, both of which arose during a breakdown of the public criminal justice system. The first example is a group that was formed in a town in Louisiana in 1964, after the Ku Klux Klan threatened violence against anyone who supported the desegregation efforts of the Congress of

Racial Equality. When it became clear that the local police would not take any action against the planned Klan violence, a group of twenty Black men formed a paramilitary group known as the Deacons for Defense and Justice. The Deacons began patrolling neighborhoods and guarding civil rights activists. Their success led to Deacon chapters forming in twenty-one other towns in Mississippi, Alabama, and Louisiana. The Deacons went on to protect Black students who were protesting segregation in high schools in Louisiana and to provide security for desegregation campaigns in Mississippi. In 1966, Martin Luther King asked them to serve as a protective force during a march from Memphis to Jackson, Tennessee.[22]

Another example of a private volunteer group occurred in San Francisco in 1973. The growing lesbian, gay, bisexual, and transgender (LGBT) community was being routinely victimized by harassments, threats, and violence. Like in the southern states during the civil rights movement, the police took no action to protect the victims or arrest the criminals who were terrorizing them. In response, a minister named Ray Broshears who ran a community service center for the gay community decided to organize his own private security force. Taking inspiration from the Black Panther Party, which had been founded in nearby Oakland just a few years before, Broshears named the group the Lavender Panthers. The group trained in martial arts and armed themselves with chains and pool cues and began to patrol areas around gay bars and other areas where individuals of the LGBT community congregated. After a number of public standoffs with the individuals who had been intimidating and attacking members of their community, the city saw a decrease in incidents of harassment.[23]

PRIVATE CRIMINAL ADJUDICATIONS

Just as law enforcement duties were originally carried out by private parties, other aspects of the criminal justice system historically had little involvement from the state. As late as the eighteenth century, crime victims usually had to prosecute their own cases, since the Crown prosecutor got involved only in rare cases.[24] This led to private individuals banding together to form "felons' associations," in which members would all agree to chip in to fund the cost of a private prosecution when one of them was the victim of a crime. This was also true of the American colonies; as one historian put it: "[e]arly colonial governments played no active role in apprehending or prosecuting lawbreakers."[25] Most citizens in the colonies did not even have access to the court system, as the courts were generally located in capital cities and were too distant to deal with most crime. Thus, private parties frequently resolved criminal disputes on their own, using restitution and reparations. If the perpetrator was indigent, the victim would receive restitution through services by keeping the perpetrator as a servant for a fixed period of time.[26]

By the time the colonies became states in an independent nation, the government had taken control over most prosecutions, but many victims chose to treat crimes as nothing more than civil disputes. Thus, many perpetrators never faced criminal charges; instead, they would be sued by the victim and be forced to pay restitution to the victim rather than a fine to the state.[27] In addition, because of a weak state apparatus, "many communities bound together by strong reciprocal ties based on religion or ethnic background (e.g., Quakers, Mormons) chose to establish and enforce their own laws."[28] As we will see in Chapter 7, these homogeneous societies still exist today, and they continue to run their own quasi-criminal justice systems in parallel with, or sometimes instead of, the public criminal justice system.

As the state governments grew stronger, examples of private criminal adjudications became rarer, although isolated examples do appear throughout American history. The most well-known example of this phenomenon took place in San Francisco in the nineteenth century. In 1851, as the city's population soared, the public sheriff lacked the resources to apprehend the vast majority of people accused of a crime, and the overwhelmed public criminal court system (which met every two months) was unable to try many of those who were ultimately apprehended.[29] In response to this growing crisis, a group of citizens formed a "committee of vigilance," which made a formal statement announcing their intention to "maintain... the peace and good order of society."[30] The committee did its work with the tacit permission of the authorities for 100 days, making arrests, conducting trials, and carrying out punishment.[31] Out of ninety-one total arrests, the committee hanged four individuals, whipped one, deported fourteen to Australia, exiled fourteen more from the state of California, handed over fifteen to the public authorities, and discharged the other forty-three.[32] By all accounts, the committee enjoyed public support and its actions helped to lower the crime rate.[33]

PRIVATE DISPOSITIONS

San Francisco's committee did not just resolve criminal disputes; it also carried out the punishments that it handed down, including punishments of violence. Thus, in addition to being a private adjudicative body, it also engaged in the third phase of private criminal justice: private dispositions. The United States has a long history of imposing private criminal dispositions, otherwise known as vigilante justice. Sometimes, as with the private prosecutions of the colonial days or the private trials in San Francisco in the 1850s, private dispositions would be enforced after an adjudicative process but, often, they would be imposed in a more summary fashion.

The term vigilantism generally carries a negative connotation, as most people are uncomfortable with the vigilante tactic of usurping the state's monopoly on force to impose a coercive punishment without due process. However, as is the case with private adjudications, most cases of private dispositions come from early in the country's history in areas where the state was weak or altogether absent, so that it was necessary for private individuals to fill the vacuum.

Historically, vigilantism was also mostly a task undertaken by the wealthier members of society. Since vigilante organizations were primarily employed to protect property rights, and because engaging in vigilante actions generally took a significant amount of resources, most vigilante organizations in this country's history "were invariably started and led by the elite and had solidly middle-class, upwardly aspiring memberships."[34] The result was impressive: One expert estimates that between 1767 and 1902, there were nearly 500 vigilante organizations throughout the country, ranging in size from 12 to 6,000.[35] These groups operated outside the public criminal justice system, but often with the knowledge and consent of those who were members of it. They used "intimidation, flogging, banishment, and execution to maintain the order they thought necessary for survival."[36] Often these groups were quite formally organized, with hierarchies of command and written bylaws. One example of such bylaws comes from 1780 in Virginia, in which the founding members decry the large numbers of "lawless men" who "deprive honest men of their just rights and property, by stealing their horses, counterfeiting, and passing paper currency, and committing many other species of villainy . . . ." The document notes that it was "almost useless and unnecessary to have recourse to our laws to suppress and punish these freebooters, they having it in their power to extricate themselves when brought to justice by suborning witnesses who do swear them clear."[37]

These vigilante groups were sometimes known as "regulators," as they saw themselves as regulating the moral balance of the community. This term was first applied to a vigilante group in colonial New Jersey that was dedicated to inflicting corporal punishment on men who beat their wives. The punishment became well known in the community, causing "no small terror" among the men who had been committing this crime, and having some deterrent effect.[38]

As states such as Virginia and New Jersey developed a more robust public criminal justice system, its vigilante committees were dissolved, only to spring up again as the country moved west, in Texas, California, Montana, and dozens of other states and territories. American vigilantism was common on the frontier, where it was employed against cattle thieves, counterfeiters, and other criminals that took advantage of the inadequate public criminal justice system of that time. Many factors contributed to the rise of frontier vigilantism: towns' isolation from major metropolitan areas, the high cost of jails and trials, the uneven quality of law enforcement and judges, and the lack of long-standing community ties among the citizens, which allowed criminals to "pack juries with their friends" and "brib[e] and intimidat[e] judges and juries."[39] Furthermore, the state's monopoly on force was not yet ingrained in the national culture, given the long Anglo-American history of private individuals enforcing the criminal law.

By the beginning of the twentieth century, the age of vigilante justice was coming to a close, although isolated instances of self-help still occurred under the right circumstances.[40] In their recent book SHADOW VIGILANTES, Paul and Sarah Robinson trace a series of vigilante actions in the 1970s and 1980s that were undertaken by private citizens to combat the drug trade when police intervention was absent or ineffective. In 1973, when drug dealing and its associated violence was endemic to downtown Baltimore, a group called Black October killed two drug dealers. After each murder, they sent messages to the local paper that the murders were meant as a punishment for the destruction that the dealers had caused in their community. Groups in other cities took less dramatic actions: In Detroit in 1988, residents burned down nearly 100 known crack houses, with the apparent support of the community. A poll shows that 87 percent of the residents found that the actions were justified, and when two people were arrested for one of the arsons, they were acquitted in the face of strong evidence in a clear case of jury nullification. Around the same time in Philadelphia, residents organized and formed picket lines outside crack houses, preventing buyers from entering, and persuaded local utility companies to cut service to the houses.[41]

As we will see in Chapter 8, instances of vigilante justice continue to this day. Even more powerfully, the myth of the vigilante has become ingrained within the American story, and it survives in modern times in many of our fictional heroes, from the Lone Ranger to Batman to countless movie characters played by action heroes such as Charles Bronson and Bruce Willis.

Of course, American vigilantism has a darker side to it as well. The term brings to mind not only movie action heroes but also domestic terrorist groups, such as the Ku Klux Klan, that use violence and intimidation to advance their own malevolent values. The 1780 bylaws that were quoted earlier in the chapter were from a vigilante group led by Colonel William Lynch, whose name ever since has been associated with extrajudicial executions by private citizens. Plenty of vigilante groups in the southern states, before and after the Civil War, were dedicated not to enforcing the criminal law but to maintaining a system of white supremacy and ensuring the continued subjugation of people of color.

I will argue in Chapter 8 that groups such as the Klan do not qualify as true vigilantes, as their purpose is not to punish transgressions of core criminal law principles but rather to enforce their own view of morality and further their own political goals. However, even if we set aside groups with an expressly racist purpose, vigilantes are often associated with reactionary politics, seeking to protect property rights and maintain the reigning social and economic structure. Throughout history, many mainstream vigilante groups were known for focusing their attention on outsiders, who all too often were Black, Asian, Latinx, Native American, recent immigrants, or some other perceived threat to the established social order. The private adjudications set up in San Francisco in 1851, for example, indisputably helped to restore order and reduce crime, but also "had as its target ethnic and religious minorities."[42]

These authoritarian tendencies in vigilante movements, and in the private criminal justice system more generally, are shameful but unsurprising. In the absence of the relative democratic accountability, procedural safeguards, and transparency of the public criminal justice system, instruments of the private criminal justice system can have the effect – or even the purpose – of targeting the less enfranchised in society. One of the recurring themes of our investigation into the private criminal justice system will be to examine these anti-egalitarian elements, compare them with their public criminal justice system counterparts, and determine potential ways of eliminating or minimizing them.

THE RISE OF THE PUBLIC CRIMINAL JUSTICE SYSTEM

Although the private sector dominated the criminal justice system up until the mid-nineteenth century, the past 150 years has seen the growth of the public criminal justice system, which began as a steady climb and then exploded into a significant aspect of our economy. At the dawn of our public criminal justice system in the middle of the 1800s, the United States had a few hundred police officers patrolling the streets of the larger eastern cities.[43] The first true federal police force – the United States Secret Service – was founded in 1865 with a few dozen agents as a branch of the Treasury Department with the mandate to enforce counterfeiting laws. A few decades later, in 1908, President Theodore Roosevelt used an executive order to create the Federal Bureau of Investigation (FBI), which began with thirty-four agents. By 1915, the FBI had grown to 360 agents and, in 1920, the Secret Service mandate grew to include enforcing prohibition, which caused their numbers to swell to 4,000 officers. Around this same time, states began to create their own police forces, which – when compared with their city counterparts – were highly professionalized, disciplined, and less prone to corruption.[44] The rest of the twentieth century is a history of the steady growth of all three levels of policing – local, state, and federal. By 2008, the total number of public law enforcement officers rose above 700,000 for the first time in history.[45]

Unsurprisingly, a larger police footprint also coincided with an increase in incarceration. In 1880, the first year for which reliable numbers are available, the total number of Americans in jails and prisons was just over 30,000 – about 0.06 percent of the population of the country. The total number slowly increased for the next ninety years, outpacing population growth by about two to one, until by 1970 our country was incarcerating 196,000 people – just under 0.1 percent of the population.[46] It then ballooned as the populist concerns discussed in Chapter 1 began to drive policy decisions and incapacitation became the primary goal of the criminal justice system. By 2009, the same year that the United States passed the milestone of 700,000 public police officers, the country had 2.3 million people behind bars – over 0.7 percent of the total population of the country[47] – and the country was spending approximately $300 billion a year on the public criminal justice system.[48]

The numbers alone only tell part of the story. Up until quite recently, public attitudes strongly supported a vigorous public criminal justice system. As noted above, the rise of professional police forces, neutral prosecutors' offices, and a robust judiciary created a widespread belief that crime control was primarily, if not exclusively, a public function. The FBI has long since surpassed the Pinkerton Agency as the elite law enforcement institution in the country, and private criminal justice became associated in the public eye with cheap, underqualified rent-a-cops, gated communities that sought to exclude the poor, and reactionary vigilante groups. Meanwhile, up until at least the mid-1990s, the general public, intent on winning the war on drugs and scared of the "superpredators" roaming their streets, supported the rapid expansion of the public criminal justice system. In 1994, President Bill Clinton signed a popular bipartisan bill that added 100,000 police officers to local agencies and proposed adding 5,000 prosecutors to communities across the country.

CONCLUSION

By almost any measure, the public criminal justice system is a powerful, influential force in our society. Throughout history, we have seen the relationship between the state and the criminal justice system wax and wane but, in our current era, this relationship appears to be as strong as ever. Engorged state and federal penal codes contain a record number of crimes, which are enforced by armies of police officers serving in every city, county, and state. Government prosecutors wield enormous power, sending hundreds of thousands of people each year into a vast prison industrial complex. Under this conventional wisdom, the public criminal justice system is as robust as any time in history.

However, that conventional wisdom is not the entire story – and it may not even be the most important part of the story. First, there is strong evidence that the power and influence of the public criminal justice system is on the decline. It turns out that 2009 was the high-water mark for growth of the public criminal justice system – since then the total number of police in the country has decreased,[49] and the number of individuals who are incarcerated has dropped by 17 percent.[50] Perhaps more importantly, political dialogue has begun about the need to end mass incarceration, repurpose the police, and reduce the number of crimes that prosecutors charge. All signs point to a continued reduction of the size and influence of the public criminal justice system in the near future.

More importantly, the private system that was the primary method of enforcing our criminal laws for centuries has remained with us, even as the public criminal justice system has grown to obscure it. The private system has changed its form and, in some ways, has become more intertwined with its public counterpart. Over the past fifty years, it has grown alongside the public criminal justice system. And most important of all, the current conditions are conducive for the private criminal justice system to become even more ubiquitous. This chapter has shown how instances of private criminal justice, from private policing all the way through to vigilante actions, become more robust in times when the effectiveness, fairness, or perceived legitimacy of the public criminal justice system has been thrown into doubt. In the next chapter, we will examine how modern-day inadequacies in the massive public criminal justice system are allowing a private system to not just survive but actually flourish.

3

Public Failings, Private Opportunities

We saw in the last chapter how the past 150 years have seen a paradigm shift in the way criminal justice was administered. For centuries, private parties shouldered the primary, if not exclusive, duty of enforcing crime, and often took the lead in adjudicating criminal disputes as well. However, as society became more urban, and as the state began to grow in size and scope, the government inexorably gained control of every aspect of the criminal justice system, from large paramilitary police forces to professional prosecutors to a sprawling prison system. However, even in the late twentieth century, as the public criminal justice system was growing exponentially, we still saw evidence of private enforcement and even private adjudication when segments of the general public perceived a gap between what they expected the criminal justice system to do and what it was actually accomplishing.

Today we can see many ways in which the public criminal justice system is failing. This is not to say that the public administration of criminal justice is on the verge of collapse or that it does not satisfactorily carry out certain necessary functions. However, it is becoming increasingly clear that the public criminal justice system is inadequate on many counts. It incarcerates an enormous percentage of our population, disproportionately affecting people of color, with almost no attempt to rehabilitate or reintegrate the perpetrators of crime. It does not satisfy – nor is it designed to satisfy – the needs of crime victims. Most recently, significant numbers of people are beginning to reevaluate the scope and mission of both the police and the prosecutors, which will likely result in at least a partial repurposing of the public criminal justice system.

In a sense, the criminal justice system is no different from many other industries in which failures of the public system inevitably lead to the development (or reinvigoration) of a private alternative. It is hard to think of any other industry or area of the economy in which there is no private alternative to the public provisioning of services. From primary education to health care, from the delivery of the mail to the maintenance of roadways to the resolution of civil disputes, nearly every service that is provided by the state also has a private alternative. If receiving the service is deemed to be a fundamental right or, as in the case of crime control, if the service is believed to provide a positive externality to society, the state offers to deliver the service for free – either to everyone or perhaps only to those who have demonstrated that they lack the ability to pay for the service themselves. Primary, secondary, and even college education fall into this category, as does health care, criminal legal defense services, the provision of libraries, and a vast array of other social services. However, even though these services are deemed to be so important that the state will guarantee them to everybody, there is a general consensus that those who wish to spend more money to obtain higher quality services should be able to do so. Although the state will always provide a free public school education, it would seem quite radical to prohibit individuals from opting out of the public school system and purchasing a private school education that is either of a higher quality or perhaps of the same quality but better tailored to the family's perceived educational needs (for example a smaller school, a school that teaches the values of a certain religion, or a school that focuses on teaching fine arts or science). In the civil justice system, our society has created and maintained a robust public civil law court system, but also allows parties the option of private alternative dispute resolution systems, which may be cheaper, faster, more flexible, or simply more responsive to the parties' needs. In many of these cases, such as education and health care, the state plays an active role in regulating the private alternatives to ensure that they are of adequate quality and do not deceive or otherwise unfairly treat their clients. Whether and to what extent this regulation would be necessary in a private criminal justice system will be discussed in Chapter 9.

From this perspective, the return of a private criminal justice system seems not only likely, but inevitable. We have already seen in the last chapter that, throughout most of history, the provisioning of criminal justice has been primarily carried out by private actors. Today, in the face of the growing failures of the public criminal justice system and the potential benefits of a private alternative, we are seeing a return to the traditional role of the private sector in dealing with criminal activity through the increased prominence of both private law enforcement and alternative dispute resolution programs for criminal cases.

Of course, when we speak of "privatizing" the criminal justice system, we do not mean a total abandonment of the state's provisioning of criminal justice services. Instead, we are talking about building alternative private methods that can be used to respond to criminal activity if both the victim and the defendant choose to use them. Given the numerous problems inherent in the public criminal justice system, it is inevitable that the key participants in the criminal justice system will demand to have such a choice.

It is this question of choice that is central to a successful private criminal justice system. In many cases, the defendants themselves choose to participate in the private criminal justice system. Sometimes this will occur because a private party has control over some aspect of the defendant's life and thus can impose costs on the defendant if they refuse to participate in the private resolution. For example, the defendant may be a member of a community such as a company, a religious organization, or a university that can impose its own sanctions if the defendant refuses to cooperate. We will discuss these possibilities in Chapter 7.

A far more common incentive for defendants to participate in the private criminal justice system is that victims will agree not to involve the public criminal justice system if the defendant cooperates. In this way, much of the private criminal justice system works in the shadow of the public system, using the ever-present threat of arrest, prosecution, and possible incarceration to induce the defendant's cooperation. This incentive cannot exist, however, unless the outcome of the private system is likely to be better for the defendant than the outcome in the public system. We will consider these occurrences in Chapters 5 and 6.

In many cases, the defendant does not make a choice as to whether to participate in the private criminal justice system. For example, as noted in Chapter 4, a defendant who violates the law might be apprehended by private police or public police, depending on where and when the crime occurs. The defendant has little say in the matter, although they might be treated very differently by private police than they would be by public police – private police, for example, are far less likely to refer the case to a public prosecutor, and thus the defendant is less likely to face incarceration for their offense. Furthermore, if the victim or some other third party decides to take unilateral action against the defendant – what is commonly known as vigilante justice – the defendant has no say in the matter, as we will discuss in Chapter 8.

Thus, depending on the context, a defendant may or may not have a choice as to whether to participate in the private criminal justice system. However, the victim almost always makes a choice to opt out of the public criminal justice system and resolve the criminal case without recourse to the public police and court system. If at any point in the process the victim believes that they will be better off in the public system, they can always initiate the necessary procedures to start a formal criminal law case. Thus, the private criminal justice system must provide the victim with a better (or additional) benefit that they will not get from the public system.

The revitalization of the private criminal justice system is thus inextricably linked to the shortcomings of the public criminal justice system, which provide incentives for victims and defendants to turn to alternatives. We have already introduced the first of these shortcomings in the last chapter: the extremely long sentences faced by defendants. The second is the failure of the public criminal justice system to meet the needs of the victims. The third, which has become far more significant in recent years, is the changes we have seen in public policing and prosecuting, which have led to a gap in the public criminal justice system that can be filled by private actors.

MASS INCARCERATION

We have already seen in Chapter 1 how rehabilitation, which was the hallmark of the corrections system for most of the twentieth century, was abandoned in the 1970s. It has been replaced by an ever more punitive system that incarcerates defendants at an astonishing rate. Over the last five decades, perhaps the most perceptive and eloquent critic of our treatment of criminal defendants has been Judge Jack Weinstein, who was a federal trial court judge in the Eastern District of New York for fifty-three years. Judge Weinstein was appointed to the federal bench in 1967, and over his long judicial career he witnessed firsthand the politicization of the public criminal justice system as populist forces pushed it into adopting ever more punitive measures. In 1993, Judge Weinstein wrote an op-ed for the *New York Times* in which he detailed how the war on drugs of the 1980s had resulted in extremely harsh sentences for first-time drug couriers – usually as long as four and a half years and in some cases a mandatory minimum of ten years. He chose to stop presiding over drug cases, as he had grown "increasingly despondent over the cruelties and self-defeating character of our war on drugs."[1] For the rest of his career, Judge Weinstein protested the draconian sentences of the federal criminal justice system, expanding his critiques beyond the long penalties for drug crimes. In his view, even violent criminals were subject to far too much prison time, and alternative sentences that would include social services and community programming were either absent or woefully underfunded. Instead, the federal system relied on a one-size-fits-all response to criminal behavior: incarceration. "Lengthy mandatory minimums, and the penological theory of incapacitation continue to be justified by a lack of sentencing alternatives for society's 'unredeemables.'"[2] As Judge Weinstein and many other reformers have pointed out, the sentencing process has become much more mechanical, with both mandatory minimums and sentencing guidelines replacing individualized, case-by-case judicial decision-making.

Lengthy sentences and mandatory minimums are powerful symbols of the public criminal justice system's reliance on incarceration. However, as Professor John Pfaff of Fordham Law School recently pointed out, the primary driver of mass incarceration is not longer sentences but the increasing number of short-term incarcerations. From 1991 to 2014, both violent crime and property crime dropped by more than a third. And the rate at which crimes resulted in an arrest remained relatively constant. However, during that time, the incarceration rate nearly tripled. The reason was not that sentences for specific crimes were getting longer – in fact, the average sentence for most crimes dropped during that time. Instead, the rising incarceration rate was primarily the result of prosecutors beginning to charge crimes as felonies at much higher rates. As Professor Pfaff points out, between 1994 and 2008, the number of arrests fell, but the number of felony charges increased by 40 percent; thus "the number of people admitted to prison rose by about 40 percent, from 360,000 to 505,000, and almost all of that increase was due to prosecutors bringing more and more felony cases against a diminishing pool of arrestees."[3]

Professor Pfaff draws a number of important conclusions from these data about the need to change both prosecutorial incentives and public attitudes about our overly punitive responses to crime. However, for our purposes, these data highlight the fact that criminals who enter the public criminal justice system face a growing certainty that they will face felony prison time for their crimes. Although the decades-long sentences that make headlines are not the norm, the "moderate" sentences that criminals face if they are convicted are still significant: a median of over a year for burglary and petty larceny, a year and a half for drug trafficking, and nearly two years for illegal possession of a weapon or aggravated assault.[4] Although these sentences do not make headlines and may not strike many individuals as being unduly harsh, they provide a strong incentive for a defendant to opt out of the public criminal justice system and make a deal with a private party that will be far less onerous than over a year in prison.

In addition to a likely sentence of incarceration, many other aspects of the public criminal justice system make it an unattractive option to criminal defendants. We have already discussed the many different collateral consequences that often accompany a criminal conviction, from loss of basic civil liberties such as the right to vote and the right to carry a firearm to the challenges of obtaining a job with a criminal record. In addition, every criminal conviction on a defendant's record will likely increase the length of a sentence for the next crime, as prosecutors and judges routinely increase sentences for repeat offenders. Thus, a defendant who opts out of the public criminal justice system can avoid building the type of record that can be used against them if they are later caught committing another crime.

Many Americans believe that these consequences are exactly what criminals deserve: harsh punishment, escalating sentences for further instances of criminal activity, and collateral consequences that arguably keep the public safe by preventing convicted felons from owning guns or working in certain professions. Others, like Judge Weinstein, argue for a rethinking of our treatment of convicted criminals – with some going as far as to say that we should abolish jails and prisons entirely.[5] However, for our current purposes, we are not concerned with these normative debates; all we are trying to establish is the relatively uncontroversial point that convicted criminals face serious, unpleasant consequences in the public criminal justice system. Thus, when offered a choice by victims, private police, or other third parties who might become aware of their criminal activity, an alleged perpetrator has a strong incentive to opt out of the public criminal justice system and agree to less onerous procedures and consequences that are offered as part of the private criminal justice system.

Indeed, even before a defendant is convicted – even if a defendant is never convicted – participation in the public criminal justice system means that they still must enter and navigate the inconveniences, indignities, and traumas of the criminal justice process. Almost all criminal defendants are arrested by police and forcibly transported to a precinct, where they are searched – sometimes strip searched – and then fingerprinted, photographed, and processed through the system. This process usually takes hours and can sometimes take days. The fact of the arrest itself is made public, and is entered on the defendant's permanent criminal record. A small number of defendants who are accused of the most minor of crimes are then given a court date and released. Everyone else is transported to court while still in custody, where they undergo arraignment and a bail hearing. A large percentage of defendants (33 percent of individuals charged on the state level and 68 percent of those charged on the federal level) will be unable to make bail and will remain in custody until their criminal case is resolved.[6] Those who gain release must return to court (usually every month) for many months while their case is continued for motions to be filed, hearings to be held, and courtrooms to be freed up for trial. Each of these appearances means a day off work (if the defendant still has a job after the arrest) and hours of waiting for a case to be called. Defendants who do not qualify for public defenders must pay for their own attorneys. And almost all defendants who are ultimately found guilty must pay hundreds of dollars in fees and fines.

A few decades ago, Professor Malcom M. Feeley of Berkeley Law School wrote an influential book entitled THE PROCESS IS THE PUNISHMENT. Professor Feeley spent a year studying the proceedings of a specific criminal courtroom in Connecticut, and he concluded that, for most defendants, the primary punishment they faced after an arrest occurred before conviction – the wasted time, lost wages, bail bondsman fees, attorney fees, and general humiliation of being required to appear in court over and over again until the case is resolved. Both prosecutors and defense attorneys commented that the mere fact of being "in the system" was enough to teach defendants a lesson, and that defendants often pled guilty early in the process to simply avoid having to come back to court every month for the next six to eight months.[7]

The process that Professor Feeley observed in the early 1990s has not changed substantially in the intervening decades. Professor Carissa Hessick of the University of North Carolina studied a Brooklyn courtroom in 2020 and saw the same phenomenon: defendants missing work and paying the subway fare to appear in court, where they would wait for hours in a courtroom for their case to be called, not being allowed to talk, eat, drink, use their cell phone, or even read, only to have the case continued for another day. And these were the defendants who were out on bail: A significant percentage of defendants were sitting in jail for weeks or months before their case could be resolved. And all of this was before the defendant was convicted – that is, before the "official" punishment was imposed.[8]

Compared with this treatment, and the strong likelihood of incarceration that awaits them at the end of this process, it is no surprise that many defendants will prefer the streamlined procedures, private resolutions, and non-carceral consequences of the private criminal justice system. Of course, this is only half of the equation; a private criminal justice system also needs the participation of the victims of crimes.

TREATMENT OF VICTIMS

An outsider who observes the skyrocketing incarceration rate might conclude that, at the very least, it gives victims what they want by imposing penalties on those who perpetrated a crime against them. Throughout most of history, victims have born all of the cost and responsibility for bringing offenders to justice, being forced to rely on volunteers or to hire private police of dubious skill. Today, the state brings a vast amount of resources, using professional, well-trained personnel to detect, apprehend, try, and punish criminals – all at no direct cost to the victim.

And yet surveys show that victims tend to be deeply dissatisfied with the public criminal justice system.[9] Although crime rates have dropped dramatically in recent years, they are still higher than in most other Western countries.[10] Meanwhile, fear of crime has remained a constant over the past fifty years, even as incarceration rates have ballooned. In 2021, 37 percent of the population reported that there was an area within a mile of their home where they would not feel safe walking alone at night,[11] 43 percent of Americans reported that they "frequently" or "occasionally" worried about having their home burglarized or their car broken into or stolen, 52 percent of the population reported that they avoid going to certain places that they would otherwise want to go to because of a fear of crime, and 35 percent purchased a gun to protect themselves or their home from criminals.[12]

The way the criminal justice system is structured – with only a small percentage of criminals apprehended and ultimately punished, but with those punishments being quite severe – ends up satisfying nobody. We have already seen that this structure is inefficient from a utilitarian point of view, as the best way to achieve deterrence is to catch more criminals, not lock up the few whom we do catch for longer periods of time. The structure also breeds contempt for the criminal justice system from both sides of the ideological divide. Those who favor rehabilitation and believe that the criminal justice system is too punitive critique the massive numbers of people in prison and the long sentences of incarceration, which often extend far longer than necessary to achieve deterrence. Those who are in favor of treating criminals harshly point out that, although the median sentence for a person who is convicted of a crime can be substantial, once you factor in the low probability of being caught and successfully prosecuted, the average expected sentence for an individual who commits a serious felony is relatively short. One commentator has calculated that the expected sentence for an individual who commits a robbery is sixty-six days, while the expected sentence for an individual who commits a burglary is thirteen days.[13]

Once a specific criminal case begins, victims are treated extremely poorly by the criminal law system. If "the process is the punishment" for criminal defendants, it is almost nearly as much for crime victims. The numerous delays inherent in our criminal justice system are both financially costly for victims, who must miss work, and emotionally costly for victims, who suffered trauma as a result of the crime and are seeking closure.[14] Because victims are not parties to the action, they are generally treated no differently from any other witness to the offense – and most witnesses are treated merely as tools in the overworked, underfunded criminal justice system. Victims have very little say in how a criminal case moves forward; throughout the whole process, they are little more than observers.[15]

In response to this dissatisfaction, victims' rights groups began mobilizing and lobbying for more power in the public criminal justice system. In the early 1980s, President Ronald Reagan convened the Task Force on Victims of Crime, which concluded that "the innocent victims of crime have been overlooked, their pleas for justice have gone unheeded, and their wounds – personal, emotional, financial – have gone unattended."[16] Since then, a majority of states have passed some form of victims' rights legislation, culminating in the federal Crime Victims' Rights Act of 2004. These laws typically provide victims with the right to be notified of key aspects of the proceedings, the right to "consult" with the prosecutor, and the right to speak at sentencing.[17] However, even with these rights, victim surveys still indicate a significant dissatisfaction with the process.[18]

As noted above, some of this dissatisfaction is due to the ineffectiveness of the public criminal justice system, which apprehends and convicts such a small percentage of those who commit crimes. However, many of the victim complaints come down to a lack of control – victims do not control how public law enforcement resources are used, how a case is adjudicated in the system, or the degree of punishment that is imposed on the criminal if they are found guilty. Victims want to both be able to control the processing of the case and have their preferences followed by the prosecutor – and all too often neither of these desires was fulfilled.[19]

This lack of victim control exists by design – the public criminal justice system is meant to reflect the will of the state, as personified by the prosecutor, not the victim. The victim is not a party in the public criminal justice system, and it is the parties – the prosecutor and defendant – who make all of the tactical decisions about how the case proceeds. At best, the prosecutor may consult with the victim on some questions – indeed, some victims' rights legislation mandates that the prosecutors give the victim input at certain stages.[20] At worst, the victim is viewed by the prosecutor as a tool, as a means to the end of getting a conviction, just like any other witness or piece of evidence. In some cases – such as domestic violence cases or other cases in which the victim may be scared or reluctant to cooperate – the prosecutor will use the power of the state to coerce the witness into testifying against their will. And, in every case, the prosecutor makes all of the final decisions about how – and if – the case will go forward.

Thus, the continuing attempts by victims' groups to have influence over the public criminal justice system will always fall short, because the entire point of the public criminal justice system is to bypass the victim and make decisions that are best for society as a whole, as determined by the prosecutor. Although prosecutors should consult with victims about their wishes, and judges should consider victim impact statements at sentencing, ultimately the prosecutor represents the state, and each judge will follow their own sentencing philosophy. Thus, both institutional actors – the prosecutor and the judge – will often make decisions that are contrary to the desires of the victim.

Given these dissatisfactions, it is easy to see why private criminal justice alternatives are appealing to crime victims. Private criminal processes use a more streamlined procedure, which is less time consuming and less emotionally draining for victims. They also allow the victim greater control of the proceedings. As we will see in future chapters, the range of victims who choose the private criminal justice system over the public system is broad, but the reasons for the choice are all strikingly similar. A college student who has been the victim of a sexual assault on campus may choose to proceed through the more victim-friendly university disciplinary system. A retail store who catches a shoplifter will impose its own swift punishment, maintaining control over the outcome without having its employees spend time and resources appearing in court. A supervisor who discovers that an employee stole company funds may want to keep the incident quiet rather than having it become part of the public record. A victim of domestic violence may want to turn to restorative justice, which will allow them to forgive their partner and perhaps demand a change in behavior, rather than let a stranger in the form of a prosecutor decide the appropriate sanction. Members of a community that has suffered vandalism or graffiti often prefer that the perpetrator make amends in the community rather than be incarcerated. All of these parties want to keep some measure of control of the proceedings and the outcome, which they cannot do if they hand the case over to the public police.

RETHINKING THE ROLE OF POLICE AND PROSECUTORS

So far we have focused on how dissatisfaction with the public criminal justice system on the part of defendants and victims provides incentives for these parties to resolve their disputes without recourse to public police and prosecutors. This in turn fuels the growth of the private criminal justice system in all of its various incarnations. However, there is one more factor that encourages the growth of the private criminal justice system: Shifting political dynamics are causing the public criminal justice system to shrink, thereby creating a vacuum that will be filled by private law enforcement and private systems of adjudication. This contraction of the public criminal justice system manifests itself in two ways: the defunding or repurposing of the police and the rise of the progressive prosecutor movement.

In the wake of massive protests in the summer of 2020, cities began to rethink the role of their police forces. Protestors called for reducing the size of police departments and changing communities' response systems so that police are not always the first responders to all 911 calls.[21] Advocates sought to enhance the role of alternative responders, such as social workers or medical or mental health providers, based on the theory that these professionals can de-escalate situations and resolve problems without arrests or confrontations.[22]

This movement to decrease police budgets was met with some initial success – in 2020, municipalities across the country reduced spending on budgets by over

$840 million in their police departments.[23] In the fiscal year 2021, cities like New York, Seattle, Denver, and Minneapolis all reduced their spending on police budgets by 10 percent or more, while dozens of others cut funding to a lesser extent.[24] The defunding process has been slower than advocates would have liked, and some cities have restored or increased their police budgets after initial cuts,[25] but the movement to reduce police footprints is still very much alive.

The main purpose of these proposed changes is to decrease the presence and influence of the police in the community. The changes also reflect a growing recognition that many of the situations to which police respond do not involve criminal activity, and so do not require a law enforcement officer with powers of arrest. Nationwide, police respond to over 240 million 911 calls a year, and they also engage in tens of millions of other interactions on the street, on roads and highways, in schools, and in housing projects. The vast majority of these calls and interactions do not result in an arrest. And even those that do result in an arrest do not necessarily require an armed public law enforcement officer: One study concluded that only around 5 percent of the arrests that police make involve serious violent crime.[26]

The term "defunding the police" can have different meanings depending on the context. At its most extreme, it means abolishing a municipality's police department altogether and creating a new agency that de-emphasizes law enforcement and prioritizes a more holistic, public health-oriented approach.[27] Even at its most moderate, it means cutting police budgets and shifting some of their current roles to other organizations, so that many calls that now go to the police would instead be routed to social workers, psychologists, and other community outreach members.[28] There is no real model for how police departments will interact with their communities after these changes,[29] but if reformers are successful in their goals, far fewer individuals will end up interacting with police officers, and thus far fewer individuals will enter the public criminal justice system.[30] To better understand how a scaled down police department might operate, it is useful to first examine the various functions of a modern police force.

Under current practices, police respond to many different types of situations, which can be divided into roughly four categories. The first is the many police functions that are unrelated to crime control, such as public safety, transportation, or health problems, which are not criminal in nature. These include responding to a car accident, a medical emergency, or a fire or other dangerous condition. A recent article by Professor Shima Baradaran Baughman of the University of Utah argues that these functions, and not crime control, are actually the primary functions of police officers.[31] She cites a recent survey that shows that police in big cities spend 37 percent of their time on noncriminal calls, and an additional 15 percent of their time on traffic issues.[32]

The second category involves situations in which an individual appears to be doing something suspicious (at least in the eyes of the witness), but no actual crime has been observed. For example, a witness may hear yelling and crashing from the apartment next door, or see an individual walking slowly along a line of parked cars, looking into their windows. Often the witness might be the police officer themselves, who is on patrol and sees what could be a drug deal or a person potentially casing a store or a home for a burglary. Upon further investigation, the officer may determine that there is probable cause to believe a crime has been committed, but it is also possible that there was no criminal activity at all, or that the intervention of the officer prevents the crime from occurring.

The third category is situations in which a crime is technically being observed, but the optimal response to that crime is not an arrest but instead a reconciliation, de-escalation, and/or a civil consequence. Reasonable people can and do differ in their opinions of what types of crimes belong in this category, but almost everyone agrees that not every act of criminal conduct should be handled by the public criminal justice system. Examples of conduct that could fall into this category include a homeowner who is hosting a late night party that causes excessive noise, a mentally ill person who is verbally threatening others, a homeless person who is sleeping on a sidewalk or the subway, an underage individual who is drinking alcohol, and so on. As society's views change, certain criminal actions move in or out of this category; for example, a few decades ago, many police officers (and society as a whole) might have placed domestic violence and drunk driving in this category, while few would do so today. Conversely, marijuana possession is unlikely to lead to an arrest today, even in those dwindling jurisdictions where it is still illegal under state law.[33]

The fourth category of conduct that police respond to is when there is evidence that a serious crime has occurred, and the officer who responds believes that an arrest is an appropriate and necessary response. These situations differ from the second category in that there is sufficient evidence to make an arrest, and they differ from the third category in that the crime is sufficiently severe that the defendant should enter the criminal justice system.

One result of the police reform movement may be to create a system in which armed law enforcement officers respond only to the fourth category of conduct. There are logistical challenges to transitioning to such a system, such as determining which category the conduct falls into before deciding what type of agency should respond. However, alternative institutions and agencies are already being created to replace police officers in responding to certain situations. Some cities in Oregon, for example, have created a program that dispatches a crisis response team that consists of a mental health professional and a medic to respond to certain 911 calls and nonemergency police calls, particularly those that appear to involve individuals with mental health problems.[34] The team seeks to resolve situations, which may involve potentially dangerous or criminal activity, without resorting to the criminal justice system.[35] Over a one-year period, the program handled approximately 24,000 calls, and only 150 required police assistance. Before the program existed, it is likely that police would have responded to a much higher percentage of such calls.[36] A group in Los Angeles has experimented with a similar system known as Community

Alternatives to 911 (CAT-911). According to CAT-911's website, its purpose is straightforward:

> The vision of Community Alternatives to 911 is a city and region where local communities have the resources and strong, interpersonal relationships needed to respond constructively and healthfully to problems together. We know that we cannot depend on the broken criminal justice system to solve our problems and that calling 911 often just makes the situation worse – if they respond at all. CAT 911 is about building transformative justice that lets us take control of our lives and our communities into our own hands and nurtures each other's growth and human possibility.[37]

CAT-911 advertises that it can provide responses to a wide range of incidents, including domestic violence, sexual violence, police violence, and "acute first aid needs when paramedics are not responding or there is a concern about police involvement."[38] Thus, we see a direct correlation between the loss of legitimacy of the public police and the rise of alternative private responders.

This transition will result in far fewer interactions between police and civilians, and a corresponding increase in the number of incidents that are handled by nonpolice entities. Some of these nonpolice entities will be other state actors, such as social workers or medical professionals, who are better equipped to deal with the noncriminal emergencies and disturbances that constitute our first category. However, if police decide to pull back – or are forced to pull back by new regulations or budget cuts – from responding to the second or third categories of incidents, where actual crime might be occurring, they will leave a vacuum that will likely be filled in part by private law enforcement – either paid police or neighborhood volunteers. In other words, reducing police presence will change the way that our society responds to suspected criminal activity. Specifically, it will mean that thousands if not millions of interactions that formerly took place between civilians and police will be replaced by interactions between civilians and private individuals. Many, if not most, of these interactions will not lead to criminal charges – indeed, one of the purposes of transitioning from police to alternative responders is to decrease the number of interactions that may lead to criminal charges. However, many of these interactions will still involve private individuals observing (or being the victims of) criminal activity.

Even if the size and influence of police departments does not significantly shrink, attitudes about the police can affect police behavior. Studies show that high-profile police shootings can have a significant effect on police response to crimes: As the police lose perceived legitimacy, community members become less willing to call 911 in response to perceived criminal activity;[39] meanwhile, the police themselves may become more reluctant to engage in proactive policing.[40] Taken together, these changes will likely result in police officers being a less common presence on our streets, in our schools, in public housing projects, and in many other public spaces.[41]

These changes in policing will often be joined by an even more significant political movement: the increasing number of progressive prosecutors, a phenomenon we briefly touched on in Chapter 1. Up until the middle of the 2010s, almost every local prosecutor in the country emphasized crime control as the primary objective of their office. Then, beginning in 2015, some urban counties began electing a new type of prosecutor with a more progressive ideology. As of 2022, progressive prosecutors have been elected in about half of the states and now run the prosecutor's office in Chicago, Philadelphia, Boston, Baltimore, San Francisco, Manhattan, Los Angeles, and Detroit.

Like many broad movements, the exact contours of what it means to be a progressive prosecutor varies from jurisdiction to jurisdiction, and some prosecutors may claim the mantle of the movement without being truly committed to substantive or structural change to the role of the prosecutor. The stated goals of progressive prosecutors include demanding greater accountability for police misconduct, eliminating cash bail, and increasing transparency in prosecutorial decision-making. However, perhaps the most common aspect of progressive prosecutors is the determination to reduce or eliminate prosecution for petty and nonviolent crime and to reduce incarceration levels through fewer prosecutions, as well as increased diversion programs, treatment programs, and uses of restorative justice. Indeed, many of these prosecutors have issued formal "decline to prosecute" policies, in which they instruct their line prosecutors to refuse to prosecute certain crimes except in extraordinary circumstances. Some of these policies include only low-level drug possession crimes and prostitution, but others are more extensive, including thefts up to $750 and simple assaults. Thus, these laws will remain on the books in these jurisdictions – so the underlying activity will still be criminal under the law – but individuals who commit these crimes will not enter the public criminal justice system.

As progressive prosecutors come to power in more cities, the footprint of the public criminal justice system will shrink even further, as fewer crimes – especially less serious crimes – are charged, and those that are charged are less likely to result in a traditional, carceral punishment. Debate will continue among academics and the general public about whether this shift is desirable, but progressive prosecutors still remain popular in many jurisdictions. This shift, like the change in policing patterns, will mean that fewer instances of criminal activity will end up in the criminal justice system, increasing the amount of crime that receives no public adjudication or punishment. This conduct will include a large number of nonviolent crimes, such as disorderly conduct, reckless endangerment, trespass, vandalism, theft, and perhaps even drug sale and possession. It will also include some crimes of violence such as domestic violence and sexual assault that, for various reasons, are not prosecuted by the state. As with the shrinking footprint of the public police, the lower numbers of criminal prosecutions will lead to a growing number of crimes that are unresolved by the public criminal justice system.

CONCLUSION

When the government's provisioning of services fails to meet the needs of those who consume those services, a private alternative will arise to fill the demand. Both defendants and victims are treated poorly by the public criminal justice system, giving each of them a strong incentive to find alternative methods of resolving criminal disputes.

The dissatisfaction with the public criminal justice system felt by defendants and victims creates the opportunity for private settlements and adjudications that make both parties better off than they would be in the public system. However, we are also learning that discontent with the system is much broader. As we saw in the last chapter, there has been a long-standing frustration with the public police among corporations and other wealthy institutions, which felt that the public police did not sufficiently deter crime, especially property crimes. This frustration gave rise to a large private security industry that grew up in parallel with the public police. However, in recent years, we have seen a growing dissatisfaction from a different political direction, especially among communities of color, who feel they are over-policed and believe that police are too quick to use force, including deadly force, when interacting with civilians. This has led to calls to defund the police or, at the very least, reduce the police footprint, and to reform the model of prosecution away from the traditional law-and-order model. The inevitable (if unintended) consequence of this movement will be to increase the growth of the private criminal justice system, including private law enforcement, private settlements, private adjudications, and private dispositions. In the next section of the book, we will consider each of these phases in turn. We begin in the next chapter with the large, growing, and diverse system of private law enforcement.

4

Private Law Enforcement

As we saw in Chapter 2, law enforcement functions have historically been a private function, and the government's involvement in deterring crime and apprehending criminals is a relatively recent phenomenon. Although public police have grown dramatically in number over the past century and a half, they never fully supplanted the vast private law enforcement system. Private individuals and private companies now conduct the majority of law enforcement functions in the United States, as they have throughout most of our history, and they are the most visible and well-known branch of the private criminal justice system.

This is not to say that private law enforcement today is the same as it was in the nineteenth, or even twentieth, century. Private law enforcement has evolved along with the needs of its clients, the politics of crime control, and the technology available. As Professor Elizabeth Joh of the University of California at Davis notes, the different types of private law enforcement we see throughout history are "distinct from contemporary private policing in their incentives, purpose, and function"; thus, "one should be cautious in tracing a continuous development of private policing from the earliest forms of community self-protection to the present day."[1]

Certainly there have always been private individuals and companies that have sought to obtain extra protection by hiring their own security guards. And private individuals have always played a role in detecting crime, dating back to the constables who were expected to raise a "hue and cry" when they saw evidence of criminal activities. However, the modern-day system of private law enforcement is far larger and more diverse than at any other time in history. In this chapter, we will focus on two distinct categories of private law enforcement: private police and volunteer community organizations. As we will see, even within these categories, there is a wide range of differences in the level of professionalism of the private law enforcement and in the goals of the companies or institutions that hire them. However, when taken together, this army of private citizens constitutes the country's primary method of deterring crime and apprehending criminals.

THE REBIRTH OF PRIVATE LAW ENFORCEMENT

At 3:15 AM on March 13, 1964, a young woman named Kitty Genovese was returning home from the bar where she worked to her apartment in Brooklyn. As she exited her car and walked toward her apartment building, a man named Winston Mosely approached her and stabbed her twice in the back. Genovese cried out for help and Mosely fled. Genovese staggered toward the rear entrance of her building and then collapsed just outside it. Mosely returned ten minutes later, stabbed her multiple times, raped her, and then stole her money and left her to bleed to death. The entire attack took nearly half an hour. Two weeks later, the *New York Times* published an investigative report about the murder, stating that thirty-eight witnesses saw the murder or heard Genovese call for help and did nothing; one witness allegedly told the reporter that he "didn't want to get involved."

Some details of the *New York Times* report turned out to be erroneous: Decades later, it was revealed that no witnesses observed the entire attack, that most of those who heard or saw something assumed that they were witnessing a domestic argument, and that Mosely initially fled because one witness yelled at him, while two other witnesses did call the police. However, at the time, the event became a national disgrace: a symbol of the lawlessness of the city and lack of compassion of Americans generally and New Yorkers specifically. For years, books, articles, and studies examined the crime. Some psychiatrists saw the event as evidence of the "bystander effect," in which the likelihood of someone reporting a crime decreases as the number of witnesses increases. Others pointed out that people at the time were less likely to get involved if a man were attacking his girlfriend or wife, as such incidents were thought to be "intra-family disputes."[2]

For our purposes, this tragic event is symbolic of a significant shift in the perception of who had responsibility for law enforcement. By the 1960s, participation by private individuals in law enforcement duties had reached its nadir, far removed from the strong role they routinely played in the eighteenth and nineteenth centuries. As the twentieth century progressed, public police began to supplant volunteer law enforcement, and gradually people began to regard the state as the exclusive provider of law enforcement services. As communities became more heterogeneous, and anonymizing urban areas grew in size, individuals became less involved in all aspects of their communities.

However, if the Genovese incident marked a new low in private participation in law enforcement, it can also be regarded as something of a turning point. One of the reasons that some of the witnesses of Genovese's assault did not contact the police was that they believed that it would serve no purpose, as the police were seen as ineffective in the face of escalating crime rates. The 1960s and early 1970s saw the most dramatic increase in crime in the history of our country; from 1960 to 1975, the annual rate of violent crime more than doubled from 200 to 500 per 100,000 citizens, and the annual rate of property crime nearly tripled.

The initial response to this rising crime rate was predictable: Cities increased their police budgets. During the 1960s, public law enforcement grew by 42 percent, while private law enforcement grew by only 7 percent. Thus, by 1969, public police officers (numbering around 500,000) officially outnumbered their private counterparts (which numbered around 300,000).[3] However, this ended up being both the first and the last time in the country's history in which public security officials outnumbered private security forces. Crime rates kept rising, and the public police could not keep up. Starting in the 1970s, city budgets began to be cut due to urban flight and shrinking tax revenue, and the number of public police officers per capita actually began to fall, dropping by 10 percent between 1975 and 1985.[4] Private citizens no longer believed that the public police were sufficient to deter crime and keep their communities secure, and they began taking their own steps to deter and detect crime, primarily by hiring more and more private security guards. By 1980, spending on private security was already 57 percent higher than what the government spent on law enforcement.[5] The growth of private security never abated and, by 2019, private security officers outnumbered public law enforcement officers by nearly a two-to-one margin, with over 1.1 million private police and around 665,000 public police.[6]

The degree to which private security has taken over law enforcement functions in this country is extraordinary. Private police are everywhere: conducting residential security patrols; monitoring shoppers in department stores; safeguarding warehouses; patrolling college campuses and shopping malls; and guarding factories, casinos, office parks, schools, and parking lots.[7] Some public entities even hire private police to conduct patrols and guard public areas – as far back as the late 1990s, government agencies were the third largest category of private police employers, after manufacturing firms and retail stores.[8] This led one commentator to classify private police into three categories: purely private police, semipublic private police (when government agencies contract with private police), and semiprivate public police (police who are employed by private entities but who are granted special deputization powers by the government).[9]

In this book, we are concerned with purely private police. Most of these officers are hired by private companies that use them to guard property, monitor their own workers and investigate employee malfeasance, and detect and apprehend theft and fraud by their customers. For businesses of all sizes, "inventory shrinkage" – an industry term encompassing retail losses from customer and employee theft, administrative error, and fraud – represents a significant cost of doing business, a cost that rose to $61.7 billion in 2020, providing a strong incentive to invest in private security.[10] To take one example, the department store Target loses an estimated billion dollars a year to shoplifters, so it is worth investing tens of millions of dollars on private security in order to limit or cut that number. Target's head of asset protection, a former FBI agent, oversees a national army of security guards and detectives with an infrastructure that rivals the capabilities of most small cities, including tens of thousands of surveillance cameras and a national forensic lab. "Property crimes generally are not a high priority for law enforcement, nor should they be," he explains. "So we took the approach that if we could do the front-end work – do the video analysis, the fingerprint and computer analysis – then give it to the law-enforcement agencies, they don't have to spend the time and effort on it."[11] Target is not an outlier – as of 2017, there were six private companies that operated their own forensic labs, including Walmart and American Express.[12] Meanwhile, the rise of the internet has created an entirely new branch of the private security industry, as companies, governments, and nonprofit organizations hire specialists to ensure that their presence on the web is secure.[13]

The "clients" of the private police are not limited to the large corporations that own casinos, office parks, and retail stores: Frequently, a neighborhood will band together to step in where public policing has failed. In the Olympic neighborhood on the Eastside of Los Angeles, for example, ordinary citizens and business owners were growing increasingly frustrated with the high number of burglaries and graffiti in their midst. One business owner commented that the criminal activity "goes in spurts depending on the visibility of the officers in the Los Angeles Police Department," adding that the police were generally "shorthanded" – "even our police substation had been defaced with graffiti."[14] In response, the business owners formed the Business Watch, in which each of the forty members contributed $1,800 per month to pay for a private security company to patrol the neighborhood at night. The result was a marked decrease in crime in the neighborhood.[15] More recently, neighborhoods in Chicago have formed neighborhood associations for the express purpose of hiring private police to patrol their community. Individuals contributed $100 a month in order to pay the $14,000 per month fee for the patrols. Studies have shown that the patrols have helped to control the crime rate when compared with similar neighborhoods without the private patrols.[16]

A number of explanations have been offered to explain this dramatic growth in private police. One of them, put forward by Professors Clifford Shearing and Phillip Stenning of Griffith University, traces the rise in private police to the rise of private spaces. Over the past half century, public spaces have been replaced with private spaces in various aspects of our life: More of us work in office parks, shop in shopping malls, and live in gated communities. And, as private corporations have grown larger, more of them have turned to hiring their own private security to patrol their warehouses, industries, and retail stores.[17]

The increase in private spaces certainly provides the *opportunity* for a greater amount of private policing, but the *motivation* that private companies have for investing so heavily in their own security forces is the same as it has always been: The public police have failed to provide the level of security and type of policing that private companies can provide and individuals want. This is consistent with the history of private policing that we traced in our last chapter. As Professor David Sklansky of Stanford University notes:

> [F]or over two centuries privately paid entrepreneurs in both Britain and America have been filling gaps in the police protection offered by public law enforcement. Private police today, moreover, tend at least in broad outline to do the kinds of things that public police departments are faulted for not doing: patrol visibly and intensively, consult frequently with the people they are charged with protecting, and – most basically – view themselves as service providers.[18]

Thus, the dramatic growth in the private security industry can be traced to the failure (or at least the perceived failure) of the public criminal justice system to satisfy the needs of the citizens. Primary among these needs is the need to feel safe and secure: If the public police are scarce or nonresponsive to crimes being committed in a certain company or neighborhood, the company or neighborhood will likely respond with its own measures to improve security by hiring private guards or contracting with a private security firm.[19]

However, as Professor Sklansky suggests, the reason for turning to private law enforcement may be dissatisfaction, not only with the *level* of response but also with the *method* of policing itself, as well as the outcome it produces. Public law enforcement has its own agenda and goals, which may differ quite dramatically from the agenda or goals of the private entity. We discussed the goals of the public criminal justice system in Chapter 1: retribution against those who commit crimes, incapacitation of offenders so that they cannot commit more crimes in the near future, and general deterrence by showing other potential criminals that committing a crime has negative consequences. Public police officers accomplish these goals by charging the alleged perpetrator with a crime so that formal criminal proceedings can be brought against them; indeed, the goal of deterrence is achievable only if the police regularly apprehend and initiate formal criminal procedures against a substantial number of criminals. In this sense, the criminal justice system is providing a public good: By expending large amounts of resources to apprehend and punish a significant percentage of wrongdoers, the system creates an expectation that committing a criminal action will (at least possibly) result in punishment.

A private entity, however, may not have any of these goals, or at least not to the same degree. The "clients" of the private security industry – that is, the company that employs the private security force or the residents of the neighborhood who hire the security guards – almost never care about retribution or incapacitation against any specific perpetrator; they want only to deter crimes from occurring in the first place. This goal of general deterrence is accomplished in a number of different ways. Companies can engage in frequent and intensive monitoring of their customers and employees, often with the aid of new technologies that reduce the amount of personnel required. Neighborhoods can have their private police engage in regular, visible patrols and invest in physical infrastructure such as barriers, lighting, and alarm systems. In both cases, the private entity will want to prominently advertise the steps it is taking so that customers, employees, and visitors are aware of the higher risk they would take if they committed a crime. None of this is inconsistent with the goals of public law enforcement; in fact, as we will see in the section "Rules Governing Private Law Enforcement" later in this chapter, private police may be able to engage in some of these activities more effectively because they are generally unconstrained by the constitutional regulations that apply to public police.

Private police officers – again, acting in the interests of their clients – also have a second goal: to ensure that perpetrators who are caught do not commit future crimes against the client. One method of advancing this goal would be to apprehend the perpetrator and hand them over to the police for formal criminal adjudication, but this is almost certainly not the most efficient method. By involving the public criminal justice system, the private entity loses control over the process, and the costs in time and money of cooperating with the public police and courts can be significant. The private entity might be able to achieve its goals more efficiently by, for example, simply removing the perpetrator from the situation, either temporarily or permanently; ejecting or banning the perpetrator from the entity's jurisdiction; or suspending or firing the perpetrator. Significantly, the private entity will not be willing to invest the resources necessary to ensure that the perpetrator is deterred from committing similar crimes against other victims, so more expensive dispositions such as incarceration hold little appeal. The private entity only has an interest in deterring anyone from committing a crime against that particular private client – but it is indifferent between shifting the criminal activity to another store or block and preventing the criminal activity altogether.[20]

Beyond having different ultimate goals, a private entity might prefer that the method of law enforcement be different from the method used by the public police. For example, the private entity may want to use more subtle methods of law enforcement so as not to disturb other customers of the corporation or lower property values in the area. Noisy arrests inside a department store – indeed, even the presence of uniformed police personnel – may project an image that drives away potential customers. Frequent drug busts in a neighborhood, with the inevitable negative publicity and high crime statistics that derive from arrests that are public records, may lower property values, thus damaging the interests of homeowners in the neighborhood.

Professor Joh, who conducted a case study of a major private security firm, learned that there were many security issues in which a private firm would prefer the police not get involved. For example, if a suspicious abandoned attaché case is seen on the street, one of the directors of the private firm explained in an interview that he would want to take care of the situation before the police got involved:

> [The police will] want to shut everything down. But was there a phone call? Was there a letter? What are the chances that it really is a bomb? The cops don't care. They figure "you never know." We don't want to just shut down for that. We want to protect ourselves from the police, to tell you the truth.[21]

Conversely, some private entities may want more blatant and ostentatious demonstrations of law enforcement; for example, local media coverage of multiple apprehensions inside a certain store might serve to deter would-be shoplifters, and frequent patrols of brightly marked cars inside a gated community might scare away potential burglars.

Finally, private entities will want their private security to respond to different types of behavior from the public police. The public police are primarily concerned with enforcing the law and maintaining order, broadly defined, and may not be responsive when private entities make requests that go beyond these mandates. As Professor Joh notes: "[w]hat counts as deviant or disorderly behavior for private police is defined not in moral terms but instrumentally, by a client's particular aims: a pleasant shopping experience, a safe parking area, or an orderly corporate campus."[22] Of course, this means that private police will have an incentive to respond to behavior and situations that are not even illegal, such as disruptive or annoying behavior, or even simply individuals who are homeless or poorly dressed or – in the most insidious manifestation – of a certain race.

In short, although the varying types of private police may share some characteristics (they generally tend to prioritize prevention over apprehension, for example), each private security force has a "client-defined mandate," and thus the goals of private police will vary depending on the needs of the client.[23] This is likely the primary reason that private law enforcement appeals to its clients: No matter how responsive and efficient the public police might be, by nature they cannot satisfy all of the various and perhaps conflicting preferences of private citizens.

VOLUNTEER ORGANIZATIONS

The high crime rates of the 1960s and 1970s – and the inability of public police to respond – were important factors in the reemergence of private policing. However, it had another important effect as well, which was to increase community involvement in law enforcement activities. The most famous of these actions was the founding of neighborhood watch programs in the 1960s – partially in response to the publicity surrounding the Genovese case in New York. These programs were organized into the National Neighborhood Watch in 1972. By 1981, 12 percent of the country's population was involved in some kind of neighborhood watch program;[24] by 2000, that number grew to 41 percent.[25] In the 2010s, there were an estimated 25,000 registered neighborhood watch groups and even more unregistered groups.[26] Such programs take many different forms, from facilitating communication between civilians and police, all the way to regular patrols organized by block captains.[27] In theory, these organizations help to prevent crime in numerous ways: by creating visible surveillance to deter criminal activity, by increasing awareness and precautions among neighborhood residents, by encouraging norms of behavior and intervention among the residents, and by improving communication with public law enforcement.[28]

The effectiveness of neighborhood watch programs in lowering crime rates varies considerably; some of them have significantly reduced crime – one study found that neighborhood watch programs decreased crime by 85 percent[29] – while others have apparently had no effect.[30] Studies have shown that neighborhood watch programs tend to be successful in reducing crime when they can encourage members to identify themselves as members of a geographic community. As Richard Shapiro, the former director of the New York City Police Department's civilian participation programs, said: "People identify with their neighborhood. If you tell them to protect their family, there's no question. So they extend their family to the neighborhood. Nobody lives in New York City. They all live in neighborhoods."[31]

The breakdown of public policing saw the rise of another volunteer private law enforcement group: the Guardian Angels. The Guardian Angels were founded in 1978 to patrol the New York City subway system, which at the time was experiencing extremely high rates of crime. By 1982, the Guardian Angels were incorporated as an official nonprofit, with a membership of over 2,000 in forty-two cities across North America. The Angels' mission is a bit more interventionist than neighborhood watch programs; volunteers in the latter are meant to patrol and report to the public police, while the Angels are trained in martial arts and first aid, and they carry handcuffs. Part of their explicit mission is to intervene to prevent crime and apprehend wrongdoers, using force if necessary, and members are taught the relevant laws governing arrest powers for civilians. During their very visible patrols, the members wear distinctive uniforms to help deter criminal activity.[32]

During the height of the Angels' popularity, most public law enforcement groups were hostile toward them, fearing that their willingness to intervene in crimes, combined with their relatively low level of training, would lead to increased violence. More than one mayor and police chief branded them as "vigilantes," a term we will return to in Chapter 8.[33] However, such fears appear to have been unfounded; the Guardian Angels have rarely been charged with a crime for their actions during their patrols. And some members of law enforcement welcomed their involvement. The Bronx District Attorney acknowledged the conditions that led to their founding: "The municipal and state governments have not met their obligations to provide the kind of security that's needed on the subway, in the parks or on the streets. How do we say to any citizens who want to do some good that they should not be involved?"[34]

The Guardian Angels' membership and influence waned in the 1990s and 2000s as crime rates dropped, but in recent years the organization has seen something of a renaissance. They are currently active in 130 cities in the United States, with new chapters forming (or re-forming) each year. Modern Guardian Angels, like their ancestors in the 1970s and 1980s, patrol where the police presence is insufficient or absent.[35] New York City, where the Guardian Angels have continuously patrolled for over forty years, boasted over 350 members in 2021, while Philadelphia's branch re-formed in 2022 after a long hiatus.[36]

Other volunteer private law enforcement organizations have continued to operate well into modern times, with groups arising from both the left and the right of the political spectrum. In Chicago, the Chicago Police Department encouraged the development of the Chicago Alternative Policing Strategy (CAPS). The city was divided into districts comprising two or three city blocks, and each district formed an "advisory council" made up of members of the community. These councils then organized various private law enforcement actions, primarily engaging in "positive loitering," in which community members occupied locations where drug sales and other crimes were occurring in order to disrupt and deter the criminal activity. Community members would hold rallies, prayer vigils, or "smoke-outs" (which involved barbequing food) in these high-crime areas. Advisory councils also coordinated private investigations of criminal activity, albeit on a small scale. When it became clear at council meetings that the police lacked the resources or the will to investigate certain crimes, citizens gathered their own evidence of criminal activity and then turned it over to the police. This led to the shutdown of a local bar that was the site of criminal activity and the arrest of a landlord who had allowed drug dealing to occur on his property. The citizens even engaged in a form of private punishment in the form of public shaming, by picketing outside the home of another landlord who allowed drug dealing and other crimes to occur on his property. We will talk more about private shaming and other forms of private punishment when we discuss vigilantism in Chapter 8. Studies showed that CAPS succeeded in lowering levels of street crime.[37]

Professor Dan Kahan of Yale University studied the CAPS program to determine why it was so successful, and he concluded that the program was an example of "reciprocity theory" in action. The conventional wisdom is that individuals in a group will rarely contribute goods or make an effort to improve the well-being of the group unless they are provided incentives or coerced into contributing. Instead, individuals will "freeride" on any contributions that others make. Reciprocity theory posits an exception to this rule: Individuals will voluntarily contribute to the group's well-being if they believe that others in the group will also contribute.[38] This theory explains, for example, why most people in developed countries willingly pay their taxes – they are not really concerned about being caught if they do not pay; rather, they are willing to pay their share because they believe nearly everyone else is also paying their share. Conversely, if a country suffers from widespread tax evasion, it is extremely difficult to convince anyone to pay, and thus the government must rely more heavily on enforcement and coercion.

Professor Kahan applied this theory to the private policing that occurred in the CAPS program:

> Whereas traditional policing strategies risk displacing community self-policing, CAPS assigned highly conspicuous elements of law enforcement to community residents themselves. As they observed their neighbors attending and speaking up at

council meetings, and thereafter participating in order-maintenance demonstrations, public shamings, and the like, citizens realized that in fact their neighbors were willing to take an active role in safeguarding their community from crime. Those who formed this impression thereafter reciprocated, either by participating in CAPS initiatives or by entering into less formal arrangements to watch out for one another's interests.[39]

In other words, by the turn of the twenty-first century, Chicago had come a long way from the situation in New York in 1964, when dozens of private citizens witnessed a brutal murder but few of them believed they had a duty to even contact the police. One benefit of private citizens engaging in law enforcement activities is the increase in communal trust, solidarity, and cooperation. Citizens begin thinking of their neighborhood as a community, rather than as an anonymous collection of individuals.

Finally, Professor Kahan mentioned another benefit of the CAPS program's community self-policing: As the community was essentially policing itself, "... there was little likelihood that this form of law enforcement would acquire the connotations of racial domination and hierarchy ... ."[40] This is a common benefit when private citizens decide to police their own community, and it is a major reason why some communities, especially among people of color, turn to private law enforcement instead of relying on the public police. This phenomenon took its most extreme form in the wake of the George Floyd murder in the summer of 2020, when protest groups created small autonomous zones where public police were not allowed. In Minneapolis, the community barricaded the four-block area around where Floyd was killed and prevented any police from entering. Instead, the community groups assigned private bodyguards to escort families into the area.[41] In Seattle, protestors established the Capitol Hill Organized Protest (CHOP), an autonomous zone about six blocks in size where public police were not allowed (CHOP actually encompassed one of the city's five police stations, which was abandoned by the police and boarded up). At least at first, CHOP remained peaceful, with volunteer medics to take care of emergency medical needs and unarmed volunteers to patrol the area at night to watch for trouble. When people engaged in criminal conduct, such as a person threatening another with a knife, the community members were able to de-escalate the situation peacefully.[42] Unfortunately, the peaceful atmosphere did not last – about two weeks into the establishment of the zone, a series of shootings occurred in or near the zone, two of them fatal. After a little over three weeks, the Seattle police, with the help of the FBI, reclaimed the area, making nearly seventy arrests.[43]

Volunteer private law enforcement can come from the other end of the political spectrum as well. One prominent example is the Minutemen Project, a volunteer organization founded in 2004 to help patrol the southern border of the United States. Over the next five years, thousands of volunteers, some of them armed, set up outposts on the Mexican border with the goal of contacting the official border patrol if they saw what they believed to be an undocumented immigrant crossing the border. The Minutemen eventually splintered into smaller, sometimes competing, groups and many of these groups are still operating on the border. For example, Arizona Border Recon has been patrolling the border since 2011, engaging in "reconnaissance" and reporting the results of their investigation to the United States Customs Border and Patrol.[44]

Cybercrime has created an entirely new type of private law enforcement volunteer – the "white hat hacker." Originally this term referred to individuals who would break into a company's internet security system without permission in order to demonstrate to the company the technical vulnerabilities in its system. Today, white hat hackers work as essentially freelance cybersecurity agents to protect organizations' cryptocurrency holders from black hat hackers who are trying to steal it. They band together in groups with names such as the Robin Hood Group or the White Hat Group and monitor cryptocurrency holdings on the internet. When they notice a hack occurring, they log on and conduct their own hack, exploiting the same vulnerability as the criminal. The white hats will then attempt to transfer as many of the assets as possible into their own accounts – essentially trying to steal the money before the criminal can. After the hack is over, the white hats return the assets to the rightful owner, sometimes in exchange for a "bug bounty," which is typically 10 percent of the money that could have been stolen. As one cybersecurity researcher noted: "We started with bug bounties of 10 k, then 100 k. Now we have bug bounties of 1 million, 10 million. Probably in the next year, we are going to see hundreds of millions – billions."[45]

The white hat hackers are the modern-day version of the posse that formed in a frontier town to chase after bank robbers. Like the private individuals who made up a posse, the white hats are stepping in with a necessary rapid response that is not being provided by the traditional public police. Indeed, this is a common thread tying together all of these various groups – the neighborhood watch, the Guardian Angels, the Black Lives Matter-inspired autonomous zones, the Minutemen, the white hats, and hundreds of other similar groups: They are created in response to a shortcoming (or a perceived shortcoming) in the public provision of policing services. As we saw earlier, this is the same motivation that inspires companies, neighborhood associations, and other private institutions to hire their own security – they are dissatisfied with the quality or quantity of public policing.

Unsurprisingly, the growth of private law enforcement organizations has led to a cottage industry of goods and services catering to their needs. One commentator has called this the "commercial surveillance market," which has "further entrenched the normalization of ubiquitous and pervasive surveillance."[46] Dozens of private companies offer drug-sniffing dogs for the home, school, or workplace – their websites promise confidentiality, meaning that if they do find drugs, they will not contact the police or other official law enforcement.[47] Other companies offer license plate readers to private communities so that the communities can record and identify every car that enters and leaves their neighborhood. One such company, Flock, has installed its cameras in over 1,400 cities and records over a billion license plates each month. They charge a neighborhood organization approximately $5,000 a year, which covers the cost of the cameras, software, and online services used to identify the owners of the cars. Flock's founder notes that, nationwide, police closed only 17 percent of all recent reported property crimes, and he argues that one of the solutions to this poor enforcement problem is more cameras on public roads. Flock's business quadrupled between 2019 and 2021, and it sees no sign of slowing down. As the founder noted: "There are 17,000 cities in America. Until we have them all, we're not done."[48]

Smartphone apps are the latest technology to be adapted to the needs of private law enforcement. Many of these apps, such as Nextdoor, began their life as neighborhood social networks, designed to allow individuals who lived near each other to share suggestions about restaurants or other services. However, within a short time, individuals began to use the app to report "suspicious" activity that they observed in their neighborhood. Nextdoor at one time even had a feature called "Forward to Police," which allowed a user to alert the local police department of anything the user believed might be indicative of criminal activity. Another app, Citizen, provides its users with real-time data from police records – its employees transcribe transmissions on police, fire, and emergency radios – and gives its users up-to-the-second information on any crime that is occurring nearby. Users who are in the area are encouraged to video and stream the incidents from a safe distance – perhaps merely for the prurient amusement of the rest of the Citizen audience, but also to document the criminal activity. Citizen claims that its primary purpose is to enhance the safety of its users by warning them of dangerous activity nearby.[49] Other new technologies, such as Amazon's Ring, which provides an online camera on its owner's front door, enhance the decades-old industry of home-security systems by providing users – and the public police, upon request – a view of the public street outside a home.[50]

By far the most significant technology enhancing private law enforcement is the internet. For nearly two centuries, police posted "most wanted" posters throughout a community, seeking help from private citizens who might know the whereabouts of known criminals. Recently, television shows expanded the reach of law enforcement's requests for assistance to millions of Americans. Perhaps the most famous of such shows, America's Most Wanted, ran for over twenty years and boasted that it had led to the capture of 1,149 fugitives.[51] The program presented viewers with information about a crime and asked them to contact the police if they had any helpful information. However, all of this pales in comparison with the use of social media, where both public police and private citizens receive help in solving crime from an army of online amateur sleuths. Often, public law enforcement agencies seek out help themselves, creating Twitter and Facebook accounts for their departments, asking private individuals to connect with them, and then regularly posting information about criminal activity with the hope of finding leads.[52] Other times, private individuals drive the investigation by posting their own details of a crime and seeking help — as of August 2022, the "Reddit Bureau of Investigation" has over 560,000 members, all sharing and seeking clues for crimes they have witnessed.[53] Professor Wayne Logan of Florida State University notes that one of the drivers of this crowdsourcing of crime control is the "frustration with the crime-solving ability of police." These private efforts are also spurred by the "sharp criticism and distrust of local police in the wake of the killing of civilians, fueling calls that departments be 'defunded' [and] prompting reevaluation of the ways in which community members can shoulder greater responsibility in maintaining public safety."[54] Once again we see how dissatisfaction with the public police leads to an increase in private law enforcement. Professor Logan sees a danger in the recent explosion of crowdsourcing crime control, because it "displace[s] responsibility for crime control and public safety," which can "undercut government accountability for public safety and foster vigilantism."[55] Whether the shift of responsibility for crime control from public to private actors represents a danger or an opportunity is an issue we will consider in Chapter 10.

All of this technology working together has led to what Professor Joh calls the "gig surveillance economy." Just as private individuals can easily rent out a room in their house on Airbnb or work as a part-time taxi driver for Uber, they can also sell data from their Amazon Ring cameras or information from their smartphone apps. As the gig economy gets more sophisticated and the devices get cheaper, private individuals may even invest in more sophisticated surveillance technology, such as installing license plate readers on their cars or even wearing body cameras to record the public areas they pass through, in order to sell that information to police departments on an ongoing basis. They could also be hired out for particular surveillance tasks, such as recording a specific location or searching for a suspect's car on a specific road, much like Uber drivers contract out for specific rides.[56]

In theory, crowdsourcing crime control could be an enormous benefit to public law enforcement agencies, serving as a significant force multiplier for their surveillance and leading to increased apprehensions of criminals. The knowledge that private citizens are actively engaged in crime detection could also deter would-be wrongdoers from engaging in criminal activity, as we have seen with the positive effect of neighborhood watch programs in many communities. However, volunteer private law enforcement initiatives also carry risks. The first is that they could target innocent people, which can cause serious problems in the era of social media. In the wake of the Boston Marathon bombing in 2013, hundreds of private individuals examined photos of the incident and falsely accused various people of having been responsible; the accused suffered harassment and damage to their reputations. More recently, Citizen users circulated a photo of a person who allegedly started a wildfire in California, with offers of a reward up to $30,000 and users being asked to "hunt this guy down." The police investigated and found no evidence that he was involved in the fire; they eventually arrested and charged someone else.[57] Professor Logan notes that crowdsourcing can lead to a phenomenon called "information cascade," in which, "instead of assessing the reliability of information on their own," internet users "rely on what they assume others have reliably concluded and transmit the possibly false information, which the internet relentlessly then perpetuates."[58]

Although these high-profile mistakes can cause real harm, a far more common and insidious feature of volunteer law enforcement is the danger of racial profiling. It is true that some intra-community private policing, such as the CAPS initiative in Chicago, can result in a more equitable and anti-racist enforcement. However, often the reverse is true, especially when volunteer law enforcement are watching for "outsiders" who enter their community. Private citizens – poorly trained, unfettered by constitutional restraints, often motivated by fear, and frequently living in de facto segregated neighborhoods – will tend to use race as a factor in deciding whether to report activity or take other actions.[59] Nextdoor eventually decided that its "Forward to Police" function violated the company's anti-racism initiative, and it discontinued the feature in the summer of 2020, stating that "it did not meet the needs of our members and only a small percentage of law enforcement agencies chose to use the tool."[60] Neighborhood watch programs have also been criticized for singling out individuals based on race,[61] a topic we will return to in Chapter 8.

RULES GOVERNING PRIVATE LAW ENFORCEMENT

As noted in Chapter 1, the conventional wisdom that policing should be primarily a public function is based on two premises: first, that the state is supposed to have a monopoly on the legal use of force and, second, that policing at least occasionally requires using force to accomplish its goals of apprehending criminals. Thus, the argument goes, private law enforcement will never be able to take over the policing function altogether. It turns out that, although this argument is generally true, both of its premises have significant caveats and exceptions and, combined together, these caveats and exceptions give private law enforcement officers nearly the same powers as their public counterparts.

The first premise, regarding the state's monopoly on the legal use of force, is overstated. Regular citizens often have broad powers to conduct arrests, and individuals engaged in private law enforcement, whether as part of paid private police or as part of a volunteer organization, are likely to be extremely familiar with the scope of these powers. Like public police, private individuals can arrest anyone who has committed a misdemeanor in their presence, and can make an arrest for a felony as long as they have probable cause to believe the arrestee has committed the felony.[62] Some private security guards have powers that go above and beyond what ordinary civilians can do; for example, most states have a "merchant's privilege" that allows security guards in many retail establishments to detain those suspected of theft crimes, even if the crime is merely a misdemeanor. For example, California's law states that a merchant can "detain a person for a reasonable time for the purpose of conducting an investigation in a reasonable manner whenever the merchant has probable cause to believe the person to be detained is attempting to unlawfully take or has unlawfully taken merchandise from the merchant's premises," and that the merchant is permitted to use a "reasonable amount of nondeadly force necessary" to prevent the suspect from escaping or to prevent the loss of property. The law also permits the merchant to search the suspect to look for the suspected stolen property.[63] And all private police – like any private citizen – are allowed to search a suspect if given consent and to interrogate a suspect in order to obtain a confession.[64]

Public police do have some powers that private law enforcement do not, such as the power to obtain a warrant to search a home or other private property (although states give some private police, such as bail bondsman, the same powers of search and arrests that public police have).[65] However, much of the power exercised by private law enforcement, especially the professional private police, is informal power. Private police officers are often in uniform, many are armed, and they usually know the extent of their legal authority to a greater degree than the suspects with whom they interact. They can use this informal power to engage in the same tactics as their public counterparts, such as asking for consent using words and intonation that imply that the request is an order or engaging in a conversation in a way that makes the suspect feel that they are not free to leave.

What really distinguishes public police from private law enforcement are the legal limits that the law places on the actions of the public police. Public police officers are governed by a complex set of rules set out by the Constitution, particularly the Fourth and Fifth Amendments. Thus, a public police officer must comply with the Fourth Amendment when searching a person or their property, and must comply with the Fifth Amendment when interrogating suspects. If they violate these rules, the evidence they uncover or the statements they hear could be excluded from any future criminal trial. However, under the state action doctrine, these constitutional rules apply only to actions by public officials; thus, the Supreme Court has held that there is no constitutional limit on the actions that private law enforcement can take when they are searching or interrogating a subject.[66] The Fourth and Fifth Amendments are meant to limit the power that the state exercises over its citizens, not to govern the interactions between private citizens. This principle has been consistently followed by all lower courts and state courts; as one lower court noted: "[t]he fact that the private sector may do for its own benefit what the state may also do for the public benefit does not implicate the state in private activity."[67]

Of course, private individuals who engage in law enforcement are still bound by the same laws as anyone else – if they enter a person's home to conduct a search without the consent of the owner, they are committing a trespass, and if they physically grab someone without the probable cause required by the citizen's arrest rules, they are committing a battery. They could, at least in theory, face criminal charges or civil liability for these actions, although such consequences are very rare.

In one case, a woman won a $2,000 judgment in a false imprisonment lawsuit against J.C. Penney after two security guards accused her of shoplifting, brought her back inside the store, and held her in a room for twenty-one minutes.[68] However, even if the actions of the private law enforcement officers are illegal, the fruits of their search or the statements they obtain are still admissible in a future criminal trial; in other words, the exclusionary rule does not apply to their conduct.

Many scholars have criticized this distinction, arguing that the state action doctrine should be relaxed or even abolished, so that the exclusionary rule would apply to private actors and any evidence they unlawfully obtained would be inadmissible in a future criminal trial.[69] As we will see in subsequent chapters, such a change may not matter very much, as individuals engaged in private law enforcement often have no intention of turning the suspect over to the public criminal justice system. Relaxing the state action doctrine would also have unintended consequences. Without some arbitrary line-drawing, it would mean that the complex constitutional restrictions and the exclusionary rule would apply to evidence of a crime found by ordinary citizens, which would complicate public criminal investigations and prosecutions.

COSTS AND BENEFITS OF PRIVATE LAW ENFORCEMENT

Does this enormous army of private police and volunteer law enforcement make society better off? Some might think that the answer to this question depends on the definition of "society." Certainly the companies that hire private police and the neighborhoods and individuals who actively engage in law enforcement believe that their efforts ultimately save them money and keep them safer. However, there is a strong argument that the private individuals who are paying money or volunteering their own time are also benefiting others: In economic terms, their actions provide a positive externality by reducing overall crime. If we return to the original purposes of the criminal justice system, we can see that private law enforcement fulfills the purpose of deterring crime, both by preventing crimes that might occur and – to a lesser extent – by helping to impose punishment on those who do commit crimes. As we noted in Chapter 1, making the punishment more severe does not increase deterrence, but increasing the chances of being apprehended (or, more specifically, the perceived chance of being apprehended) significantly increases the deterrent effect. Professor Daniel Nagin of Carnegie Mellon University argues that public police have two distinct functions: that of "apprehension agent" and that of "sentinel." The job of sentinel can be fulfilled by anyone "whose presence discourages a motivated offender from victimizing a criminal opportunity," including not just public police but also any "person ... with no official crime control authority who are personally willing to intervene or to summon those with the authority to intervene."[70] The army of private law enforcement officers, both paid and volunteers, vastly increases the number of sentinels deterring crime. And society gets this benefit without needing to expend any tax dollars or state resources.

Supporters of private law enforcement tout further benefits. As we have already seen, private law enforcement is more responsive than public police; thus, it provides its clients with the service they want and is more directly accountable for its mistakes. Private law enforcement can also be more flexible than the public police, being less burdened by large bureaucracies and less restricted by municipal and constitutional regulations. This – along with the standard market incentive – allows private law enforcement to innovate with new technologies and streamlined procedures at a much faster rate than its public counterparts.

Of course, as Professor Sklansky notes, for most of these benefits there is a corresponding downside:

> [T]he greater flexibility of private guard companies stems from their freedom from regulations and traditions that have developed largely because they were thought necessary to control the uniformed, armed, quasi-military forces patrolling our streets. Where some see the greater flexibility of private policing, others see the threat of policing that is uncontrolled. Indeed, the most persistent complaint about private guard companies ... is that they are insufficiently regulated.
>
> ... [T]he supposed accountability of private policing has a troubling side as well. Private companies are thought more accountable than government because they answer to their particular customers instead of to the general public. But this is not clearly to everyone's advantage. In particular, those who come into contact with private guards but do not help to pay for them may not welcome the fact that such guards are accountable exclusively to their customers.[71]

This last point deserves some elaboration. Almost no private law enforcement organization is exclusively concerned with deterring and detecting crime. Instead, it seeks to fulfill the mandates of its private client. As noted above, this could include harassing customers or visitors who are deemed undesirable for one reason or another. While such actions do not detract from the crime control benefits that private law enforcement provide, they are still socially undesirable behaviors that are justifiably condemned when engaged in by public police officers.

Some detractors of private law enforcement also disagree with the premise that private security and volunteer law enforcement provide the positive externality of reducing crime. Instead, private law enforcement may simply divert crime from a privately protected neighborhood to a nearby neighborhood or store without private law enforcement.[72] This is known as the "deterrence vs. diversion" debate. Ironically, private law enforcement will be most effective at deterring overall crime if the prospective criminals do not know which neighborhoods and companies have increased their security. However, it is often in the best interest of the private institutions to advertise their use of private law enforcement, whether it is with visible patrols or prominent signs advertising the existence of extra security.

There is also a danger that we have seen from other industries that have undergone partial privatization: that those who can afford to pay for improved private

Conclusion

services will be less likely to politically support state funds for broader public services. For example, if a significant percentage of wealthier individuals send their children to private schools, they may be less willing to support tax increases to improve the public schools. Similarly, if wealthy neighborhoods rely on their own private security, residents of those neighborhoods may not support maintaining a public police presence, thus lowering the quality of the public police for everyone. Of course, such reasoning would be short sighted in both instances, since universal education and low crime rates have positive externalities for everyone, even those who do not directly benefit. Nevertheless, there is a danger that widespread use of private police will crowd out the perceived need for public police.

In contrast, private volunteer law enforcement, such as neighborhood watch groups or the Guardian Angels, do not raise the same economic equity concerns as private police; any neighborhood or community can form a neighborhood watch organization. However, these volunteer groups highlight the other critique of private law enforcement: the lack of training and oversight of these groups.[73] Both private police and private volunteer groups insert themselves into dangerous situations, occasionally confronting suspected criminals. Occasionally, the private law enforcement individual is armed; sometimes they are armed with a firearm. The training these individuals receive varies considerably. On one end of the spectrum are off-duty police officers who moonlight as private security guards, bringing all of their training and skills to their second job. On the other end are everyday individuals engaged in neighborhood watch programs who patrol their neighborhoods with at most a few hours of training about how to react when they suspect a crime is occurring. All of these private individuals are subject to the same implicit biases and subjective preconceptions that public police are subjected to, and this can result in racial profiling, unfounded accusations, and unnecessary violence. We will discuss this in further detail in Chapter 8, when we discuss private criminal dispositions – that is, what happens when private individuals deliver punishment in response to perceived criminal activity.

CONCLUSION

The widespread support for public policing remains in force, but it has been tempered somewhat as the inadequacies of purely public policing have become more apparent. Today, nearly everyone will agree that a strong, competent public police force is a necessary element of our society, but nearly everyone will also agree that it should be permissible and is probably desirable to allow individuals to supplement public police protection with private security. The result is a law enforcement system that is predominantly private in nature, but that is supported by a robust public police force at its core.

Perhaps the most important aspect of private law enforcement agents is not the sheer number of people engaged in this activity, but their goals and objectives in engaging in their duties. Public police officers are inextricably tied to the public criminal justice system – after they make an arrest, their cases almost always end up in court, with a prosecutor and a defense attorney usually agreeing to a plea bargain that is approved by a judge. All of these actors – the police, the prosecutor, the judge – are (at least in theory) acting to advance the interests of the community, and their decisions are guided by the utilitarian and retributive goals we discussed in Chapter 1. However, the private police – whether paid or volunteers – do not necessarily share those goals. Paid private police officers are mere agents of their employers, and they will act in accordance with their employers' needs. Volunteer groups may be furthering the needs of their own microcommunity (as with neighborhood watch programs) or perhaps trying to further their own political agenda (as with the Minutemen or the organizers of the police-free "autonomous zones" in cities). Thus, when private police apprehend a suspected wrongdoer, they may not turn them over to the public police. Instead, they will often engage in their own forms of dispute resolution – whether it is a form of private plea bargaining or a more formal process. Occasionally they will even carry out a punishment on their own – actions that transform them from mere private police into true vigilantes. The next few chapters trace the different possible paths that suspects might travel through the private criminal justice system.

5

Private Criminal Settlements as Plea Bargains

The last chapter discussed scenarios in which private law enforcement apprehend suspected criminals, and it noted that often private law enforcement organizations (and their clients) do not have an incentive to report the alleged crime to the public police. In this chapter and the next three chapters, we will discuss what happens next – that is, what are the options that private law enforcement (and the alleged perpetrator) have if they opt out of the public criminal justice system?

As we will see, this question applies to more cases than those involving private law enforcement. There are many crimes that go undetected by both public police and private law enforcement but are observed by a victim or a witness. As with private law enforcement, often the victim or witness will report the crime to the public police and begin a criminal investigation and/or prosecution. However, as noted in the Introduction, this course of action is the *atypical* response to criminal activity.

We have already seen in the last chapter that private law enforcement will often catch and release suspected criminals with little more than a warning, as the very act of being apprehended may be sufficient to deter the suspect from committing the crime again, at least in the jurisdiction that is patrolled by the private actor. Frequently, a victim or witness will likewise decide not to take any action at all when they see a crime being committed. They may believe that reporting the crime will be a waste of time because the police response will be weak or nonexistent. Perhaps the alleged perpetrator is a friend or a family member and the victim wishes to forgive and forget. Sometimes, the alleged perpetrator is able to intimidate or otherwise persuade the witness not to report the crime. Alternatively, perhaps the injury – whether to person or property – is so slight that it is simply easier to move on rather than call the police or take any private action (especially if the witness was not a victim of the crime). This final reason has probably become more prevalent in recent decades as the state continues to criminalize more conduct, thus creating more "crimes" that victims and witnesses do not think are worth reporting.[1] This is an example of the law of unintended consequences: When the state over-criminalizes conduct, victims and witnesses may be less likely to report criminal activity. It is also another example of the phenomenon we discussed in Chapter 1 – that what we treat as criminal activity in reality depends more on the beliefs of private individuals than on what the legislature has decided to criminalize.

However, if these private individuals – whether they are private law enforcement, witnesses, or victims – want to take some action but do not necessarily want to call the public police, they have four options. First, if they are victims of the crime, they have the right to sue the alleged perpetrator in civil court. Most victims choose not to exercise this right, as often the offender does not have the assets available to pay any damages, and thus the time and expense required to hire a lawyer and file a case is not worthwhile. If a victim does decide to sue the alleged perpetrator, they will almost always contact the police as well, as a criminal conviction will be admissible in the victim's subsequent civil suit, thus lowering the cost of winning a judgment.[2]

Second, the private individual could refer the case to a private organization that engages in its own form of criminal adjudication, such as the adjudicative procedures followed by professional associations, religious institutions, or universities. The individual could do this with or without notifying the public police, depending on their preference. We will discuss these private adjudicative procedures in Chapter 7.

Third, the individual could impose their own private punishment, either by taking a privilege away from the alleged perpetrator or by inflicting harm upon the perpetrator. This could mean acting as a vigilante and essentially committing a crime against the alleged perpetrator, but it could also take the form of something more mild and less controversial. For example, if the witness or victim has a preexisting relationship with the alleged perpetrator, they may sever or alter that relationship, as when a wife leaves her abusive husband or a company fires or penalizes an employee who embezzled money. As with the first two options, the victim or witness could also notify the public police, although often they will not when they are imposing their own punishment. We will talk more about these potential private dispositions in Chapter 8.

Finally, the victim or witness could bargain with the alleged perpetrator to gain a benefit in exchange for not reporting the crime to the police. All of the first three options are available whether or not the public police get involved – that is, civil lawsuits, private adjudications, and private punishments could either be a substitute for or merely supplement the public criminal justice system. In contrast, private criminal settlements cannot be combined with a public prosecution, as the crux of making such a bargain is that the witness or victim promises to refrain from reporting the alleged perpetrator to the public authorities if the alleged perpetrator takes (or abstains from taking) some action. In making these agreements, the private party is essentially harnessing the power of the state and converting that state authority into a more flexible, personalized power over the alleged perpetrator. A good amount of energy is lost in this conversion process, as the method only works if the alleged perpetrator believes that (1) agreeing to the bargain will be less onerous than being apprehended by the public authorities and (2) the state will not learn about the crime from another source. However, because the alleged perpetrator has so much to gain from making a private agreement – and because the victim or witness who negotiates with them gains so little from instituting a public prosecution – there is quite a bit of room for negotiation. The results of these negotiations are the subject matter of this chapter and the next chapter: private criminal settlements.

Private criminal settlements come in many varieties. They may occur between two private individuals who have (and wish to maintain) a preexisting relationship, as in the case when the victim and the perpetrator are family members. They may involve a corporate client of a private police officer who decides that referring the case to the public criminal justice system is too expensive and time consuming. The witness may not even be the victim of the crime; they could be a third party who either accidentally discovered evidence of the crime or actively sought the information in order to extract a payment from the perpetrator.

Should these private criminal settlements be permitted? I will ultimately argue that they should be not only permitted but encouraged, as the benefits they offer to society outweigh their costs. However, I realize that this is a controversial view. The general public may react to the idea of private criminal settlements in different ways, depending on the context. A wife who was abused by her husband but decides to give him another chance if he agrees to undergo counseling may seem sympathetic and even laudable, while a retail store bullying a shoplifter into paying their way out of an arrest may seem unsavory. A neighborhood association that fights back against drug dealers by threatening them with criminal prosecution if they do not leave the neighborhood might seem understandable, while a mercenary who investigates criminal activity and asks for money instead of calling the police seems greedy. However, it is not entirely clear how to legally distinguish between these different kinds of cases – or, indeed, whether we should draw any distinctions between them at all.

Before making a case for why these settlements should be encouraged, we will first take some time to describe them and evaluate them from a number of different perspectives. First, this chapter will provide an overview of how these agreements work and provide some real-life examples. We will then examine these settlements through two different lenses in order to fully explore their costs and benefits to society. First, they can be analogized to their public counterpart: plea bargaining. As with plea bargaining, the alleged perpetrator who agrees to a private settlement is voluntarily relinquishing certain rights in exchange for a lesser punishment. However, the private agreements are a more extreme version of public plea bargaining, since the alleged perpetrator is both sacrificing more rights and gaining more benefits. The alleged perpetrator gives up not just the right to trial, as they do in traditional plea bargaining, but also the right to an attorney, the right to have their charges formally presented to them, and the right to have a neutral judge review the case and approve the agreement. On the other hand, the alleged perpetrator is avoiding not only the full punishment they would receive after a criminal trial, but also even the collateral punishments that the criminal justice system imposes on any individual unwise or unlucky enough to be caught up in it: the inconvenience of arrest, the possibility of pretrial incarceration, the innumerable court appearances, and the stigma of a criminal accusation.

After we examine private criminal settlements through the lens of plea-bargaining theory in this chapter, the next chapter will consider them from a different perspective: as a form of blackmail. The structure of a private criminal settlement is that the witness possesses incriminating information about the perpetrator, and the witness is agreeing to keep that information secret if certain demands are met. Most scholars consider private criminal settlements to be blackmail,[3] and legislators concur; these arrangements have been criminalized in every jurisdiction in the country, although some states provide limited exceptions.[4] I will ultimately challenge this viewpoint, arguing that the standard justifications for criminalizing blackmail – which are weak to begin with – are particularly unpersuasive in the context of private criminal settlements.

Before we conduct these analyses, we must first define exactly what we mean by private criminal settlements and understand why they are likely to be more widespread than most people may believe.

ANATOMY OF A PRIVATE CRIMINAL SETTLEMENT

We will start by discussing the incentive structure of the witness who observes the criminal activity. (From now on, we will refer to any private individual who learns about a crime as a "witness," which will include witnesses who are private police officers and witnesses who are victims of a crime.) First, it is important to note that private criminal settlements are available to a witness only if (1) the witness knows the identity of the alleged perpetrator and (2) the witness has exclusive control over whether or not the crime is reported. If there are other witnesses who can report the crime to the police, or the police already know about the crime, the alleged perpetrator has no reason to agree to the deal.

Because these arrangements are almost always made in secret, there is no way of knowing how common these arrangements are. However, bargaining theory suggests that both parties have a great incentive to enter into these agreements when the preceding two conditions are met.[5] The witness receives some consideration from the defendant if an agreement is reached, whereas the witness's alternative to an agreement – reporting the crime to the police – looks much less appealing. Table 5.1 summarizes the costs and benefits to a witness of reporting a crime to the police.

The alleged perpetrator, of course, must give up something of value in order to make a private agreement, but they are even more at risk if they reject the agreement. Table 5.2 summarizes the alleged perpetrator's costs and benefits of refusing to make a deal with a witness who is willing to bargain.

The alleged perpetrator has the more difficult calculation to make: Whereas an arrest and a brief incarceration before arraignment are relatively certain, the possibility of conviction and ultimate sentence are dependent on a number of factors,

TABLE 5.1 *Witness/victim decision-making in choosing the public criminal justice system*

Cost	Benefit
Immediate requirement of interview and paperwork with police officer.	Victim or witness is contributing to prevention of crime generally, making crime slightly less likely in this jurisdiction, and thus making victim or witness slightly safer (theory of general deterrence).
Strong possibility that witness will need to interview with prosecutor.	This specific alleged perpetrator will know that the victim will call the police if a crime occurs and will be less likely to commit crimes against this victim. This incentive applies only to victims who report, not to other kinds of witnesses (theory of specific deterrence).
Remote possibility that witness will need to testify at trial.	The victim or witness will feel that they are fulfilling a duty by contributing to public justice and helping to ensure that those who commit crime are punished.
Remote possibility that perpetrator will seek retribution.	

TABLE 5.2 *Alleged perpetrator's decision-making in choosing the public criminal justice system*

Cost	Benefit
Discomfort/humiliation of arrest.	Agreeing to terms of private settlement means certain and immediate consequences, while most of the negative aspects of public punishment are not definite and are far in the future.
Possibility of being held in jail until arraignment (if no summons given).	
Cost of attorney (if not eligible for public defender).	
Chance of being convicted (through trial or plea bargain) and creating or adding to criminal record.	
Expected sentence after conviction.	
Collateral consequences of conviction, including stigma of being labeled a criminal.	

such as the strength of the case against them, the willingness of the prosecutor to strike a deal, and the disposition of the sentencing judge.[6] Furthermore, the alleged perpetrator has additional risks in agreeing to the private settlement: There is always the possibility that the witness will take the consideration and report the crime anyway. Finally, there is the possibility that another witness – including a public police officer – will become aware of the crime independently and commence a public prosecution. The likelihood of this possibility obviously depends on the facts and circumstances of the case – thus, the more likely it is that a third party could report the crime, the less likely an alleged perpetrator will be willing to negotiate.

When the witness and the alleged perpetrator are both willing to make a deal, there is a wide bargaining range for them to work with – certainly a wider bargaining range than exists in the contexts of traditional plea bargains between a prosecutor and a defendant. During private negotiations, a witness is free to offer any kind of deal, unconstrained by legal or institutional requirements. The only limit is what the alleged perpetrator is willing to accept. A prosecutor, on the other hand, has institutional limitations on what they can or cannot do, and usually must choose among a limited number of punishments: fine, community service, probation, and/or incarceration.

For their part, alleged perpetrators at the point of private apprehension have more to lose by not making a deal than those defendants who are negotiating with a prosecutor. An alleged perpetrator who agrees to a private criminal settlement can avoid all of the punishments – both direct and indirect – of the public criminal justice system. The defendant in a public plea-bargaining setting has already been arrested, charged, and brought to court. An alleged perpetrator bargaining with a private witness has the possibility of avoiding all of those impositions. For low-level crimes, the initial processing in the public criminal justice system – which, unlike the possibility of conviction and sentencing, are certain to occur – are often the harshest aspect of the interaction. In Chapter 3, we discussed Professor Malcolm Feeley's argument that, for lower level crimes, "the process itself is the punishment," since "the time, effort, money, and opportunities lost as a direct result of being caught up in the system can quickly come to outweigh the penalty that issues from adjudication and sentence."[7] By its very nature, public plea bargaining imposes this "punishment" even before the negotiation begins. And, once a defendant has suffered the punishment of the initial proceedings, they must then bargain with a prosecutor – and, even in the best case, when a deal is struck, the defendant faces a criminal conviction and the accompanying stigma and collateral consequences.

Given this incentive structure, it is likely that private criminal settlements – whether formal or informal – occur quite often. This is true even though, as we will see later in this chapter, they are almost always illegal.

TYPES OF PRIVATE CRIMINAL SETTLEMENTS

So far we have been talking about private criminal settlements quite broadly, which means that we have been lumping together very different types of bargains. However, as alluded to earlier, private criminal settlements come in many different shapes and sizes. For our purposes, it is useful to place them into three different categories: private police settlements, close-quarters settlements, and entrepreneurial settlements. Private police settlements occur when the private police apprehend a suspected criminal, but their clients do not want to spend the time and money engaging with the public criminal justice system and so try to accomplish their goals (usually specific and general deterrence) through less formal means. Close-quarters settlements refer to agreements between two individuals who already know each other, such as family members or an employer and an employee. Entrepreneurial settlements involve those who try to discover criminal activity with the purpose of extracting concessions from the alleged perpetrator. Essentially, the various types of private settlements differ in the motivations of the parties who deal with the alleged perpetrator: Private police usually want to deter future criminal activity, family members or employers generally want to avoid the harshness of the public criminal justice system, and entrepreneurs simply want to gain a benefit from the alleged perpetrator.

As I noted in Chapter 4, private police always have the option of turning the suspect over to the public authorities for adjudication and punishment, but this course of action is often not in the best interest of the private employer. Cooperation with the authorities takes time – time that the private employer will likely have to pay for – and the benefits of cooperating are diffuse, contributing to a general deterrence model that helps society, but that otherwise does not help the employer specifically.

A common example of private police settlements is the "civil demand letter" that many major retail stores send out to customers whom they catch shoplifting. After store security guards apprehend a suspected shoplifter, they will often take two separate actions. The first is to impose their own punishment, such as banning the person from the store. This is a type of private disposition, which we will discuss in Chapter 8. However, the real punishment will be come in the form of an "offer" contained in a letter that the store sends to the suspect a few days after the incident. Many states have passed special laws to deter shoplifting that allow retailers to recover up to $500 from shoplifters in addition to the actual damages – which may be nonexistent if the perpetrator is apprehended and the property recovered.[8] However, actually paying an attorney to sue a person in civil court is expensive, and would probably cost far more than $500, so the stores send these letters ostensibly to settle the civil case. The letter states that the store could sue the suspect in civil court if the suspect does not pay a certain amount of money:

> In order to save you additional time and expense, a demand is hereby made upon you for $500. If we do not receive this payment within 20 days from the date of the letter, we may hire a local attorney to take all necessary legal steps, which includes a civil court action to collect the full amount allowed by the statute.

Often, these letters use wording that is intentionally ambiguous, threatening "all necessary legal steps," which "include" a civil action (but by implication could include other steps as well). Thus, suspects who receive these letters often believe that if they do not pay the requested amount, they will be charged with a crime – a belief that the store encourages in order to encourage payment. Certainly the store owners seem to think that these letters also foreclose criminal charges: A representative of one retail store says that the "fine" that the store is demanding is "the penalty for committing a crime," while supporters of the program note that the shoplifter benefits from the procedure because, by participating, the shoplifter "avoids criminal prosecution."[9]

In almost all cases, the letters are a bluff. Stores that send out these letters usually have no intention of actually suing these suspects, much less contacting the police to bring criminal charges. Instead, these stores are indirectly using the public criminal law as a threat to coerce the recipients into paying a civil settlement. If the accused pays up, the store gets some amount of restitution – but, even if not, there is some deterrent effect on the alleged shoplifter, thus helping to prevent further crime against the store.

As noted in the Introduction, a company called the Corrective Education Company (CEC) tried to commercialize this process. Starting in 2010, large retail companies such as Walmart, Bloomingdale's, and Kroger contracted with the CEC to outsource their private plea bargaining process.[10] After the store's private security guards apprehended a suspected shoplifter, the security officer offered the accused the option of "enrolling" in the CEC's restorative justice program.[11] If they consented, the accused paid between $400 and $500 and completed an online class of six to eight hours.[12] After completion, the store agreed that the shoplifting case was "closed for all purposes" and that the store would not "pursue the matter with law enforcement" or seek civil recovery.[13] If the accused refused to take the class, the CEC referred the matter back to the store, informing the accused that the store "may pursue other legal rights to seek restitution and resolve this crime at their discretion."[14] In its first four years, 90 percent of the accused who were presented with this option chose to take the class, resulting in approximately 20,000 participants.[15]

Many people critiqued the CEC for exacerbating the economic inequities of the criminal justice system, as the very poor might have been unable to enroll with the CEC and thus were forced to enter the more punitive public system. (The CEC offered scholarships to a small percentage of its enrollees, but its model relied on the vast majority of them paying the full rate.)[16] Indeed, this is a recurring critique of private criminal settlements generally – as they often rely on monetary payment in order to avoid criminal punishment, suspects with resources can more easily avoid entering the criminal justice system. Others have portrayed the CEC's methods as nothing more than blackmail – a question we will explore in the next chapter.

However, the data show that the CEC brought some benefits as well. First, it saved the retail store time and money; in fact, the CEC paid the store for every "customer" that the store referred to the company. The program also saved the state money, as the police, prosecutors, public defenders, jails, and courts never got involved.

Shoplifting is an extremely common but relatively minor crime, and if police officers and the rest of the public criminal justice system got involved in every infraction, the drain on criminal justice resources would be severe. On the other hand, shoplifting costs retailers over forty billion dollars a year, so in the aggregate it is a significant economic problem that requires some kind of response. And the CEC's methods did seem effective: Some evidence showed that CEC "graduates" had a significantly lower recidivism rate than accused shoplifters who went through the public criminal justice system.[17] Finally, at a time when many scholars believed that mass incarceration has become a moral, political, and economic crisis, the CEC offered a response to criminal activity that did not involve incarceration or any other kind of monitoring by the state.

The second category – close-quarters settlements – consists of agreements made by individuals who already have a preexisting relationship with the perpetrator: a friend or family member or a neighbor, employer, or teacher. The witness may value the relationship with the perpetrator and not want to jeopardize that relationship by calling the police and potentially being required to testify against the perpetrator. Additionally, the witness may be concerned that the public criminal justice system will treat the perpetrator too harshly, whether because of unfair (or even dangerous) treatment at the hands of the police[18] or because of an overly punitive sentencing regime. However, although the witness might believe that the public criminal justice system will treat the perpetrator too harshly, they still could demand something from the perpetrator in return for not contacting the authorities. For example, if the witness is a victim, they may ask for restitution or require the perpetrator to undergo treatment or counseling. The informal nature of the bargaining procedure, combined with the ongoing relationship between the victim and the perpetrator, allows for an extraordinarily broad bargaining range and a high level of flexibility in the negotiations. Most observers would consider this type of settlement to be the least objectionable, as the motives of the bargainer are benevolent and because, in many cases, the deal that is struck between the bargainer and the suspect may be more effective in rehabilitating or deterring the suspect than any disposition that might be handed out by the public criminal justice system.

Finally, entrepreneurial settlements consist of agreements made by those who seek out evidence of a crime for the express purpose of extracting concessions from the perpetrators in exchange for not contacting the authorities. Frequently, these witnesses are motivated purely by financial gain, but not always. Consider the following two hypothetical cases:

(A) Residents of an urban neighborhood are fed up with the drug dealers and sex workers who are present on their block. The police occasionally arrest the criminals, but the dealers and sex workers simply return a few days later. Residents decide to take matters into their own hands and form a neighborhood watch organization. Members of the organization take turns observing and recording the criminal activity that occurs in the area. When cars come through their neighborhood to buy drugs or hire the sex workers, the observers take pictures and then write down the license plates of the cars. Every week the residents determine the owners of the cars and then send letters to all of them. The letters include pictures of the illegal transactions and explain to the customers that the neighborhood watch organization will contact the police unless the customer contributes $500 to the neighborhood watch organization. The organization then uses the money it collects to hire part-time security guards, install better lighting, and create after-school programs for the neighborhood youth.

(B) A stockbroker in a midsized brokerage firm notices some unusual patterns in the trades made by her officemate. She does some investigation and learns that her officemate is illegally trading on inside information given to him by his brother-in-law, who sits on the board of several major publicly traded corporations. She confronts her colleague and threatens to report him to the SEC unless he agrees to pay her $50,000.

In both cases, the bargainer seeks incriminating information with the purpose of obtaining resources from a potential criminal and, in both cases, the bargainer receives money in exchange for their silence. In the first example, the bargainer has ulterior motives that are generally consistent with the public criminal justice system – deterring crime, increasing security – but has determined that the best way to advance those motives is to arrange a private criminal settlement rather than contact the authorities. In the second example, the individual is simply motivated by personal gain, seeking to uncover the secrets of another in order to personally profit from them. Do we approve of the first and condemn the second? What if the stockbroker takes the $50,000 and donates the money to a children's hospital or some other worthy cause? What if the neighborhood watch organization uses the money it collects to throw hedonistic block parties instead of increasing security? Finally, even if we do want to encourage one type of entrepreneurial settlement but not the other, how do we draft laws that distinguish between the two?

There is another difference: In the first example, the neighborhood watch association (like the retail store that is eliciting a payment for shoplifting) is eliciting a payment for a wrong committed against them, while the stockbroker in the second example has not been harmed by her officemate's actions. Thus, some might argue that the neighborhood watch "deserves" the money from those who have perpetrated crimes that harmed them, while the stockbroker is merely obtaining a windfall that she has no moral claim to receiving.

Because of either the difference in motivation or the difference in the harm suffered by the private party, some would condemn the stockbroker and seek to criminalize and punish her behavior. However, just like with the retail store that coerces a shoplifter into paying "tuition" to enroll in an anti-shoplifting program, the actions of the stockbroker actually further many of the broader societal goals of the criminal justice system. In both cases, the alleged perpetrator faces consequences for the crime; in both cases, these consequences help to deter the perpetrator from future criminal behavior; and, in both cases, these consequences are achieved at no cost to the taxpayer.

Of course, even if entrepreneurial settlements do bring benefits, they are still flawed in many ways, as we will see in the next chapter. In fact, all three types of private criminal settlements are controversial; although they all may help contribute to deterrence or rehabilitation, they are all also vulnerable to similar critiques: the lack of transparency in the process, the risk of an uninformed waiver of valuable rights by the suspect, and the possibility that the bargainer may not share the same goals as the public criminal justice system. In analyzing these settlements, we can draw on an existing and well-developed body of scholarship that can be used as lens through which to evaluate private criminal settlements: the theory of plea bargaining.

PRIVATE CRIMINAL SETTLEMENTS AS PLEA BARGAINS

In one sense, private criminal settlements are simply a more extreme version of public plea bargains. The public plea bargain short-circuits the traditional path of criminal adjudication by allowing the defendant to waive certain rights in exchange for a lower punishment, and is perhaps less of a formal condemnation, as there is never a formal pronouncement of guilt by a jury of the defendant's peers. On the other hand, a private criminal settlement asks the perpetrator to waive even more rights and in return receive an even lower punishment, including the complete absence of a formal condemnation. In this sense, the formal condemnation is merely one more chip on the bargaining table and one more unpleasant consequence that the perpetrator seeks to avoid, thereby increasing the bargaining position of the victim or other private party who is conducting the settlement. Private criminal settlements allow the parties to gain flexibility and efficiency by eschewing the formalities of the "traditional" criminal justice system. Because prosecutors and defendants can already use the plea-bargaining process to potentially barter away all aspects of the criminal justice system – constitutional rights, incarceration, the stigma of a criminal conviction – it is hard to argue that any of these aspects are fundamental and essential parts of the process. Thus, the difference between public plea bargains and private criminal settlements is properly seen as one of degree and not of kind.

Private criminal settlements are of course distinct from plea bargains in one significant respect: They remove the state – and specifically, the prosecutor – from the negotiation altogether. In public plea bargaining, the prosecutor plays a critical role in selecting which cases should be prosecuted, how they should be charged, and what sentences are appropriate. Prosecutors have traditionally been considered a necessary arbiter of justice in the public criminal justice system, although recently there has been significant criticism of the prosecutor's role in the plea-bargaining process.[19]

5 Private Criminal Settlements as Plea Bargains

Plea bargaining is ubiquitous in the public criminal justice system – estimates are that between 90 and 98 percent of all criminal cases are resolved through plea bargain rather than trial.[20] Despite their widespread use – or, to put it more accurately, primarily *because* of their widespread use – plea bargains have been routinely criticized by scholars and in the popular press. The process has been labelled as an "impediment to the effective operation of the criminal justice system" that prioritizes efficiency over justice in order to impose punishment without bothering with the constitutional requirements of a trial.[21] Many of these criticisms apply, with even greater weight, to the process of private criminal settlements. However, plea bargaining also has a smaller number of (somewhat less passionate) supporters,[22] and some of their arguments about the benefits of plea bargaining (including the saving of resources and the increased flexibility) also apply to private criminal settlements.

CRITIQUES OF PLEA BARGAINING

Critiques of plea bargaining fit into four different categories that are particularly pertinent to the question of private criminal settlements: (1) plea bargaining results in a lack of transparency, (2) plea bargaining leads to inequality in result based on income, (3) plea bargaining can become coercive, resulting in innocent defendants pleading guilty, and (4) the results of plea bargaining do not accurately simulate the results of a trial. As we shall see, most of these criticisms apply with even more weight to private criminal settlements.

Lack of Transparency

Plea bargaining makes the criminal justice system less transparent in two ways. First, the negotiations are conducted in private, so criminal cases are resolved in relative secrecy – in contrast with the constitutionally guaranteed public nature of a criminal trial. Second, the ultimate disposition of a case is frequently misleading: A defendant will frequently agree to plead to a charge that is less severe than (and perhaps completely unrelated to)[23] what they were actually charged with – and thus the defendant's criminal record will not be an accurate record of their actual criminal conduct.[24]

Unlike other rights that the defendant waives in exchange for the plea bargain, such as the right to confront witnesses, the right to a public trial does not belong exclusively to the defendant. Thus, resolving the case in secret affects society as a whole, not just the defendant. In a full-fledged trial, the judge can monitor both sides to ensure fairness in the proceedings, the public can monitor the judge and both parties, and a record is made, which can be consulted in the case of an appeal. None of these applies in the plea-bargaining context, so abuses by either side go unchecked and unnoticed unless one of the attorneys brings it to the attention of the court. More broadly, secrecy in the process threatens the integrity of the entire system, decreasing its legitimacy in the eyes of lay people. As one critic noted "the concern is that we fundamentally alter the quality of justice when we take enforcement away from a public audience."[25]

The need for transparency in the labeling of convictions is a bit more subtle. Professor Albert Alschuler of the University of Chicago notes that correctional facilities rely on the name of the crime when classifying prisoners and setting parole dates, and the "mislabeling" of the crimes during the plea-bargaining process makes this task less efficient.[26] A greater problem arises later in the process, when a defendant is arrested and convicted for a new crime, and the judge (or prosecutor, if the new crime is being plea bargained) is attempting to determine the appropriate sentence for the new crime. A defendant's prior criminal record is perhaps the most important factor in determining what sentence is appropriate, and past plea bargaining can disguise the actual nature of much of the defendant's prior conduct. For example, a defendant who has committed three acts of domestic violence in the past may have a criminal record of three disorderly conducts, and the prosecutor or judge seeking to set an appropriate sentence for the fourth domestic violence conviction will be acting with imperfect information.[27]

These critiques apply with even greater force to private criminal settlements. The parties conduct the negotiation and private resolution even further from the public eye. For the parties, this is likely one of the benefits to the process – both the witness and especially the perpetrator might prefer not to be involved in a public process. However, from the perspective of the public criminal justice system, the secrecy of private criminal settlements detracts from their legitimacy. There is no way to monitor the process for abuses and no way to ensure that the process is fair and impartial.[28] Those who are inexperienced with the criminal justice system are more likely to be abused, especially if the party with whom they are negotiating is a repeat player. For example, if a first-time shoplifter is apprehended by an experienced store security guard, the guard could employ bullying and other inappropriate tactics to unfairly influence the perpetrator.

Similarly, the defendant's criminal record is completely unaffected by a private criminal settlement, so a prosecutor or judge in a future case will not have any hint as to the nature of the defendant's previous criminal activity – or even that the defendant previously committed a crime at all. In the plea-bargaining context, the prosecutor and judge at least know enough about the system to realize that past convictions are not always what they seem, and they can take that into account when reviewing a criminal record littered with arrests for certain conduct and guilty pleas for different conduct. In contrast, the prosecutor and judge will never know if a defendant has past private criminal settlements. This could lead to under-sentencing of recidivist defendants, as well as different treatment of criminals who were able to settle their previous criminal disputes privately from those who could not.

Of course, this is one of the factors that makes private criminal settlement so appealing to the perpetrator in the first place; avoiding a criminal record is one of the intangible benefits the perpetrator derives from making a deal with the private actor. By agreeing to a private settlement, the perpetrator not only lessens the punishment on this occasion, but also lessens the punishment for the next crime or crimes that they commit. In other words, this secrecy gives the parties even more room to negotiate, further increasing the incentives to enter into these agreements.

Inequality Based on Income

Another critique of the plea-bargaining system is that it creates disparities based on the economic class of the defendant.[29] Plea bargaining allegedly does this in two ways. First, those who can afford a good lawyer can negotiate a better deal with the prosecutor if only by filing more motions, requesting more hearings, and generally making the litigation longer and thus more expensive for the prosecutor – which should, under the logic of plea bargaining, result in a prosecutor who is more willing to do a deal. Second, and far more importantly, defendants who are able to post bail fare much better than those who cannot. Defendants who are held in jail pending trial are less able to participate in their defense and are more willing to plead (especially in misdemeanor cases, where the time spent in jail awaiting trial may begin to approach the maximum sentence for the crime charged).

It is debatable whether this critique of plea bargaining is well taken, however. Good lawyers will certainly help a defendant get a better plea bargain, but they will also just as certainly help the defendant's chances at trial, and it is not clear whether the disparity is greater for plea bargains than for trials. In fact, one could argue that public defenders – who cost nothing to the defendant – are the most skilled plea bargainers of all, as they are repeat players in the system and know exactly what each case is "worth" in the system. Likewise, the problem of pretrial detention leading to a coercive plea is more of a critique of pretrial detention than of plea bargaining itself.

However one resolves this dispute with regard to public plea bargains, it seems at first glance that disparity based on income inequality is a far greater problem for private criminal settlements. In fact, the effect of income disparity may be the primary objection that most individuals have to allowing such agreements. Allowing the wealthy to buy their way out of criminal liability might result in one type of justice for the rich, who can pay off their victims and avoid even the inconvenience of an arrest, and another type of justice for the poor, who will be unable to strike a deal and will inevitably end up in the public system, incarcerated and burdened with a criminal record.

Upon closer analysis, however, the dynamic between income and disposition in a private criminal settlement is a bit more complex. First of all, it is not clear that less wealthy perpetrators would be unable to reach a private agreement. As noted above, many victims/witnesses receive very little benefit (or even suffer costs) when they report the crime to the police and would potentially be willing to accept a very small amount of consideration in exchange for their promise not to report the crime. And the consideration given by the perpetrator need not be monetary – as noted in some of the hypothetical cases described earlier, it could be a promise not to engage in certain activity, to stay away from a certain commercial establishment, or to perform some service. These low-cost or nonmonetary resolutions are common for less severe crimes, which likely make up the bulk of crimes that are resolved by private criminal settlements.

In fact, if private criminal settlements were to become more widespread, it is likely that wealthy perpetrators would face harsher consequences than their less wealthy counterparts. A wealthy individual faces greater opportunity costs if arrested and incarcerated, and would therefore be willing to pay more money than someone less wealthy in order to avoid criminal liability. Even more important, however, would be the increased enforcement that would occur against wealthy criminals. If private criminal settlements were common, one could imagine private individuals or companies conducting their own investigations into criminal activity for profit. These private parties would surely target the wealthier members of society, investigating every possible indiscretion on their part in order to determine whether criminal activity has occurred.[30] Granted, these individuals will be able to pay money in order to avoid arrest, incarceration, and a criminal record, but, if private criminal settlements are banned or discouraged, the private party will never have the incentive to investigate the conduct in the first place and the wealthy perpetrator will never have been detected at all. Thus, it is certainly possible that wealthy individuals will be punished more often, and thus deterred more effectively, if private criminal settlements were to become widespread.

Danger of Wrongful Convictions

One of the most powerful critiques of plea bargaining is that it can lead to innocent defendants pleading guilty. There are a number of variants to this argument. Some commentators argue that plea bargaining is coercive, as the defendant faces such a severe potential sentence if they do not agree to the deal that even an innocent defendant may feel forced into taking the plea.[31] Others argue that a defendant who is offered a plea bargain will make their decision based not on whether they are guilty or innocent, but on their level of risk aversion – and, as innocent defendants are likely to be more risk averse than guilty defendants, the plea-bargaining process leads to more innocent convictions than the trial process would.[32]

Of course, trials can also occasionally result in the conviction of an innocent person, and there is no way to know which method in fact leads to a greater percentage of false convictions. Fundamentally, this critique is not based on the numbers of false convictions; instead, it focuses on the very nature of the plea-bargaining process.

Because the defendant has so much to lose merely by going to trial, even if the case against the defendant is weak, there is almost always some offer that the prosecutor can make that will be more attractive than the prospect of going to trial and would therefore induce the defendant to plead guilty – even if they are in fact innocent. As one commentator puts it:

> [Prosecutors] merely have to offer each defendant a settlement he prefers to trial. Only very rarely is the highest acceptable sentence of a defendant zero; in fact many innocent defendants are willing to accept minor punishment in return for avoiding the risk of a much harsher trial result. Therefore, prosecutors can extract guilty pleas even from defendants who are likely to be found not guilty at trial.[33]

This problem is only exacerbated in the context of private criminal settlements, as a defendant has so much more to lose by not reaching an agreement. In other words, the very same factors that make a private criminal settlement so attractive will also increase the likelihood that an innocent defendant will agree to pay some consideration in exchange for not having to become involved in the system. In the plea-bargaining context, a defendant knows that the alternative to a negotiated settlement is undesirable only if a prosecutor can convince a jury of their guilt beyond a reasonable doubt – a very high standard and one that at least some innocent defendants might be willing to gamble on. In the private criminal settlement context, the perpetrator's alternative to a negotiated settlement is undesirable if the witness or victim can simply convince a police officer that there is probable cause to make an arrest – a much lower standard that even innocent defendants may not care to test.

On the other hand, the consequences of an innocent person agreeing to a private criminal settlement are far less severe than when an innocent person accepts a plea bargain, since, in the former case, the accused does not end up with a criminal conviction. In fact, private criminal settlements provide a valuable opportunity for an innocent person who is accused of a crime. In the absence of a private criminal settlement, if the accused cannot convince the victim/witness of their innocence, then the likely result is arrest and the very real possibility of a criminal conviction. Thus, the chance to agree to a private criminal settlement could prevent an innocent person from being convicted.

Dissonance between Plea Bargain Result and Potential Trial Result

Defenders of plea bargains frequently respond to these first three criticisms by arguing that plea bargaining is a voluntary process, so the defendant is perfectly free to reject the agreement and go to trial. The same response applies with regard to private criminal settlements – by their nature, these settlements are voluntary and so, if a defendant is not satisfied with the offer, they can call the other party's bluff and take their chances in the public criminal justice system.

This argument, however, rests on a fundamental assumption that may not be true: that private criminal settlements and plea bargains take place in the shadow of the law and therefore the results from these agreements are similar to the results of a public trial (minus some discount in exchange for the perpetrator saving the state resources by forgoing a trial). Once again, the literature on plea bargaining is a rich source of analysis on this question. Commentators have debated this issue for decades in the plea-bargaining context, as it directly affects the desirability of plea bargaining. If the plea-bargaining process is indeed a reasonable replacement for a trial, then plea bargaining should be encouraged, as it can achieve the same result with far fewer resources.[34] On the other hand, if the results are dependent on factors unrelated to what would occur at trial, then society should work to reform, limit, or abolish the practice.[35]

The idea that plea bargains mostly reflect what would happen at trial was perhaps best identified by Judge Frank Easterbrook, although others have endorsed the model as well.[36] The essential argument is as follows: Both prosecutors and defense attorneys are repeat players in the system, and so they both have a good idea of what would happen if the case went to trial – with regard to both the chances of conviction and the likely sentence. Thus, they are able to bargain within a relatively narrow range to reach a result that is more or less equivalent to what would happen at trial, discounted by the possibility of acquittal and discounted again in exchange for the defendant's willingness to forgo their right to trial and thereby save the state time and money. For example, if the defendant has a 90 percent chance of being convicted of a crime, and the crime carries an average sentence of ten years, the defendant might be offered a plea deal of six years: nine years as an approximation of the result at trial, minus three years in exchange for saving the state the resources of going to trial. Under this theory, attorneys use the handful of trials that do occur as the standard to guide the hundreds or thousands of plea bargains that they strike – much like real estate appraisers use actual sales of neighboring houses to estimate the value of a specific property. Plea bargains are therefore a relatively efficient method of disposing of cases – the state gets almost the same amount of justice, having to settle for slightly lower sentences in exchange for the time and money that is saved. Under this model, giving the defendants more procedural rights – a more robust *Miranda* right, for example, or more extensive discovery rights – is in reality simply giving the defendant more to bargain away, effectively lowering the ultimate sentence.

Of course, Judge Easterbrook's contract theory of plea bargaining rests upon the assumption that the attorneys who are bargaining are veterans of the criminal justice system who can easily determine (and agree upon) the expected result at trial. In criminal law, this is generally a valid assumption, as most defense attorneys and all prosecutors are repeat players or at the very least have an opportunity to consult with more experienced colleagues.

More fundamentally, however, commentators have attacked the contract theory for ignoring agency costs in plea bargaining.[37] Prosecutors and defense attorneys have other, more personal, incentives when they engage in plea bargaining, which could tend to skew the outcome of the plea bargain far from what might happen at trial. Prosecutors might be willing to give too deep a discount because they wish to reduce their workload or because they are afraid of losing a case at trial.[38] Defense attorneys might be overburdened and under-resourced, and may enjoy close relationships with the judges and the prosecutors, which they do not want to jeopardize with aggressive bargaining tactics.[39] To make matters worse, these agency costs vary from case to case based on factors that are completely unrelated to the goals of justice or even to what might happen at trial. Some prosecutors may have political ambitions and be more risk averse than others, while some private defense attorneys may be much more willing to go to trial than their state-funded counterparts.[40]

Judge Stephanos Bibas, when he was a professor at the University of Pennsylvania Law School, launched an even broader attack on the contract model of plea bargaining (which he calls the "shadow-of-trial" model). In addition to arguing that the agency costs are far more significant than other commentators are willing to acknowledge, Judge Bibas also examines psychological factors that tend to skew the results of plea bargaining. He concludes that there are four "structural and psychological forces" that influence plea bargaining – uncertainty, self-interest, money, and demographic variation – and he proposes a number of structural changes to reform the plea-bargaining process to align its results more closely with those of a trial.[41]

First, uncertainty on behalf of both parties leads to many psychological pitfalls: overconfidence and risk taking in some cases, and risk aversion and anchoring in others. The two primary remedies that Judge Bibas proposes to combat the pitfalls from uncertainty are liberalized discovery rules, to be enforced before the plea bargaining takes effect, and more determinant sentencing regimes. The problem of self-interest is somewhat trickier. It is closely related to the agency costs discussed earlier, in that both prosecutors and defense attorneys have their own personal goals and motivations beyond what is best for their clients, but it also means something more – defendants will act in irrational ways during the plea bargaining session, and attorneys must work to de-bias them and overcome their denial of the risk or overconfidence. Judge Bibas suggests taking steps to reduce agency costs by supervising the line prosecutors more carefully, changing the fee structure for defense attorneys, and giving judges a more active role in reviewing the plea bargain. He also suggests that defense attorneys work harder to overcome a client's irrational psychological biases.

The other two issues Judge Bibas discusses – money and demographic variation – tend to exacerbate the first two problems. Defendants with money can hire attorneys with better information, thereby reducing uncertainty during the bargaining process. These attorneys may not have the same self-interest to accept an unfairly low offer. Demographic variation can also aggravate problems because variation between different defendants creates a wider range of biases and irrationalities, sometimes with perverse results. For example, repeat offenders are likely to be less risk averse, meaning that they will not take a deal unless the prosecutor offers a steep discount. In contrast, first-time offenders will be more likely to take a much harsher deal in order to avoid the potentially severe sentences after trial.[42]

Most of these critiques apply with even greater force in the case of private criminal settlements. In plea bargaining, both negotiators are almost always repeat players with legal training and extensive knowledge of the chances at trial and the expected sentence. However, this is generally not the case in the context of private criminal settlements because the parties are private citizens, and private citizens who are negotiating are unlikely to have information pertaining to the expected outcome at trial. Consequently, the negotiations may lead to results that are completely unrelated to what might happen at trial. Even more troubling is the possibility that one of the private parties (such as a recidivist criminal or an experienced security guard) has this kind of information and the other does not, leading to asymmetrical results.

This lack of information will only increase uncertainty, leading to a greater level of the psychological biases that Judge Bibas discusses: overconfidence, risk taking, risk aversion, and anchoring. And, although the parties are negotiating on behalf of themselves, which should eliminate agency costs, Judge Bibas' problem of self-interest is even more pronounced. Without defense attorneys present to de-bias the alleged perpetrator away from these skewed perceptions, the party will likely act irrationally.

Even if the private parties had perfect information, and even if they were able to overcome the irrationalities inherent in negotiation, private criminal settlements may still result in sentences that are more severe than what a perpetrator would receive at trial. For example, if the perpetrator is charged with a crime that would result in a light sentence from the public authorities but would be embarrassing to the alleged perpetrator, such as soliciting a prostitute or indecent exposure, they may be willing to concede a good amount during the negotiation in exchange for keeping the incident secret. This also brings a benefit to the alleged perpetrator, of course, as they get to avoid that aspect of the "sentence" that they would be subjected to if they entered the public criminal justice system.

BENEFITS OF PLEA BARGAINING AND PRIVATE CRIMINAL SETTLEMENTS

As we have already seen, there is ample evidence that the contract model of plea bargaining is flawed. Contract model theorists would freely acknowledge that other factors (such as the caseload of the court and the prosecutor) will also influence the bargain that is struck – the more overloaded the prosecutors are, the more they will discount their offer; that is, after all, the entire point of plea bargaining. Contract model theorists would also acknowledge, perhaps a bit more grudgingly, that other factors unrelated to the chance of conviction and possible sentence will affect the offers made and the outcomes that are reached, but they tend to downplay these other factors. Opponents of the contract model go much further, arguing that these other factors are so significant that they overwhelm the "legitimate" factors, thus rendering plea bargaining illegitimate.

There are good reasons to believe that private criminal settlements, even more so than plea bargains, are likely to produce dispositions that are inconsistent with what would happen at trial. However, perhaps both sides are viewing the situation from the wrong perspective by assuming that, ideally, plea bargaining – or private criminal settlements – should approximate the results of a trial. Certainly that is the original goal of plea bargaining, and there should be a presumption that the results at trial are the socially optimal results – that is, the results that are most consistent with our ideals of achieving justice while still protecting the rights of the defendant.

However, plea bargaining does more than merely increase the efficiency of the criminal justice system, as it provides unique benefits that the traditional adversary trial does not provide. Traditionally, plea bargaining has been seen as little more than an inexpensive way of producing rough justice – a process that is accepted as a necessary evil because the criminal justice system cannot afford to provide every defendant with a trial. However, like other forms of alternative dispute resolution, plea bargaining creates the chance for a more creative and flexible resolution to the dispute. By allowing defendants more input into the process, plea bargaining can increase the parties' belief that the process is fair – a concept known as "procedural justice." Plea bargaining also allows prosecutors to exercise broad discretion and seek justice in each individual case.

As with the costs of plea bargaining, some of these benefits apply to private criminal settlements, while some do not. Although private criminal settlements provide even more flexibility than plea bargains, they do not increase procedural justice or allow prosecutors to exercise discretion. They do, however, provide one additional benefit not afforded by trials or plea bargains: the chance of maintaining long-term relationships between the perpetrator and the victim, leading (perhaps) to a greater chance of rehabilitation and lower recidivism rates.

Flexibility in Reaching a Resolution

One obvious benefit of plea bargaining is that it allows for greater flexibility in resolving the criminal dispute. When a judge sentences a defendant after a guilty verdict, the judge is limited by statutory restrictions as to the sentence that can be imposed. A prosecutor and a defense attorney who work out a plea bargain, however, can agree to alter the charge in order to accommodate any disposition that the two parties agree upon. Thus, if a prosecutor believes incarceration is inappropriate, they can amend the charge to a crime that does not carry mandatory jail time. A prosecutor may also amend the charge to avoid what they believe is an overly harsh mandatory sentence. For example, in a three-strikes jurisdiction, if the defendant has two prior felonies and then commits a burglary that would result in life in prison, the prosecutor could amend the charge to a misdemeanor in order to avoid the lengthy prison time that the three-strikes law would require.

Similarly, if the crime that the defendant committed carries with it a collateral consequence that is unjust under the particular circumstances of this case – such as deportation for a legal permanent resident who is a productive member of society or lifelong sexual registration for a juvenile who committed a relatively minor sex crime – the prosecutor has the power to adjust the charge and allow the defendant to plead guilty to a different offense. In return, the prosecutor may demand concessions from the defendant that would be impossible or at least unlikely after a conviction at trial, such as agreeing to engage in a specific kind of community service, voluntarily entering counseling, restitution beyond what is required by law, or cooperation in the investigation and prosecution of others. None of these arrangements would be possible without the use of plea bargaining.

Of course, in the criminal law context, flexibility can be both positive and negative. On the one hand, flexibility may allow the parties to reach a more just result than would occur if a judge were to formally follow strictly enforced sentencing guidelines. This is especially true if one accepts the premise that prosecutors are seeking to do justice in individual cases, which would mean that allowing them broad discretion in selecting charges and proposing dispositions only increases their ability to reach a just result in each case. On the other hand, this kind of flexibility leads to inconsistent results for identical crimes, even within the same jurisdiction, and consistency is a key element of fairness, particularly in the context of criminal law. Furthermore, whenever a prosecutor and a defense attorney become creative in crafting a resolution specifically for their particular case, they are ignoring the intent of the legislature, which sets out a specific sentencing range, perhaps including particular collateral consequences, for a given crime.

For better or for worse, private criminal settlements allow for even greater flexibility than plea bargains. Although prosecutors have more freedom to craft dispositions during plea bargaining than judges do at sentencing, they are still somewhat restricted by the law and by institutional office policies. Private parties who are settling a criminal dispute, on the other hand, are free from any institutional limitations whatsoever. This enhanced flexibility is one of the reasons why private criminal settlements are so attractive; if the public authorities are not involved, the parties can come up with any sort of resolution, as long as they both agree to it. However, while flexibility is potentially a positive element in the plea-bargaining context – when one of the parties is (at least in theory) attempting to reach a just resolution – there is less reason to believe that it will lead to a more just result in the case of private criminal settlements, in which each party is simply trying to maximize gain (or, in the case of the alleged perpetrator, minimize punishment). Instead, the flexibility inherent in private agreements merely leads to inconsistent results for identical crimes.

This inconsistency problem is only magnified by the secretive nature of these agreements. Prosecutors and defense attorneys in the same jurisdiction can, and often do, compare the proposed disposition of their cases to past cases that have been resolved by a plea bargain to ensure that a potential plea agreement is not severely out of line with the "going rate" for that crime. In contrast, most (although not all) individual private parties will have no idea how other private parties have resolved their criminal disputes, and will therefore begin from a blank slate for every negotiation, resulting in inconsistent results. Of course, private criminal settlements can result in consistent results in certain situations involving repeat players; for example, when security guards for a specific retail store catch shoplifters, they probably have a standard deal to offer the perpetrator. Even in these situations, however, there is only consistency for perpetrators apprehended by the same repeat players. To take the same example, different stores in the same jurisdiction would likely have different policies regarding shoplifting.

Procedural Justice

A second benefit that plea bargaining provides is that it endows the defendants with a greater sense that they have been treated fairly in the dispute. This may at first seem counterintuitive; after all, plea bargaining is generally seen as a quick and dirty alternative to the due process and fairness of a criminal trial. However, psychologists have devoted a significant amount of study to determining what factors lead participants to believe that they have been treated fairly; they have concluded that the primary factor is not the actual substantive outcome of the case, but rather whether or not the individual believed the procedure was fair. This has led to a field of study known as procedural justice. It is a method of evaluating dispute resolution systems based not on the substantive outcomes they produce (which is known as "distributive justice"), but instead on whether the individuals who were affected by the resolution believed the procedure that was used was fair.[43]

The name of the discipline is somewhat misleading, as the studies are focused only on the perception of fairness and not on the actual fairness of the process. Of course, just because most victims and defendants believe that certain procedures are fair does not make them so. Obviously, the question of whether the parties involved are in fact better off is a critical one. However, the issue of perceived fairness should not be overlooked, as it is critical to the legitimacy, and therefore to the long-term survival, of the criminal justice system. In other words, even if the traditional criminal justice system were to utilize procedures and produce outcomes that all experts agreed were fair and just, the system would have no long-term viability if the individuals within the system – victims and defendants – perceived it to be unfair.

Studies in the field of procedural justice have demonstrated that there are three factors that determine whether or not an individual believes that a given procedure is fair. The first is known as "process control," which is the individual's opportunity to participate in the procedure, whether or not their participation affects the actual outcome. For example, one study found that allowing victims to testify at sentencing hearings increased the victim's perception of the fairness of the process, even if their arguments had no effect on the ultimate sentence given to the defendant. The second factor is whether the participant views the decision-maker as neutral and unbiased, that is, whether the rules are impartially followed and the decision-maker seems to be motivated to be fair to both sides in a given case. The final consideration is whether the individual is treated with dignity and respect during the process.[44]

Professor Michael O'Hear of Marquette University has noted that plea bargaining has the potential to fulfill the criteria for procedural justice better than the traditional criminal trial, at least with respect to the defendant. Professor O'Hear divides plea bargains into two different categories: "routine case processing" and the "adversarial interaction."[45] Routine case processing, which is more common for high-volume misdemeanors and low-level felonies, does not really involve bargaining or negotiating, but merely involves reviewing the police report to determine the key facts of the alleged crime and then informing the defense attorney of the preestablished offer for that particular offense. This process resembles "less a Middle Eastern bazaar than shopping in a supermarket."[46] This category of plea bargains does not fulfill many of the requirements of procedural justice, mostly because the defendant has "no real voice in the process."[47]

Adversarial interaction, on the other hand, occurs when the prosecutor and the defense attorney cannot agree quickly on the going rate for the specific offense with which the defendant is charged. In these cases, the prosecutor has three options: They can engage in "horse trading" by simply offering a lower sentence than the going rate; they can withdraw from negotiations altogether; or they can "adopt a position of principled engagement" by discussing the merits and equities of the case with the defense attorney and the client.[48] Principled engagement, unlike the other two options, creates a situation in which the prosecutor is at least willing to listen to the defendant's story and is potentially amenable to the idea of reducing or changing the offer in response to what the defendant says.[49]

Obviously it is only this final option – adversarial interactions in which the prosecutor and the defense attorney enter into principled engagement – that has any hope of increasing the level of procedural justice for the defendant. As O'Hear notes, the prosecutor usually decides what type of bargaining will occur and what stance they will take in that bargaining, as the pressures of the system almost always result in a guilty plea for the defendant regardless of how the prosecutor conducts the negotiation. Therefore, to enhance the level of procedural justice in the plea-bargaining context, O'Hear proposes training prosecutors in the importance of giving defendants a meaningful opportunity to convey their side of the story (what he calls providing "meaningful voice opportunities") and encouraging prosecutors whenever possible to adopt a position of principled engagement.[50] He also encourages prosecutors to treat defendants with respect and dignity throughout the process. In addition, O'Hear argues that prosecutors should develop – and convey to defendants – objective criteria to guide plea-bargaining decisions.[51]

What proportion of plea bargains already involve principled engagement? And how many prosecutors currently refer to objective criteria and treat the defendants with respect during the process? These are open questions, but at least these factors are possible in the process of public plea bargaining. In addition, as O'Hear points out, if procedural justice is a desirable goal, then it would be relatively inexpensive in most jurisdictions to adjust the methods of plea bargaining to enhance these elements of the process.

Private criminal settlements have the potential to offer an enhanced level of procedural justice, but they also create different challenges in this regard. Whether defendants are treated with respect in these private negotiations will depend on the private party who is conducting the negotiation. Some private parties will treat the alleged perpetrator with dignity and avoid unnecessary threats and humiliation, but some will not. The challenge is to change the system in order to ensure that the person negotiating with the alleged perpetrator treats them with respect during the process. Unlike prosecutors, the private parties who conduct these negotiations cannot be trained to act in a certain way or sanctioned if they fail to do so. Likewise, these private parties may or may not be neutral and unbiased – they are seeking to further their own interests, not uphold specific procedural rules, and this may or may not lead them to treat every defendant alike.

Other elements of procedural justice will still be present in private criminal settlements. The defendant will probably have more opportunity to tell their story than in most public plea-bargaining situations. And private criminal settlements certainly enhance the level of procedural justice for the victims, who experience very little procedural justice in the public criminal justice system, whether a case is involves a plea bargain or goes to trial.

Shifting Power from Judges to Prosecutors

A third potential benefit that plea bargains provide to the criminal justice system is a shift in adjudicatory power from judges to prosecutors. The traditional criminal justice system divides power among various actors: Prosecutors have the original charging power, juries decide guilt or innocence, and judges set the appropriate sentence if the defendant is convicted. During the plea-bargaining negotiation process, the prosecutor assumes all three roles, as they become de facto adjudicator and sentencing authority. Given the ubiquity of plea bargaining in the current system, this represents a significant shift in the balance of power.

Critics of plea bargaining see this shift as a negative development. Professor Alschuler argues that the process:

> tends to make figureheads of judges, whose power over the administration of criminal justice has largely been transferred to people of less experience, who commonly lack the information that judges could secure, whose temperaments

have been shaped by their partisan duties, and who have not been charged by the electorate with the important responsibilities that they have assumed.[52]

The lack of experience and legitimacy are important concerns, but probably the most troubling aspect about this shift in power is that a prosecutor is meant to be both an advocate for the state and a neutral adjudicator, zealously pursuing the case but at the same time willing to offer a plea deal that represents the most "just" disposition for the case. It is certainly not impossible for a prosecutor to take on both roles – indeed, most prosecutors are committed to ensuring a just resolution for each of their cases. However, at the very least, the breakdown of the separation of powers between the judge and the prosecutor gives an appearance of impropriety.[53]

Other commentators have seen the shift in power from prosecutors to judges as a positive development. In the modern criminal justice system, plea bargaining involves more than just a reduction of a sentence based on the risk of acquittal; it also involves the exercise of discretion on the part of the prosecutor. In other words, a prosecutor who offers a plea bargain is making a determination that the proposed disposition is a just and fair resolution of the case – a determination based on their expertise and their duty to do justice for the citizens of their jurisdiction.[54]

A prosecutor's exercise of discretion at the plea-bargaining stage can be broken down into three different categories. First, the prosecutor makes a calculation about the risks of going to trial and the cost to the system of litigating a case, and offers a discount to the defendant based on these two factors. How much each factor weighs into this discount will vary widely depending on the case. For example, in a rape case that relies heavily on the testimony of a victim with credibility problems, the prosecutor may be quite concerned about the risk of acquittal and offer a significantly reduced sentence. On the other hand, if the crime is a minor one, such as shoplifting an item of small value, a guilty verdict may be assured – but the prospect of using up even a few hours of a judge's and jury's time on the case may convince the prosecutor to offer a similarly sized reduction. As repeat players in the system, prosecutors will develop quite a bit of expertise in making these calculations – in terms of both the chances of conviction and the likelihood of conviction.

The second way a prosecutor will exercise discretion in the plea-bargaining process is by choosing among a number of different crimes to find the most appropriate one to which the defendant can plead. The prosecutor (or police officer) has already exercised discretion in the charging decision, selecting the appropriate crime from the vast (and growing) list of criminal prohibitions passed by the legislature. Professor William Landes and Judge Richard A. Posner have called this the problem of "discretionary nonenforcement." According to Landes and Posner, the criminal justice system requires a great deal of discretionary nonenforcement because it is impossible for legislatures to write laws with sufficient precision to perfectly cover only those who are guilty of crimes and not also potentially cover those who are innocent.[55]

Landes and Posner argue that a public monopoly on criminal enforcement is a necessary condition for the practice. However, this argument overlooks the possibility of private criminal settlements also fulfilling this role of discretionary nonenforcement. Because they operate in the shadow of the public criminal justice system, private criminal settlements are impossible unless the crime in question involves conduct that the local prosecutor will be willing to charge. In other words, if a private party sees a person smoking marijuana in a jurisdiction where public consumption of marijuana is illegal, the private party could try to make a deal with the person in exchange for not reporting the incident to the police. However, the marijuana user will be willing to make the deal only if the local prosecutor would in fact bring charges for this crime. Thus, private criminal settlements are a way that prosecutors can leverage their power of discretionary nonenforcement, essentially acting by proxy through private parties who threaten prosecution in their name.

The third and related way that prosecutors exercise discretion in conducting plea bargaining is in setting punishment. In theory, a prosecutor will seek the socially optimal punishment for each crime based on the culpability of the defendant. Critics of plea bargaining, of course, see this as a cost of plea bargaining, if not an outright travesty of justice: The judge is the neutral party who is supposed to set the punishment, and delegating this power to one of the parties in the case (who may only be a few years out of law school) subverts the adversarial nature of the system. On the other hand, prosecutors have a sworn obligation to seek justice, and many of them take that duty seriously when plea bargaining. In theory, prosecutors are able to listen to equitable arguments from the defense attorney and the victims, and – compared with judges – they have the time to investigate these arguments and greater discretion to respond to them. On the local and state level, all prosecutors and most judges are elected, so both of them have some accountability to the public.

In recent years, the amount of power wielded by the prosecutor in the plea-bargaining process has come under severe criticism. Many scholars consider modern prosecutors' motives to be not to seek the fairest and most just sentence possible, but instead to pander to the public by charging the highest possible crime and imposing the harshest possible sentence. As noted in Chapter 3, there is strong evidence that prosecutors have been the primary drivers behind mass incarceration for the past twenty years.[56]

In the end, whether the delegation of power from judges to prosecutors is a negative or positive development remains an open question. Although prosecutors are supposed to always keep the best interests of the community in mind when they conduct plea negotiations, their record on that count is mixed, either because they are forced to engage in assembly-line justice or because they believe they must be overly punitive in order to gain reelection.

When the same analysis is applied to private criminal settlements, it is likely that a further delegation of power from prosecutors to private parties results in a net loss of justice. As noted above, the parties in a private criminal settlement will frequently have limited or no experience in the criminal justice system, and thus may end up with settlements that bear very little relation to the expected eventual outcome at trial. More significantly, the private individual who bargains with an alleged perpetrator – whether a victim or a witness – is presumably only trying to get the greatest possible gain from the transaction, without any concern for whether the ultimate disposition is fair to the alleged perpetrator or beneficial to society. In contrast, a prosecutor can (and does) think about whether it is sensible to expend a certain amount of public resources to prosecute a minor crime. A private party will have no such consideration – they will decide to settle the case privately or call the police based only on their own individual incentive.

Furthermore, the parties who negotiate a private criminal settlement do not practice selective nonenforcement, at least not knowingly. As long as the private party negotiating with the perpetrator believes that they could receive some consideration in exchange for the private criminal settlement, they could threaten to report perpetrators for every minor infraction of the broadly worded (and extensive) criminal law, leading to over-enforcement. The private party is not likely to seek justice in setting punishment. Instead, they will seek to maximize the amount they can get from the perpetrator, regardless of how culpable the perpetrator is. A private party will (presumably) not care about factors that mitigate the moral guilt of the defendant, about the true cost to society of the crime, or about any of the other many factors that make up the complex calculus of prosecutorial discretion. Of course, as noted earlier, the private party's threat to contact the police is valid only if the police and the prosecutor will actually arrest and prosecute, respectively, the alleged perpetrator for the crime, which will limit the bargaining power of the private party.

Preserving Relationships

Private criminal settlements do offer one potential benefit that plea bargaining does not provide: Parties who engage in private criminal settlements are more likely to maintain any preexisting long-term relationships, whether it is a personal relationship (such as husband and wife) or a professional one (such as an employer and employee or a school and student). Contacting the authorities frequently causes significant, and perhaps irreparable, damage to these relationships. After the first contact, the public criminal justice system puts additional strain on these relationships by putting the victim and the defendant in adversarial positions and forcing the victim to make statements against the perpetrator and (at least occasionally) to testify against the perpetrator in court.

In contrast, private criminal settlements create a situation in which the victim and the perpetrator are working together – both to resolve the dispute in the first place and to ensure that the perpetrator ultimately satisfies the obligation they have undertaken. The victim-centered nature of the resolution may also help to mend the relationship rather than tearing it further apart, allowing the victim to feel that the perpetrator is atoning for their actions.

Of course, not all of these relationships are worth preserving – in many cases, it may be best to fire the embezzling employee or leave the abusive spouse. Moreover, many private criminal settlements do not involve a preexisting relationship at all. However, under the right conditions, private criminal settlements could help to preserve certain relationships if both parties are inclined to do so.

CONCLUSION

Comparing private criminal settlements to public plea bargains has helped us to identify many of the advantages and disadvantages of this particular form of alternative dispute resolution. First, we have seen the powerful incentives that witnesses and alleged perpetrators have to strike a deal without involving the public criminal justice system. More importantly, we have gained insights into whether these deals are good for society. They certainly suffer from a lack of transparency, and they may not accurately simulate the results that would occur if the case were to go to trial. By cutting the prosecutor out of the picture, these deals remove prosecutorial discretion from the equation, which could result in dispositions that serve the parties' narrow interests without taking into account broader questions of justice and deserts. However, the critique that private criminal settlements could lead to more innocent people being punished is not backed by evidence – such settlements might in fact allow innocent people to avoid the harsh consequences of arrest and prosecution. The concern that private criminal settlements favor the wealthy is open to debate – in fact, the widespread adoption of private criminal settlements could result in more private parties investigating wealthier individuals to seek lucrative entrepreneurial settlements. At the same time, private criminal settlements offer greater flexibility than public plea bargains (and far more than public criminal trials), provide the victim and the defendant with a greater sense of procedural justice, and have a better chance of preserving preexisting relationships than if the criminal dispute is referred to the public authorities.

We will revisit the costs and benefits of these settlements in Chapter 10, including an examination of the effect on society if such agreements were to become even more widespread. However, first, we need to consider the elephant in the room – whether or not these criminal settlements are themselves a crime. In each of these cases, a private party is threatening to reveal information unless the alleged criminal takes some action, a threat that is considered to be blackmail in most jurisdictions. In the next chapter, we will examine whether it make sense to criminalize these agreements. As it turns out, the crime of blackmail itself is a controversial topic. After decades of scholarship on the topic, there is still no consensus among legal scholars as to whether any kind of blackmail should be a crime. And the controversy over criminalizing this conduct only becomes more intense in the context of private criminal settlements.

6

Private Criminal Settlements as Blackmail

In the last chapter, we examined the phenomenon of private criminal settlements, which occur when a witness to a crime agrees not to report the crime to the authorities in exchange for some action on the part of the alleged criminal. This phenomenon is common enough that it became institutionalized, with companies such as the Corrective Education Company (CEC) contracting with large department stores to act as a private diversion class for shoplifters. As we saw in the last chapter, the CEC model has some merits and drawbacks, and reasonable people can disagree about whether it is a net benefit to the justice system to allow criminal disputes to be resolved in this way. However, regardless of where you come down on that debate, one point is indisputable: The CEC was breaking the law.

In 2015, five years after the CEC began operation, the City Attorney for San Francisco filed a lawsuit against the company, demanding that the company pay restitution to every customer that enrolled in its courses. The City Attorney had three objections to the CEC business model. First, he noted that the CEC's program "ha[d] not been approved by any California court or prosecutor," that it "operate[d] without the knowledge or involvement of the criminal justice system," and that its rehabilitative classes "flout[ed] many of the laws that regulated pretrial diversion programs."¹ He concluded that "[w]henever we privatize our justice system, especially criminal justice, you run the risk of intimidation from people who are motivated by nothing but profit and I think this is a perfect example of that." Essentially, the City Attorney was putting forth the premise that the state should have a monopoly on responding to criminal activity. We addressed this argument in Chapters 1 and 2, in which we noted that, although the state currently enjoys a near-monopoly on the legal use of coercion and force, private actors have traditionally played a significant if not dominant role in responding to criminal actions, and the mere fact that these private actors may have a profit motive does not preclude them from pursuing policies that coincide with the goals of the public criminal justice system.

Second, the City Attorney argued that the CEC and the stores that hired this company were deceiving and coercing those who were accused of crimes. According to the City Attorney's lawsuit, the CEC made "false and misleading statements to people detained by private security guards in the back room of a store to induce them to sign unlawful and unconscionable contracts confessing to crimes."[2] As noted in the last chapter, there were certainly instances in which the CEC and its clients used misleading language, and it is likely that most people do feel a degree of coercion after being apprehended by a private security guard and threatened with criminal prosecution. Of course, individuals who are apprehended by public police and threatened with criminal prosecution likely feel at least the same degree of coercion, and public police are allowed to engage in a great deal of deception in order to obtain a confession, so these tactics alone are not sufficient to morally condemn private criminal settlements. Nevertheless, Chapter 9 will propose some reforms that can increase the transparency of private criminal settlements and reduce the level of coercion that occurs.

The City Attorney's third critique of the CEC's private criminal settlements, and the one that formed the basis of his lawsuit, is more substantive: He claimed that the CEC was blackmailing its customers and that the deals it was offering were noting more than extortion. He was not alone in this legal analysis: The Attorney General of Indiana also sued the CEC under the same legal theory. In the end, the courts agreed: In 2017, a trial judge in San Francisco ruled that the CEC's practices were "textbook extortion under California law, and ha[d] been so declared for at least 125 years."[3] The CEC began winding down operations that year and eventually filed for bankruptcy. In 2018, the company sued its own lawyers over allegations about what the founders were told regarding the legality of their business plan.[4]

The CEC's fate will likely serve as a warning to other companies that try to commercialize private criminal settlements. And yet it is likely that private criminal settlements will continue to take place on a smaller and less formal scale for two reasons. First, as we have seen, both parties have a strong incentive to engage in private criminal bargaining. Second, the laws against private criminal settlements provide little in the way of deterrence because the chances of the blackmail being detected are very small. As with other forms of blackmail, private criminal settlements usually occur in secret, often with no witnesses aside from the two contracting parties. Both parties to the agreement have reasons to keep the agreement confidential – in fact, the "victims" of this type of blackmail arguably have an even greater incentive than other blackmail victims, as they will face arrest, prosecution, and punishment if the information is revealed. It is only when private criminal settlements are scaled up and become public – as was the case with the CEC – that they are likely to attract the attention of the authorities. The unintended consequence is that private criminal settlements will likely remain widespread, but decentralized and secretive, which will only exacerbate their flaws. I will argue in this chapter that the blackmail statutes should be changed to allow private criminal settlements under certain circumstances, so that these agreements can be institutionalized in the same way that private police have been institutionalized. Partly this is because, as noted in the last chapter, these agreements can be beneficial to both sides and can advance the goals of the criminal justice system, even if the parties have different motivations. However, mostly, it is because the justification for criminalizing blackmail, which is already weak, is even weaker in the context of private criminal settlements.

SHOULD BLACKMAIL BE A CRIME?

Blackmail occurs when an individual possesses information about the prospective victim that the victim would prefer not be made public, and the individual offers to keep the information quiet in exchange for some action on the part of the victim. This private information could be anything – a person's sexual orientation, an affair, or even information that a person has committed a crime. Agreeing not to report a crime to the police in exchange for some benefit is explicitly illegal under blackmail statutes in every jurisdiction in the United States, generally with potential penalties of a year or more of imprisonment. The federal statute is typical: "Whoever, under a threat of informing, or as a consideration for not informing, against any violation of any law of the United States, demands or receives any money or other valuable thing, shall be fined under this title or imprisoned not more than one year, or both."[5]

Blackmail is a crime that has puzzled commentators and scholars for decades.[6] It is an offense that feels intuitively immoral to many individuals, but it is difficult to explain why the activity should be criminalized. Most scholars begin their discussion of blackmail by describing the "blackmail paradox": it is generally not a crime to keep information secret, and it is not a crime to ask for payment in exchange for doing something you are legally permitted to do, but it is a very serious crime to combine the two legal activities by asking for payment in exchange for not disclosing information.[7] Given this anomaly, dozens of law professors, philosophers, and economists have all struggled to come up with a theory to explain why blackmail should be criminalized, while others have concluded that none of these theories is sufficient and so blackmail should be decriminalized.[8] The rest of this chapter will review the justifications for criminalizing blackmail, and then apply those potential justifications to private criminal settlements. As with most crimes, the justifications for criminalizing blackmail can be grouped into two categories: those based on utilitarian reasons and those based on retributive reasons.

UTILITARIAN JUSTIFICATION 1: WASTED RESOURCES

The primary argument for criminalizing blackmail from a utilitarian perspective is that blackmail is an economically inefficient activity. In the paradigmatic case, the blackmailer will invest resources in finding out about the victim's activity and then ask the victim to pay them money to not disclose the information. As one commentator argues, this is akin to "digging up dirt, at real resource cost, and then reburying it."[9] If blackmail were legalized, entire industries would spring up devoted to finding the most embarrassing and damaging secrets about individuals, extracting payment for these secrets, and then destroying the information they found.

There are two possible responses to this utilitarian argument. The most powerful response is to simply ask, so what? Economic inefficiency is hardly a sufficient justification for criminalization. People engage in economically inefficient behavior all the time – from taking long drives through the country to making trades on their fantasy football team – and nobody argues those behaviors are criminal.[10] As a voluntary transaction between consenting adults,[11] blackmail should not be criminalized unless – as is at least arguably true for selling drugs, making pornography, or engaging in prostitution – there is some negative externality caused by the transaction that is damaging to society.

Another response to the economic inefficiency argument is that it paints with too broad a brush. Here it is important to distinguish between different kinds of blackmail. In the last chapter, we differentiated between three different types of private criminal settlements. "Close-quarters" private criminal settlements are agreements that are made between individuals with preexisting relationships. "Private police settlements" occur after a private arrest, when the clients of the private police would prefer a quicker, cheaper resolution to the criminal activity that was observed by the private police than would be achieved through the public system. "Entrepreneurial settlements" occur after a private party actively seeks out evidence of criminal activity in order to gain a benefit from the criminal. Scholars categorize the crime of blackmail in similar ways, differentiating between "opportunistic blackmail," in which the blackmailer unintentionally obtains the private information – as either a victim or a witness – and then decides to capitalize on what they observed, and "commercial research blackmail," in which the blackmailer invests time and money in discovering the private information. For opportunistic blackmail (which would include most close-quarters settlements), there is no wasted use of resources, as the blackmailer expends no resources to obtain the incriminating information. In the case of commercial research blackmail, the blackmailer does indeed invest resources to find information, only to hide it again; thus, assuming the agreement does not serve any socially useful purpose, the practice would be socially inefficient.

However, as we saw in the last chapter, private criminal settlements *do* serve a socially useful purpose, even if that is not always the motivation of the individuals who undertake the agreements. By forcing the accused to take some action that they do not want to do, the blackmailer is both deterring future crimes – a utilitarian purpose – and punishing the past crime – a retributive purpose. However, because the defendant would not agree to the deal unless it provided better terms than they would receive from the public criminal justice system, private criminal settlement penalties cannot be as severe as those in the public system. This therefore leads to a lower level of deterrence and punishment in private criminal settlement than what the accused would face in the public criminal justice system.

Professor William Landes and Judge Richard Posner add another point to this under-deterrence argument. They assume that a private blackmailer can extract only financial consideration – that is, money – from the alleged perpetrator, and they note that many alleged perpetrators may not have sufficient resources to pay a price that is equivalent to the punishment that they deserve. Thus, the private blackmailer will be forced to settle for even less than they would otherwise demand. In contrast, the state can incarcerate a perpetrator for an appropriate period of time regardless of the perpetrator's financial resources.[12]

One flaw in this argument is that it assumes that money is the only consideration that the perpetrator can give to the blackmailer. In fact, one of the appealing aspects of incriminatory blackmail (as with any form of alternative dispute resolution) is its flexibility: The blackmailer could demand services from the perpetrator, require that the perpetrator abstain from certain behaviors, or request any other kind of consideration. Therefore, even the very poor who have no financial resources could still suffer some punishment – and also be deterred – by private criminal settlements.

However, even if each individual private criminal settlement provides a lower level of deterrence and punishment than would be achieved through the public criminal justice system, the execution of these settlements could still increase the overall level of deterrence. The important variable is the extent to which the private settlements are displacing the traditional public criminal justice response.[13] For opportunistic blackmail, this is an unknown variable. Opportunistic blackmailers acquire evidence of a crime through chance, usually by being witnesses or victims of a crime. If a private criminal settlement were effectively banned, some of these victims and witnesses would contact the police, which would lead to a higher level of deterrence and punishment, but some would do nothing, thus leaving the perpetrator unpunished altogether. Many crimes between friends and family members, for example, will always go unreported, as the victim often does not want law enforcement to get involved in the case. Some commentators have disputed the very premise of the under-deterrence argument for this very reason, noting that, in many cases of opportunistic blackmail, the victim or witness would never call the police, even if the private criminal settlement option were unavailable.[14]

Of course, even if we assume that the existence of opportunistic blackmail results in a lower level of deterrence and punishment than if we were able to ban the practice altogether, it is not clear that these arrangements are a net loss for society. Opportunistic blackmail achieves at least some level of deterrence and costs far fewer state resources than would be expended in the public criminal justice system. In other words, in the same way that public plea bargaining offers a defendant a reduced sentence (and thereby provides less deterrence) in exchange for a saving of resources, opportunistic blackmail offers an even lighter sentence in exchange for not using any state resources.

Instances of commercial research blackmail – what we have termed entrepreneurial private criminal settlements – unequivocally increase deterrence. Unlike the opportunistic blackmailer, the commercial research blackmailer would not have even known about the crime, much less reported it, if they did not have the incentive of payment from the perpetrator.[15] Legalizing and encouraging these settlements would encourage third parties to seek out evidence of a crime that by definition would otherwise remain undiscovered by public law enforcement. This would result in an increase in private detection of criminal activity, and a corresponding increase in private payments from perpetrators to blackmailers, thus raising the cost of crime in general and achieving a greater level of deterrence. Furthermore, commercial research blackmailers would be able to profit only from crimes that were undiscovered or unsolved by the public authorities, so any investigations they were to undertake would focus on these crimes, thus automatically filling in the gaps in the public criminal justice system.

In other words, opportunistic blackmail agreements – including close-quarters settlements – do not waste resources, as they require no private investment of time or resources. Commercial research blackmail agreements, which include entrepreneurial settlements and most private police settlements, require some private investment of resources, but they are not wasted: They result in certain crimes being discovered and indirectly punished through a blackmail payment. And both types of blackmail contribute at least modestly to the goals of the criminal justice system, as they punish and deter.

UTILITARIAN JUSTIFICATION 2: BLACKMAIL ENCOURAGES FRAUD, THEFT, AND SECRECY

Some utilitarians, notably Professor Richard Epstein of New York University, have argued that blackmail should be criminalized, not because it is inherently harmful, but because its practice leads to socially undesirable results, such as theft and secrecy. It leads to theft because blackmail encourages otherwise law-abiding citizens to steal in order to pay the blackmailer's demands, and it encourages secrecy because the blackmailer will have an incentive to ensure that the victim's secret (for example, the victim's criminal activity) is kept safe, and so will encourage the victim to keep silent about their crime and advise them on how to do so.[16]

This argument is not unique to blackmail – it can be used to justify other, so-called victimless, crimes such as drug use, sex work, and gambling – but in most other cases it is not offered as the sole reason for criminalization. Although drug addicts and compulsive gamblers can and do commit theft to support their habits, these acts are also criminalized because they are inherently damaging to the individual – that is, they have a paternalistic justification as well. And, at least traditionally, there is a strong moral component to the criminalization of these actions: Gambling or using drugs or hiring sex workers is considered to be morally wrong by many people. In short, utilitarians would find it hard to justify laws against drug possession, sex work, and gambling on utilitarian grounds alone, especially because there is a reasonable argument that criminalizing these actions creates more harm to society than the underlying act itself.

Similarly, it is hard to justify criminalizing blackmail solely based on the theft that it might encourage. Unlike drug addiction or compulsive gambling, there is no real argument that the blackmailer needs to be protected from themselves. Furthermore, not all blackmail leads to theft, nor is there any evidence that it leads to fraud or theft more often than other perfectly legal activities. In the end, the underlying theft is already itself criminalized, and presumably punishments for theft and fraud could be increased if the state wanted more deterrence.

Epstein's other point – that blackmail leads to secrecy – is self-evident. Obviously a blackmailer has an incentive to help the victim keep the information secret – it is valuable information to the blackmailer, after all – and so this would conceivably encourage the blackmailer to give advice and even assistance to the victim on how to prevent others from discovering the information. However, this argument has very little force in justifying a general ban on blackmail outside the context of private criminal settlements. Secrecy in and of itself is not against the law; in fact, we value secrecy and privacy in many contexts. For example, a person may privately enjoy certain activities that would be embarrassing to them if their coworkers or family members knew about them – anything from unorthodox hobbies, such as knitting or playing bagpipes, to unusual sexual practices. On a more serious level, businesses keep trade secrets and governments keep state secrets. Both types of secrets are generally considered to be beneficial, if not necessary, in a modern society. If a blackmailer assists their victim in protecting information that the victim would prefer to keep private – perhaps the victim's sexual orientation or a sexual indiscretion in the past – the assistance would probably be welcomed by the victim as a positive byproduct of the blackmailing process.

However, when applied to private criminal settlements, the secrecy concern becomes more legitimate. In this case, blackmailers are not merely helping victims keep embarrassing information secret; they are helping to cover up crimes. The blackmailer may even become an accessory after the fact by helping to prevent detection of the crime by law enforcement.[17] This problem is particularly acute for commercial research blackmailers, as they are likely to be repeat players in the industry who invest resources to unearth evidence and track down witnesses that could incriminate the perpetrator. In order to maintain secrecy, these blackmailers could destroy the evidence and deter witnesses from testifying if the perpetrator pays the asking price. In this sense, under Epstein's utilitarian theory, private criminal settlements are the worst kind of blackmail, and commercial research blackmailers are the worst kind of blackmailers. Opportunistic blackmailers – victims or others who just happen to witness a crime – are far less likely to be able to provide any useful assistance to the perpetrator. They can guarantee their own silence, of course, but they will generally not be in a position to help the perpetrator cover up the crime or hide it more effectively from the authorities.

Even so, Epstein's objection still covers only a byproduct of blackmail, not the blackmail itself. Just as the theft that sometimes accompanies blackmail is independently criminalized, so is the crime of hindering the apprehension or prosecution of a crime. If commercial research blackmail were legalized, penalties for assisting in the cover-up could be increased.[18] Additionally, a jurisdiction could criminalize any further compensation after the initial payment to the commercial research blackmailer. This would effectively eliminate the blackmailer's incentive to help with any cover-up, as they would have no interest in whether the perpetrator was ultimately apprehended.

In the end, utilitarian theories do not seem to sufficiently explain why most individuals believe that blackmail should be illegal.[19] Blackmail has been criminalized not because it wastes resources or because it could lead to other crimes, but because people believe it is morally wrong. As one scholar notes: The utilitarian justifications "fail even to approximate common intuitions regarding what's wrong with blackmail."[20] We therefore turn our attention to the retributive justifications for criminalizing blackmail.

RETRIBUTIVE JUSTIFICATION 1: THE ILLEGAL OFFER

At the outset, many of the retributive justifications for criminalizing blackmail fail because of a mischaracterization of the act itself – specifically, a conflation of extortion with coercion.[21] If an individual blackmails their victim by threatening to carry out an illegal act against the victim unless a payment is made, then the individual has coerced the victim, not blackmailed them. For example, if A threatens to burn down B's house, break B's kneecaps, or kidnap B's child unless B pays A $100,000, the transaction may look like blackmail, but it is not. True blackmail consists of the blackmailer threatening to take an action that is not criminal, which the blackmailer has every legal right to do – usually the disclosure of information – unless the victim complies with the blackmailer's demand. This is the essence of the "paradox" of blackmail – two legal actions can combine to create a crime.

At least one commentator has attempted to justify the criminalization of blackmail on retributive grounds by narrowing the definition of blackmail to cover only those cases in which the action that the blackmailer threatens or offers to undertake is itself illegal.[22] As noted earlier, a threat to do something illegal transforms the blackmail into coercion, which provides an easy case for justifying criminalization. However, for the purposes of criminalizing private criminal settlements, the definition could potentially be useful if failing to report a crime were itself a crime. If so, the incriminatory blackmailer who offers to remain silent in exchange for consideration is offering to commit an illegal act for money. In a sense, the blackmailer is offering to enter into an illegal conspiracy with the victim.

However, this justification for criminalizing private criminal settlements is not very persuasive, because modern criminal law does not impose a general duty to report a crime. The common law offense of failure to report a crime – known as misprision of a felony – was created centuries ago during a time before professional police forces existed.[23] As we saw in Chapter 2, ordinary citizens were required to apprehend felons themselves or, barring that, to raise a "[h]ue and cry" so that other citizens could respond.[24] The crime of misprision of a felony was ultimately abolished by twentieth-century judges who applied the principle that a mere omission cannot be a crime. Only two states have laws that criminalize the non-reporting of a crime,[25] and federal law only prohibits active "concealment" of the crime, which courts have interpreted to mean more than merely the omission of nondisclosure. To be convicted, a defendant must also commit some kind of affirmative action, such as lying to investigators or concealing evidence.[26] The modern criminal law rejects the idea that the mere non-reporting of a crime should itself be a crime, following the basic criminal law principle that omissions cannot themselves be criminal.[27]

There are some exceptions to this principle, of course, and the "illegal offer" justification is sensible in the rare circumstances when specific individuals are legally bound to report evidence of a crime. For example, law enforcement officers (who have a duty to report and enforce the criminal law) are obviously making an illegal offer when they request money in exchange for not reporting a crime. In addition, many states impose a specific crime-reporting duty on certain professions. For example, physicians who see evidence of gunshots or other violence are frequently required to report the incident to the police, while certain professionals are mandated reporters for child abuse.[28] Furthermore, a handful of states require eyewitnesses to report certain violent felonies, although prosecutions under these statutes are extraordinarily rare.[29] We will discuss the wisdom of these laws – and their implications for the private criminal justice system in general – in Chapter 9. But, for now, it is enough to acknowledge that if an individual has a statutory duty to report a crime, then it should be a crime for that individual to agree to violate that duty by withholding the information in exchange for money. However, there is nothing in this justification to suggest that all private criminal settlements should be illegal.

RETRIBUTIVE JUSTIFICATION 2: THE BLACKMAILER AS "PARASITE"

Professor James Lindgren of Northwestern University School of Law has argued that blackmail is morally wrong because the blackmailer is offering to sell something that does not truly "belong" to them – that the blackmailer "interposes himself parasitically in an actual or potential dispute in which he lacks a[n] ... interest."[30] For example, if an employer would want to know about an employee's drug problem and the blackmailer demands and receives money from the employee in order to keep the drug use secret from the employer, then the blackmailer has in a sense profited from information that would be valuable to the employer. Or, to use one of Professor Lindgren's examples, if a woman were to learn that a company is criminally polluting the air and seek $1,000,000 in exchange for her silence, she may deserve some amount of compensation (if she lives near the smokestack herself), but she has "stolen" money that belongs to the state. In other words, the blackmailer has inserted themselves as an unwanted intermediary between the victim and the person who would like to have this information, thus effectively stealing the money from both of them.[31]

The "parasitical" argument has intuitive appeal, but it does not fully explain why this particular type of exploitation should be considered criminal.[32] For example, if it is immoral – even criminal – to profit as a "parasite" for not revealing information, then why is it not immoral to profit by *revealing* the information? What if, for example, the blackmailer learned about the employee's drug use and offered to sell the information to the employer? What if the woman invested time and money to discover which companies were polluting and offered to sell this information to the state to aid in enforcement efforts? What about a company that spends resources to locate untapped lucrative oil reserves, finds them underneath a farmer's fields, and then offers to sell the precise location to an oil company? There are plenty of legitimate situations in which an individual learns information about one person that would be valuable to another and offers to sell the information – in effect bargaining with someone else's information.[33] Why is it then criminal to offer to *not* disclose the information?

However, once again, although this argument is a relatively weak justification for the criminalization of blackmail generally, some would argue that it carries more weight for private criminal settlements specifically. In those agreements, the blackmailer is inserting themselves between the perpetrator and the state – thus, the blackmailer is not merely bargaining with chips that belong to an employer or a wronged spouse, but is bargaining with chips that belong to the state. The blackmailer in this case is using a unique type of leverage that comes from the criminal justice system, a leverage that has been put into place to further the cause of justice and is now being subverted to further the blackmailer's own personal goals.

From another perspective, however, private criminal settlements are less objectionable than other types of blackmail under this rubric. If the blackmailer is receiving money in exchange for keeping information secret that would benefit another private party, you could argue that they are "stealing" that benefit from the private party. The private party morally deserves the benefit that they would enjoy if the information came to light. However, in a criminal case, the state does not actually gain anything of monetary value from the defendant. Although it has a right to punish the defendant, exercising that right actually *costs* the state money. The state's interest in learning about and pursuing the criminal case is not financial; its interest is to further the goals of the criminal justice system, that is, making the defendant suffer for the crime that they already committed (from a retributivist standpoint) and deterring the defendant from committing more crimes (from a utilitarian standpoint). When a third party – the victim or a witness – supplants the state in a criminal case, they are furthering those same goals by extracting something of value from the alleged perpetrator, or by requiring the alleged perpetrator to do something they do not want to do. Granted, the third party will not impose the exact same punishment that the state would if the case were reported (in fact, by definition, the punishment will be less severe), but, as discussed earlier, this is no different from traditional plea bargaining: The state pays less (in this case nothing) and the defendant is deterred less and punished less severely. Whether it is worth it to reduce the punishment so drastically in exchange for dropping the cost imposed on the state to zero is an empirical question – one already discussed in the context of the utilitarian justifications.

It is true that the third party is (probably) not doing this out of a sense of justice – perhaps they are doing it out of pure greed – but, once again, the motivations of the third party are irrelevant.[34] The state (that is, the alleged victim of this "misappropriation" under this theory) has no interest in the third party's motives. In other words, even in the private criminal settlement context, this reason for criminalizing blackmail falls short. Nothing is actually being "stolen" from the state; instead, the third party is advancing the state's goals (at least part of the way) and saving the state money.

RETRIBUTIVE JUSTIFICATION 3: THE BLAMEWORTHY ACTOR

Throughout this book, we have seen that private criminal settlements can further the goals of the public criminal justice system, even if the motivation of the private actor has nothing to do with those goals. Private police are motivated by the commercial needs of their clients; those who engage in commercial blackmail are motivated by profit; those who engage in close-quarters private criminal settlements want to rehabilitate their friend or loved one. One of the premises of this book is that these motivations are irrelevant as long as the result of these actions is to punish and deter offenders. However, the most compelling argument for criminalizing blackmail challenges this premise, proposing that motivation is actually central to our understanding of blackmail.

This argument comes from Professor Mitchell Berman of the University of Pennsylvania Law School, who proposes an "evidentiary theory" of blackmail. Under Berman's theory, one sufficient set of criteria for criminalizing any action is that the act (1) tends to cause or threaten identifiable harm and (2) is undertaken by a morally blameworthy actor.[35] By adding the second criterion, Berman resolves the paradox of blackmail. If B discloses an embarrassing fact about A, then B causes identifiable harm to A – in reputation, if not financially – but B may or may not be disclosing the fact as a morally blameworthy actor. B may be disclosing the fact because B believes it is important for the world to know the truth, or because B is a friend of the person they are disclosing the fact to and wants that person to know the information. Likewise, if B keeps the information secret, B may be causing harm – there may be a spouse or employer who remains deceived and makes poor decisions as a result of the deception – but B may be doing so for noble and admirable purposes, such as to protect A from wrongful discrimination that would occur if the secret was revealed.

However, if B threatens to disclose the information in a way that will damage A unless A gives B some consideration, we can now assume that B's motives are morally blameworthy. The circumstances of the blackmail make B's motives clear. As Berman puts it, "[a] reasonable fact-finder could infer with confidence sufficient for purposes of criminalization that if B carried out his threat he would be engaging in harm-causing conduct with bad motives."[36]

Berman's evidentiary theory sufficiently resolves the blackmail paradox, as it provides a principled way to explain why two legal actions – withholding information and agreeing to carry out a legal act – become illegal when combined together. Berman even discusses the specific case of private criminal settlements – which he calls "crime exposure blackmail" – and concludes that it fits perfectly within his model. When B fails to report a crime to the authorities, we know that B's silence will prevent a perpetrator from being brought to justice, which causes an identifiable harm. However, once again, we have no way of knowing why B remained silent – B might have been afraid to come forward, might be a good friend of A and selflessly does not wish to harm A, or might believe that the act that A committed should not be a crime and so the failure to report could be seen as a subtle form of civil disobedience. Under Berman's scheme, it would be unfair to punish B under any of these scenarios – whether B disclosed or not. However, when the failure to report the crime is combined with a request for money or some other benefit, Berman claims that we can infer from the very fact of the blackmail demand that an individual who threatens to disclose a crime unless payment is made is motivated by "pure selfishness."[37]

However, in order to justify criminalizing incriminating blackmail using Berman's theory, one must make two assumptions, neither of which is self-evident. First, we have to agree that a person's motive should be relevant in determining whether or not an action is criminal. Second, we must assume that when the victim or witness demands something of the perpetrator in exchange for not calling the authorities, the act of blackmail itself triggers an evidentiary presumption that the blackmailer is acting with a "bad" motivation.

The first assumption is, at the very least, controversial – as Berman himself admits, it is contrary to the general rule that "motive is immaterial in the substantive criminal law."[38] Berman does little to defend himself against this point, merely stating that motive is relevant in some specific criminal contexts, such as euthanasia, justification defenses, and determining punishment.[39] These are, however, narrow exceptions to a very broad and well-established rule. Euthanasia defenses are relatively modern and not widely accepted, for example,[40] and the fact that motive is a valid consideration in determining the proper sentence once liability is established is quite different from arguing that it is relevant in determining whether liability exists in the first place. Professor Berman also engages in a bit of circular reasoning. First, he concludes that blackmail ought to be illegal because the act of blackmail demonstrates the bad motive of the actor. Then, to justify this conclusion, he argues that it must be proper to consider the motive of the actor since doing so helps to justify the illegality of blackmail.[41]

However, more significantly, Berman's second assumption – that the very act of incriminatory blackmail proves that the blackmailer has a "bad" motive – is suspect. Simply put, when a person demands something from the perpetrator in exchange for not calling the authorities, the blackmailer may not be acting out of "pure selfishness" or any other improper motive. They may be the victim, seeking to receive compensation for physical, economic, or emotional harm that was suffered. Or the blackmailer may be an "entrepreneur" who invested time and money into investigating this case and now feels that they deserve compensation for all the work. Are either of these two motives "morally blameworthy"?

The Model Penal Code, which is meant to be a model for criminal codes across the country, acknowledges the possibility that a blackmailer may not have an improper motive, at least with respect to a victim-blackmailer. The code includes a special provision for criminal exposure blackmail, which it calls "compounding," and creates a defense for a victim who blackmails the criminal who victimizes them, as long as the pecuniary benefit demanded by the victim "did not exceed an amount which the actor believed to be due as restitution or indemnification for harm caused by the offense."[42] Some state codes also make even broader exceptions for criminal exposure blackmail if the blackmailer was acting in good faith. Ohio, for example, allows for a victim or a witness to engage in criminal exposure blackmail for a number of reasons, including if "the actor's purpose was limited to ... [c]ompelling another to refrain from misconduct or to desist from further misconduct ... [or] to [p]revent ... or redress ... a wrong or injustice."[43]

Professor Berman is not convinced. Because we all have a moral duty to report criminal activity, he believes that the failure to do so "tends to bespeak a disregard for the common good and the concrete interests of actual and potential victims."[44] Even a victim who is merely seeking compensation for their injuries suffered – someone who would fit perfectly into the Model Penal Code's defense – is acting with an improper motive: "[Since] all members of the community have a civic duty to report crime, then it cannot be morally acceptable for a victim to offer to ignore her obligation for personal gain – even if that gain is in some sense compensatory."[45] In other words, Professor Berman's justification for criminalizing incriminatory blackmail is contingent upon the premise that we all have a civic duty to report crime, and it is morally wrong to fail in that duty in order to pursue one's goals.

Professor Berman acknowledges that moral blameworthiness is a "nebulous concept" – he says it is comprised of a "conscious willingness to cause [or risk] harm without adequate moral justification," or "an unjustifiable failure to appreciate the risks [one] creates."[46] However, Professor Berman does not allow for the possibility that the victim or witness could be serving the public interest in reaching a private settlement. Although he later acknowledges the possibility of "public interest blackmail" that would not be criminalized – cases where both "the act threatened ... and the condition demanded ... would serve the same public interest" – he fails to consider whether criminal exposure blackmail could fit into that category.[47]

In the end, whether Professor Berman's theory can justify criminalizing private criminal settlements depends not only on accepting the proposition that motive should be relevant in determining whether an action is criminal, but also on how one defines "improper motive" and whether a victim or even a witness is presumptively acting with an improper motive when they receive compensation in exchange for not reporting a crime. Like most judgments made on retributive grounds, this may be a question that it is impossible to objectively resolve, but there is certainly reason to believe that Professor Berman's presumption may be overbroad, particularly with respect to victims of a crime. Consider the following two hypothetical situations:

> Sam and Diane are married. Sam has an alcohol problem, and when he drinks he tends to become verbally abusive toward Diane. One night his verbal abuse turns into physical abuse, and he hits Diane in the face with a beer bottle, breaking her cheekbone. Diane goes to the hospital, but does not call the police and refuses to tell the doctor how she got injured. When she gets home, she gives Sam an ultimatum: he must immediately enroll in an alcohol treatment program and he can never drink again. If he fails to comply with either demand, she will call the police and report his assault on her.
>
> Timothy is a sixteen-year-old high school student. One day a teacher catches him spray-painting graffiti on the outside wall of the school. Timothy has decent grades, and has never been in trouble before. A criminal conviction will lead to him being suspended from school and hurt his chances of going to college. Even a mere arrest will humiliate him in front of his friends and family. The teacher tells Timothy that she will refrain from calling the police only if Timothy buys a can of paint remover, comes to school next Saturday, and cleans off his own graffiti as well as the rest of the graffiti on the wall.

These examples certainly meet the definition of criminal exposure blackmail, but would we really say that the victim or witness in these cases is acting with a "morally blameworthy" motive? Are Diane or the teacher "ignoring their obligations" and failing in their "civic duty" to report these crimes – and, if so, do we really feel a need under the retributive model to punish them for these omissions?

Even in the case of commercial research blackmail, the "moral duty" of the blackmailer to report the crime is questionable. Consider a case in which private investigator Smith is hired by ABC Company to determine whether a certain employee is stealing corporate funds. After a week of surveillance and combing through bank records, Smith reports back to his corporate employer, providing mounds of evidence that the employee is indeed embezzling money. The company pays Smith for the work and, as a condition of this payment, requires the results of the investigation to be kept secret, even from the authorities, so that the company can handle the matter internally. In accepting money for the work – and in agreeing to abstain from reporting the crime as one of the conditions of payment – has Smith acted with morally blameworthy motives? Some people, presumably including Professor Berman, would perhaps say yes – investigator Smith, like every other citizen, has a moral duty to report every crime they discover to the proper authorities. By receiving payment, which is partially in exchange for the agreement to remain silent, Smith is providing evidence of improper motive. However, many others would be uncomfortable saying that Smith has committed a crime in this situation.[48]

To take this one step further, suppose that XYZ Company hired investigator Jones for similar work, and after Jones' report, the company made no request one way or the other about keeping the information secret. Jones, however, decided not to contact the authorities because it would be too much of a hassle – Jones would have to be interviewed by law enforcement, respond to subpoenas, and perhaps testify at a trial. Under Professor Berman's analysis, the investigator in the second scenario is presumably not acting with blameworthy motives – since Jones' compensation was not in any way dependent upon silence[49] – but it is hard to see how Jones' actions are all that different from Smith's. In fact, Jones is refraining from contacting the authorities out of sheer laziness, while Smith is fulfilling a contractual promise made to the employer. If Professor Berman claimed that avoiding the time and inconvenience of getting involved was a "morally blameworthy motive," he would be criminalizing the conduct (or nonconduct) of an enormous number of nonreporting witnesses by equating their conduct with extortion.

In short, the "morally blameworthy motive" is a problematic justification for criminalizing private criminal settlements. Sometimes, an individual who makes a private criminal settlement will be acting out of purely selfish motives, sometimes they will be trying to repair the damage from the crime, and sometimes they may even have the perpetrator's best interests at heart. Determining the motive of an actor is a tricky thing, and presuming a specific motive simply from the type of crime that was committed is bound to lead to inaccuracies – which is one of the reasons why motive is almost never relevant for criminal liability.[50]

CONCLUSION

In summary, the utilitarian and retributive justifications for criminalizing private criminal settlements are not very strong. On the other side of the ledger, private criminal settlements offer a number of benefits to society. In many cases, the public criminal justice system would be unlikely to learn of the crime, even if there were no private criminal settlement. For example, if the victim or witness is a friend, family member, or employer of the perpetrator, they may decide not to report the crime even if there were no possibility of a private criminal settlement. In addition, if the blackmailer learns about the crime because they engaged in commercial research blackmail, the crime would likely have gone undetected by anyone if not for the incentive provided by the potential blackmail payoff. In these kinds of cases, allowing private criminal settlements imposes some punishment on the perpetrator (a punishment the perpetrator would not otherwise suffer) and – in cases in which the victim participates in the agreement – a rough sort of restitution.

Our analysis has revealed only two dangers that may arise from allowing private criminal settlements: first, that the blackmailer will become an accomplice after the fact and assist with covering up the crime and, second, that the blackmailer may be violating a moral or statutory duty to report the crime. However, lawmakers could address these potential dangers easily enough. The danger of the blackmailer becoming an after-the-fact accomplice could be solved in two ways: by increasing the punishments (and thus the deterrence level) for actively concealing criminal activity and/or by banning ongoing, continuing requests from the blackmailer – that is, by allowing the blackmailer to make only a single demand of the perpetrator. This would remove any incentive on the part of the blackmailer to help the perpetrator avoid detection. Lawmakers can avoid the second risk by criminalizing any attempt to blackmail using incriminating information if the blackmailer has a statutory duty to report the crime in question, for example if a police officer attempts to blackmail a suspect instead of arresting the suspect or if a mandatory reporter sees evidence of child abuse and uses the evidence to blackmail the perpetrator.

Like the crime of blackmail itself, private criminal settlements at first seem unsavory and harmful, but further examination reveals that there are few legitimate reasons to criminalize them. And, unlike the crime of blackmail, private criminal settlements provide tangible benefits to society: As we saw in the last chapter, they allow for flexible resolutions to criminal disputes, they provide a greater sense of procedural justice, and they can preserve long-term relationships between the victim and the alleged perpetrator. They also further the goals of the criminal justice system – providing a degree of deterrence, retribution, and perhaps restitution – at no cost to the state. The previous two chapters have also revealed significant concerns about private criminal settlements, including the lack of transparency and the fact that prosecutors are unable to represent the state's interest in crafting the resolution. However, before we pass judgment on private criminal settlements, there are still two major types of private criminal resolution that we have not yet discussed: those that come from private adjudications and those that are imposed unilaterally onto alleged perpetrators without their consent. The next two chapters will examine these aspects of the private criminal justice system.

7

Private Adjudications

On February 19, 2014, a celebrity news website released a video showing Baltimore Ravens football player Ray Rice pulling his unconscious fiancée out of the elevator in an Atlantic City casino.[1] Rice later admitted that he had struck his fiancée in the elevator after an argument. Amidst growing public concern, the National Football League (NFL) suspended Rice for two games in July 2014.[2] The lenience of this punishment caused a storm of media criticism against the NFL and its commissioner, Roger Goodell. Columnists called the decision "appalling" and a "colossal mistake."[3] A commentator on Fox Sports summed up the public sentiment by saying that the light punishment sent the message that "violence against women is acceptable" and noted that Rice's suspension was shorter than that of players who had received cash while playing in college or tested positive for marijuana.[4] Three United States senators wrote an open letter to Goodell calling for a more severe punishment, saying that the two-game suspension "reflects a disturbingly lenient, even cavalier attitude towards violence against women."[5]

The outcry only intensified two months later, when another, more graphic, video surfaced showing the actual assault in the elevator, which showed Rice hitting his fiancée with a powerful left hook. That same day, the Baltimore Ravens cut Rice from the team and the NFL imposed an "indefinite suspension." Even before the new evidence arose, Commissioner Goodell admitted that he had made a mistake with the initial suspension and announced a new policy: a mandatory six-game suspension for a first domestic violence offense and a lifetime ban after a second offense.[6] Although Rice would ultimately win his appeal of the new sentence, no team would hire him, even after he promised to donate his entire first-year salary to domestic violence charities.[7] His career was over.

Although the Rice incident received a significant amount of publicity, it was not an outlying case. Nearly every year, the NFL faces questions about the degree of punishment it should mete out after its players commit a crime, including cocaine use,[8] animal abuse,[9] manslaughter,[10] child abuse,[11] drunk driving,[12] and obstruction of justice.[13] And the NFL is not the only one making these decisions – the National Basketball Association (NBA), Major League Baseball (MLB), and many other professional sports leagues routinely suspend or fine players for drug use and assault.[14] Often, the punishment that the players receive from their employers is the only significant repercussion for their actions; even if the player is punished by the criminal justice system, the league punishment receives far more media attention and, as the commentators in the Rice case noted, sends a far more powerful message.

In the Ray Rice case, almost nobody paid any attention to what happened to his actual criminal case. As it turned out, Rice was allowed to participate in a one-year pretrial diversion program, which included anger management classes, and the felony aggravated assault charge was dropped.[15] This is a program meant for nonviolent offenders; fewer than 1 percent of all assault and aggravated assault charges in New Jersey are disposed of in this way.[16] Therefore, even though the assault was captured on video and resulted in the victim being knocked unconscious, Rice did not end up with a criminal record and did not have to spend any time in jail or on probation. And yet there was no public outcry about the decision made by the Atlantic City Prosecutor's Office; no senators or any other public figures critiqued the handling of the criminal case; almost none of the comments on cable news or Twitter castigated the prosecutor for not holding Rice accountable or for sending a message that violence against women was acceptable. News accounts rarely even mentioned the status of Rice's criminal case.

When the NFL's vice-president defended the original two-game suspension imposed by the league, he argued that it was in fact a substantial financial penalty for Rice, as it would cost him hundreds of thousands of dollars in lost salary. He went on to note, correctly: "The discipline that was taken by the NFL is the only discipline that occurred with respect to Mr. Rice in this case.... Were he not an NFL player, I don't know that he would have received punishment from any other source."[17]

In Rice's case, there were two parallel institutions responding to Rice's criminal activity – the public criminal justice system and Rice's private employer. Both institutions failed to impose a punishment that was appropriate for the act of extreme violence that he had committed. However, the response of the private institution – the NFL – was the only one that mattered to the public. For some reason, society looked to the perpetrator's employer with the expectation that it would carry out the traditional roles of the criminal justice system – punishing a person who had committed a violent, immoral action; sending a message to the public that this behavior is inappropriate; and deterring others from committing this crime in the future.

This chapter will examine the influence of third-party institutions on the private criminal justice system. In the previous two chapters, we examined the phenomenon of private criminal settlements, when a witness or a victim and the alleged perpetrator agree on a resolution to a criminal case – what could be called a bilateral response to criminal activity. In the next chapter, we will consider the unilateral response of vigilante action, when the victim or another private party imposes their own punishment on the alleged perpetrator without the cooperation or consent of the alleged perpetrator. Third-party institutions (the subject of this chapter) represent a multilateral response – when the victim and the alleged perpetrator turn to a third party to adjudicate the case and determine punishment.

The Ray Rice case highlights two important points about this aspect of the private criminal justice system. It shows that third parties – such as employers, professional organizations, colleges, religious institutions, neighborhood associations, and a wide variety of other organizations – often carry out their own adjudicative procedures and impose their own punishments on those who are accused of committing a crime. And it also demonstrates that society often looks to these third parties to impose such punishments, sometimes expecting more from the private institutions than they do from the public criminal justice system. Unlike private criminal settlements, which rely on the witness not involving the public criminal justice system, private adjudications can occur in parallel with a public criminal case, although the punishment imposed by the private adjudicator is often more severe than what the perpetrator receives in the public system.

As noted in Chapter 3, the public criminal justice system treats victims relatively poorly. On some level, this dissatisfaction is unsurprising, as victims are not a party to a public prosecution and so the public system is not designed to meet the needs of the victims. Private criminal adjudications create a more streamlined procedure, which is less time consuming and less emotionally draining for victims. They also usually give the victim greater control of the proceedings, which enhances the sense of procedural fairness that victims feel about the process.

Private criminal adjudications are distinct from private criminal settlements in a number of important ways. First, private criminal adjudications derive their authority over the alleged perpetrator independently rather than exercising power derived from the public criminal justice system. Private criminal settlements exist as a parasite of the public system – the only reason that defendants agree to the deals that are offered is because they believe (usually correctly) that they will face far greater consequences if the case is turned over to the public system. Private criminal adjudications impose their own punishments independent of the public criminal justice system, so their authority is not dependent on threatening to involve the public criminal justice system.

This leads to a second difference between private criminal adjudications and private criminal settlements – the latter tend to be secretive and work only if the public criminal justice system does not learn of the alleged criminal activity, while the former can be open and can occur in parallel with a public criminal case. Finally, private criminal adjudications tend to have specific rules and policies, if not complex procedures, that guide the decision-makers in resolving the dispute, and often have rules and precedents that they seek to follow when imposing punishment.

Roughly speaking, third-party private adjudications can be broken down into two categories. The first involves adjudications by an institution or community against one of its own members, such as a professional association or company against an employee, or a religious institution against a parishioner. The institution is able to apply its own rules and impose its own punishment, disciplining or even expelling the alleged perpetrator if they are found to be guilty of criminal activity. Therefore, unlike private criminal settlements, these processes are not dependent on the threat of the public criminal justice system to provide an incentive for the accused to participate, because they can enforce their own consequences independent of the public system.

The second category of private adjudications comprises mediations and restorative justice programs that are sponsored by the state but that involve no state participation, in which the state agrees not to formally pursue criminal charges as long as the alleged perpetrator and victim reach an agreement. These programs, such as Victim–Offender Mediation, almost always begin after a crime has been reported to the public police, and they sometimes occur after a certain level of adjudication has occurred in the public courts. They essentially involve the state deferring to a private dispute resolution system to resolve the criminal dispute.

THIRD-PARTY ADJUDICATORS

On August 27, 2012, two Columbia University students, Emma Sulkowicz and Paul Nunsegger, engaged in intimate sexual activities in Sulkowicz's dorm room. A few months later, in April 2013, Sulkowicz filed a complaint with Columbia's Office of Gender-Based and Sexual Misconduct, charging Nunsegger with rape and seeking to have him expelled from the university. In her description, the August encounter began as a consensual sexual activity but then Nunsegger slapped her, choked her, held her wrist, and had non-consensual anal intercourse with her. Nunsegger maintained that there was no violence and all sexual activities were consensual. A hearing was held in October and, in November, the university found Nunsegger "not responsible" and took no action against him. Sulkowicz appealed the decision, but her appeal was denied.

Sulkowicz's case gained national attention. In May 2014, Senator Kirsten Gillibrand of New York appeared with her at a press conference to highlight the problems of sexual assault on campus; Senator Gillibrand later invited her to attend the State of the Union address as the senator's guest. Sulkowicz's story was on the front page of the *New York Times* and *New York* magazine, and she wrote an op-ed for *Time* magazine. During her final year at Columbia, Sulkowicz, who was a visual arts major, created a performance art piece in which she carried a dormitory mattress everywhere she went on campus, both to symbolize the burden of rape survivors and to protest Columbia's handling of the case. She argued that Columbia's disciplinary process was deeply flawed and that she was asked inappropriate questions during the hearing and was not permitted to admit relevant evidence. She stated that she would carry the mattress until Nunsegger was expelled or until she graduated; as Nunsegger was never expelled, she carried the mattress for nine months, including on her graduation day.

As with the Ray Rice case, a topic that was rarely covered was the response of the public criminal justice system to this alleged crime. The incident clearly traumatized Sulkowicz, and she cared so passionately about justice in her case and for others like her that she spent years as a national spokesperson for the issue. And yet the institution she turned to for justice was her university, not the police and the criminal courts. Eventually, Sulkowicz did report the incident to the police in May 2014, thirteen months after she reported the incident to Columbia. The police concluded that they did not have reasonable suspicion, much less probable cause, to support the charge, and the district attorney decided not to proceed with the case. Sulkowicz said the officers were dismissive of her story and mistreated her.[18] However, her extensive public advocacy had nothing to do with her disappointment with the police and the district attorney; her short-term goal was to have Nunsegger expelled, not arrested, and her long-term goal was to reform campus disciplinary proceedings, not police charging practices or state rape law. Why did she – and the thousands who supported her protest, including Senator Gillibrand – seek justice from her university, rather than from the state institutions that literally exist for the sole purpose of responding to criminal activity? And why did the public response to her advocacy also focus on the university's response?

Professor Malcolm Feeley of the University of California coined the term "segmented societies" to describe relatively homogeneous communities or specific institutions that develop their own form of social control, including their rules and punishments to maintain that control.[19] If the alleged perpetrator is a member of the community, the community is able to impose its own punishments without resorting to the public criminal justice system. Often, these institutions will be more friendly to the accused because of the segmentation – the accused is part of their homogeneous subculture and so the institutions have an interest in protecting them. However, in other contexts, the segmented societies will prioritize protecting their own community over protecting the alleged wrongdoer, and so may mete out punishments that are more severe than what the wrongdoer would face in the public criminal justice system; for example, a licensing agency that is primarily interested in preserving its industry's reputation may suspend or ban the accused from working in their industry for relatively minor offenses such as drug use or simple assault.

This chapter opened with a prominent example of third-party adjudicative procedures: professional sports leagues that judge alleged criminal activity by athletes and impose punishment in the form of fines or suspensions. The Ray Rice case involved the simplest and arguably the least fair of the many types of third-party adjudications: Under the NFL rules in place at the time, the league commissioner had the sole and exclusive power to determine the procedure that was followed and the punishment that was imposed. For decades, the commissioner would conduct his own factfinding, including interviewing the alleged perpetrators, impose punishment based on a vaguely worded league personal conduct policy, and even decide the appeals from his own rulings.[20] After sustained criticism of this process from both players and the general public, the NFL and the players' union agreed to set up a slightly more sophisticated process in 2020, in which the union and the commissioner would jointly appoint an independent arbiter to adjudicate the case, along with stricter guidelines on the appropriate punishment for various types of violations.[21] The independent arbiter was also more tightly bound by precedent, as evidenced by the 2022 adjudication of the quarterback DeShaun Watson, who was accused of over two dozen cases of sexual assault: After imposing a six-game suspension, the independent arbiter wrote that Watson deserved a much more severe penalty, but that she was bound by the league's guidelines and the precedents of its prior suspensions. Even so, the procedure still left much to be desired from an impartiality standpoint; the NFL (run by the commissioner) then appealed the decision to the commissioner. Before the commissioner could rule on the appeal, the NFL and Watson agreed to settle the case for an eleven-game sentence and a $5 million fine.[22]

The NFL process highlights another important point about private adjudications: The degree of punishments for different types of offenses will reflect the goals and perceived needs of the organization conducting the adjudication, which often will not coincide with the goals and needs of the public criminal justice system. On the one hand, the NFL frequently punishes players for noncriminal conduct in order to maintain the integrity of the game or protect its brand; thus, it has sanctioned players for using performance-enhancing drugs[23] or violating the league's social media policy against hate speech.[24] Some of these punishments may far exceed the punishments imposed for serious criminal conduct; for example, suspensions for (legally) gambling on NFL games last for an entire season, while a suspension for killing a person while driving under the influence (which was punished by the public criminal justice system by 180 days in jail) led to only a ten-game suspension.[25] On the other hand, the NFL has an interest in returning its star players to the field, and also has to manage its labor relations with the players' union, which consistently pushes for more lenient punishments – so many of the sanctions for violent crimes appear to be overly lenient, such as six-game suspensions for domestic violence or child abuse.[26]

The dissonance between the institution's goals and the traditional goals of the public criminal justice system can be seen in many different types of third-party adjudications, which often seek to downplay the severity of criminal activity and keep the incidents confidential. Cruise ships, for example, have an incentive to maintain a reputation as being safe for their vacationing passengers. As there are no public police on board cruise ships, private police working for the cruise ship company investigate allegations of criminal activity, from disorderly conduct to assault to theft to sexual assault. These private police generally have an "adversarial relationship" with the victim, as they are seeking to avoid civil lawsuits against the company.²⁷ Victims and defendants are often brought to a "dispute resolution facilitator," that is, another company employee who seeks to resolve the criminal dispute with fines, restitution, and the occasional banning of the defendant from certain parts of the ship.²⁸ Crew members who commit crimes against passengers are "often just fired and sent home," after restitution is provided to the victim.²⁹ By the time the ship reaches port, the parties involved are generally ready to move on, and public law enforcement is almost never contacted.³⁰

Religious institutions provide another prominent example of a segmented society. Many churches have their own procedures to deal with lower level criminal activity among their clergy and parishioners. For example, if a teenager vandalizes the building, the church will work with the parents to encourage the perpetrator to do service projects to atone; if a clergy member learns that a parishioner is using drugs, the clergy member will try to get the parishioner treatment and community support. Calling the public police and involving the public criminal justice system is viewed as a punitive action that could unduly harm members of their community and that is inconsistent with the religious principles of forgiveness and redemption.

Occasionally, these laudable principles can be taken too far, as famously exemplified by the Catholic Church's response to sexual assaults by its priests. By one count, there were over 10,000 alleged child victims of sexual assault by priests in the United States alone.³¹ It took decades for this abuse to come to light, and another decade after that for the church itself to begin conducting its own investigations and change its policies. Up until the early 2000s, the church's standard response to reports of abuse was to move the priest to a different parish, either with or without some form of counseling.³² This response – or lack of response – came under intense criticism as news of the scandal broke. Critics of the Vatican argued that the church should instead have removed them from the priesthood in order to prevent them from using their clerical position to prey on vulnerable and trusting children.³³

The inaction and complicity of the bishops in this story is certainly reprehensible, and the church is still dealing with the massive social, moral, and economic fallout of its response to the scandal.³⁴ However, at least as significant for our purposes is the fact that neither the church nor most of the victims chose to involve the public criminal justice system. The church came under fire for not defrocking its priests, but why should the criticism stop there? Why did the bishops and other supervisors not immediately contact the police when they heard credible (and often multiple) accounts of crimes being committed?³⁵ Even more notable is that the victims themselves almost never called the police.

Consider the example of Mark Belenchia, who was a twelve-year-old boy in Mississippi in 1968 when he was sexually abused by Bernard Haddican, the new Catholic priest in his parish. The crimes continued over the next three years, and Mark, who was traumatized, confused, and ashamed, remained silent about the abuse. Finally, some time after the abuse had stopped, he told his mother and uncle about what happened. His mother drove to Jackson, the state capital, to report the abuse to the Vicar General of the diocese (a Vicar General is the principal deputy of the bishop, and exercises administrative authority over the diocese). The Catholic Church took no action against Haddican, who continued to serve as a priest in Mark's parish.[36]

In 1985, over a decade after the abuse ended, Mark sought counseling from a different priest because he was experiencing marital problems. Over the course of the counseling, he told the priest that Haddican had abused him as a child. The priest advised him to speak to the new Vicar General, who sent Mark to receive specialized counseling. Once again, the Vicar General took no action against Haddican.[37] Haddican served as a priest until his retirement in 1991, working in nearly a dozen different parishes, and he died in 1996 having faced no repercussion for his actions, either from the Catholic Church, which knew of his crimes, or from the public criminal justice system, which did not.[38]

The possible reasons that the Catholic hierarchy had for not reporting Haddican to the police are relatively straightforward: It wanted to avoid scandal and (more generously) it believed in redemption rather than punishment.[39] What is more curious is the decision made by Mark's mother and then later by Mark himself. When Mark reported the crime to his mother in the early 1970s, she did not contact the police or the local prosecutor, even though she had just learned that her son had been sexually assaulted over seventy times. Instead, she drove 135 miles to report the offense to the next rung of the Catholic hierarchy. And, over ten years later, Mark again reported the crimes after being encouraged to do so by his priest – but, like his mother, he reported them only within the Catholic Church. He never contacted the police even after it was clear that the church was not going to confront Haddican with his crimes, and even though a criminal case could still be brought against Haddican.[40] Mark and his family were not alone in this decision; by one estimate there are over 4,000 priests accused of this conduct, and ultimately only about 1,000 of them were reported to the police, usually years or decades after they or their family members reported it to church authorities.[41] Why did all of these victims choose to keep the matter within the church?

This question is not meant to criticize Mark or his mother, or any of the other thousands of victims and parents who decide not to contact the police in this situation. But it is also not merely a rhetorical question. Why – and under what conditions – do individuals decide to report criminal activity to private institutions rather than avail themselves of the extensive and easily accessible public criminal justice system, especially if the response by the private institution is inadequate? The answers surely depend on the context, and will probably vary from person to person. However, the answers also reveal something important about our faith in the public justice system, and about what we believe is the proper response to crime.

The most prominent example of third-party adjudicative procedures is the one that opened this section: university disciplinary proceedings. These proceedings can be based on alleged criminal conduct ranging from underage drinking and petty vandalism to rape. The Sulkowicz case is typical in that the public police are rarely contacted about criminal activity on college campuses, and the public prosecutors rarely become involved. Instead, criminal violations "are handled by campus police, deans of students, and internal 'dispute resolution' mechanisms run by colleges themselves."[42] For example, the private police at Ohio Wesleyan University are charged with "upholding University policies and State and federal laws" and regularly make arrests for illegal activity, such as underage drinking, marijuana possession, and disorderly conduct.[43] Once a suspect has been apprehended for one of these crimes (or for a violation of a university policy), they appear in front of a "judicial board" of five students, which adjudicates the case and decides on the appropriate punishment.[44] Some schools have delegated these procedures to private law firms or consulting firms creating a "cottage industry" of private adjudicators.[45]

If the crime does not involve a victim, the campus police must decide how to proceed with the case, and they usually decide to refer the defendant to university disciplinary proceedings rather than the public police. This is a direct result of the segmentation effect: The subculture wants to discipline its own members. For crimes against individuals, such as assault or sexual assault, the victim must decide whether to pursue the case through the university or through the public police, or both. There are plenty of reasons to choose the former, including a faster resolution of the dispute and a system that will pay more attention to their needs as victims. This can be especially acute for alleged victims of sexual assault, given the public criminal justice system's poor treatment of sexual assault victims and the low conviction rate.[46] As one advocacy group notes:

> Colleges and universities can act quickly to protect students. Schools, unlike the criminal justice system, are in the position to take action quickly to ensure a safe campus; if they had to rely on the criminal justice system to try the case, the college would have to wait years for the assailant to be taken to prison . . . . As the school waited for the trial to conclude, the victim would be left on campus with their perpetrator – or perhaps forced out of school for their safety – and other students would be vulnerable to repeat violence by the assailant.[47]

Just as a victim often believes a private criminal settlement will meet their needs more effectively than calling the police, many victims decide that a third-party adjudicator will provide a faster and more satisfying result than the public criminal justice system. In some cases, as with religious institutions or universities, the victim knows and trusts the third-party institution to some degree – at least more than they know and trust a large, anonymous, and mysterious collection of police, lawyers, and courts, and a seemingly impenetrable system of rules and procedures.

The simpler rules and procedures are another important aspect of private criminal adjudications. Part of the appeal of third-party adjudications is that they use procedures that are simpler and more streamlined than their public counterpart, and since they do not impose traditional criminal sentences such as incarceration, they are not required to provide the same level of due process as the public criminal courts. Often, the "adjudication" is nothing more than a decision-maker gathering facts and then making a ruling, but, in some cases, the third-party institution institutes formal procedures to guide its decision-making process. For the most part, third-party institutions are free to set their own procedures, but occasionally they are constrained by state or federal law. Such cases highlight the tension that often exists between criminal adjudications conducted by third-party institutions and criminal trials in the public criminal justice system.

In the university disciplinary context, public universities face constitutional constraints on their procedures. As the defendant has a property interest in not being suspended or expelled from the university, the public university – which counts as a "state actor" – cannot violate that property interest unless it follows a minimum standard of due process. According to the Supreme Court case of Matthews v. Eldridge,[48] the due process clause of the Fourteenth Amendment requires a public university to give the defendant notice and an opportunity to be heard by the decision-maker. The university's procedures must also pass a balancing test that considers (1) the interest of the defendant in maintaining their good standing at the university, (2) the risk of an erroneous deprivation of the defendant's property interest given the procedures used, and (3) the university's interest, including the fiscal and administrative burden of the alternate procedures.[49] Public universities must also meet the standard set out by the Supreme Court in Goss v. Lopez,[50] which held that a defendant must be given a greater level of due process if they are facing a more serious punishment, but that – consistent with Matthews v. Eldridge, even the possibility of a short sentence requires notice and an "informal give and take" through which the defendant is able to give their own version of the events.[51] However, these protections still fall far short of what is seen in public criminal trials; for example, most circuit courts have held that a right to cross-examine is not required by the due process clause in school disciplinary hearings.[52]

Private universities are not subject to any constitutional due process requirements, but often they promise a certain level of due process in their student handbook, and they could be held liable if they fail to meet those standards. For example, in Fellheimer v. Middlebury College,[53] the college handbook stated that when a student is charged with violating college rules, they will receive a statement "of the charges with sufficient particularity to permit the accused party to prepare to meet the charges."[54] The defendant received a letter saying that he had been charged with rape, and a later letter said he was being charged with sexual assault. After a disciplinary hearing, the defendant was notified that he was not guilty of rape, but was guilty of "disrespect for persons, specifically for engaging in inappropriate sexual activity."[55] The defendant argued that he never received notification that he was also being charged with "disrespect of persons" and he was not told the elements of that offense. The court held that the college was liable for breach of contract, as its procedures did not conform with the commitments it made in its student handbook.

If a student is facing a charge of sexual assault, the federal government imposes even greater requirements for the procedure. Title IX of the Education Amendments of 1972 prohibits sex-based discrimination by any school that receives federal funding[56] (a category that includes nearly every college and university in the country). Beginning in 2011, the Department of Education required all colleges and universities to use a preponderance of the evidence standard when adjudicating sexual misconduct claims, and discouraged the schools from allowing cross-examination in the hearings. The guidance also discouraged schools from using mediation to resolve disputes involving sexual assault, even if both sides agreed to it.[57] After a political battle surrounding these requirements, President Donald Trump's administration issued a new policy in 2020 that required live proceedings with cross-examination, an express presumption of innocence, sufficient time to prepare for the hearing, and the ability for the defendant to choose a legal advisor to assist in their defense. The new policy also allowed schools to return to the "clear and convincing" standard of evidence that many of them used before 2011.[58] After more controversy, the Biden administration in 2022 proposed requiring new standards that would change some of the requirements back to the 2011 rules.[59]

Given the highly partisan environment of the country and the influence of the #MeToo movement in the late 2010s, it is no surprise that the appropriate level of process for sexual assault allegations became a political flashpoint. However, the political dispute masks a deeper question: What sort of procedures should be provided by third-party adjudicators in general, and what role (if any) should the state have in setting those procedures? On the one hand, one of the benefits of third-party adjudications is that their procedures can be more streamlined than the byzantine process of the public criminal justice system, which has to set up a complex and byzantine set of procedural protections to protect criminal defendants who may be facing incarceration. On the other hand, many individuals who are the subject of third-party adjudications could be subjected to sanctions that are more severe than what they would face if they were convicted in a criminal court, and so some degree of procedural protection is appropriate. We can also see how third-party institutions could be limited in the types of procedures that they institute, whether through agreements they have made with their employees, through commitments they have made to those who joined their community, or through direct regulation by the government. And, just as third-party institutions will adjust the substantive offenses and the severity of punishments based on the interests and needs of the organization, it will follow its own institutional needs to create procedures and due process protections that are more victim-friendly or more defendant-friendly.

RESTORATIVE JUSTICE AND PROCEDURAL JUSTICE

Our second category of private adjudications – restorative justice programs – are derived from the public court system rather than the private sector, and thus are not dependent on the existence of a segmented community. In addition, unlike third-party adjudications, which are designed and run by institutions with their own interests and agendas, restorative justice programs are administered by neutral administrators who – in theory, at least – are merely attempting to reach a resolution that is acceptable to the victim, the defendant, and the local community.

Restorative justice represents a serious paradigm shift in how society responds to criminal behavior.[60] The traditional criminal justice system focuses on the defendant, imposing a penalty upon them as punishment for past wrongdoing and to deter them from future criminal actions. Restorative justice focuses on both the defendant and the victim, seeking (as the name implies) to restore the affected individuals to their pre-crime condition.[61] The theory is not to punish the defendant, but rather to lead them to atone for their crime, work to repair the damage they have done, and reintegrate them into the community. Restorative justice has been defined as "a process to involve ... those who have a stake in a specific offense and to collectively identify and address harms, needs, and obligations, in order to heal and put things as right as possible."[62] According to John Braithwaite, a leading restorative justice theorist, "restorative justice is about restoring victims, restoring offenders, and restoring communities."[63] As proponents put it, the goal of this distinct ideology is to "find... hope, meaning, and healing in the process of creating justice and promoting accountability."[64] Howard Zehr, a leading advocate in the restorative justice movement, has set out the primary ways in which restorative justice differs from traditional criminal justice (Table 7.1).[65]

Some of the outcomes of restorative justice – forcing the defendant to pay financial restitution to the victim, to attend a drug treatment program, or to perform community service – are also part of the traditional criminal justice system, but that is where the similarities end. The process of restorative justice is generally informal, without lawyers or judges present, and involves the victim and the defendant sitting together with a mediator and telling each other their stories. After the victim explains how the crime has affected their life, the defendant explains their own actions and (hopefully) takes responsibility for the crime committed.[66] The two of them together

TABLE 7.1 *Comparing the traditional criminal justice system with restorative justice*

Criminal justice	Restorative justice
Crime is a violation of the law and state.	Crime is a violation of people and relationships.
Violations create guilt.	Violations create obligations.
Justice requires the state to determine blame (guilt) and impose pain (punishment).	Justice involves victims, offenders, and community members in an effort to put things right.
The central focus is offenders getting what they deserve.	The central focuses are the victim's needs and the offender's responsibility for repairing harm.

then attempt to create a plan that will make the victim whole again.[67] As restorative justice proponents concede, this is an aspirational goal because often a crime victim cannot be truly restored to the emotional, psychological, or even material condition that they enjoyed before the crime occurred.[68]

A diverse collection of interest groups supports the restorative justice movement. Many proponents are drawn to the theory because it focuses on rehabilitating and thus reintegrating the perpetrator – goals that have been all but discarded by the traditional criminal justice system.[69] On the other hand, victims' advocates have been supportive of restorative justice programs because – again in contrast with the traditional criminal justice system – they allow the victim to play a central role in the process and in the outcome.[70]

Perhaps the most surprising lesson from the small but growing restorative justice movement is in the substantive sentencing results that it produces. As noted in Chapter 2, the traditional criminal justice system has grown more and more punitive in the past few decades, ratcheting up minimum sentences, annually setting new records for prison populations, and criminalizing more and more types of behavior – while the restorative justice movement has grown in popularity by giving victims exactly the opposite.[71]

However, the restorative justice revolution is more fundamental than a change in sentencing policies. The underlying theory focuses on the process as much as – and perhaps more than – the outcome. Restorative justice programs gives both the victim and the defendant what the traditional criminal justice system denies them: the ability to tell their stories to each other directly and to work together to try to repair the damage – whether physical, material, or psychological – that the crime has caused.[72] Thus, restorative justice programs fundamentally change the way criminal cases are resolved, in addition to changing the substantive resolutions themselves.

There is evidence that this change in process is the true secret to the success of these programs. As noted in Chapter 5, studies in the field of procedural justice have demonstrated that there are three factors that determine whether or not an individual believes that a given procedure is fair: the participant's opportunity to participate in the procedure, whether the participant views the decision-maker as neutral and unbiased, and whether the participant is treated with dignity and respect during the process.[73]

Restorative justice programs satisfy the first and third criteria, especially when compared with the traditional criminal justice system. Defendants and victims get a chance to participate fully in the process, and a major tenet of restorative justice is recognizing the humanity and dignity of all the participants – treating both victims and defendants as individuals with significant needs and limitations.[74] By contrast, in the public criminal justice system, nearly all of the cases are resolved through plea bargaining between a prosecutor and a defense attorney, a process in which victims and defendants almost never participate. Even if the case goes to trial, the victim and the defendant participate in only a very limited way by testifying as witnesses under strict and formal rules. Both the victim and the defendant frequently find the criminal justice process rather dehumanizing; the victim may feel simply like a tool that the prosecution uses to obtain a conviction (which essentially is the case), while the accused is merely another faceless defendant to be processed in the vast criminal justice machinery.[75] Whether or not the decision-maker – or in the case of restorative justice programs, the mediator – is seen as neutral and unbiased can vary widely depending on the specific program. As we will see, the success of restorative justice programs depends in large part on the identity, training, and behavior of the mediator.

Overall, however, surveys indicate that restorative justice programs score quite high on the procedural justice metric. Participants – both defendants and victims – tend to be extremely satisfied with the process, with a satisfaction rate of between 90 and 95 percent.[76] However, this high level of satisfaction is not due to self-selection – even when cases are randomly assigned to courts or to restorative justice programs, satisfaction levels and perceptions of fairness are higher for participants in the restorative justice programs.[77]

Of course, just because most victims and defendants believe that restorative justice programs are more fair does not make them so. The question of whether victims or defendants are in fact better off in such programs – or in any other alternative to the public criminal justice system – depends on many different factors. However, the issue of perceived fairness should not be overlooked, as it is critical to the legitimacy – and therefore to the long-term survival – of any criminal justice system. In other words, even if the public criminal justice system were to utilize procedures and produce outcomes that every expert agreed were fair and just, the system would have no long-term viability if the individuals within the system – victims and defendants – perceived it to be unfair. The procedures inherent in the public system – procedures that marginalize the victim, prevent both the victim and the defendant from participating directly in the process, and dehumanize victims and defendants alike – create a dissatisfaction that will inevitably result in change. As noted in Chapter 3, surveys of victims over the past twenty years have shown that victims' dissatisfaction with the criminal justice system stems overwhelmingly from these procedural justice concerns:

> [Victims] say they are unhappy about their lack of a legitimate role in the processing of their cases beyond that of witness for the prosecution, the lack of opportunity to be consulted about the progress of their cases, the lack of recognition of the emotional, as well as material, harm they have experienced, and the lack of fairness and respect they receive at the hands of the justice system as a whole.[78]

Restorative justice provides other benefits besides making victims and defendants feel as though they are being treated fairly. Professor Thalia González of Occidental College has conducted extensive research on these programs and has concluded that, in addition to improving victim satisfaction, they "maintain community safety, promote healing and reintegration, and reduce the use of punitive practices, including incarceration."[79] The programs are also far less expensive than the public criminal justice system,[80] and result in a lower level of recidivism.[81]

In these ways, the restorative justice movement has a lot in common with other aspects of the private criminal justice system, such as private law enforcement, private plea bargains, and private third-party adjudications. It has gained in popularity because of perceived failures of the public criminal justice system, and it can provide resolution to a criminal dispute in a way that better meets the needs of both the victim and the defendant without resorting to incarceration. For those victims and defendants who choose the restorative justice route, the public system is too punitive, ignores the root causes and human effects of crime, and makes little attempt to either assist the victim or rehabilitate the defendant.[82] And, like other aspects of the private criminal justice system, restorative justice is a return to older concepts of criminal justice.

As noted in Chapter 2, before King Henry I decreed that certain actions were "offenses ... against the King's peace," criminal behavior was "viewed as conflict between individuals, and an emphasis upon repairing the damage by making amends to the victim was well established."[83] Even after certain harms became criminalized, private prosecution was still common; as late as the seventeenth century, both the English and the colonial criminal justice systems depended upon "a system of private prosecution, where the victim or interested individual had the right to bring and prosecute the case against a criminal offender."[84] John Langbein describes pre-eighteenth century criminal trials as "lawyer-free contests of amateurs" in which the victim of the crime served as the prosecutor.[85] Although the state had some involvement in criminal cases throughout the medieval and colonial period, it was not until the eighteenth century that public prosecutors first began to appear.[86]

Not all restorative justice programs fit neatly into our model of private criminal justice, as many of them operate under the aegis of state supervision. For example, in some cases, a criminal action is initiated by the prosecutor's office before it is diverted into a restorative justice program, and the ultimate resolution usually requires the approval by the prosecutor and/or the court.[87] Generally, these state representatives are unwilling to dismiss the formal criminal complaint unless they believe the resolution properly reflects the harm the defendant did to society.

In practice, restorative justice programs are generally limited to juvenile crimes or to relatively minor crimes such as vandalism, theft, and minor assaults, although they have also been applied to adults and (rarely) to serious violent felonies. Restorative justice programs can take many different forms.[88] In its most radical incarnation, known as "sentencing circles" or "peacemaking circles," the defendant and the victim each invite numerous members of their support group (family members, peers, etc.) to the dialogue, and other interested members of the community also participate. A "talking piece" is handed from person to person as each interested member has their say about how the crime has affected their life or the community.[89]

Somewhat less unwieldy is the process of "group conferencing" or "community group conferencing," which tends to be more structured and includes fewer members of the victim's and defendant's support groups. However, by far the most popular form of restorative justice in this country is Victim–Offender Mediation, which is somewhat similar to civil law mediation.[90] There are, however, important differences. A civil law mediator tends to be a neutral facilitator who does not pass judgment on either side, whereas the Victim–Offender Mediation process is undertaken with all participants – including the mediator – fully aware that the defendant bears the responsibility of repairing the damage done.[91] The mediator is also aware that there is a third interest unrepresented in the mediation – that of society – and will endeavor to ensure that the resolution addresses not only the damage to the victim but also the breach of the social contract caused by the crime.[92]

Emboldened by these successes, restorative justice proponents are understandably seeking to multiply and expand the scope of these programs by establishing them in more jurisdictions and by enlarging the categories of crimes that could be referred into Victim–Offender Mediation, including crimes of violence.[93] A study in 2020 revealed that forty-five states have incorporated some form of restorative justice into their public criminal justice systems, authorized by over 250 different laws and regulations.[94]

However, one tantalizing possibility for a dramatic expansion of restorative justice programs would be to create an industry of private mediators to resolve criminal disputes even before they entered the public criminal justice system, thus bypassing prosecutors, judges, and courts altogether. This industry could adjudicate and enforce dispositions for the substantial (and increasing) number of individuals being apprehended by private law enforcement officers and not being turned over to the public system. The private individuals, companies, and communities that employ private police would no doubt be willing to utilize – and pay for – an option that would allow them to resolve the dispute without resorting to state action. Similarly, defendants who face the possibility of the long delays, lack of participation, and retributive punishments of the state-sponsored criminal system might be more willing to enter into a private adjudication process.

CONCLUSION

Like other aspects of the private criminal justice system, third-party adjudicative procedures and punishments either bypass state involvement altogether or, in the case of many restorative justice programs, involve the state voluntarily divesting itself from the adjudicative and punitive process. In so doing, these adjudications shrink the scope of the criminal dispute, although not to the same degree as private criminal settlements. Instead of seeking an outcome that represents the interests of the state or of society at large, these adjudications serve a narrower subgroup in society. In the case of third-party adjudicators, the adjudicative process and the potential dispositions are designed to further the needs of the segmented society that set up the process, whether that is a licensing board that needs to protect the integrity of its profession, a religious organization that wants to emphasize forgiveness and foster a sense of community, or a university that seeks to prioritize the safety and psychological well-being of its students. In the case of restorative justice procedures, the process and potential dispositions are designed to meet the needs of an even narrower circle of individuals: the defendant, the victim, and their immediate circle of family and friends.

However, these procedures are not immune to influence from society, as they have the highest public profile of any aspect of the private criminal justice system. Private police tend to work outside the public eye, and most private criminal settlements remain secretive. Private criminal adjudications and dispositions are often widely publicized, and therefore are more likely to be affected by public opinion, as evidenced by the upward revisions of punishments for domestic violent assaults in the NFL, the paradigm shift in the way the Catholic Church dealt with accused sex offenders, and the shifting procedural rules that the Department of Education imposes on university disciplinary proceedings. Thus, third-party adjudications are indirectly encouraged to reflect the preferences of broader groups of society.

Even so, private party adjudications represent a way of decentralizing the criminal justice system, making it more responsive to the individuals and groups that are most affected by the criminal activity, but less of a reflection of the values of society as a whole.[95] They still serve a broader group than the private criminal settlements that we discussed in the previous two chapters, which only serve the needs of the defendant and the witness, and they serve a much broader group than the unilateral dispositions of the vigilantes that we will discuss in the next chapter. However, they are still vulnerable to the same critique that we considered in Chapter 1 – because the state is not a party to the action, the results of these adjudications may or may not coincide with the goals of the public criminal justice system. We will consider this critique, as well as other costs and benefits of private adjudications, in Chapter 10.

8

Private Dispositions

The final and most controversial phase of the private criminal justice system involves private parties imposing their own punishment on alleged criminals. Sometimes these private punishments are classified as vigilante actions, but, as we will see in the next section, "Private Criminal Dispositions versus Vigilantism," most definitions of vigilantism are both narrower and broader than our definition of private criminal dispositions. Prior chapters have already touched on other types of privately imposed sanctions. In Chapters 5 and 6, we saw that defendants have to sacrifice something of value in order to fulfill their side of a private criminal settlement. However, those privately imposed punishments are distinct from the private dispositions we are discussing in this chapter, as they involve some participation by the defendant: The defendant is consenting (albeit under threat of being turned over to the public criminal justice system) to the punishment. Also, in Chapter 7, we discussed institutions that conduct private adjudications and thus have the power to impose their own punishment on the defendant. While those private punishments do fall under the broad definition of private criminal dispositions, they are not the focus of this chapter. In the context of a private criminal adjudication, the defendant is a member of the organization that is imposing the punishment, and the scope of the punishment is limited to restricting or terminating that membership. The private dispositions we are exploring in this chapter are punishments imposed on defendants without their consent or participation.

PRIVATE CRIMINAL DISPOSITIONS VERSUS VIGILANTISM

The first term that comes to mind when most people think of private criminal dispositions is vigilante justice. Before we compare these two concepts, we need to answer a challenging but critical question: How do we define vigilantism? The term is an anglicization of the Spanish word *vigilante*, which means watchful or watchman, and which in turn comes from the Latin *vigilare*, which means to keep awake – a reference that calls to mind the ancient volunteer night watchmen who would raise a hue and cry if they observed criminal activity. The dictionary definition of vigilante is "a member of a volunteer committee organized to suppress and punish crime summarily (as when the processes of law are viewed as inadequate)."[1] Professor William E. Burrows, who wrote one of the seminal works on the subject of vigilantism, argued that vigilantism is difficult to define, as it can be "all things to all men, and anyone who attempts to force it into some nice, near scholarly slot soon sees that the task is impossible."[2] Nevertheless, Professor Burrows boldly makes an attempt, arguing that a vigilante is a member of an "organized, extralegal" group "which takes the law into their own hands."[3] Professor Burrows also argues that violence or the threat of violence is a necessary element of vigilante groups, since "[w]ithout violence in some form, actual or potential, vigilante action would mean next to nothing, because it would be incapable of intimidation and, therefore, of 'regulation.'"[4] This definition is consistent with how vigilante justice has been viewed for most of history. However, it turns out to be a bit too limited for our purposes, as we want to encompass any private action taken against an alleged perpetrator of a crime, whether or not it is undertaken by an organized group and whether or not it is extralegal. Furthermore, even though the traditional vigilante uses violence to accomplish their ends, this is not a requirement of a private criminal disposition: As we will see, there are plenty of ways in which an individual can regulate behavior and even intimidate an alleged perpetrator without resorting to threats of violence.

Professor Paul Robinson and Sarah Robinson offer a somewhat different definition of a vigilante in SHADOW VIGILANTES.[5] In their view, vigilantes are always committing illegal actions, but there is a critical distinction between moral vigilantism and immoral vigilantism. They provide a list of ten rules to serve as criteria to differentiate between the two types of vigilantism, including acting only when there is a "serious failure of justice" and when there is "no lawful way to solve the problem."[6] Thus, all moral vigilantism comes from what they call the "doctrines of disillusionment," which is when "the criminal justice system seems to many to advertise an indifference to the importance of doing justice."[7] This disillusionment "undermines the criminal justice system's moral credibility."[8] The Robinsons conclude that, under these conditions, we should be sympathetic to moral vigilantes, because the public criminal justice system has failed its obligations under the social contract and so it is justifiable for vigilantes to break their side of the social contract and take the law into their own hands. The Robinsons also argue that vigilantism serves a valuable instrumentalist purpose, as it forces the public criminal justice system to "pay attention to ordinary people's disillusionment with a system that they see as failing to give serious offenders the punishment they deserve."[9] Thus, moral vigilantes can show the public criminal justice system where it needs to improve.

The Robinsons also identify a quasi-vigilante phenomenon that they call "shadow vigilantism." This is when individuals express their disillusionment with the public criminal justice system by undermining it in subtler ways than direct vigilante action. Examples include private individuals who refuse to report vigilante actions to the police or refuse to indict or convict individuals who they believe have engaged in moral vigilante actions. Public officials also engage in this conduct, such as when prosecutors choose not to bring charges against those who act as vigilantes. Shadow vigilantism can work against defendants as well if a public official perceives that the criminal justice system is failing to properly convict and punish criminals. For example, a police officer who is frustrated with the technicalities of search and seizure rules could commit perjury in order to avoid evidence from being precluded and to ensure that a person who is factually guilty does not escape on a technicality.[10]

Although the Robinsons, are occasionally sympathetic to vigilante action, they also recognize the significant costs of vigilante justice, even moral vigilantism. Vigilante actions cause a systemic distortion in the public criminal justice system, and can lead to a further breakdown in the system's credibility, especially if the vigilantism goes unpunished. This causes a vicious circle, which they call the "vigilante echo," in which insufficient law enforcement leads to disillusionment, which leads to vigilante action, which leads to further disillusionment in the system.[11] It is far better, in the Robinsons' view, for the public criminal justice system to take notice of the areas where vigilantes are forced to act and then repair the system in those areas. To the Robinsons, moral vigilantism – whether of the active or shadow variety – is a necessary and justified evil, but it is still an evil, and so the job of the police and prosecutors should be to remove its necessity.[12]

Both Professor Burrows' and the Robinsons' definitions of vigilantes are somewhat narrow for our purposes, in three ways. First, not all vigilantes are members of a formal group or an organization. Some act on their own or in small groups. Indeed, the popular culture vision of a vigilante – from action heroes portrayed in dozens of vigilante movies to modern superheroes such as Daredevil and Batman – is usually of an individual fighting crime on their own. And many of the real-life vigilantes also acted alone or in small groups, such as George Zimmerman and Kyle Rittenhouse. Second, vigilantes do not always engage in violence or threat, nor is doing so necessary, as Professor Burrows claims, in order to regulate or affect the behavior of potential criminals. As we will see in the section "Nonviolent Private Criminal Dispositions," many vigilante groups use non-violent tactics, such as shaming, to punish criminals and deter future wrongdoers. Finally, not all vigilantes are "extra-legal," especially those who do not employ violence.

Therefore, this book will use a broader term than vigilantism: private criminal dispositions. This term will encompass any action by a private citizen or group that imposes punishment on those who allegedly perpetrate crimes. A private criminal disposition occurs when the private individual or group is seeking to punish a person whom they believe has committed actual crimes as defined by the state – theft, assault, burglary, and so on. The term does not include individuals or groups that are trying to further their own idiosyncratic values by imposing punishment on people of whose conduct they disapprove. Thus, members of fringe political groups – such as the Ku Klux Klan – are not true vigilantes. Paul and Sarah Robinson make this one of the distinctions between moral and immoral vigilantes, as a moral vigilante must "respect the full society's norms of what is condemnable." The Robinsons give an example of animal rights activists who believe that animals should not be farmed or used for medical research, and so commit crimes in order to punish companies who engage in these activities. Under the Robinsons' view, a moral vigilante "cannot in a democratic society substitute their own values for those of the larger society."[3] My definition of private criminal dispositions shares this criterion of moral vigilantism – a private disposition must be imposed in response to a perceived violation of the actual criminal law, not a violation of the actor's subjective view of morality. This distinguishes private criminal dispositions from domestic terrorist acts – the former intend to enforce the criminal law, while the latter act to further a political agenda, maintain the terrorist's power in a social order, or even prevent legitimate law enforcement from enforcing certain crimes.

On the margins, there may be some dispute as to whether an actor is punishing an alleged criminal for "transgressing the law" or for merely violating the actor's individual moral code. If we adopt a purely positivist view of the law, in which a crime is nothing more or less than what the legislature says is the law, then it is easy to distinguish between an idiosyncratic punishment and a true private criminal disposition. However, as we saw in Chapter 1, a broader definition of "criminal activity" includes violation of established social norms, not just the specific laws on the books. Thus, in some cases, there may be some dispute as to whether a private party is engaged in enforcing society's norms or their own minority views.

Although there may be controversial cases on the margins, in most contexts it is easy to distinguish between private parties acting to enforce their own minority worldview and those acting consistently with the goals of the public criminal justice system. One simple measure is the popular support for the groups that carry out these actions – the modern Ku Klux Klan, for example, has consistently polled at lower than 10 percent support among Americans, even during the Civil Rights Movement, when the country was in turmoil about racial issues.[14] Another measure is whether the level of punishment imposed by the private party is significantly greater than what any significant number of Americans believe is appropriate. In the late 1970s, domestic terrorists opposed to abortion committed arson against multiple women's health clinics[15] and, over the next thirty years, antiabortion radicals killed eleven people and injured dozens more, including doctors who performed abortions, staff members at abortion clinics, and their family members.[16] Even among those who believed abortion was a crime, these actions were considered extreme in their severity, placing them well outside our definition of private criminal dispositions.[17]

Even if we exclude from our definition the extremists who are trying to enforce their own idiosyncratic values, this does not mean that everyone who is targeted by a private punishment is in fact guilty of a crime. As with other aspects of the private criminal justice system, there may be few, if any, safeguards to ensure that the private actor is punishing an actual criminal, rather than merely an individual who the private actor believes to be a criminal. Private criminal dispositions are defined by their focus on the belief of the private actor, not on the actual guilt of the suspected criminal; because the private actor is punishing a person whom they believe violated an actual crime as defined by the state, the action will be classified as a private criminal disposition.

Furthermore, this definition does not depend upon the *purpose* of the private actor. As long as the private actor is imposing punishment in response to perceived criminal activity, it does not matter if they are trying to further the aims of the public criminal justice system, such as deterring crime or imposing punishment on the guilty. They could be acting out of a desire for personal vengeance, such as when a boyfriend attacks a man who sexually assaulted his girlfriend; they could be engaging in a blood feud, such as when a gang member responds to the murder of one of their gang's own members by killing a member of the rival gang that was responsible for the original murder; or they could be acting in their own narrow self-interest, such as when a retail store bars a suspected shoplifter from entering the store property. All of these acts would qualify as private criminal dispositions under our definition.

As we will see later in this chapter, the type and degree of punishment that is imposed will vary widely. Almost always, private individuals impose a different level of punishment from the level that would be imposed by the state – often it is less severe (such as when a company fires an employee for theft, compared with the jail sentence the employee might receive from the state), but occasionally it is more severe (such as when a private actor imposes physical punishment or even death for a property crime). A private disposition is almost always going to be different in kind from any punishment imposed by the state – the latter's default response to criminal activity is incarceration, which is not available to private actors.

Thus, even limiting the definition of private criminal dispositions to actions that are intended to enforce the criminal law does not ensure that these actions are normatively desirable. As noted earlier, by definition these dispositions take place without any official adjudication or declaration that their target is guilty of a crime, and so they could often punish a person who is not in fact guilty of anything. And even if the target of the action is guilty, the private actor – whether an individual or an organization – determines the appropriate punishment based on their own preferences, not based on the degree of punishment set by a democratic legislature or imposed by a legitimately appointed judge. Finally, even if the target is guilty and the punishment is reasonable, the very existence of private dispositions could be corrosive to the criminal justice system.

MOTIVATIONS FOR PRIVATE PUNISHMENTS

Although there is wide disagreement about how to define vigilantism, there is surprising unanimity on the reason why individuals and groups turn to this type of behavior. It is a reason that is very familiar to us at this point in the book: a belief that the public criminal justice system is unable or unwilling to enforce the criminal law, either in its handling of one particular case or more generally.[18] As the Robinsons put it, citizens have a natural right to respond to wrongdoing, and they give up that right as part of the social contract they make with the government. However, this surrender of rights is not irreversible; if the government fails to meet its end of the bargain and does not properly respond to criminal activity, individuals are justified in reclaiming this natural right and acting on their own.[19]

We already discussed the most extreme examples of this failure in Chapter 2, where we discussed private criminal justice on the frontier during the earliest history of the country. In that context, state power was weak or absent, and private citizens had to band together to impose their own punishments for violations of the law. Vigilante justice tended to exist "when the legally constituted authority was weak and corrupt," leading citizens to set up a private criminal justice system to enforce existing laws.[20]

As an author at the beginning of the twentieth century saw it, Americans had not just the right but a *duty* to become involved if the criminal justice system failed to properly maintain law and order:

> The courts, or rather the juries, into whose hands we have put the law, are not dealing the law. They are withered hands, or rather they are imitation hands made for show, with no life in them, no grip. And so when your ordinary citizen sees this, and sees that he has placed justice in a dead hand, he must take justice back into his own hands where it once was at the beginning of all things. Call this primitive, if you will. But so far from being a *defiance* of the law, it is an *assertion* of it – the fundamental assertion of self-governing men, upon whom our whole social fabric is based.[21]

On a deeper level, private punishments also fit well with the democratic ideology of the country – as the power of the government ultimately comes from the people, it makes sense for the people to exercise that power themselves in the absence of governmental authority. As Professor Burrows put it:

> The concept of popular sovereignty – democracy – was the single most important political element contributing to the vigilante reaction. Obviously, no monarch would have allowed a bunch of armed subjects to ride around the countryside hanging the people they hated ... So one of the key reasons for vigilantisms' taking hold in America was the belief that the rule of the people superseded all other rule. And from that followed the premise that they had the authority to act in their own best interest in the absence of effective constituted authority.[22]

However, if private punishments can be partially justified by pointing to a broken social contract, it is also important to remember that the historical record of private punishments is decidedly mixed. Chapter 2 traced the history of private criminal dispositions in this country, which included laudable groups such as the "regulators" in colonial times who inflicted corporal punishment on husbands who beat their wives, all the way to the twentieth-century vigilantes such as the Deacons for Justice during the Civil Rights Movement, the Lavender Panthers who protected the LGBT community, and the residents of inner city neighborhoods who burned down crack houses during the drug epidemic of the 1980s. However, the history also includes the slave patrols in the antebellum South, the "committee of vigilance" that took over the criminal justice system in San Francisco for a few months in the nineteenth century and disproportionately targeted ethnic and religious minorities, and the strike-breaking violence of the Pinkerton Agency. As noted earlier, the institutions and individuals who engage in private punishments tend to be the wealthier, more enfranchised groups punishing alleged criminal activities of the poor, immigrants, and racial minorities, and private criminal dispositions often disproportionately protect the property rights of the wealthy at the expense of those with fewer political and economic resources.

LEGAL STATUS OF PRIVATE CRIMINAL DISPOSITIONS

No state allows for a formal "vigilante defense." An instruction from a North Carolina trial court is typical of how a judge will guide a jury in cases in which an individual has broken the law in carrying out a private criminal disposition:

> Now, Ladies and Gentlemen of the Jury, you should not decide this case upon the basis of your own standard of morals, nor upon what you might like the law to be. No person is justified in taking the law in his own hands. No person is justified to constitute himself the keeper of the morals of his fellowman. No person is justified in acting as judge, jury and executioner. You should not decide this case upon the basis of sympathy for anyone, nor upon the basis of anger at anyone. You should decide this case upon the basis of the law that I have given you and the facts as you find them to be.[23]

A justice from another state supreme court decried private punishments as "one of the most unfortunate phenomena" of recent times, as "[p]ublic safety is the business of government."[24] Criminal courts tend to be hostile to the idea of private citizens enforcing the criminal law. The term vigilantism generally carries a negative connotation, as most people associate vigilante action with violence and they are uncomfortable with private citizens using violence to enforce the criminal law. This is because within the last 150 years, the United States (as well as most Western industrialized states) has achieved what one commentator refers to as a "monopoly of punishment, policing, and military force."[25] As the state enjoys a legal monopoly on using force, only the state can lawfully use coercion to apprehend and punish criminals. Thus, the argument concludes, any vigilante who punishes an individual for committing a crime is usurping the state's proper role and acting illegitimately.

However, as noted in Chapter 1, this argument is flawed in two ways. First, there is no particular reason that vigilantes need to use force or violence to achieve their ends, and many private citizens punish criminals without violence. Even if the state did have a complete monopoly on the legitimate use of force (which in fact it does not, as we will see later in this section), this does not mean that it would have a monopoly on punishing criminal conduct. Even the public criminal justice system does not always use force to enforce the criminal code and punish criminal behavior.[26] And private individuals and institutions punish individuals for criminal conduct all the time without using force or violence. As we have seen in earlier chapters, colleges expel students who commit sexual assault, retail stores ban shoplifters from returning to their stores, and employers impose professional sanctions on employees who embezzle funds. These actors are not considered vigilantes under the traditional definition, as they do not employ threats or violence, but their actions easily fit into our definition of private criminal dispositions. Because their "punishments" consist solely of removing a privilege that the perpetrator used to enjoy, their actions are relatively uncontroversial.

Even private criminal dispositions that move beyond the removal of privileges and seek to actively make the suspected criminal suffer generally do not involve force. We have already seen in Chapters 5 and 6 how individuals threaten criminal prosecution in order to obtain some consideration from the alleged criminal, a tactic that most jurisdictions consider to be blackmail. Other groups use shaming tactics to punish and deter criminals or hack into their computer systems to cause damage.

Most surprisingly, even the private criminal dispositions that use force are not always illegitimate, as the state's supposed "monopoly on the legitimate use of force" is not in fact a monopoly. We noted in Chapter 5 that all states allow private citizens to make arrests, which could involve detention through force, and some states have supplemented these rights with greater powers to use reasonable force to retrieve stolen property. And some private individuals, such as George Zimmerman, have been able to successfully claim self-defense even when they used deadly force in their attempts to enforce the criminal law. Thus, it is important to categorize different types of private criminal punishments to see which ones violate the law and which do not. Private criminal dispositions come in all shapes and sizes – some violent and some not – and their legality varies depending on both the type of punishment being inflicted and the laws of the state where they occur.

NONVIOLENT PRIVATE CRIMINAL DISPOSITIONS

We will start with the mildest form of private punishments: when the private actor simply removes a benefit or a privilege that the alleged perpetrator originally enjoyed. Retail stores frequently engage in this type of private punishment. Macy's department store, for example, used to have a policy that imposed a seven-year ban on shoplifters entering their store.[27] Similarly, an employer who catches an employee stealing from the company might terminate the contract of that employee, and a parent who catches a teenage child taking drugs might forbid the child from leaving the house for two weeks. In Chapter 7, we examined institutions, such as universities and professional associations, that conduct their own private adjudications in response to alleged criminal conduct and suspend or revoke the privileges of the defendant if they are found culpable. These private dispositions are the least controversial, and usually receive approval from the general public – in fact, as we saw in Chapter 7, private institutions are often criticized when they do not take action against suspected criminals in their midst. They also do not violate the criminal law, as the "punishment" they impose merely involves taking away a benefit.

The next level of private criminal dispositions involves inflicting a level of suffering onto the suspected criminal without causing physical harm to the suspect or their property. A useful example of this private punishment is public shaming of alleged criminals. This has been an effective tool for local communities since at least the 1980s. Residents of neighborhoods facing an influx of sex workers or drug dealers sometimes grow frustrated with the lack of police response. Instead of confronting the criminals directly, they write down the license plate numbers of the individuals who drive into their communities to buy sex or drugs, look up the names of the owners of the cars, and then advertise the customers' names, addresses, and phone numbers in fliers around town.[28] On the more progressive side of the political spectrum, communities can enforce their social norms on their own members through "social pressure and exclusion," including "prevent[ing] truancy and confront[ing] individuals disturbing the peace without resorting to police."[29]

The rise of the internet created new opportunities for private shaming punishments. Once again, the need for private criminal dispositions arose in a context where there were large gaps in the public enforcement of crime. In other chapters, we have seen examples of strong vigilante movements in the early days of the Republic, either in colonial times or in the western territories before the public criminal justice system was established. The early days of the internet created an analogous situation, as criminals were able to exploit the anonymity and global reach of the world wide web, while public police were struggling to keep pace. This advantage was perhaps nowhere more significant than in the area of sex crimes, as child pornographers could more easily store and transmit their contraband and child molesters could contact and groom their victims from the secrecy of their online accounts. As public law enforcement could not immediately counter these advantages, a group calling themselves the "Cyberangels" became "the first cyber-neighborhood watch" and recruited thousands of volunteers to monitor the internet looking for individuals who were victimizing children. The Cyberangels were the beginning of one of the largest vigilante movements in our country's history: online pedophile hunting. For over two decades, volunteers in various organizations have logged into chat rooms and online meeting places, posing as children in order to lure potential cyberpredators. One of the most prominent of these organizations was a group called "Perverted Justice." Their volunteers then attempted to gather (in role) a photograph of and contact information about the individual who was soliciting them, and representatives of the organization would then call to confirm the intentions of the potential child solicitor. Once the organization was convinced of the individual's guilt, it posted the alleged perpetrator's name, contact information, and picture on their website, alongside a transcript of the sexually explicit chat that the individual had with the volunteer. Originally, the organization suggested the possibility of contacting the alleged perpetrators and their friends and families, and later it worked with local and national media outlets to put some of the perpetrators on television. It eventually contracted with NBC to create a show called *To Catch a Predator*, which featured video footage of the sexual predators showing up at a house where they had made plans for a meeting with an underaged girl and being confronted in dramatic fashion by the show's host.

After a few years, Perverted Justice increased its cooperation with law enforcement and began to publicize the number of criminal convictions that it had assisted in, making it more of a private law enforcement group than a group engaging in private dispositions. However, it never stopped publicizing those whom it caught soliciting underage sex. Its reasons were both retributive and utilitarian: Its members thought it was important to punish those who attempted to solicit children and to deter potential perpetrators from engaging in internet solicitation by "poisoning the well," so that individuals who wished to engage in the conduct would abstain because of the fear that they would be exposed by an adult volunteer posing as a child.[30]

Although Perverted Justice is no longer operational, other individuals and groups have taken up its cause, migrating from network television to YouTube and Facebook, where they are known as "pedophile hunters" and have amassed tens of thousands of followers. One recent study found over a 160 different pedophile hunting groups, all of which followed the same pattern: A private individual poses as an underage girl or boy online, chats for a few days or weeks with a potential sexual predator, and then sets up a meeting. A member of the group then goes to the meeting and videos (sometimes live streaming) their confrontation with the suspect. Once posted, the videos often amass hundreds of thousands of views. In 2022 alone, these groups conducted nearly 1,000 stings of suspected predators. Although most of the hunters share their evidence with police, their ultimate goal is to publicize the actions of the suspects; as one hunter put it, he wants "street justice," so that "a guy walks around the street and people know who he is."[31]

Unsurprisingly, these online pedophile hunters are not without their critics. Like any vigilante group, these individuals may accuse – and punish – someone who is actually innocent. Even when their target is guilty, the public shaming they perform can ruin the lives of those they expose, occasionally with dire consequences. At least ten suspected predators have committed suicide over the last six years after their actions were exposed by these groups – in fact, the original *To Catch a Predator* ceased operation after a district attorney who had been exposed on the program killed himself when police came to serve him with a search warrant. Finally, critics point out that the confrontations these vigilantes set up can occasionally be dangerous for the vigilantes when the targets of the investigation react violently. These are all legitimate concerns, although it is worth noting that they also occur in the public criminal justice system.

The next category of private criminal dispositions involves punishments that cause physical damage to property but stop short of force or violence. The early days of the internet again provide an illustrative example. In 2001, as the internet was exploding across every industry, one online security expert explained that "[d]efending a modern information system could also be likened to defending a large, thinly-populated territory like the nineteenth century Wild West: the men in black hats can strike anywhere, while the men in white hats have to defend everywhere."[32] The government found it very difficult to identify, track, apprehend, and prosecute hackers; the technical and jurisdictional hurdles were just too formidable.[33] A senior security manager at a major financial institution, echoing the sentiments of vigilantes throughout history, told a reporter that "[t]here's not a chance in hell of us going to law enforcement with a hacker incident .... They can't be trusted to do anything about it, so it's up to us to protect ourselves."[34] As one commentator put it: "traditional law enforcement schemes simply do not work in cyberspace because of the speed by which attacks cause damage to e-commerce sites and also because hackers can stage attacks from multiple jurisdictions with varying cybercrime laws and procedures for prosecuting internet crimes."[35]

In the absence of effective public law enforcement, many companies pursued a strategy of "counterstrikes" or "hack-backs" against suspected hackers. The essential idea was to respond immediately to any unauthorized entry onto their systems with a counter-hack that damages the computer instigating the attack. A 1999 article described a survey of 320 of the Fortune 500 companies, which indicated that 32 percent of the companies used "counteroffensive software."[36] These actions provided instant deterrence and punishment against further attacks, but they were not without their risks; for example, the counterstrike could hit an innocent computer, especially if the original hacker routed their attack through a third party.[37]

Nonviolent private punishments are generally premeditated, that is, they are purposeful impositions of punishment on the alleged criminal, generally after some period of reflection, and often pursuant to a preexisting institutional policy. Thus, they are also more likely to be legal, especially for repeat players such as retail stores or cyber-hunters, as the institutions and individuals that engage in these actions take the time to understand what is permitted and what is not. Even the online pedophile hunters with their controversial tactics are careful to conduct themselves legally when they pose as underage decoys or when they ultimately confront their suspects. However, as we saw in Chapter 6, some types of nonviolent punishments cross the line into blackmail, and thus are technically criminal actions. Furthermore, the private dispositions that involve property damage – from the sophisticated hack-backs discussed earlier to the person who intentionally scratches the paint of a car that is illegally parked in a handicapped spot – almost certainly violate the law.

Even when nonviolent private punishments violate the law, criminal prosecution is unlikely for at least two reasons. First, the perpetrator who is suffering the punishment might realize that if they report the punishment to the police, they may be arrested for the underlying crime.[38] Thus, many instances of illegal private punishment go unreported and so never enter the public criminal justice system. Second, if the private punishment seems proportionate to the original crime, prosecutors may be reluctant to bring charges, either because they believe a jury would not convict the private punisher or because they are exercising their own discretion as to whether it is just to bring charges under such circumstances. We will discuss this "informal defense" to private dispositions in greater detail in the next section.

VIOLENT PRIVATE CRIMINAL DISPOSITIONS

Violent private punishments also take a variety of forms. Some are carried out by institutions and some by private parties. Because of the state's near-monopoly on the legitimate use of force, private criminal punishment that involves violence is more likely to be illegal.

However, a few types of violent private dispositions have been expressly sanctioned by law, in situations where the state has authorized specific exceptions to its monopoly on the legitimate use of force. The contours of these exceptions vary from state to state, and they have evolved over the past decades, with significant repercussions for those who conduct private punishments. We already noted in Chapter 4 that many states have "merchant codes" that permit a retailer to detain a suspected thief or use force in order to regain stolen property. As with self-defense law, private actors must prove that force was necessary and that the threat to their property was imminent, or that the forcible repossession of the property occurred immediately after the perpetrator stole it – otherwise the proper course of action is to contact the public police. Recent changes in state law have shown an evolution toward a more lenient rule for the legitimate use of force. Originally, the party who used force to protect or recover property must have had a reasonable belief that force was necessary; more modern statutes only require the party to have an honest, good faith belief that force was necessary, even if they were unreasonable in that belief.[39]

On the other side of the spectrum are plainly illegal private punishments, such as a street gang committing a murder in retaliation for a member of their own gang being killed or a group of friends or family members who physically attack a man after he sexually assaults a woman.[40] On rare occasions, the guilt of the victim will persuade a prosecutor not to press charges or (more rarely) will lead to jury nullification, especially if the force used by the private individual was reasonable under the circumstances (for example if a man punches another man in retaliation for an unwanted sexual advance against his wife). However, the criminal law in every state is clear: Committing an act of violence in retaliation for a past wrong is itself a criminal act.

In between these two extremes are a number of different types of forcible punishments that straddle the line between legal and illegal. Some of them are relatively mild and are so close to being legal that it would be hard to bring criminal charges against the person inflicting the punishment. Private security guards may be trained to hold alleged perpetrators in custody for longer than necessary while taking statements and processing paperwork, effectively imprisoning them for a few hours and making them less likely to return to the store. Bouncers at a bar might inflict some extra physical pain on rowdy patrons when ejecting them from the establishment in order to deter them (and others who are watching) from engaging in unwanted behavior in the future. Although these actions technically violate the law, the amount of excess force used is minimal enough that prosecution and conviction of any of these individuals would be very unusual. Even if a prosecutor is convinced that the actor used excessive force and violated the law, the prosecutor will often face practical evidentiary challenges at trial. When the alleged conduct is so close to being legal, not only is there a concern over the triviality of the charge or convincing a jury to convict a defendant that they don't consider morally culpable, but the prosecutor may also have a difficult time obtaining sufficient evidence to prove that the conduct actually crossed the line into illegal conduct. For example, even if the prosecutor believed it was warranted to charge a bouncer for using excessive force, and even if they were in front of a jury generally willing to convict for such a crime, there may not be sufficient evidence to convince the jury that this "edge case" was indeed illegal excessive force, particularly because the line between lawful and unlawful use of force is itself somewhat unclear.

The most interesting – and high profile – cases of private dispositions involve private individuals who set out to enforce the law as volunteer private law enforcement and end up using lethal force against a suspected criminal. These individuals then attempt to rely on a self-defense claim or similar legal provisions to protect them from conviction. For lack of a better term, we will call these individuals "private enforcers," as their motivation seems to go beyond merely patrolling and observing to include actively enforcing the law and occasionally using deadly force. Sometimes these individuals are part of a private militia or paramilitary organization, with such groups having been growing in popularity in recent years;[41] sometimes they are part of neighborhood watch organizations; and occasionally they are individuals acting on their own. Private enforcers fall along a spectrum based on the degree to which they provoke – or even initiate – violence in their encounters with suspected criminals. A few well-known case studies provide examples of private individuals at different points along this spectrum.

In August 2020, during the height of the Black Lives Matter movement, police officers in Kenosha, Wisconsin, were responding to a domestic dispute when they shot and seriously injured Jacob Blake, a Black man. Many members of the community in Kenosha believed the shooting was unjustified, and multiple days of protests followed. Although the protests were mostly peaceful during the daytime, they turned violent at night, with dozens of buildings and hundreds of vehicles being set on fire. A citywide curfew and the activation of the National Guard on the second day were ineffective in stemming the violence, and the widespread looting and violence continued into the second night. In response to the public police's failure to contain the violence, a private militia group called the Kenosha Guard set up a Facebook page that quickly grew to 5,000 members. The group then met in person and assigned its members different locations of the city to protect, despite the protest of the county sheriff. By the third night of violence, many armed civilians were patrolling the streets and guarding businesses, claiming their presence was necessary because of the vacuum left by law enforcement.[42]

One of these private volunteers was a 17-year-old named Kyle Rittenhouse. Rittenhouse's permanent residence was just across the state line in Illinois, but at the time of the unrest he was staying in Kenosha with his girlfriend's brother, a man named Dominick Black. Rittenhouse and Black had become very close, and a few months earlier, Black had bought Rittenhouse an AR-15-style rifle, as Rittenhouse was too young to legally purchase the weapon for himself. After watching footage of the unrest on television, the two men went downtown during the day to help clean up the graffiti, and then made a decision to return at night to guard one of the businesses that had already suffered some damage the night before.[43]

Rittenhouse had some experience shooting firearms, and he had participated in his city's Police Explorer's Program when he was in the ninth grade, but he had no actual training or experience in law enforcement. During the night, events quickly spiraled out of control. As he patrolled the property of the Car Source business that he had appointed himself to protect, he was confronted by a mentally ill man who had just been released from a psychiatric hospital hours before and who had threatened both Rittenhouse and other armed civilians earlier that night. The man, shirtless and screaming, chased after Rittenhouse and threw a plastic bag containing toiletries at him. Rittenhouse turned just as the unarmed man lunged at him, and Rittenhouse shot him four times, killing him. Demonstrators who witnessed the killing began chasing Rittenhouse, who started running toward the police vehicles nearby. A demonstrator hit Rittenhouse in the back of the head and he fell; another man tried to kick him in the head and missed. A third demonstrator hit Rittenhouse in the head with a skateboard, and Rittenhouse shot him in the chest, killing him; a fourth approached Rittenhouse and pointed a gun at him and Rittenhouse shot him in the arm. Rittenhouse fled the scene, eventually turning himself in later that night.[44]

Rittenhouse was eventually tried for intentional homicide and related charges, but he was acquitted on all charges after successfully presenting a case of self-defense. His case was similar to another instance eight years earlier, when George Zimmerman, the coordinator of his community's neighborhood watch program, fatally shot Trayvon Martin in a gated community in Florida. The community had created the neighborhood watch program in 2011 in response to a number of burglaries and attempted break-ins.[45] In February 2012, Zimmerman was driving through the neighborhood on a personal errand when he saw Martin walking through the neighborhood. For reasons that remain unclear, Zimmerman believed Martin looked "real suspicious" and was "up to no good," and he called the police to come investigate. Zimmerman then left his car and followed Martin on foot, against the advice of the 911 operator. He then hung up the call.[46] What transpired over the next few minutes is unclear; unlike in Rittenhouse's case, there was no video, and witnesses provided conflicting accounts about the events leading up to the shooting. Zimmerman claimed that after he left his vehicle to see where Martin was going, Martin approached him, threatened him, punched him, knocked him down, and repeatedly pounded his head into the sidewalk. Zimmerman then stated that he reached for his weapon and shot Martin in self-defense. Most witnesses supported Zimmerman's account that Martin was on top of him and hitting him just before the shooting, but there were contrary reports as to who started the violent confrontation.[47] A trial jury acquitted Zimmerman of all charges, apparently accepting his argument that he acted in self-defense.

Like Rittenhouse, Zimmerman claims that he did not set out that night to inflict punishment on criminals. However – like Rittenhouse – his actions went beyond the usually "patrol and report" duties of most private police. By arming themselves and intentionally inserting themselves into volatile and dangerous situations, these two private law enforcement volunteers were inviting – some would say instigating – conflict with individuals whom they suspected might be about to commit a crime. It is therefore difficult to categorize their actions. It is possible that their stories belong in Chapter 4, in our discussion of private police. However, their aggressive tactics suggest that they were ready and willing to use deadly force in the course of their self-appointed duty, thus putting them nearer on the spectrum to those who impose private punishment on suspected criminals. Zimmerman is certainly closer to a person engaged in private criminal dispositions than Rittenhouse: Zimmerman shot Trayvon Martin while engaging in specific private enforcement against Martin, while Rittenhouse was not attempting to specifically engage in enforcement against any of the men he shot.

Some private enforcers fall even further along the spectrum toward those who intentionally set out to impose a private punishment. A few months before Kyle Rittenhouse shot three people in Wisconsin, three men in Georgia named Gregory McMichael, Travis McMichael, and William Bryan pursued and then killed Ahmaud Arbery. Gregory and Travis McMichael, who are father and son, observed

Arbery walk inside a house in their neighborhood that was under construction. Arbery left the house and then jogged away. Incorrectly believing that Arbery had committed a crime inside the house, the two men called 911, armed themselves, and starting chasing Arbery in a truck. They were soon joined by Bryan, who was driving his own truck. Once the men caught up with Arbery, Travis McMichael confronted him while holding his shotgun. After a brief altercation, which was partially captured on video by Bryan, Travis McMichael shot Arbery in the chest multiple times, killing him. Like Zimmerman and Rittenhouse, the three men involved in the shooting claimed self-defense, arguing that they had probable cause to believe that Arbery committed a crime, that they were trying to detain Arbery until the police arrived, and that Arbery was aggressively trying to take Travis McMichael's gun such that Travis had no choice but to shoot Arbery to protect himself. Unlike in the Zimmerman and Rittenhouse cases, the jury rejected their claim and convicted all three men of murder.[48]

On the furthest end of the spectrum is the case of Joe Horn in Texas. In 2007, Horn observed two men breaking into his next-door neighbor's house and called 911 to report the crime. While he was still on the phone waiting for the police to arrive, he saw the two men exit his neighbor's home carrying a pillowcase full of items. Ignoring the police dispatcher's repeated warnings for him not to go outside, Horn armed himself and went out onto his lawn to confront the burglars. He yelled at them to freeze, and at least one of them ran toward him before beginning to move away. Horn shot and killed them both. Horn's intent to use deadly force to punish the two burglar's is the clearest of all of the case studies in this chapter. During his conversation with the dispatcher, Horn was warned that he might get shot if he went outside and he responded: "You want to make a bet? I am going to kill them."[49] A grand jury heard two weeks of testimony in the case and then voted not to indict Horn for any crime.

In evaluating these private enforcement actions, we will put aside for now their morality and social desirability, and examine them first from a purely legal perspective. The legality of these actions is heavily dependent on the specific facts of each case, but it also depends on the laws on self-defense and the defense of others in the relevant jurisdiction. Traditionally, a person acting in self-defense or to defend others must meet four criteria: (1) the action must be taken in response to an imminent threat, (2) the action must be proportionate to that threat (that is, deadly force cannot be used unless deadly force is threatened), (3) the action must be necessary to avoid that threat, and (4) the actor may not be the initial aggressor in the altercation. These criteria were originally meant to create a very narrow exception to the bar on private use of force, under the theory that the public police should be summoned to respond to any act of violence unless it was absolutely necessary to act. If a person had time to call the police before the violent act would occur, if the person could retreat or take any other action to avoid the violent act, or if they could have prevented the violent act by not provoking the attacker, then they were not allowed to use force themselves.

In recent decades, however, many states have adjusted these requirements to broaden the use-of-force exception. The most well-known examples of these changes are the "stand-your-ground laws," which hold that an actor need not retreat in the face of an imminent use of force, even if they could safely do so, as long as the actor is in a place where they have a lawful right to be. As of 2022, thirty-six states had some version of this law, which significantly waters down the "necessity" requirement. Stand-your-ground laws make it more likely that a private law enforcement officer will turn into a private enforcer – as one commentator put it: "While concerns over a single, vigilant neighbor, keeping a watchful eye out for criminal activity may not pose many concerns, legitimate concerns for civil liberties do arise when that neighbor joins an organized group charged with protecting the neighborhood and is allowed to carry a concealed weapon and to refuse to back down in a confrontation."[50]

However, a more significant legal shift for our purposes comes from the evolution of the "initial aggressor" doctrine, which is meant to ensure that an individual could not avail themselves of a self-defense claim if they had provoked the violence. The key question that prosecutors, judges, and juries must answer is what counts as being the "initial aggressor," especially for individuals engaged in private law enforcement, such as security guards or participants in neighborhood watch programs. The traditional perception of a self-defense claim involves an innocent person who is not looking for trouble and who is violently accosted and compelled to use force – or deadly force – to protect themselves. However, what if the person were actively patrolling a neighborhood or a commercial establishment and initiated contact with a suspected criminal? What if the person were armed or threatened to use force against the suspected criminal? At what point do the person's actions cross the line into becoming the "initial aggressor" under the law? Professor Noah Feldman of Harvard University cites this as the critical question in the Rittenhouse case, as Rittenhouse was able to use the self-defense doctrine after he purposefully put himself into a dangerous situation.[51] Professor Feldman notes that it was only the fact that Rittenhouse chose to enter into a "hot environment" with a deadly weapon that ultimately allowed him to argue that he was in fear for his life – thus, Rittenhouse created some of the conditions that he later claimed created the necessity for him to use deadly force.[52] This critique applies with even more force as we move along the spectrum from Rittenhouse to Zimmerman to the McMichaels and ultimately to Horn.

The initial aggressor doctrine has evolved into different forms in different states, making it difficult, if not impossible, to find a universal rule of when a private enforcer has crossed the line into criminal activity. However, Professor Cynthia Lee of George Washington University Law School was able to create a useful taxonomy of the different initial aggressor rules in the United States after conducting an in-depth analysis of the rule across the country. She distinguishes between "provocateurs," who goad their victims into committing an act of physical violence and then counterattack, and "aggressors," who are the first to use or threaten force against their victim.[53]

The classic example of a provocateur is a white supremacist who travels to a funeral for a Black civil rights leader, begins shouting racial epithets at the mourners attending the funeral, and then shoots members of the crowd when they charge at him.[54] Most jurisdictions do not define the term "provokes," although, as Professor Lee notes, hostile words and insults alone can occasionally be enough to classify a person as a provocateur.[55] Courts appear to require a bit more than a causal relationship between the defendant's actions and the ultimate victim's violent reaction – the violent reaction by the victim must be foreseeable or at least reasonable. Ultimately, the question of whether a private enforcer's actions provoked a violent response will be decided by a jury, and so might vary significantly from jurisdiction to jurisdiction or even within a jurisdiction.

Professor Lee does point out that the "provocateur" category is significantly limited by the fact that almost every jurisdiction requires proof of the intent of the private enforcer – that is, it is not merely enough that the private enforcer actually did provoke a person to violence; the prosecutor must prove that the private enforcer meant to provoke them or at least knew that their acts would provoke them.[56] This requirement would probably exempt all of the case studies we examined above, with the possible exception of Joe Horn, who appeared to be attempting to provoke his victims into a conflict. However, a minority of states consider a provoker to be an initial aggressor even if there is no evidence that they knew they were provoking the violent conduct. Professor Lee gives the example of Minnesota, which bars a self-defense claim if the actor "provoke[ed] the difficulty in which he finds it necessary to use deadly force."[57] This broader definition could arguably include all of the members of our case studies, but would also include a much broader category of people who unwittingly – perhaps even unforeseeably – create a dangerous situation. It would also include those – such as trained private law enforcement – who justifiably create a dangerous situation during their routine duties of apprehending wrongdoers.

Lee's second category, that of "aggressor," describes private enforcers who are the first to use or threaten physical force. This is the traditional definition of initial aggressor, and it disqualifies the use of self-defense in most states. Unfortunately, as Lee points out, there is no agreement among different jurisdictions as to what conduct constitutes "threatening physical force." Some jurisdictions allow words alone to be sufficient to constitute a threat;[58] other jurisdictions look to whether the actor reasonably believed they were starting a fight.[59] However, most states use language that defines a threat as an action that "creates a reasonable belief in another person's mind that physical force is about to be used."[60] Like with the definition of "provocateur" – in which a jury must decide whether the private enforcer's acts reasonably led the victim to use violence against the private enforcer – this definition of "aggressor" requires a jury to ultimately determine whether the private enforcer's action created a "reasonable belief" that physical force was about to be used.

These definitions mean that whether an action is construed as "provoking" or "threatening" will differ from case to case, especially when the brandishing of a firearm is part of the action. For example, Professor Lee argues that the provocateur category should include any individual who "display[s] a firearm in a threatening manner or point[s] a firearm at another person."[61] Certainly some of the individuals who point a firearm are intending to provoke a reaction from their counterpart, but others may be acting in genuine fear or out of a desire to deter criminal activity. And the first part of that phrase – "displays a firearm in a threatening manner" – is troublingly ambiguous, especially as it is meant to mean something different from pointing a firearm at someone. What is a "threatening manner?" To some, the mere holding of a firearm would seem threatening; others would not see such an act as threatening unless the defendant literally made specific threats against someone.[62]

The starkly divergent reactions to Rittenhouse's acquittal stem in large part from this difference. Some individuals, especially those who do not own guns or do not live in areas where gun ownership is commonplace, believe that simply displaying a firearm, or perhaps even just carrying it in an area where protests are occurring, is provoking or threatening violence. Others – who apparently include the Rittenhouse jurors – are more accustomed to the presence of firearms and thus do not see Rittenhouse's actions as provoking or threatening. Unsurprisingly, familiarity with guns breaks down across partisan lines, as did the reactions to Rittenhouse's verdict: 48 percent of Republicans own guns, while only 20 percent of Democrats do.[63] Another factor to consider is the lawfulness of openly carrying a firearm in the location of the confrontation. Obviously, in places where openly carrying a firearm is illegal, producing a firearm would reasonably constitute a threat. In places where openly carrying a firearm is permissible, many would argue that such conduct alone is reasonable and would not be a threat. At any rate, denying a self-defense claim on the grounds that the defendant was openly carrying a firearm in a jurisdiction in which such conduct is permitted raises serious constitutional difficulties.[64]

As Professor Lee points out, legal scholars are also divided about what could make someone a "provocateur" under self-defense laws. Professor Michael Mannheimer of Northern Kentucky University wrote that Zimmerman was not the initial aggressor if all he did was follow Martin down the street asking him questions.[65] In contrast, Professor Alafair Burke of Hofstra University concludes that Martin may have reasonably perceived Zimmerman following him as a threat of force, which would make Zimmerman the aggressor in the confrontation.[66]

On the other hand, when private enforcers instigate physical contact, as with the McMichaels and William Bryan, the legal ambiguity disappears, and the result under the laws of any jurisdiction (and the conclusion of almost any prospective juror) would be that the private enforcer has crossed the line from enforcing the criminal law to becoming a criminal. In other instances, such as the Zimmerman case, the facts are ambiguous – without the video footage that was available in the Rittenhouse and McMichaels cases, it may be impossible to know whether the private enforcer was the first to use or threaten force, or whether the private enforcer acted in a way that foreseeably provoked the victim to use force against them. In such cases, much will depend on the burden of proof for the self-defense claim. If the prosecutor has the burden of disproving self-defense, then private enforcers will have more leeway to act; if defendants are required to prove that they were not the initial aggressor, they will use force or deadly force only if the facts are strongly in their favor. Judges also sometimes take the decision out of the hands of the jury: In the Zimmerman case, the trial judge did not even give the jury an instruction on initial aggression, as there was no evidence that Zimmerman initiated the physical conduct or that he intended to elicit a violent response.[67] Of course, any private enforcer who unjustifiably initiates physical contact or explicitly threatens force, like the McMichaels, will be barred from asserting self-defense if the situation turns violent.

There is one other type of defense that private enforcers can use, which is less formal but perhaps no less important. As noted earlier, prosecutors may be reluctant to bring charges if a jury is likely to see the private punishment as proportional to the perpetrator's crime. No state recognizes an official "vigilante defense," so jurors are technically not allowed to consider whether a private enforcer's action is morally justified, but jurors always have the power to acquit even if there is no legal justification for doing so. Thus, prosecutors or juries might unofficially sanction the private enforcer's action if they believe it is proportional to the severity of the crime to which they were responding. For example, a prosecutor or jury is unlikely to hold a woman accountable for punching a man in the face in response to unwanted sexual touching, whereas a private enforcer who engages in physical violence in response to a minor property crime is likely to be treated as a criminal by prosecutors and juries. This is another example of what Paul and Sarah Robinson call shadow vigilantism (which, as we saw in Chapter 8, refers to individuals who do not engage in acts of private criminal justice themselves but who enable others to do so).

It is worth noting that, in all of the case studies of private enforcers described earlier, the public officials engaged in varying degrees of shadow vigilantism. Kyle Rittenhouse was allowed to walk past the police officer blockade at the scene and was arrested only when he turned himself in hours later. Prosecutors initially refused to bring any charges against George Zimmerman and only did so months after the event in response to public outcries. Bryan and the McMichaels were not arrested until two and a half months after they killed Ahmaud Arbery. Horn's case was not presented to a grand jury until six months after the shooting, after significant public controversy in response to the release of the 911 recording.

Before concluding the chapter, there is one other aspect of violent private dispositions that must be acknowledged. As with other forms of private criminal justice, violent private dispositions have historically benefitted the enfranchised more than the less powerful in society. Those who have surplus time and the resources to impose private punishment tend to be those who already have greater monetary assets. Although there are no statistical studies or databases of violent private criminal dispositions, anecdotal evidence suggests a racial component to the actions of private enforcers: White people are more likely to engage in private dispositions and Black people are more likely to be the victims of such actions.[68] This is not unique to private enforcers: There is statistical evidence that, although the public police have shot and killed more white individuals than individuals of all other races combined (since white individuals make up a much larger percentage of the population than any other race), police shoot and kill people of color at a higher rate than they kill white individuals. The rate of police killings of Black people is twice that of white people, and when one examines the subset of police killings in which the suspect was unarmed (which is a rough proxy for unjustified killings), the disproportionality grows to three and a half times the rate of white individuals. This is at least partially explained by the persistent stereotype of Black people being dangerous or violent – we now have decades of studies showing that when observing Black and white people engaging in identical conduct, a person is far more likely to describe the conduct of the Black person as violent or threatening. This contributes to "threat perception failure" – when an individual believes that a suspect is holding a weapon when the suspect is in fact unarmed.[69] Given the well-documented disproportionality of unjustified police killings of people of color, and the ubiquity of this particularly harmful type of implicit bias, it is quite likely that violent private criminal dispositions also disproportionately involve people of color as victims. However, there is no evidence that this problem is more acute for private enforcers than it is for public police officers. In theory, this racial disproportionality should be easier to eliminate in the public police, through screening, training, and changes in institutional culture, but after years of awareness and political activism, this has not yet been the case.[70]

CONCLUSION

Like other aspects of the private criminal justice system, private criminal dispositions come in many different forms. They include any time a private party or institution imposes its own punishment in response to perceived criminal activity – from nonviolent punishments, such as removing privileges, public shaming, or damaging property, to violent and even lethal actions against the suspected criminal. This part of the private criminal justice system is the most controversial, partly because it is often conflated with domestic terrorist acts, which have little or nothing to do with enforcing the criminal law, but also because the punishments carry a sense of finality. When private police officers patrol, investigate, or even apprehend a suspect, they can be seen as merely supplementing the job of the public police. When parties engage in private plea bargaining, there is at least a sense that the suspected criminal is consenting to the punishment or at least choosing it over less palatable alternatives. And when private institutions adjudicate a dispute and determine that a suspect's criminal activities violate the institution's rules, their punishments are well within the rights of the private institution. However, in the case of private dispositions, the private party acts as the judge, jury, and executioner, offering the suspect no real choice and inflicting real harm on the suspect without any input from the public criminal justice system. Private criminal dispositions are thus the most extreme version of private criminal justice. They also represent the culmination of many of the themes we have been discussing throughout the book: the need (or perceived need) of private individuals to take action when the public criminal justice system is unable to perform its functions; the potential for effective enforcement of the criminal law at no cost to the state; and the countervailing potential for these actions to disproportionately benefit those with resources at the expense of the less enfranchised, including people of color. These themes in turn bring us back to the critical question we began with at the start of the book: How should we regulate the private criminal justice system to harness its beneficial aspects and discourage its harmful aspects? And, overall, does the private criminal justice system have a positive or a negative impact on society? The next two chapters take up these two questions.

9

Regulating Private Criminal Justice

Over the past few chapters, we have examined how private individuals and organizations act without any government involvement to enforce the criminal law, resolve criminal disputes (through settlement or adjudication), and punish criminal activity. These various aspects of the private criminal justice system have their advantages and disadvantages, which we will consider in more detail in the next chapter. Those who conclude that the disadvantages far outweigh the advantages, and therefore that a private criminal justice system should not exist, might be tempted to try to create rules that would reduce or even eliminate private responses to criminal activity. However, given the ubiquitous nature of the private criminal justice system and the sheer diversity of ways in which private parties respond to criminal activity, such an effort seems unwise if not impossible. We have seen throughout this book that the incentives to opt out of the public criminal justice system – for defendants, victims, and witnesses – are so great that any attempt to abolish these practices would likely only drive them underground, decreasing their transparency and their accountability even further.

Thus, regardless of whether private criminal justice is a net benefit, there is no question that private police, private dispute resolution, and private punishment will be with us for the foreseeable future. However, this does not mean that the private criminal justice system cannot be regulated to optimize its benefits and minimize its costs. A primary purpose of this book is to shine a light on the different parts of the private criminal justice system so that we can better understand their strengths and weaknesses. In this chapter, we will revisit these weaknesses and examine ways in which they can be mitigated or eliminated.

PRIVATE POLICE

Chapter 4 discussed two different types of private police: paid private law enforcement, such as retail store detectives and security guards, and volunteer organizations, such as the Guardian Angels and Neighborhood Watch programs. In that chapter, two primary distinctions stood out between private police and their public counterparts. First, the level of training of private police was generally far below the level that public police receive, especially for volunteer private police. Second, as non-state actors, private police were not bound by the constitutional limits that restrict the public police.

Improved training for private police could provide a number of benefits. As we saw in Chapters 4 and 8, private police officers often become involved in confrontations, and they occasionally resort to force or violence. They must also interact with a large cross-section of society, sometimes under situations of great stress, and they are subject to the same implicit biases as the rest of the population. Despite this, training requirements for private police range from weak to nonexistent, depending on the type of private police and the jurisdiction in which they operate.

As we saw in Chapter 4, there is a wide range of private parties who engage in law enforcement actions, from individuals who happen to observe a crime and decide to make a citizen's arrest, to volunteer Neighborhood Watch organizations of 5 to 100 people, to giant corporations that provide security guards to hundreds of companies. For example, Allied Universal, the largest provider of security guards in the country, employs 140,000 private security officers who provide security services to "commercial office buildings, stores, universities, defense plants, banks and many other locations" throughout the United States.[1] None of these individuals receives any special powers from state or local legislatures; thus, they have no greater legal rights than an average citizen. This also means, however, that they are hard to regulate, as there are virtually no statutes specifically designed to empower or regulate private security forces.

This stands in stark contrast with the extensive qualifications and training required for those who become public police officers. Although the requirements vary from state to state and even within states, almost all police officers must have at least a high school education; some police departments require associate degrees as well. Recruits must also pass a physical and psychological evaluation and are subjected to a background check. Finally, recruits are sent to a police academy where they receive an average of twenty-one weeks of instruction on how to do their job, including firearms training, lectures on criminal law, the development of leadership and communications skills, training on de-escalation tactics, and diversity training.[2] In addition, police officers must complete a certain number of hours of training every year to ensure their skills remain sharp.

The only universal regulation that applies to private police, oddly enough, is a restriction on the types of uniforms they can wear. Many states have passed statutes to ensure that private security guards cannot be confused with public police.[3] This emphasis is perhaps not too surprising given the history of controversy surrounding the uniforms of public police when they first came into existence. Other than this relatively uncontroversial rule, private police are only subjected to a patchwork of regulations.[4] Some states or municipalities require licensing for private security who carry firearms;[5] many more require licensing for private detectives.[6] However, the vast majority of private police are not subject to any training requirements at all.

Of course, state-enforced regulation is not the only way to encourage training for private police. Traditional market forces have led many private security firms – or private companies that employ their own security – to ensure that the private police they employ have at least a minimum level of qualifications and competence. Private police do not enjoy the qualified immunity protections of their public counterparts, so any abuse of authority could lead to an expensive amount of liability, to say nothing of the reputational hit suffered by their client. As noted by Farhang Heydari, the Executive Director of the Policing Project at the NYU School of Law:

> At a policy level, because the private sector is subject to market pressures, private entities can show greater responsiveness to potential for civil liability and even media scrutiny .... This is likely why there are examples of private industry implementing their own accountability mechanisms, such as ethics boards, codes of conduct, impact statements, and whistleblowing. These mechanisms are particularly prominent around emerging technologies, where government regulation struggles to keep pace.[7]

These dramatically divergent levels of training have a positive aspect as well: Private police perform such a wide variety of tasks, from guarding warehouses overnight to patrolling residential neighborhoods, that a one-size-fits-all regulatory scheme does not really make sense. At one level, it seems appropriate for the employers of private police to demand (and pay for) the level of training they believe is necessary, based on the financial risk of civil liability. Critics of private law enforcement often point to the significant number of tort cases against private security guards as proof that private police do in fact violate the rights of suspects.[8] Although these cases surely provide evidence that some private security guards do abuse their power, the fact itself is not too surprising – with over a million private police interacting daily with the general population, frequently in confrontational situations, it is inevitable that some of them will mistreat civilians. The large number of successful tort cases could equally be seen as evidence that the tort system is working: Suspects whose rights are violated by public police are able to bring suit and win damages.

Nonetheless, some scholars have argued that the potential for civil lawsuits brought against members of a neighborhood watch or a private border patrol who overstep their legal powers is an insufficient tool for regulating their conduct. As Professor Sharon Finegan of South Texas College of Law noted:

> A civil suit is ... unlikely to be an effective remedy for conduct that violates an individual's civil rights under these circumstances. Just as a criminal suspect is unlikely to have the resources or knowledge to file a § 1983 action against a public officer who violates his or her civil liberties, it follows that a suspect would also be unlikely to file such an action against private individuals who encroach upon his civil liberties. In addition, even if an individual has the resources to take the case to

trial and has the evidence to support liability, the likely recovery in such a case is typically quite small. Thus, there is not great financial incentive for an individual to file a civil suit to recover for civil rights violations committed by private neighborhood watch members.[9]

Professor Finegan has a number of suggestions for enhancing the regulatory oversight of private police, including passing laws that limit their ability "to carry weapons while on patrol" and to "confront suspects in the course of their duties"; mandating arrest when private police violate the criminal law; reducing the burdens on filing a civil suit against private police (or providing for a minimum level of statutory damages for those civil suits); and requiring certification of neighborhood watch programs, which would "mandate... a certain amount of training to participate in law enforcement activities."[10]

These suggestions are no doubt well intentioned, but in practice most of them would require a nearly impossible degree of line drawing. When exactly is a private citizen engaging in "law enforcement duties"? This book has used a very broad definition of "private police," encompassing both paid security guards and individuals who volunteer in neighborhood watch programs. Would the registration requirements apply to individuals who put a neighborhood watch sticker in their window and spend a few hours each week looking out their window for suspicious activity? When exactly is a private police officer "on patrol"? Furthermore, restrictions on carrying weapons in public areas would likely be unconstitutional given the Supreme Court's current interpretation of the Second Amendment.[11]

The best solution among Professor Finegan's proposals is to increase incentives and lower burdens for those who wish to file civil suits against private police. Public police receive extra protection from civil suits through the doctrine of qualified immunity: As long as public police officers do not act in bad faith, they are immune from tort or criminal liability for assault, false imprisonment, or trespass.[12] However, there is little reason why private police should have any special license to negligently cause another person harm.[13] As we saw in Chapter 4, private security guards enjoy some special immunities through what are known as "merchant's privilege" statutes, but, for the most part, statutory law treats private police no differently from any other private citizens.[14] Thus, if a private officer searches private property without the consent of the owner, their action generally constitutes a trespass, and if a security guard wrongfully arrests or detains another individual, they may be exposed to civil liability for false imprisonment.[15] In theory, the private tort system could be an effective method of regulating the conduct of private police by deterring unlawful trespasses and detentions. In practice, barriers to filing civil lawsuits and the often-nominal level of damages that are awarded for one instance of trespass or one instance of wrongful detention mean that such lawsuits are uncommon, and thus they are an insufficient deterrent for careless actions by private police. Lowering the procedural barriers to filing a civil suit and creating a statutory minimum for damages would encourage more lawsuits, and thus allow the civil torts system to be a more effective regulator of private police conduct.

The second significant distinction between public police and private police is that private police are not bound by the Fourth Amendment's restrictions on search and seizure or *Miranda*'s restrictions on interrogations. Scholars who study private police frequently call for a change to this policy, arguing that, as private police have taken over so much of everyday policing, our constitutional rights will become almost meaningless unless they also protect us from private actions.[16] Nevertheless, the Supreme Court has consistently held that the protections of the Fourth and Fifth Amendments apply only to public employees and private parties who are deemed to be "state actors." The courts use three factors to determine if a private actor qualifies as a state actor: (1) the extent to which the private party relies on governmental assistance and benefits, (2) whether the private party is performing a traditional governmental function, and (3) whether the injury caused is aggravated in a unique way by the incidents of governmental authority.[17]

At first, it seems as though most private security guards would qualify as "state actors" under these factors: They often work closely with public police to perform their duties;[18] criminal law enforcement is arguably a "traditional governmental function";[19] and the injury caused by improper searches or coercive interrogations is certainly aggravated by the state when the tainted evidence is used to convict a defendant in court.[20] However, as pointed out by Professor Sklansky, this argument ends up proving too much: If applied literally, it becomes nearly impossible to distinguish between private police and ordinary private citizens who happen to carry out a law enforcement function.[21] Public law enforcement provides assistance not just to private security companies but to many individuals and groups: commercial establishments, neighborhood associations, schools, individual citizens, and so on.[22] Even if we concede that policing is a "traditional governmental function" (and, as noted in Chapter 2, given the long history and current dominance of private policing, this is not a self-evident proposition), why would the state action doctrine apply to private security guards who make arrests, but not to an ordinary citizen who makes an arrest? After all, by making the arrest, both are engaging in the same traditional governmental function.[23] And the same argument applies to the "unique aggravation" prong – although the state may ultimately use its unique authority to punish defendants as a result of the actions of private security guards, it uses the same authority to punish defendants when any private citizen provides evidence to the courts.[24] Thus, given the current status of the state action doctrine for criminal procedure cases, there is no way to legally distinguish between private police and private citizens.[25]

It is possible that courts may find their way out of this doctrinal dilemma,[26] but the more fundamental question at this stage is whether they should. The Bill of Rights was adopted explicitly to protect citizens from government action, not from each other; thus, enforcing its protections against private citizens seems contrary to its purpose. And, even in modern times, there is no significant political pressure to change the status quo. Only one state (Texas) has passed a law that applies the exclusionary rule to bar evidence uncovered by private parties that engage in illegal searches.[27] When a court in California ruled that the state's exclusionary rule applied to private police, the people overturned the decision in a referendum.[28] In segmented societies, such as private companies, individuals have often consented to searches of their offices or computers by their employer.

Furthermore, applying the exclusionary rule to the actions of private police would not necessarily have a significant impact on their behavior; as we saw in Chapter 4, often, the private police (and their clients) have no intention of bringing formal criminal charges against a suspected criminal, preferring to work out a private agreement or engage in a private disposition. Of course, constitutional protections could also be enforced through civil lawsuits, but, as noted earlier, private police are already subjected to private lawsuits when they violate a person's common law rights; thus, creating more causes of action based on violation of constitutional rights seems unnecessary. In addition, statutes already exist to ban the most severe violations of privacy – for example, wiretapping a phone is expressly illegal unless conducted by public police who have obtained a special court order.[29] Thus, the need to enforce constitutional protections against private police is not as great as it might at first seem.

PRIVATE CRIMINAL SETTLEMENTS

Unlike the enforcement arm of our private criminal justice system, which can be roughly quantified in terms of numbers and cost, there is no way to know the amount of private criminal settlements that take place each year. As noted in Chapter 6, almost all of the private criminal settlements that do occur are technically illegal under state laws that prohibit blackmail. Therefore, the first question to resolve in deciding how to regulate private criminal settlements is whether these agreements should be legalized. Chapter 6 examined in depth the various utilitarian and retributive arguments in favor of criminalizing blackmail in general and private criminal settlements specifically. It turns out that, although many people have an intuitive belief that blackmail should be illegal, the doctrinal justifications for criminalizing this behavior are weak.

Therefore, the first step toward regulating private criminal settlements is to legalize them. Obviously, this is a controversial proposition, especially for those who are not convinced that these settlements can further the goals of the criminal justice system. However, as noted in Chapter 5, these settlements offer multiple benefits, such as deterring future criminal behavior and punishing those who commit crimes. Also, there is good reason to believe that these settlements will continue in some form, whether they are legal or not.

One obvious danger of allowing private criminal settlements is that the party who is being paid not to report the crime would have an incentive to help keep the crime secret, and might assist the alleged perpetrator in covering up the crime. This danger would not be as great as it may first appear – once a party has been paid to remain silent, they would have little incentive to ensure that others did not learn about the crime. However, there is a possibility that a potential blackmailer would work to destroy evidence or otherwise thwart public law enforcement *before* they approached the alleged perpetrator – such actions would strengthen their hand in negotiations, as they would be able to show that they were the only way that the public authorities would learn about the crime. Therefore, existing laws that prohibit someone from assisting in covering up a crime should be strictly enforced – in fact, sentences for these crimes should be increased in order to increase deterrence against this kind of crime.

The final challenge with private criminal settlement is the information asymmetry that often exists between the parties. Often, the private criminal settlement involves a repeat player with sophisticated knowledge of the criminal justice system negotiating with an accused person who has far less experience and understanding of the process. In an ideal world, before the accused agreed to a private criminal settlement, they would have a complete understanding of both the procedural protections they would receive in the public criminal justice system and the punishment they would be likely to receive if they were formally charged. Attaining this level of understanding for every alleged perpetrator would be impossible; even in the public plea-bargaining context, where the defendant is advised by an attorney, the complexities of the law and the true level of risk faced by the accused is challenging to convey. However, an important first step would be to establish rules that prohibit either party from making misleading statements during the course of the private negotiations. Thus, the laws that outlaw private criminal settlements could be amended to merely criminalize fraudulent statements that are made to induce a person to enter into an agreement.

Legalizing private criminal settlements will require more than just amending the laws prohibiting blackmail; it would also require limiting the spread of so-called mandated reporter laws. Almost every state has some version of these laws, which make it illegal not to report a crime under certain circumstances. The most common of these are narrowly targeted to protect the most vulnerable or to focus on crimes that are unlikely to be detected by other witnesses, such as laws that require certain professionals to report signs of child abuse.[30] However, other states have instituted far broader laws that make it a crime to fail to report a felony once someone learns that a felony has occurred,[31] and there is wide support for extending existing laws to cover more people and more criminal activity.[32]

Scholars are divided on the wisdom of these laws. On the one hand, forcing private citizens to report crimes to the public police would certainly increase the effectiveness of law enforcement, resulting in more arrests, more convictions, and ultimately more criminals in prison.[33] However, as Professor Wayne Logan of Florida State University argues, there are significant downsides to broad mandated reporter rules. To start with, these laws infringe on our personal autonomy, requiring citizens to take an action instead of merely prohibiting specific acts. However, their true effect on our society is more insidious: "The duty [to report] would perpetuate the sense that we are a nation of 'citizen spies,' as in the former East Germany or modern China. Ultimately, if allowed to come to full fruition, the duty to report would help promote what philosopher Michel Foucault called 'responsibilization,' a way of 'managing the public by having it manage itself.'"[34]

In addition, broader mandated reporting rules would de facto criminalize private criminal settlements, as the very essence of these agreements requires the private party to agree to *not* report the crime to the police. Of course, some of Professor Logan's critiques of mandated reporting rules would also apply to allowing widespread private criminal settlements: Every private citizen could theoretically be a citizen spy – but, instead of working for the government, they would be working freelance in order to enrich themselves. This may not be as ominous as the state forcing all of its citizens to become government informants, and it certainly does not infringe on personal autonomy – in fact, giving private parties the option to enter into consensual agreements to resolve a criminal dispute increases the autonomy of both the witness and the accused.[35] However, allowing private criminal settlements could encourage individuals to increase their surveillance of their fellow citizens, which could significantly fray societal bonds. As Professor Logan notes in the context of mandated reporter laws: "the imposition of a legal duty to report could significantly diminish social trust and interpersonal relations."[36] Giving private parties the freedom to settle criminal disputes could end up having the same effect.

PRIVATE CRIMINAL ADJUDICATIONS

Although private criminal adjudications are not always completely transparent, they are not nearly as secretive as private criminal settlements, so it is easier to set up rules to regulate their procedures. Possible improvements can be grouped into three categories: protecting the rights of the accused; ensuring that the proceedings are privileged; and training and licensing the individuals who act as judges or mediators in the proceedings.

The most controversial question regarding private criminal adjudications involves the level of procedural protections given to the alleged criminal. On the one hand, one of the primary benefits of an alternative criminal dispute resolution is to create a streamlined, more efficient system. Also, the stakes are usually not as high for private criminal adjudications as they are for a criminal trial – the accused will not be facing months or years of prison time, but merely the suspension or revocation of certain benefits that they had been enjoying. On the other hand, some minimal level of due process seems appropriate before labelling someone a criminal, even if it is only a private organization that is doing the labelling.

The protections set out in Matthews v. Eldridge seem like a good starting point for determining the appropriate level of due process for private criminal adjudications. Legally, these factors apply only to state actors who are seeking to revoke a property interest, but the case sets out a set of standards that serve as a good compromise between the strict rules that apply to the public criminal justice system and the scant protections that some private criminal adjudications provide. Under these standards, the adjudicative body must give the defendant notice and an opportunity to be heard by the decision-maker, and the process must balance the interests of the defendant, the risk of an erroneous deprivation of the defendant's privacy rights, and the fiscal and administrative burden to the private organization conducting the adjudication.[37] These factors are flexible enough to ensure that defendants facing greater consequences from a private adjudication – expulsion from a university or being banned from their profession – will be afforded greater protections than those who face only a minor censure or a small monetary fine.

Significantly, these standards do not specifically mandate a right to an attorney. Although this right is critical in public criminal law cases, with their complex procedures and formal rules, it is not necessarily appropriate for most private criminal adjudications. Private criminal adjudications offer many benefits: They can be less adversarial than a public criminal proceeding, they can address broader issues beyond the narrow legal questions that gave rise to the initial conflict, and they can encourage greater participation by the parties. Attorneys can interfere with these potential benefits – adjudications become more confrontational, the dispute becomes narrowly focused on the specific legal issues, and parties become more passive as the attorneys drive the process forward. Attorneys can influence the nature of private adjudications in a more subtle way as well – they can lead institutions to promulgate more procedural rules, which in turn leads to a greater need for attorneys to participate, and so the increased complexity of the proceedings and the increasing dominance of lawyers can reinforce each other in a feedback loop.

The other two proposals for private criminal adjudications are less controversial. First, statements and testimony in private criminal adjudications should be privileged so that they cannot be used in any future public criminal case. The concept of privileging communications and statements in alternative dispute resolutions is nothing new: Mediations depend on such confidentiality, and the Model Standards of Conduct for Mediators protects the confidentiality of all information obtained during mediation.[38] Meanwhile, the Federal Rules of Evidence and all of the state counterparts of these rules preclude all statements made during civil settlement and plea negotiations from being admitted at trial under almost all circumstances.[39] This confidentiality allows communication to be more open during these proceedings, and also makes it possible to tolerate lower procedural protections, as statements made in the more informal procedures cannot later be used against the parties in the higher stakes of an actual trial.

As it turns out, the privilege for private criminal adjudications needs to be even stronger than the privilege that exists for private mediation, as the mediation privilege has an exception if the evidence is used in a court proceeding involving a felony.[40] The privilege for private criminal adjudications would have to extend to all future court cases – civil and criminal – as does the evidentiary privilege for settlement conferences and plea bargaining. The contours of this privilege would have to be clearly communicated – for example, the facilitators of a private adjudication might need to affirmatively inform all of the parties at the outset that all statements in the official proceedings are privileged, but that other statements made during the investigation or informal meetings between the parties are not.

The final proposal would be to encourage a training and licensing scheme for private criminal adjudicators. This could be a top-down regulation imposed by Congress or a president for certain types of adjudications (for example, Title IX proceedings in university settings), or it could be a decision made by each institution that conducts private criminal adjudications to ensure that those who preside over these proceedings are qualified to do so. Many such institutions, from colleges to professional associations, conduct private criminal adjudications with employees who do not have extensive training in adjudicating or mediating disputes. The results are often disastrous. As one commentator noted:

> [Anyone] who has sat on a university disciplinary committee knows just how amateur and haphazard these institutions can be. They work adequately for some kinds of issues; indeed, it is useful, even edifying, to participate in an untutored group of faculty and students on a disciplinary committee trying to struggle with issues of academic cheating, dress codes, how much robust speech should be allowed in classrooms, or whether a fraternity prank has gone too far. But college hearings are often disasters when dealing with more serious criminal matters, such as harassment, theft, stalking, assault, and especially sexual assault.[41]

This stands in stark contrast with the civil side of alternative dispute resolution, in which there is a well-established industry that provides a deep pool of certified mediators and arbitrators to those who seek to resolve their disputes.[42] After decades of growth, civil alternative dispute resolution is a large and well-respected industry. Ideally, private criminal adjudicators should be as plentiful and well trained as their counterparts on the civil side.

PRIVATE CRIMINAL DISPOSITIONS

Of all of the aspects of the private criminal justice system, private criminal dispositions will be the hardest to regulate. Under the traditional conception of vigilantism, vigilante conduct by definition involves illegal conduct, and so it would be impossible to set up legal rules to control and legitimate such actions. Paul and Sarah Robinson, the authors of SHADOW VIGILANTES, are sympathetic to at least some of the individuals who undertake private criminal dispositions; although they concede that every vigilante action erodes respect for the law[43] and that vigilantes often lack the necessary training,[44] they argue that vigilante actions can sometimes be morally justified.[45] As noted in Chapter 8, they propose ten "rules for the moral vigilante" that are meant to limit vigilante actions to situations in which they are necessary and likely to do the least amount of harm. However, the Robinsons are not proposing a set of legal regulations; they are merely creating guidelines for when vigilante actions are morally appropriate. Under their definition, vigilante conduct is always illegal. Of course, as the Robinsons point out, just because the law does not recognize a vigilante defense, juries often do. As long as juries have the power to nullify a crime, the distinction between moral vigilantes and immoral vigilantes will always have at least some practical significance.

However, our definition of private criminal disposition – any private action taken in response to criminal activity that punishes the alleged perpetrator – is broad enough to encompass both legal and illegal actions. An individual or a group that removes privileges that had been granted to an alleged perpetrator or engages in the public shaming of an alleged perpetrator does not violate the law. Other types of private criminal dispositions, such as causing property damage or doing physical violence, are usually (but not always) illegal. The key to "regulating" private criminal dispositions is to craft the criminal law and its defenses in such a way as to encourage the type of private criminal dispositions that we believe are beneficial to society and criminalize the types of private criminal dispositions that are not.

One relatively uncontroversial method of regulating private criminal dispositions is to extend the civil liability proposal that was made for private police and ensure that anyone who imposes a private punishment on an alleged perpetrator is liable for damages that might occur to third parties. Professor Jay B. Kesan of the University of Illinois and Professor Ruperto Majuca of Weber State University propose this rule in the context of companies that "hack back" against those who break into their computer systems.[46] Professors Kesan and Majuca believe that private criminal dispositions are a necessary evil in the context of cybercrime: "[T]raditional law enforcement schemes simply do not work in cyberspace because of the speed by which attacks cause damage to e-commerce sites and also because hackers can stage attacks from multiple jurisdictions with varying cybercrime laws and procedures for prosecuting internet crimes."[47] They also argue that the company conducting the hack-back must "only use force necessary to defend their property and not needlessly destroy the hacker's digital assets."[48] In short, they propose rules for the private use of "violence" in cyberspace that are nearly identical to the rules that exist for the private use of violence in the physical world: proportionality and civil liability for damage to innocent parties. They support these acts for the same reason that acts of private violence are allowed in the physical world: Under certain conditions, public law enforcement is unable to react in time and so the only way for innocent victims to protect themselves is to engage in their own limited use of force.

This leads us to the most challenging aspect of the private criminal justice system to regulate: the rules regarding the use of force in self-defense or the defense of others. The basic concept of self-defense – that innocent people have a natural right to defend themselves against the imminent use of violence – has been around for centuries. Moreover, the theory behind the self-defense doctrine is consistent with the theory behind private criminal justice more broadly: Under certain conditions, the public police are not able to ensure that the law is enforced and so private individuals must enforce the criminal law on their own. On the other hand, as we saw in the last chapter, private enforcers sometimes initiate violent encounters and then use broad self-defense laws to shield their aggressive actions.

Unfortunately, society is unlikely to come to any consensus about when a private party is "initiating a violent encounter." The extremely polarized reaction to the high-profile instances of private use of force in the Zimmerman and Rittenhouse cases show that Americans have different conceptions of what types of actions will brand a person as an initial aggressor, thus rendering them ineligible for a self-defense claim. However, as a general rule, ambiguity in the law is a thing to be avoided, and the ambiguity surrounding the initial aggressor rule is no exception. Professor Lee suggests resolving this ambiguity by proposing two reforms to self-defense law:

(1) Judges must give an "initial aggressor" instruction if the defendant's words or acts created a reasonable apprehension of physical harm in another person.
(2) Judges must give an initial aggressor instruction whenever an individual claiming self-defense displayed a firearm in a threatening manner or pointed that firearm at another person outside the home, unless the defendant displayed or pointed the firearm in response to a credible threat of physical harm and the defendant's intent in pointing the firearm was to avoid a physical confrontation.[49]

The first proposal sets out an objective "reasonableness" standard that creates a negligence *mens rea* for every private enforcer. In other words, even if the private party does not believe and is wholly unaware of the fact that others might see their actions as threatening, they will be barred from claiming self-defense if a reasonable person found their behavior threatening. Although this standard will almost certainly deter individuals from engaging in private law enforcement in dangerous situations, it appears to be a fair standard to impose on self-declared private enforcers. If a person takes it upon themselves to enter dangerous situations to enforce the law, they can be legally required to take care that their actions do not appear personally threatening to others. However, even with such a consistent, unambiguous standard in place, there will still be differences from jurisdiction to jurisdiction – actions that a Massachusetts judge believes creates a reasonable apprehension of harm may not lead a Texas judge to the same conclusion. And, of course, this proposal merely changes the law that is given to juries; different juries in different jurisdictions – or even in the same jurisdiction – will have different ideas of what kind of conduct is objectively threatening.

Professor Lee's second proposal is less compelling. As noted in Chapter 8, the term "displayed a firearm in a threatening manner" on its own will do little to resolve the current ambiguity in the law – the mere presence of a firearm may seem threatening to some individuals, while others may not feel threatened unless the gun is pointed at them. Professor Lee limits this ambiguity by imposing a reasonableness requirement on the proposal, saying that "the judge will instruct the jury on the initial aggressor doctrine in instances where the defendant's acts created a *reasonable* apprehension of physical harm . . . ."[50] However, if this is the case, then the second proposal seems unnecessary; the first proposal already mandates an initial aggressor instruction when the defendant's actions create a reasonable apprehension of physical harm. The exceptions in the second proposal make sense, especially the intent requirement, as the only legitimate purpose for using force or deadly force in the self-defense context is to prevent violence.[51] Thus, the proposal may be more concisely stated as follows: Judges must give an initial aggressor instruction if the defendant's words or acts created a reasonable apprehension of physical harm in another person, unless the defendant displayed or pointed the firearm in response to a credible threat of physical harm and the defendant's intent in pointing the firearm was to avoid a physical confrontation.[52]

CONCLUSION

As a general rule, the private criminal justice system is not particularly transparent and not especially subject to regulation. Private police often act with discretion and seek to bypass the public criminal justice system in large part because they want to avoid the rules and regulations that it imposes. The competitive advantage of private criminal adjudications is their streamlined procedure and lack of regulations. Private criminal settlements and private criminal dispositions are often illegal, and as long as they remain so there is little hope of regulating them so that they can be more fair.

Nevertheless, the future of the private criminal justice system can still be shaped by rules that we adopt to monitor and regulate it. As with any other type of regulation, the exact contours of these regulations depend on the specific values that we want to further, and in many ways the values that we are balancing are not that different from those that we consider when we discuss the laws of the public criminal justice system: security, civil rights, efficiency, personal autonomy, and equality. The rules that we choose to adopt will reflect how we balance these sometimes conflicting values.

The most significant value judgment that we need to make, of course, is whether each of the aspects of the private criminal justice system are beneficial or detrimental to society. A consistent theme of this book is that the existence of the private criminal justice system is inevitable – it has always existed and, although its extent and influence may wax and wane, it will always continue to exist. However, we can develop rules that encourage its growth or rules that limit its impact. Private police – both paid security guards and volunteers – can be given wide discretion in deciding how to proceed when they observe criminal activity, or we can restrict how private police interact with suspects and impose mandated reporter laws to reduce private police officers' discretion after they apprehend those they accuse of a crime. We can encourage private criminal settlements by legalizing them, or we can crack down on them by enforcing existing laws against extortion. We could tighten the self-defense laws to criminalize more instances of private criminal dispositions and thus deter private citizens from getting involved when they observe suspected criminal activity, or we could loosen the self-defense laws and encourage such involvement. This leads us to the ultimate question posed by this book: Does the private criminal justice system make the country a better, safer, and fairer place or would we be better off if it had a smaller footprint? The final chapter proposes some answers to this question.

10

The Verdict on Private Criminal Justice

This book has detailed the various manifestations of the private criminal justice system, from the millions of paid security guards and volunteers who make up a vast private law enforcement network, to the private settlements, adjudications, and dispositions that are the natural and inevitable outgrowth of that network. The reasons for the growth of the private criminal justice system can be traced directly to the perceived and actual failures of the public criminal justice system. Private individuals, institutions, and companies are seeking criminal justice services that better meet their needs, while the draconian punishments of the public criminal justice system lead defendants to opt into private settlements and private adjudications in which they have more control over the process and outcome.

The very existence of an alternative criminal justice system is admittedly a controversial proposition, even if it is meant only to supplement and not replace the traditional criminal justice system. Up until now, this book has presented the private criminal justice system as inevitable, but, as noted in the previous chapter, the size and influence of the private criminal justice system are the result of the types of laws and regulations we create. Thus, some normative decisions must be made as to the desirability of different aspects of the private criminal justice system.

As we have seen throughout this book, every phase of the private criminal justice system has its strong detractors. And many of the critiques have merit: Private police are often poorly trained and are subject to little government regulation; the power and information asymmetry of private criminal settlements can lead to unfair dispositions; many private criminal adjudications lack basic due process protections; and private criminal dispositions usually take place without any formal or even informal procedure to determine guilt. Even the nontraditional approach to adjudication and post-conviction resolution offered by restorative justice has been rejected by many practitioners and commentators. Given these current debates, there is no doubt that a private industry of criminal dispute adjudication and resolution to accompany the current private policing network would be extremely controversial. Many academics, prosecutors, defense attorneys, judges, and lawmakers would be opposed to the very existence of such an industry. In this chapter, we will evaluate these critiques of a private criminal justice system and discuss the potential benefits that the system provides.

REPRESENTING THE "COMMUNITY INTEREST"

Our first step is to return to the very first question we initially asked about a private criminal justice system: Is it even possible to have a "criminal justice system" without the state? As we noted in Chapter 1, the theoretical objections to a private criminal justice system are threefold: first, that a crime is, by definition, defined by the state; second, that a criminal justice system requires coercion and violence, tools that are traditionally reserved for the state to employ; and, third, that a criminal action is an offense against the state and so the state must have a say in the response to such activity. The primary reply to the first objection is that society has reached a general consensus of what is considered criminal activity, even without state legislatures passing laws that officially define it. The reply to the second objection is that a response to criminal activity does not have to include coercion or violence and, even if it does, the state has legitimized the use of private force in a number of different contexts. However, it is the third objection that concerns us in this chapter: whether a criminal justice system can be legitimate if the state is not involved. We know that a crime is distinct from any other harmful activity because it is an action that violates the social contract. The perpetrator has transgressed not just against another individual, but rather against all of society. Thus, it seems wrong to cut the state actor out of the process that responds to crime. As we have seen, private actors – victims, witnesses, and perpetrators – often choose to opt out of the public criminal justice system because a private response to criminal activity better suits their individual needs. In prior chapters, we have seen how these private needs often serve society's needs as well, by punishing wrongdoers and deterring future criminal conduct. However, for many critics of private criminal justice, this confluence of results is insufficient. The public criminal justice system serves an explicit function that is absent from the private criminal justice system: ensuring that the response to criminal activity meets the norms and expectations of society.

Many crimes, such as sex work, the use or sale of contraband such as drugs or firearms, and gambling, have no individual victim and are a transgression only against society. Other crimes, such as illegal dumping of pollution or securities fraud, have only a large and ill-defined group of individual victims.[1] In other words, all crimes cause a "moral injury" against society, but only some crimes cause physical, emotional, or financial injury to a victim or victims.[2] While a private criminal justice system could repair a victim's physical, emotional, or financial injury, it would be unable to address a moral injury – the very element of the action that defines it as "criminal." Many current restorative justice programs recognize this fact and include a community representative at the mediation,[3] and when cases are referred to restorative justice proceedings from court, the ultimate resolution must almost always be approved by a judge before the criminal case is dismissed.[4]

There are a number of responses to this argument. The first and most radical response is to question the need for a tort/crime distinction at all. As far back as the 1970s, commentators were proposing a "restitutive theory" of criminal justice, in which the victim and the defendant would be the two parties and the primary (if not only) goal of the criminal justice system would be to repair the harm done to the victim.[5] Proponents of this new theory of criminal law pointed out that the tort system is ineffective in compensating crime victims; in reality, the vast majority of crime victims do not bring civil suit against the perpetrators and are left only with what the criminal justice system gives them.[6] There is also a legitimate question about why the system should force victims to bring an entirely separate action: Why, after being interviewed by detectives, prepared and placed on the stand by prosecutors, and cross-examined by defense attorneys, should the victim then need to find a lawyer and start all over again in order to repair the harm that was done?[7]

Although there seems to be little popular support for such a major paradigm shift in criminal law, there is certainly evidence that the distinction between crimes and torts is blurring somewhat: The growing popularity and effectiveness of the victims' rights movement has led the public criminal justice system to be more focused on private harms rather than public harms.[8] Nearly forty years ago, it was observed that "the wide acceptance and use of restitution within the criminal justice system has already resulted in the partial merger of criminal and tort law."[9] Now, with restitution even more common and victims' rights legislation allowing victims to participate in various stages of the criminal process, the merger is even more apparent. The shift toward a more punitive public criminal justice system could even be seen as evidence of a desire to provide "moral restitution" to the victim rather than focusing on more utilitarian goals, such as rehabilitation, which might be better for society as a whole. Furthermore, as the criminal codes expand ever further into regulating more and more aspects of our life – economic activity, environmental activity, and so on – unlawful acts that have traditionally been thought of as private torts or civil regulatory violations are being reclassified as crimes.[10] Once again, when we look at the historical evolution of the criminal justice system, there is nothing inevitable or preordained about the state having a role in criminal prosecutions. It has been nearly nine hundred years since King Henry I declared that certain harms were crimes against both the state and the victim, but, for most of the time since then, both in England and later in the United States, the primary responsibility for prosecuting crimes fell to the private party who had been wronged.[11]

Admittedly, this response only goes so far. Whatever the extent that private interests have infiltrated the public criminal justice system, there is a general consensus among lay people and criminal law experts alike that the state or community interests should be represented in a criminal adjudication and ultimately reflected in the resolution.[12] However, this consensus does not necessarily lead to the conclusion that a public criminal justice system is better able to serve the needs of society than a private criminal justice system. The real question is as follows: How are community interests currently represented in the traditional public criminal justice system, and how are they represented in an alternative private system?

This question leads to the second response to those who believe the state must be involved in criminal proceedings. We have already seen that the public criminal justice system has its own problems: the marginalization of victims' needs, the overly punitive sentencing of defendants, and the lack of real participation by victims and defendants alike. Perhaps the most damning critique of the public criminal justice system – and the one that is most relevant to the question of privatization – is a criticism that is inextricably tied to its public nature: the pervasive politicization of the public criminal justice system.[13] This politicization affects every aspect of the public criminal justice system – the writing of criminal legislation, the policies of public police, the charging decisions by prosecutors, and the sentencing by judges – and calls into question whether or not the public criminal justice system can in fact represent the interests of the "community."[14]

In this context, "politicization" refers to two separate but related phenomena. Chapter 1 described how criminal justice policy was transformed in the final third of the twentieth century into a populist political issue, with dramatic results. Before the 1960s, criminal policy was left more or less to the expertise of the professionals – career police officers, prosecutors, judges, and even academics. Crime control was, for the most part, not mentioned in political campaigns, and legislators on the federal or even state level did relatively little to change the substantive or procedural aspects of criminal law. Indeed, the greatest change to substantive criminal codes during the first seventy years of the twentieth century was the Model Penal Code, which was designed by academics and other professionals to simplify and streamline substantive criminal law.[15]

Perhaps in a democratic society, the eventual capture of crime policy by the voting public was inevitable. What is not inevitable – indeed, what seems curious – is why the politicization of crime led so quickly and directly to an abandonment of rehabilitation and an increase in the severity of sentences. Various scholars have attempted to explain this phenomenon. For example, David Garland of New York University has hypothesized that the United States went through a "cultural shift" in how people viewed crime, resulting in an internalized crime consciousness and overly emotional reactions toward crime.[16] However, there is no question that police, prosecutors, legislators, and judges – most of whom are elected to their office – feel populist pressure to adopt a very punitive level of criminal justice.

The other meaning of the term "politicization" in this context refers to the institutional incentives that are created by the public criminal justice system. Legislators can appear tough on crime by criminalizing more and more behavior and then counting on prosecutors to wisely choose which crimes will be prosecuted and which will not. Prosecutors find it easier to seek convictions with more crimes to choose from (many of which have overlapping elements or are simply traditional crimes with a difficult-to-prove element removed) and so they encourage legislators to criminalize more behavior.[17] The same incentive structure exists for sentencing policies: By increasing sentences, legislators can impress their constituents while relying on prosecutors to charge crimes appropriately.[18] Prosecutors can then use these higher sentences during the plea-bargaining process to get exactly the sentence they want with less effort, thus increasing the efficiency of the office. As the late William Stuntz of Harvard Law School explained, "prosecutors are better off when criminal law is broad than when it is narrow. Legislators are better off when prosecutors are better off."[19]

The result of these two political realities is well known: a public criminal justice system with an overly broad penal code and an incarceration rate far higher than any other country in the world. It is fair to ask whether this system truly represents what the "community" actually wants. Indeed, it is fair to ask what kind of "community" we seek to represent in the criminal justice system, or even whether a country as heterogeneous as ours could even have one monolithic "community."[20] Certainly one of the most significant effects of the politicization of crime over the last six decades has been the centralization of crime policy, as the federal government has become more and more involved in criminal law.[21] The public criminal justice system has taken on a life of its own, fueled by populist politics and sustained by institutional incentives, which continue to criminalize more behavior and punish more severely those who transgress.

Paradoxically, a private criminal justice system could actually enhance the influence of community interests in our criminal justice policy – but only if the private and public criminal justice systems can work together. It is true that if the private response to criminal activity is hidden from the state, it might deviate substantially from what society considers appropriate. On the other hand, if a state actor (such as a public police officer or a prosecutor) is aware of the private response to criminal activity, the response will have to be within a range of acceptable actions, or else the public criminal justice system will intervene and interfere with the private response. Therefore, in evaluating the desirability of private criminal justice, it is useful to divide the system into two categories: the "hidden" segments and the "open" segments. The more open the private criminal justice system is, the more likely it is to conform to societal norms.

Chapter 7 explored how private criminal adjudications and restorative justice programs share many attributes, including a greater focus on the needs of the defendant and the victim, and the bypassing of the complex procedural thicket of rules that govern the traditional public criminal justice system. The chapter also began to speculate about a new industry of private mediators that could resolve criminal disputes using restorative justice principles before they ever reached the public criminal justice system. It is now time to ask what such an industry would look like, and whether it would be a positive development for society.

Restorative justice supporters, like supporters of other alternative dispute resolution programs, frequently trumpet the fact that the process is "flexible, transparent, and creative in its approach,"[22] which allows participants to experiment with procedures and resolutions outside the traditional criminal process. Restorative justice advocates also emphasize the need for accountability – in fact, restorative justice procedures not only insist on making the defendant accountable for their actions, but also look to the community to be accountable for the causes and the solutions to the criminal activity.[23] And just as private policing empowers those who take responsibility for their own security, restorative justice empowers both victims and defendants to resolve their dispute – in fact, empowerment is perhaps the primary tenet behind the restorative justice movement.[24]

Given these similarities in attributes and ideologies, the next logical (and perhaps inevitable) step in this evolution is for private criminal adjudications to adopt the methods and goals of the restorative justice movement. In discussing potential reforms to private criminal adjudications, the previous chapter noted that, although these proceedings ought to provide a basic level of due process, such as the right to be notified of the charges and the right to be heard, it does not make sense to apply most of the strong procedural protections that are found in the public criminal justice system. Restorative justice proceedings, with their informal procedures and their focus on meeting the needs of the victim rather than punishing the defendant, also eschew many of the formal rules of the public criminal justice system. The previous chapter also pointed out that many of the organizations that currently conduct private criminal adjudications – such as universities and professional associations – may not have the expertise to mediate these disputes. Thus, these organizations may choose to contract out their adjudicative procedures with a new private criminal mediation industry.

At first, these private mediators would operate completely independently of public norms and community input. Private criminal mediators would be in charge of resolving the criminal dispute between the victim and the defendant and crafting a solution satisfactory to both of them. Like the actors in the public criminal justice system, these individuals would be professionals and specialists, applying their own expertise to make critical decisions about what kind of disposition would be appropriate.

However, these private actors will be different from public actors in very important ways. When individual actors in the public criminal justice system make decisions, they are in theory acting as the voice of the community – acting in conformance with their own belief of how the community would like them to respond. Sometimes this is a centralized decision – such as when a police chief institutes a policy of mandatory arrest for all domestic violence cases. Other times it is an individual decision, based on the professional's expertise and experience – such as when a prosecutor decides not to bring charges in a rape case because the evidence is too weak. In the end, there is a check on their individual exercise of power: The public individuals and institutions must ultimately answer to those who elected or appointed them[25] and thus they cannot stray too far from societal expectations.

In contrast, the actors in the private system would have different constraints on their decision-making. Unlike prosecutors and judges, the private mediators in the system would have to ensure that both sides are satisfied with the process and the outcome, as either the defendant or the victim would be able to choose to opt out at any time if they did not like what was happening. In the public system, of course, neither the victim nor the defendant has any say over the process, and each has very little say over the outcome.[26]

However, the public criminal justice system would provide even greater restraints on private criminal mediators. If these mediations were open, and the public prosecutors were aware of the dispositions that occurred, mediators would be forced to consider societal norms in crafting their resolutions. We have already discussed how resorting to the private criminal justice system would be optional, such that if either of the parties was not satisfied with the result, the case would be turned over to the public criminal justice system. In the case of the victim's or the defendant's dissatisfaction, either side could call off the mediation at any time, and the police would be called in to arrest and process the defendant under the public system. In the case of a resolution that both the victim and the accused agree to but that is outside the acceptable norms of the community, the process would be a little more indirect: On learning of the crime, the public police or prosecutor would investigate to determine how the dispute was resolved and, if the resolution was contrary to the interests of the community, the prosecutor would be obliged by public duty (and ultimately political considerations) to step in and bring formal public charges.[27]

The public prosecutor will not have unfettered power to overrule the results of the private adjudication; if the victim is satisfied with the outcome of the mediation, they may be much less willing to cooperate, thereby making the case much harder, although not impossible, to prosecute. Thus, the public criminal justice system will likely not get involved unless one or more of the following factors is present: the crime is so severe or affects enough individual citizens that it requires incarceration as a punishment, the private resolution is severely out of line with societal norms, or the private mediator who ran the dispute has a long record of repeatedly ignoring the community interest in crafting resolutions. The private criminal justice system will thereby be somewhat insulated from the public criminal justice system, as, in many contexts – particularly for smaller crimes or crimes isolated between a defendant and a victim – the prosecutor will determine that it is not worth the time or the resources to second-guess the result of the private adjudication and file public charges. However, any private criminal mediator (or private criminal mediation company) that wants to avoid its resolutions being made moot by a subsequent public prosecution will work to ensure that the community interests are taken into account when crafting solutions to criminal disputes. The more often and more dramatically a private mediator ignores the community interests, the more they will attract the disapprobation of public prosecutors, until ultimately the public prosecutor in the jurisdiction will routinely reject every one of that mediator's outcomes, thus lessening the incentive for either the defendant or the victim to participate in the private alternative, and eventually running the private mediator out of business.

This process of checks and balances could even work to regulate private criminal settlements. As we saw in Chapter 5, many employers of private police choose to reach a private agreement with the alleged perpetrator rather than call the authorities. After the accused is arrested by a private police officer or security guard, the private entity decides whether to turn the accused over to the public criminal justice system or handle the case privately. The accused has the same choice – agree to a private resolution or force the private entity to either call the public police or dismiss the case altogether. If both sides decide to handle the case privately, the parties resolve the case without state intervention. Both parties would always know that the default system – the public criminal law system – was available, and thus either party could choose to take their chances in the public system if they lost faith in the private resolution process.

Currently, almost all of these private resolutions are "hidden" segments of the private criminal justice system, as the public authorities never learn about either the crime or the agreement reached by the parties. As noted in Chapter 5, this lack of transparency can lead to information asymmetry between the private party and the accused, leading to unfair resolutions. It can also result in dispositions that are contrary to society's interest. One solution to this problem would be to force the private criminal settlements to be open, so that prosecutors would ultimately know about both the crime and the resolution that was reached. Although this would seem to remove the accused's incentive to participate in the process, in reality an open public settlement would still offer substantial benefits for the accused. The procedure would be streamlined, with the accused having more control over the process and the result. And the punishment would almost certainly be less than what the defendant would receive in the public criminal justice system. Public prosecutors would be notified of every case that was resolved by private settlement, and they would monitor the outcomes. As long as these outcomes were within a range that was acceptable to the prosecutor, the prosecutor would not need to intervene with their own charges. This would both constrain private settlements from straying too far from public norms and also provide valuable feedback to the actors in the public system on what most victims believed was a fair disposition for any given crime. In this way, private criminal resolutions could work within the public criminal justice system rather than hiding in the shadows.

This open version of the private criminal justice system will exist only at the suffrage of the public criminal justice system. If the public authorities in any given jurisdiction believe that a private criminal justice system is inappropriate, all they need to do is monitor the activities of every case processed through the private criminal justice system and bring formal criminal charges against all the defendants regardless of the outcome of the private mediation. No defendant would agree to private adjudication in such a jurisdiction, and the private criminal alternative (at least past the law enforcement stage) would simply wither away. A more libertarian jurisdiction might take the opposite view: As long as neither the victim nor the defendant complained, there would be no need to intervene in most cases, thus allowing private criminal adjudication and resolution systems to flourish (and thereby saving the public authorities a significant amount of money). Most jurisdictions, of course, will end up somewhere in the middle, allowing private criminal mediators free reign for misdemeanors or for certain specific crimes, such as theft or vandalism. As the authorities and the public get more comfortable with private criminal adjudications, and as certain private criminal mediators build reputations for incorporating the community interest into their resolutions, the types of crimes for which the public criminal justice system will allow private resolutions will probably increase.

In a universe of finite government resources, prosecutors will need to decide if it is worth the money to track down every single privately brokered resolution or if it is better for public authorities to only overrule the private criminal justice industry in egregious cases. It is this budgetary concern, more so than any ideological shift, that will eventually allow the open private criminal adjudicators to establish themselves. Once again, there is evidence that this interaction between the private and public criminal justice systems is already occurring. Consider the evolution of the Walmart retail chain regarding shoplifters caught in their stores (almost all of whom, of course, are apprehended by private security guards working for Walmart).[28] Originally, Walmart pursued an aggressive strategy toward thieves: The store managers would call a police officer and engage the public criminal justice system for every instance of shoplifting, whatever the amount of the loss or potential loss. Then, in the summer of 2006, Walmart changed its policy so that first-time thieves who stole merchandise worth less than $25 were let off with a warning instead. Walmart's reasoning was simple: Formal prosecution of an individual who steals a $6 magazine costs tens or hundreds of times that amount in salary for the private guards who process the arrest and lost work time for employees who must go to court. The reaction from the public criminal justice authorities to this shift in policy was frequently supportive – under the old policy, many small police departments had been forced to hire an additional officer just to process arrests from the local Walmart and prosecutors' offices and courts were no doubt equally burdened. In changing its rules, Walmart was simply falling into line with the policy of almost every major retail chain in the country for first-time petty thefts: handling the case privately instead of publicly.[29] In a very real sense, the public criminal justice authorities were more than happy to delegate this aspect of criminal justice response to the private sector.

It does not take too much imagination to envision the next step in this process. What should Walmart (or other retailers) do with individuals who are caught a second time stealing a $25 product? The warning was ineffective the first time, but it still seems like a waste of public and private resources to begin a public prosecution. What if the offender were told that if they worked for an hour stacking boxes or retrieving shopping carts from the lot, the police would not be alerted? Most of the accused would (rightfully) conclude this deal was in their best interest, the retailer would be compensated for the loss caused by the offense, and the government would save resources. Would police or prosecutors object that the "community interest" was not served by such an arrangement?

In order to bypass the state on even more serious crimes, it would probably be necessary – or at least helpful – to call in a private criminal mediator to help settle the dispute. What if an employee were caught by in-store detectives stealing hundreds of dollars from the company? The resolution might not be so simple as before – the offender may be willing to pay the money back, but the employer would likely want something more. The offender, for their part, may be unwilling to simply agree to whatever terms the employer sets out – perhaps the offender would be happier taking their chances in the public criminal justice system if the employer asked for too much. In such a situation, both sides could turn to a private criminal mediator, who could work to find a solution acceptable to both sides – restitution plus a fine, counseling and demotion but not a firing, and so on. The offender's ability to participate in the mediation directly would make them much more likely to accept the ultimate outcome, the retailer would get more than it could by laying out a one-sided demand (and certainly more than it could by simply calling the police), and once again the police and prosecutor would likely find that the community interest was sufficiently served by the outcome.

The next step would be to broaden the application of the procedure to crimes of violence: What if one worker assaulted another in the company's warehouse? The offender would likely be apprehended by store security and again a private solution would likely be impossible without the assistance of a professional criminal mediator. If both the victim and the offender consented, they could both agree to work with the mediator to craft a private resolution. Such a forum would be superior to a public criminal adjudication in many ways: It would be faster and more efficient, saving time and resources for both the offender and the victim; both the victim and the perpetrator would have greater control over the process; the result would likely be some restorative-justice-type repair of the physical and emotional harm done to the victim; the perpetrator could avoid incarceration; and (perhaps most importantly) the process might address some of the deeper emotional or behavioral issues underlying the assault.

And what of the "community interest" in the resolution of such a crime? In the case of a crime of violence, the prosecutor would examine the private outcome more carefully to ensure the offender was sufficiently punished to satisfy the community interest. The fact that all of the private parties agreed to the outcome would probably create some inertia on the part of the public officials, thus giving the private criminal system a bit more leeway to depart from what the prosecutor believes to be in the public interest. However, any extreme deviation from societal norms – for example, the offender merely having to apologize after an assault that put the victim in the hospital – would cause the prosecutor to take action in order to ensure the community's interest in terms of deterrence and retribution was met. The very fact that the prosecutor might be monitoring the situation would force all sides to consider the community interest in forging a resolution, as they would be aware that the prosecutor holds an effective veto over the result.

Once private criminal mediators (or private criminal mediation companies) are established, their relationships with the public prosecuting agents in the jurisdiction will become more predictable, and may perhaps even be formalized. Each jurisdiction could assign a prosecutor whose sole job would be to review the hundreds of private dispositions reached by the private criminal justice system and bring formal charges for any case in which the result did not adequately reflect the community interest. Private criminal mediators, who as repeat players would know the limits set out implicitly or expressly by the prosecutor's office, could counsel the victim and offender during the mediation process, explaining that certain proposed resolutions would not be acceptable to the public authorities and suggesting ideas that could make the resolution more palatable. The influence of the community would still be present, although it would be somewhat muted.

Thus, private criminal settlements and private criminal adjudications would operate outside the public criminal justice system, but could still be monitored by the public authorities. This monitoring would not only serve to keep the private resolutions roughly in line with community norms, but would also likely have a feedback effect on the public system itself. As prosecutors monitored the private resolutions, they would begin to notice trends, perhaps repeated deviations from the dispositions handed down in the public system. Prosecutors and defense attorneys could use these deviations as evidence of how local community norms might be shifting – if victims were consistently agreeing to dispositions for a certain crime that were far less severe than what prosecutors had been recommending in the public system, it might be worthwhile for the prosecutor to reconsider their policies for that particular crime.

Farhang Heydari from New York University School of Law has pointed out a number of ways that the private criminal justice system could increase transparency and community control of criminal justice policy. He notes that private actors were driving forces in causing police departments to publish crime data, and that the filming of police misconduct, from Rodney King to George Floyd, can encourage police reforms.[30] However, even more significantly, he argues that "decentralizing control of the criminal system from purely government hands into private hands allows for more localized control over criminal justice priorities," leading to "greater public accountability not at the municipal or county level, but at the community or neighborhood level."[31]

Indeed, although the current primary model for a private criminal legal system envisages the victim as a large company (such as a retail store, an amusement park, or the owner of a corporate park or warehouse), there are many opportunities for smaller entities to utilize the private system. In recent decades, some neighborhoods have established "neighborhood justice centers," which represent a grassroots movement toward private criminal adjudication.[32] These privately run organizations mediate criminal disputes between members of their community, with the goal of keeping the dispute out of court altogether.[33] For example, a crime victim in San Francisco could contact the neighborhood Community Board instead of calling the police.[34] A case developer will interview the victim and, if appropriate, call for both sides to attend a "hearing," at which both the victim and the perpetrator will tell their stories to a panel of mediators known as "neutrals." The neutrals will help to guide the discussion, but will leave it up to the parties to resolve the dispute – a result that occurs 90 percent of the time. The Community Boards in San Francisco hear a wide range of cases, from purely civil disputes such as excessive noise and landlord/tenant disputes to decidedly criminal behavior such as threats, harassment, vandalism, property damage, and assaults.[35] These neighborhood justice centers tend to specialize in a category of crime that the public criminal justice system is ill-equipped to handle: relatively minor criminal cases in which the victim and defendant know each other, including disputes between neighbors and friends.[36]

Likewise, intra-family violence is another area where the public system has failed to provide adequate resolutions for criminal activity. Any practitioner in the field of domestic violence is familiar with the scenario that occurs when a husband or boyfriend commits an act of violence against a victim.[37] Frequently, the victim does not call the police at all, as they do not want the authorities to be involved. If the police are called in, they will usually make an arrest,[38] but then the victim is asked to participate in a criminal case against their abuser. Many of these victims refuse to cooperate because they do not want to see their loved one go to jail. Others are scared that they will put themselves in even more danger if they testify against their abuser – after all, even if the defendant is convicted, they are likely going to jail only for a few months and may seek retribution when they are released.[39] Long delays inherent in the criminal justice system give the defendant ample time to reconcile with the victim, thus making ultimate prosecution even less likely.[40] The sad result is a large number of domestic violence cases in which charges are dropped after a significant amount of police and prosecutorial effort and resources are devoted to the case[41] – or the case is pled down to a minor violation, with the defendant forced to enter into "anger management" as a condition of probation.[42]

No doubt many domestic violence cases belong in the public criminal justice system, and some of the defendants deserve to be incarcerated, particularly if the injury is severe. However, the public criminal justice system is simply not serving the needs of a good number of the victims and defendants involved in these disputes.[43] Indeed, when these crimes go completely unpunished, the public system is not even serving the needs of society. If a credible private criminal mediation system were to handle these cases, victims would be much more willing to cooperate – and probably more likely to report the abuse in the first place. The mediator could help the parties reach a resolution that actually helps the defendant rehabilitate themselves and provides some amount of restitution to the victim – neither of which occur very often in the current public model.[44]

Private criminal mediations could even be used for crimes of sexual assault. Professor Aya Gruber of the University of Colorado has proposed a "neofeminist" approach to such crimes. She is adamant that instances of sexual misconduct are "pressing social problems that reflect and reinforce women's subordination," but she is also wary of the criminal justice system as a response to these acts. Under her paradigm, criminal law should be a "last, not a first, resort" to acts of sexual assault.[45] Professor Gruber acknowledges the feminist gains that have been made in the past few decades, as the public criminal justice system has instituted mandatory arrests for domestic violence cases and broadened the rape laws to make it easier to convict those who commit these crimes. However, she is concerned with the contributions that these changes have made to the phenomenon of mass incarceration, particularly among men of color. And, as society moves toward further empowering women – by instituting "affirmative consent" requirements for intimate activity, for example – she is becoming uneasy with the use of the blunt tools of criminal convictions and incarceration as the only way to deal with unwanted sexual contact, especially given the pace at which social mores are changing in this context.[46]

Another category of crimes that could be better dealt with by private, victim-centered adjudication are cases in which a legitimate violation of the social contract has occurred, but the criminal court system is ill-equipped to deal with the problem. These include "quality of life" crimes committed by the homeless, disorderly conduct offenses committed by the mentally ill, and narcotics possession committed by drug-addicted defendants. The criminal justice system has proven to be a poor tool for adjudicating these crimes and crafting appropriate and constructive resolutions to them,[47] but, in most situations, the criminal justice system is the only viable mechanism for dealing with them. These crimes could probably be better handled by a private system, in which the local community can receive some benefit from the disposition, the defendant can play a role in the process, and the disposition will force the defendant to take responsibility for their actions while still helping them to reintegrate into the community.

A private criminal justice system could thus blunt the effect of the politicization of the public criminal justice system in two ways. First, although prosecutors will review the decisions by private mediators (thus providing some incentive for the private system to take the community interest into account), the prosecutors would likely overrule the private resolution and bring public charges against the defendant only in cases that deviate egregiously from the public interest. Thus, the prosecutors' effect on the process would be indirect, providing private dispositions with a layer of insulation from the political process.

Second, private criminal justice systems would be able to craft more flexible and creative solutions to problems, dampening the public desire for punitive measures against the defendant. Under the public criminal law regime, sentencing tends to be a rigid process, with only a few options: incarceration, a fine, and/or probation. In such an institution, "justice" tends to be conflated with a certain number – one defendant "deserves" five years in prison, while another deserves ten years. Under a private criminal justice system based on restorative justice principles, mediators would be empowered to take a much broader view of justice, crafting resolutions that not only help to restore victims to their pre-crime status but also are more likely to rehabilitate the defendants.

PROCEDURAL PROTECTIONS FOR DEFENDANTS

Critics of both private police enforcement[48] and restorative justice programs[49] are already worried about diverting so much criminal justice activity out of the public courts, where defendants are protected by a myriad of constitutional and statutory protections. Expanding the privatization of the adjudication and disposition phases of criminal justice would no doubt exacerbate these concerns. For example, although the private police are immune to the constitutional restrictions on search and seizure and on interrogation, the debate over this immunity is currently of little more than academic interest. Most of the evidence obtained by private police is never intended for public courts, and so applying the exclusionary rule would have little effect. However, if improperly gathered evidence were to be used in a private criminal proceeding, the harm from such behavior would be much more real. Similarly, there would be no guarantee that a defendant in a private mediation would receive even the most basic rights during the process, such as the right against self-incrimination, the right to an attorney, or the right to confront witnesses against them, as the Constitution provides for those rights only when the state is prosecuting a defendant.

The first response to this criticism is to again point out the reality of the public criminal adjudication system, which rarely involves an actual criminal trial. Over 95 percent of all criminal cases are plea-bargained,[50] a process that provides very few procedural safeguards to the defendant. A full-fledged criminal trial, with all of its robust constitutional protections, has proven to be too costly and time consuming for the state to provide in most instances;[51] thus, it is somewhat unfair to compare a private criminal adjudication to a criminal trial. Rather, it makes more sense to think of a private criminal adjudication as merely another method of dispute resolution that would be available to the defendant. A defendant could choose to go to trial, to authorize their attorney to accept a plea deal in exchange for a guilty plea (and a simultaneous waiver of many trial rights), or to opt out of the public criminal law system altogether. Although the plea-bargaining system has been consistently criticized for over sixty years,[52] it is by now a well-established aspect of our criminal justice system, based on the legal principle that the defendant is always allowed to waive their rights in exchange for something that they want (generally, a lesser sentence).

This perspective highlights a broader point in defense of private criminal mediations: Defendants can always opt out of the private proceeding (or rather choose not to opt out of the public system) and thereby receive the added constitutional protections (and harsher retributive penalties) of the public system. Because the state maintains its monopoly on coercion, neither the victim nor the mediator can force the defendant to agree to even participate in the private mediation, much less force them to agree to specific terms.

Some commentators, however, reject the "voluntariness" of alternatives to public adjudication, arguing that the uncertainty of the resolution in the public courts creates a coercive atmosphere that pressures defendants to agree to proposals that are not in fact in their interest.[53] This uncertainty is exacerbated by the lack of informed consent requirements in most existing restorative justice programs, so that defendants may not have a clear understanding about the rights and potential plea bargains they might receive if they choose the public route.[54] It is true that a defendant who accepts a plea bargain is waiving many of their constitutional rights, but they are usually still given the opportunity to consult with an attorney,[55] and the attorney can ensure that the defendant's ultimate decision to forgo a trial is the result of informed consent. If an attorney is not present in a restorative justice mediation – or in a privately sponsored criminal settlement or criminal mediation – there could be a legitimate concern that the defendant's ultimate acceptance of the disposition is not truly voluntary.

One important but insufficient response to this concern would be to point out the difference between substantive outcomes under the traditional criminal justice system and the likely outcomes under a private system. The extraordinarily punitive nature of the traditional justice system and its heavy reliance on incarceration are both well documented, while a resolution under a private criminal justice system will preclude incarceration. If current restorative justice programs are any guide, giving victims a greater say in the resolution will usually result in a more lenient sentence. This trend is supported by surveys of victims, which show that many would be happy to find a resolution that does not involve incarceration as long as they have a greater say in the crafting of the resolution.[56]

However, it is hard to conclude that the substantive benefits that the defendant will likely receive under a private criminal mediation make up for the loss of procedural safeguards built into the public criminal system. Rather, for those rights to have any meaning, each defendant must understand the rights they could have in the public system and knowingly waive those rights, just as they do when they agree to a plea bargain. As noted in the previous chapter, private criminal mediators should be required to provide the defendant with an explanation of the rights they are forgoing by choosing to opt out of the public criminal justice system. Imposing such a requirement on private mediators would not be a very onerous burden, and it would go a long way toward legitimizing the private criminal justice system by ensuring that defendants were making an informed choice to bypass the public courts. Prosecutorial monitoring of private criminal proceedings – whether private mediations or private criminal settlements – could provide another layer of protection by ensuring that the accused were given appropriate information about the rights they were giving up by rejecting the public system.

ACCOUNTABILITY FOR PRIVATE POLICE

There is no shortage of critiques of the army of private security forces that now dominate the law enforcement stage of our criminal justice system. Critics argue that private security guards violate the constitutional rights of suspects, receive little or no training for their jobs, and are paid so little that the quality of personnel is low and turnover rates are high.[57] The regulation of private security guards is haphazard, with states enforcing widely varying (but mostly minimal) standards as regards licensing, screening, and training.[58] As private police are not controlled by any public agency – indeed, they are answerable only to their clients – some have argued that they are far less accountable for their actions and far more likely to mistreat civilians with whom they come into contact than public police. The perceived lack of accountability of private police is further exacerbated by the fact that most private police operate in the hidden segment of the private criminal justice system.

As it turns out, the truth about private police accountability is somewhat more complex. In some ways, the private nature of security guards makes them more accountable than the public police. Unlike public police officers, who are insulated from the communities that they patrol by the large government bureaucracy that employs them, many private guards must treat the public as customers of the client who hired them.[59] In other words, it is too simplistic to simply state that public police are accountable for their actions and private police are not – both are accountable to the individuals they interact with in different ways and to varying degrees.

However, this is again only a partial response to the concern about the private police. In reality, the only way to regulate private police agents effectively is through the private tort system, incorporating the reforms mentioned in the previous chapter. A few scholars have already claimed that tort actions are the only effective and reasonable method of regulating the *public* police, arguing that the exclusionary rule is insufficient or ineffective in deterring police conduct.[60] The Supreme Court itself noted that "as far as we know, civil liability is an effective deterrent [against public police misconduct], as we have assumed it is in other contexts."[61] Although there are few published cases of successful lawsuits against the public police,[62] many such lawsuits are settled before they go to trial, as reflected in the budget expenditures by large cities to pay settlements for police misconduct.[63]

Nevertheless, it is fair to question whether these lawsuits are an effective deterrent against public police misconduct. Plaintiffs in such cases face significant legal hurdles in bringing such lawsuits, including the qualified immunity enjoyed by public police officers and the sovereign immunity doctrine that protects state agents. Juries may be more willing to believe a police officer's version of the events than those of an individual plaintiff, thus making success in such cases difficult. Even when the plaintiff wins an award or receives money in a settlement, the money may be paid out by the city or county that employs the police, thus only indirectly impacting the police department itself and thereby lessening the deterrent effect of such lawsuits.[64]

Whatever the efficacy is of relying on private causes of action to regulate the conduct of public police, there is good reason to believe the tort system would be effective in regulating private police, especially if the tort reforms proposed in the previous chapter are adopted. Almost all of the significant legal and strategic hurdles that plaintiffs face in suing public police do not exist for suits against private police: Private citizens do not enjoy qualified immunity and are not protected by sovereign immunity, and juries are unlikely to show any special sympathy for them. More significantly, the damages awarded as a result of these lawsuits will be levied directly against the party most responsible for the private police's actions: the client. Unlike a city or county, which can absorb large damage awards into its budget, the private client will be affected much more severely by negative verdicts or large settlement payments – not to mention the attorney's fees in defending against such lawsuits. In addition, private clients will be eager to avoid the negative publicity associated with such lawsuits, thus providing an even greater incentive to ensure that their private security forces are properly screened and trained.

INEQUALITIES IN THE CRIMINAL JUSTICE SYSTEM

Another argument against further privatization of the criminal justice system is that the significant income and wealth disparities in our society will result in an unacceptable disparity in the provision of criminal justice services. Critics contend that the rich will be able to pay for a much higher level of protection from private law enforcement and will be far safer from crime. Companies, neighborhoods, and individuals that can afford to hire private police will be rewarded with greater security. When criminals are apprehended, the private police will ensure that the process and the consequences are victim-friendly. If poorer communities do purchase private security, the quality will likely be poorer: It will be less effective, less consumer-friendly, and perhaps less responsive. We see this phenomenon in other private enterprise contexts: If a supermarket chain has a store in a wealthy neighborhood and a store in a poorer neighborhood, the customer experience will be far better in the wealthy neighborhood, as the chain will give that store more resources.[65] While we are perhaps willing to accept the fact that wealthier individuals have bigger houses and better cars – or even better supermarkets – most of us believe the right to be free from crime is a fundamental entitlement that should not depend on the size of one's bank account. At the same time, a rich person and a poor person who are each apprehended and accused of the same crime could be treated quite differently in a privatized criminal justice system. Wealthier defendants could opt out of the public system and then conceivably pay their way out of their crime by offering a monetary settlement to the victim, while those with less means would be stuck in the public courts.[66] The public institutions that the poor would remain dependent upon – police, prosecutors, judges, prisons, etc. – could become even more resource-starved as privatization saps money from the public system. In other words, as the rich and middle classes decide to pay more for their own private criminal justice institutions, they will be less willing to support government expenditures for public criminal justice institutions.

This is a familiar argument against any movement toward privatization – most prominently with regard to schooling,[67] but also in the debate about how far to go in providing free medical care[68] and in the discussion about civil law alternative dispute resolution programs.[69] One possible response by more conservative supporters of privatization movements is that even if something is a fundamental right – or especially if it is a fundamental right – individuals should be allowed to spend more money to get more of it if that is how they choose to spend their resources. However, this response is not as persuasive to those who do not subscribe to a libertarian economic philosophy – the idea that the rich will be safer from crimes (and perhaps not have to answer for their crimes to the same degree as those with less resources) seems fundamentally unfair.

A better response would be to once again more closely examine the reality of the current criminal justice system, which reveals two unpleasant facts. The first is that the rich already get far more protection from crime than the poor in our public criminal justice system. This is partly due to geography because, for a variety of reasons, the poor tend to live in high-crime neighborhoods.[70] Currently, one of the strongest indicators of whether an individual will be the victim of a violent crime is the individual's level of income.[71]

The second unpleasant fact is that, under our public system of criminal justice, the poor who are arrested get nothing like the treatment of the middle or upper classes. They are dependent on court-appointed defense attorneys, who are famously overworked and underpaid,[72] and, after they are arraigned, they will be held in jail (even though they are presumed innocent) unless they can pay the government a certain amount of money to be released on bail.[73] Those with more resources will be able to hire a private attorney and will be much more likely to make bail after the arrest. A person's bail status is not just a matter of being able to remain at liberty for the few months until one's trial is concluded; it also has a fundamental effect on the ultimate outcome of one's criminal case, partly because incarcerated defendants are less able to assist in their own defense.[74] One study found that defendants who are incarcerated prior to trial are 35 percent more likely to be convicted than those who are not – if the defendant is facing a felony charge, they are 70 percent more likely to be convicted if they are in jail before trial and are much more likely to plead guilty.[75] For misdemeanor cases, the amount of time that defendants will wait until trial could easily equal or exceed the likely sentence for their crime.[76]

Once again, simply highlighting the deep inequities of the current system and claiming that an alternative system could not possibly be much worse is not the most persuasive argument in favor of privatizing the criminal justice system. As it turns out, however, a private criminal justice system will likely be much better for individuals of a lower income than the current system. The reason is straightforward: The current public system relies primarily on incarceration as punishment, and incarceration is extremely (and disproportionately) punitive to people with a lower income. Even a short jail sentence can mean that a low-wage worker might lose their job, while longer sentences make criminals unemployable when they are released.[77] The effect on family members of those who are convicted of crimes is even more dramatic (and, of course, completely unjust): Families may lose their primary breadwinner for months or years at a time, while parents are forced to raise children on their own, helping to maintain a cycle of poverty.[78]

An alternative criminal justice system that cannot use incarceration could dramatically improve the lives of lower-income defendants and their family members.[79] Instead of being locked up for months or years at a time (including being in jail for months before conviction) and then released into society with a criminal record and poor employment prospects, criminals who enter the private criminal justice system can work out more flexible arrangements with their victims that may allow them to continue working and stay with their families while their punishment is being carried out. This will lead to a "soft decriminalization" of many crimes – criminal activity will be punished not by the state with harsh penalties, but by an informal network of private companies, profit-seeking entrepreneurs, and neighborhood associations through a combination of fines, restitution, and other restorative justice dispositions.

The possibility that the rich will be able to pay their way out of criminal liability is indeed troubling. However, there is far more to restorative justice "penalties" than monetary fines, and many of the resolutions involved in restorative justice – apologies, shaming, providing a service to the victim, etc. – would have the same effect on any individual, regardless of their economic class.

As the private criminal justice system continues to evolve, there is no reason to think its effects will fall more heavily on the less wealthy – in fact, quite the opposite. When a private company or institution catches a perpetrator and seeks monetary compensation in exchange for opting out of the public criminal justice system, they will no doubt increase their demand based on the economic status of the perpetrator. Professor Malcolm Feeley of the University of California at Berkeley makes this argument for department stores that punish shoplifting (a crime committed by the rich at least as often as the less affluent):[80]

> [I]f Bloomingdale's or Neiman Marcus were more successful than they currently are in specifically screening for high-income shoppers, they should be able to extract higher [fees] from their shoplifters. Why [only] $400 or $500? Why not $1,500 or $2,500? All things equal, the desire to avoid an arrest record is in part a function of social status, so why not differential rates for different stores? Or even a differential rate for different items taken, or for items taken from different parts of the store (for example, the clearance section in contrast to the boutiques)?... While this may sound unusual, consider that punishments are usually tailored to the seriousness of the crime and that Nordic countries have long imposed "day fines" established as increments of an offender's average daily income – both policies that are widely viewed as progressive.[81]

This is especially true if some private firms begin to engage in "entrepreneurial private law enforcement," in which they independently seek out criminal activity and then contact the alleged perpetrators seeking payment as an alternative to turning them over to the public criminal justice system. These entrepreneurial private police could seek out criminal activity in many different contexts, from monitoring chat rooms or the dark web for child pornography to scrutinizing stock trades to look for patterns that indicate insider trading. Private law enforcement companies could set up speed traps or red-light cameras, sending letters to those who are caught violating the traffic laws and threatening to share the information with the police unless the perpetrator pays a fee (perhaps half of the fine that would be levied if the police issued a ticket). Other entrepreneurs could set up surveillance cameras in high-crime areas to detect narcotics purchases or the hiring of sex workers. These freelance private investigators will inevitably look for criminal activity in areas that are currently under-policed, as that is where they are most likely to find individuals who are not already being detected by the public police. And, not incidentally, they are far more likely to look for criminal activity among the wealthy than among the poor, for the same reason that Willie Sutton robbed banks – that's where the money is.[82]

WIDENING THE NET OF SOCIAL CONTROL

Another concern about a growing private criminal justice system is the potential that it will lead to an increase in the number of people who are surveilled and punished for criminal activity. Private individuals engaged in volunteer law enforcement, armed with new technologies such as doorbell cameras and license plate readers, are able to keep track of the actions of their fellow citizens to an unprecedented degree.

Meanwhile, private entrepreneurial law enforcement companies will use substantial resources to monitor our activities and surveil our actions – all without having to worry about constitutional protections. The overall result throughout society would be an increase in surveillance. According to Professor Wayne Logan of Florida State University, this will result in a "displacement of responsibility for crime and public safety," which will "undercut government accountability for public safety."[83]

A proliferation of entrepreneurial private police will also result in an increased amount of criminal activity being punished, although the degree of punishment will be significantly less than what the public criminal justice system sets out. Especially at the lower range of the penal code, public police and prosecutors occasionally decide not to pursue charges against a perpetrator, calculating that the cost of prosecution is not worth the minimal breach of the social contract. Police officers may let a speeder off with a warning, while prosecutors may agree to drop charges in minor cases based on equitable considerations. Entrepreneurial private police will not have the same motivation to exercise a similar level of discretion – every perpetrator they catch represents a potential payment. Of course, like most aspects of the private criminal justice system, these decisions will take place in the "shadow of the law" – if the accused knows that the public police or public prosecutor are unlikely to press charges, the private entrepreneur is unlikely to be successful in their demand for payment. To take the simplest example, it is general knowledge that the police are very unlikely to pull over a driver who is only exceeding the speed limit by five miles per hour; thus, an overzealous entrepreneurial private police officer who demands payment from someone driving five miles an hour over the limit is unlikely to make any money. However, in many other contexts, the accused may not be certain of the outcome of a public prosecution; many will prefer to pay a small fee rather than risk a far greater punishment in the public system.

Thus, a larger private criminal justice system will result in a wider "net of social control,"[84] even if (as seems likely) it is accompanied by a smaller number of public police. On the surface, this will increase the footprint of the criminal code, ensnaring more people who commit even the most trivial of crimes. The long term effect, however, may be beneficial. More crimes will be detected, more criminals will face consequences, and those consequences will be less severe. This will be a far more efficient method of deterring criminal conduct: As noted earlier in the book, increasing the penalty for criminal activity has little effect on deterrence, while increasing the chance of getting caught has a significant impact. Thus, an expanded private criminal justice system will cast a wider, more effective net – but a far less punitive one.

Furthermore, increased enforcement of nearly every crime could lead to another salutary effect: a reevaluation of the vast extent of our penal codes. As noted in Chapter 1, over-criminalization is a significant problem in the public criminal justice system, encouraged by the desire for legislators to be seen as "tough on crime" and abetted by prosecutors who use their discretion to keep the application of these laws under control. However, if a wider net were cast – a net that would include middle-class and upper-class voters who are currently under-policed and under-prosecuted in the public system – it would create a political counterweight to the constant pressure to expand the criminal code. This could lead to a true reimagining of the public criminal justice system, which could reduce overcriminalization and pare down the penal codes to only cover acts that are truly worthy of public condemnation. Professor William Landes and Judge Richard Posner foresaw this possibility nearly half a century ago in their landmark article *The Private Enforcement of Law*.[85] In their view, the primary problem with competitive private criminal enforcement is overproduction: "Thus, carried to its logical extreme, if law enforcement becomes more costly to society than the criminal activity, legalization of the criminal activity should follow. This, of course, is just another way of saying that society should change laws that do more harm than good; hardly a novel proposition."[86]

PRIVATE DISPOSITIONS

The most challenging aspect of the private criminal justice system to justify is the punishment stage: the act of a private citizen unilaterally imposing a punishment onto another private citizen without any adjudication process or settlement with the alleged perpetrator. Ironically, although many of those who engage in private dispositions claim to be acting to enforce and uphold the law, their actions weaken legal institutions by bypassing the procedures that are constitutionally and legally required before criminal punishment can be imposed.[87]

The previous chapter discussed a few reforms that could limit the most destructive aspects of private dispositions, such as increasing the civil liability for illegal private dispositions and clarifying the initial aggressor instruction in self-defense cases. If the worst abuses of private dispositions can be brought under control, this aspect of the private criminal justice system can provide some social good. One of these benefits – which is shared with other aspects of the private criminal justice system – is that private dispositions can expose gaps and weaknesses in the public criminal justice system. If we operate under the assumption that private dispositions generally occur when the public criminal justice system is failing to meet the needs of ordinary citizens, then the public officials who set criminal justice policy should take notice of areas in which private dispositions are commonly occurring.

One reason why private dispositions proliferate for certain crimes is that the social costs of the crime have increased but legislatures have not reacted to the increased social cost. Kelly D. Hine, a lawyer who applied economic analysis to the question of vigilantism, describes the phenomenon this way:

> The time lag inherent in governmental administration effectively freezes funding levels .... [E]ven if the legislature approves funding to increase enforcement, the

lag persists because of the need to train additional police and build additional infrastructure. These governmental restrictions on the supply of criminal justice . . . permit more crime to take place.

As in any instance where artificial controls limit the availability of a desired good, the "price" of that good rises. This higher price means greater benefits for those willing to circumvent the established system. If these benefits become sufficiently large, individuals may begin to engage in "black market" behavior – here vigilantism – to supply the pent up demand.[88]

As Hine concedes, this analysis is valid only if the vigilante "bases his actions on an accurate perception of social need, and if he keeps the imposed sanction within socially tolerable bounds." Under these circumstances, the vigilante is providing a benefit to society. Thus, Hine proposes a "justified vigilante" defense for those who engage in private dispositions under the right conditions.[89]

The social cost of a given crime might increase for a number of different reasons. First, the direct harm caused by the crime might increase, either because the crime is becoming more widespread (like when a more addictive type of drug becomes available) or because the harm caused by each instance of the crime is greater (like when the rise of the internet gave computer viruses access to millions of computers at once). Second, the cost of committing the crime might decrease, perhaps with the advent of new technology, leading more individuals to engage in that crime. Finally, societal values might change, such that behavior that was once thought to be acceptable or only a minor transgression becomes more egregious under new societal mores (as was the case with drunk driving or domestic violence in the final quarter of the twentieth century). The current proliferation of vigilante punishments involving the shaming of child predators demonstrates that the sexual abuse of children is a crime that many people currently believe is being under-enforced or under-punished, which motivates private citizens to spend their own time and energy catching and punishing these individuals. Policymakers observing these vigilante punishments should take notice and increase the public law enforcement resources dedicated to this particular crime.

CONCLUSION

Given the shortcomings of the public criminal justice system and the strong appeal of a private alternative, the continued evolution of a private criminal justice system is inevitable. The private police currently apprehend hundreds of thousands of criminals each year, and restorative justice theory provides an ideal blueprint for adjudicating and resolving their cases. Mediation has already revolutionized the way that civil law disputes are resolved, and private restorative justice programs would offer the same efficiency and flexibility to the parties of a criminal dispute, providing a more satisfactory process and better results for victims and defendants alike.

Conclusion

It is long past time to reimagine how our criminal justice system operates. Chapter 3 detailed the familiar problems with the public criminal justice system: mass incarceration, poor treatment of victims, and systemic racism. Traditional progressive solutions – reducing the footprint of the police; dramatically shortening prison sentences, especially for nonviolent crimes; and increasing government funding for anti-poverty programs and education – provide only half of the solution. Indeed, the more we shrink the public criminal justice system, the more the private criminal justice system will expand to fill in the gaps that are left behind. Contrary to conventional wisdom, this evolution will be a positive development. Instead of a Leviathan state apparatus, with a vast surveillance state and over a million people in prison, crime control in the future will be accomplished primarily through a diverse, decentralized private criminal justice system. Lawbreaking will be punished more mildly, leading to a soft decriminalization of many of the crimes currently in the penal code. This overlapping network of private companies, organizations, and individuals will provide a similar or greater level of deterrence than what the public criminal justice system currently provides, and it will do so without relying on incarceration and at no cost to the state, while being more effective in meeting the needs of crime victims.

Notes

INTRODUCTION: THE RISE OF PRIVATE CRIMINAL JUSTICE

1. Rachel Morgan & Alexandra Thompson, US Department of Justice, STATISTICAL BRIEF: THE NATION'S TWO CRIME MEASURES, 2011–2020, NCJ 303385 (2022), https://bjs.ojp.gov/content/pub/pdf/ntcm1120.pdf. These numbers are determined by household surveys in which respondents are asked whether they have been victims of crimes and, if so, whether they reported the crime to the police.
2. This reason has probably become more prevalent in recent decades as the state continues to criminalize more conduct, thus creating more "crimes" that victims and witnesses do not think are worth reporting. This is an example of the law of unintended consequences: When the state overcriminalizes conduct, victims and witnesses may be less likely to report criminal activity. See, e.g., Erik Luna, *The Overcriminalization Phenomenon*, 54 AM. U. L. REV. 703, 725 (2005): "Mistrusting citizens are less likely to assist law enforcement and to obey legal commands, which undermines the efforts of police and prosecutors and, paradoxically, renders the law counterproductive."
3. See, e.g., Elizabeth E. Joh, *Conceptualizing the Private Police*, 2005 UTAH L. REV. 573, 589–91 (2005) (noting that Macy's private response to shoplifters is to ban them from the store for seven years); David A. Sklansky, *The Private Police*, 46 UCLA L. REV. 1165, 1277 (1999): "The sanctions [imposed by private companies in response to criminal behavior] range from dismissal or ejection, to a return of purloined merchandise, to fines or restitution extorted by the threat of criminal complaint."
4. Amelia Pollard, The Rise of the Private Police, *The American Prospect* (Mar. 3, 2021), https://prospect.org/justice/rise-of-the-private-police/.
5. See, e.g., Michael Barbaro, Hot Off the Shelves: Shoplifting Gangs Are Retailing's Top Enemy, *New York Times* (Nov. 8, 2005), C1 (discussing retail security efforts); Michael Leahy, Crimes and Misdemeanors: High School Security Chief Wally Baranyk Says Most of the Wrongdoing in Suburban High Schools Goes on in the Shadows. So How Dark Does It Get?, *Washington Post* (June 4, 2006), W08; Suzanne Smalley, A Force of Their Own: Neighborhood's Private Guards Help Keep the Peace, *Boston Globe* (May 26, 2006), B1 (discussing residential security patrols); William Yardley, Does It Work? Campus Security: Finding Safety in Numbers, *New York Times* (Jan. 8, 2006), A18 (discussing security on college campuses).
6. See John Rappaport, *Criminal Justice, Inc.*, 118 COL. L. REV. 2251, 2272–76 (2018). The CEC was founded in 2010. Its other clients included DSW, Abercrombie & Fitch, Burlington Coat Factory, Whole Foods, American Apparel, Goodwill Industries, Sport Chalet, Kroger, Sportsman's Warehouse, and H&M.

7. Heather Strang & Lawrence W. Sherman, *Repairing the Harm: Victims and Restorative Justice*, 2003 UTAH L. REV. 15, 19 (2003) (citing John M. Boyle, CRIME ISSUES IN THE NORTHEAST 1 [1999]).
8. Jeffrey M. Jones, In U.S., Black Confidence in Police Recovers from 2020 Low, *Gallup: Social & Policy Issues* (July 14, 2021), https://bit.ly/3LoKros.
9. See, e.g., Jim Parsons & Tiffany Bergin, *The Impact of Criminal Justice Involvement on Victims' Mental Health*, 23 J. TRAUM. STRESS 182 (2010).
10. Linda R.S. v. Richard D., 410 U.S. 614, 619 (1973).
11. Michael E. O'Neill, *Private Vengeance and the Public Good*, 12 U. PA. J. CONST. L. 659, 681–82 (2010).
12. E. Ann Carson, US Department of Justice, BUREAU OF JUSTICE STATISTICS BULLETIN: PRISONERS IN 2019, NCJ 255115, 26 (2020) https://bjs.ojp.gov/content/pub/pdf/p19.pdf (referencing data from the last year before the COVID-19 pandemic). As of 2019, over 115,954 prisoners in the United States were under private management. The second largest commercial provider of corrections services, CoreCivic (formerly the Corrections Corporation of America [CCA]), made approximately $1.8 billion dollars in revenue and controlled about 69,000 prison beds at the end of 2021. CoreCivic claims to run one of the nation's largest prison systems. See CoreCivic, ANNUAL REPORT (Form 10-K), 7, 71 (Feb. 18, 2022), https://bit.ly/40DVVns.
13. For example, a defendant convicted of drug possession might be given probation on the condition that they attend substance abuse programs at Phoenix House, a national nonprofit organization that treats individuals in nine different states and the District of Columbia. See *Phoenix House*, www.phoenixhouse.org (last visited Sep. 15, 2022). Their California office alone treats 44,000 people per year (Our Story, *Phoenix House California*, https://phoenixhouseca.org/our-story/ [last visited Sep. 15, 2022]). A defendant convicted of domestic violence assault might be required by the court to complete an anger management program run by a private organization. In either case, however, the sentence is determined, monitored, and enforced by a public court.
14. The only difference between a government agency that hires a corporation to provide security or correction services and a government agency that hires and manages its own police force or prison system is that, in the former situation, the agency is contracting for a bundle of services to be managed and coordinated by a profit-seeking entrepreneur instead of a civil service bureaucrat.
15. For example, the entrepreneur may be able to provide the same level of services more efficiently and therefore more cheaply, but might have an incentive to provide a lower quality service if the consumer (the state agency) does not set sufficient standards in its contractual agreement. The bureaucrat, on the other hand, is immune from the temptation to cut costs in order to increase profits but is no less immune to corruption and far less likely to innovate in order to increase efficiency.
16. Contracting out does present its own set of opportunities and challenges. A private company's drive to innovate can increase efficiency and thereby reduce costs in an industry that is, for better or for worse, growing dramatically and taking up larger portions of state and federal budgets. On the other hand, if contracts with private corrections companies are not structured properly, the private incentive to cut costs could lead to unacceptable conditions for the prisoners. See, e.g., Sharon Dolovich, *State Punishment and Private Prisons*, 55 DUKE L. J. 437, 460–62 (2005) (detailing "cost-cutting" measures by the CCA such as rationing bread and toilet paper, or reclassifying maximum security prisoners as medium security, possibly leading to greater violence). Professor Dolovich also levels a more profound critique of the contracting out of state prisons, arguing that

they fail to meet the two basic principles of liberal legitimacy, which are that the state must avoid punishments that are gratuitously inhumane or gratuitously long (*id.* at 444–46).
17. As two leading economists on the issue of so-called private prisons have noted: "It is important to remind ourselves here that we are not discussing the legislative and judicial allocation of punishment, but only its delivery" (Mick Ryan & Tony Ward, PRIVATIZATION AND THE PENAL SYSTEM: THE AMERICAN EXPERIENCE AND THE DEBATE IN BRITAIN 69 [1989]).

1 CRIMINAL JUSTICE WITHOUT THE STATE

1. "Crime," BLACK'S LAW DICTIONARY (5th ed. 1979). Many legal scholars consider crime to be, by definition, a transgression against the state. See, e.g., Juan Cardenas, *The Crime Victim in the Prosecutorial Process*, 9 HARV. J. L. & PUB. POL'Y 357, 371 (1986).
2. See R. A. Duff, THE REALM OF CRIMINAL LAW (2018).
3. Henry M. Hart, Jr., *The Aims of the Criminal Law*, 23 L. & CONTEMP. PROBS. 401, 404 (1958). See also George K. Gardner, *Bailey v. Richardson and the Constitution of the United States*, 33 B.U.L. REV. 176, 193 (1953):

    > The essence of punishment for moral delinquency lies in the criminal conviction itself. One may lose more money on the stock market than in a court-room; a prisoner of war camp may well provide a harsher environment than a state prison; death on the field of battle has the same physical characteristics as death by sentence of law. It is the expression of the community's hatred, fear, or contempt for the convict which alone characterizes physical hardship as punishment.

4. The state's monopoly on force has been a mainstay of liberal political thought for centuries. As the prominent sociologist Max Weber noted: "The modern state is a compulsory association which organizes domination. It has been successful in seeking to monopolize the legitimate use of physical force as a means of domination within a territory." (Max Weber, ESSAYS IN SOCIOLOGY 78 [Hans H. Gerth & C. Wright Mills trans., 1958].) See also Robert Nozick, ANARCHY, STATE, AND UTOPIA 26, 138–39 (1974); Clifford J. Rosky, *Force Inc.: The Privatization of Punishment, Policing, and Military Force in Liberal States*, 36 CONN. L. REV. 879, 895–96 (2004). Rosky adapts Weber's concept of a "monopoly of force" and applies it to the private law enforcement context, noting that, in the twentieth century, "[t]he West fought two world wars and developed a massive network of military, policing, and punishment institutions, which were characterized by unprecedented levels of specialization, professionalism, bureaucratization, and strength." (*Id.* at 896 [citations omitted].)
5. "Crime," BLACK'S LAW DICTIONARY (5th ed. 1979).
6. See, e.g., Jennifer Gerarda Brown, *Blackmail as Private Justice*, 141 U. PA. L. REV. 1935, 1967 (1993): "To say that a public authority enforces the criminal law is to state a near tautology. Many define criminal prohibitions not just by the severity of their associated penalty, but also by the state's exclusive entitlement to enforce them."
7. See, e.g., Jeff Bleich, *The Politics of Prison Crowding*, 77 CAL L. REV. 1125, 1168–69 (1989).
8. John Braithwaite, *A Future Where Punishment Is Marginalized: Realistic or Utopian?*, 46 UCLA L. REV. 1727, 1735–42 (1999) (arguing that restorative justice is an alternative that can and should marginalize the use of punishment).
9. A. Warren Stearns, *Evolution of Punishment*, 27 J. CRIM. L. & CRIMINOLOGY 219, 220 (1936). Crimes of blasphemy and sacrilege still exist in many societies today. See

Ryan Jacobs, When Governments Go after Witches, *Atlantic* (Oct. 30, 2013), http://bit.ly/3K69TbF.
10. Stearns, *supra* note 9, at 220.
11. These crimes are still on the books in many states, although they are never enforced and are probably unconstitutional. See Joanne Sweeney, Adultery and Fornication: Why Are States Rushing to Get These Outdated Laws off the Books?, *Salon* (May 6, 2019), http://bit.ly/3nF6xoj (noting that, as of 2019, eighteen states still criminalized adultery and six states still criminalized fornication). Nevertheless, prosecutions for adultery occurred throughout the twentieth century, with successful convictions occurring at least through the 1960s. See State v. Ronek, 176 N.W.2d 153 (Iowa 1970). See also Jeremy D. Weinstein, *Adultery, Law, and the State: A History*, 38 HASTINGS L.J. 195 (1986).
12. See James Nevius, The Strange History of Opiates in America: From Morphine for Kids to Heroin for Soldiers, *Guardian* (May 15, 2016), http://bit.ly/3GeiyHT.
13. Thomas Hobbes, LEVIATHAN 230 (Herbert W. Schneider ed., 1958):

> [T]he civil law ceasing, crimes cease, for there being no other law remaining but that of nature, there is no place for accusation, every man being his own judge and accused only by his own conscience and cleared by the uprightness of his own intention.... [W]hen the sovereign power ceases, crime also ceases, for where there is no such power there is no protection to be had from the law.

14. Thomas Aquinas, SUMMA THEOLOGIAE, question 94, articles 2–4.
15. John Locke, TWO TREATISES OF GOVERNMENT AND A LETTER CONCERNING TOLERATION 102 (1689; Ian Shapiro ed., Yale University Press 2003).
16. *Id.* at 108.
17. Hobbes, *supra* note 13, at 230.
18. W. David Lewis, FROM NEWGATE TO DANNEMORA: THE RISE OF THE PENITENTIARY IN NEW YORK, 1796–1848 7–8 (1965). See also Snell Putney & Gladys J. Putney, *Origins of the Reformatory*, 53 J. CRIM. LAW CRIMINOLOGY POLICE SCI. 437, 441–43 (1962).
19. David Garland, PUNISHMENT AND WELFARE: A HISTORY OF PENAL STRATEGIES 15 (1985).
20. Francis A. Allen, THE DECLINE OF THE REHABILITATIVE IDEAL: PENAL POLICY AND SOCIAL PURPOSE 6–7 (1981).
21. Williams v. New York, 337 U.S. 241, 248 (1949).
22. American Friends Service Committee, STRUGGLE FOR JUSTICE 86 (1971).
23. Sanford H. Kadish, *Fifty Years of Criminal Law: An Opinionated Review*, 87 CALIF. L. REV. 943, 948 (1999).
24. Herbert L. Packer, *The Model Penal Code and Beyond*, 63 COLUM. L. REV. 594, 604–05 (1963) (quoting Jerome Michael & Herbert Wechsler, CRIMINAL LAW AND ITS ADMINISTRATION 12 [1940]).
25. Federal Bureau of Investigation, US Department of Justice, CRIME IN THE UNITED STATES 1972: UNIFORM CRIME REPORTS 61, table 1 (1973).
26. In October 1951, only 1 percent of respondents thought crime was the most important issue facing the United States. Gallup Poll Public Opinion Database, Scholarly Resources, Wilmington, DE (March 31, 2001).
27. As Professor William Stuntz points out, there is evidence of this shift in focus in the histories of presidential elections (William J. Stuntz, *The Pathological Politics of Criminal Law*, 100 MICH L. REV. 505, 524, note 85 [2001]). Historian Theodore H. White wrote a series of books about presidential elections in the 1960s, and the word "crime" does not even appear in the index for the 1960 election. See Theodore H. White, THE MAKING OF THE PRESIDENT: 1960 (1961).

28. Elizabeth Hinton, Why We Should Reconsider the War on Crime, *Time* (Mar. 20, 2015), https://time.com/3746059/war-on-crime-history/.
29. White's book on the 1968 election dedicates an entire chapter to Richard Nixon's and George Wallace's positions on the issue of crime. See Theodore H. White, THE MAKING OF THE PRESIDENT: 1968, 188–223 (1969). See also Stuart A. Scheingold, THE POLITICS OF LAW AND ORDER: STREET CRIME AND PUBLIC POLICY 37–57 (1984).
30. David Garland, THE CULTURE OF CONTROL: CRIME AND SOCIAL ORDER IN CONTEMPORARY SOCIETY 145 (2001).
31. *Id.* at 151.
32. See James A. Strazzella, American Bar Association, THE FEDERALIZATION OF CRIMINAL LAW 7 (1998).
33. For example, statistics from the United States Department of Justice show that state courts reported 583,000 convictions in 1986 and over 829,000 convictions in 1990 (Bureau of Justice Statistics, US Department of Justice, BUREAU OF JUSTICE STATISTICS BULLETIN: FELONY SENTENCES IN STATE COURTS, 1990 1–2 [1993]). From 1973 to 1990, the national incarceration rate skyrocketed, increasing by 186 percent (US Advisory Commission on Intergovernmental Relations, THE ROLE OF GENERAL GOVERNMENT ELECTED OFFICIALS IN CRIMINAL JUSTICE 9–10 [1993]).
34. See Garland, *supra* note 29, at 151. The New York Rockefeller drug laws of the 1970s and the federal sentencing guidelines of 1984 are two of the more well-known examples of this phenomenon.
35. Allison Young, The Facts on Progressive Prosecutors, *Center for American Progress* (Apr. 23, 2020), http://bit.ly/435QqAA (describing the progressive prosecutor movement from a progressive political perspective).
36. Growth in Mass Incarceration, *The Sentencing Project*, www.sentencingproject.org/criminal-justice-facts/. As of 2019, the United States incarcerated 639 out of every 100,000 citizens. Most European countries have a rate under 100; the rates for the totalitarian states of Russia and China, respectively, are 331 and 121.
37. Bureau of Justice Statistics, US Department of Justice, HISTORICAL CORRECTIONS STATISTICS IN THE UNITED STATES, 1850–1984 34, tables 3–6 (1986), https://bjs.ojp.gov/content/pub/pdf/hcsus5084.pdf.
38. Wendy Sawyer & Peter Wagner, Mass Incarceration: The Whole Pie 2022, *Prison Policy Initiative* (Mar. 14, 2022), https://www.prisonpolicy.org/reports/pie2022.html.
39. *Id.*
40. GianCarlo Canaparo et al., Count the Code: Quantifying Federalization of Criminal Statutes, *The Heritage Foundation* (Jan. 7, 2022), https://herit.ag/3VgJjln.
41. See 15 U.S.C. § 330a; 18 U.S.C. § 336; 40 U.S.C. § 5104(e)(2)(C).
42. See 21 U.S.C. § 331(k) (held to be strict liability in United States v. Park, 421 U.S. 658 [1975]).
43. Robert Leider, *The Modern Common Law of Crime*, 111 J. Crim L. & Criminology 407, 425 (2021).
44. Sandra G. Mayson & Megan T. Stevenson, *Misdemeanors by the Numbers*, 61 B. C. L. REV. 971, 985–86 (2020).
45. *Id.* at 979.
46. *Id.* at 1018. Other common categories of misdemeanors include disorderly conduct, resisting arrest, prostitution, vandalism, trespass, public intoxication, underage drinking, and unlawful possession of weapons, drug paraphernalia, or crime tools.
47. Leider, *supra* note 42, at 419.
48. Stuntz, *supra* note 26, at 508.

49. See, e.g., Stuntz, *supra* note 26, at 509. "As criminal law expands, both lawmaking and adjudication pass into the hands of police and prosecutors; law enforcers, not the law, determine who goes to prison and for how long. The end point of this progression is clear: criminal codes that cover everything and decide nothing, that serve only to delegate power to district attorneys' offices and police departments." As I argue in this chapter, although the police and prosecutors do wield considerable power in the public criminal justice system, they are restrained by social and cultural norms.
50. Leider, *supra* note 42, at 425–26.
51. See 720 Ill. Comp. Stat. Ann. 5/11-40; Miss. Code Ann. § 97-29-1; N.D. Cent. Code § 12.1-20-08; S.C. Code Ann. § 16-15-60 (outlawing fornication); Ala. Code § 13A-13-2; Ariz. Rev. Stat. § 13-1408; Fla. Stat. Ann. § 798.01; 720 Ill. Comp. Stat. Ann. 5/11-35; Kan. Stat. Ann. § 21-5511; Mich. Comp. Laws Ann. § 750.30; Minn. Stat. Ann. § 609.36; Miss. Code Ann. § 97-29-1; N.Y. Penal Law § 255.17; N.D. Cent. Code Ann. 12.1-20-09; Okla. Stat. Ann. Tit. 21, § 871; 11 R.I. Gen. Laws Ann. § 11-6-2; S.C. Code Ann. § 16-15-60; Va. Code Ann. § 18.2-365; Wis. Stat. Ann. § 944.16 (outlawing adultery). See Douglas Husak, OVERCRIMINALIZATION: THE LIMITS OF THE CRIMINAL LAW 18 (2009).
52. See Miss. Code Ann. § 97-29-47; Mich. Comp. Laws Ann. § 750.103; Okla. Stat. Tit. 21, §§ 901–05 (outlawing swearing); Me. Rev. Stat. Tit. 17, § 3203 (outlawing selling cars on Sunday); Mass. Gen. Laws Ann. Ch. 136 §§ 2–4 (outlawing sports and entertainment on Sunday without a license); Mass. Gen. Laws Ann. Ch. 136 §§ 5–6 (outlawing all business on Sundays).
53. Leider, *supra* note 42, at 437–38.
54. *Id.* at 440.
55. Jonah E. Bromwich, *Manhattan D.A. Acts on Vow to Seek Incarceration Only for Worst Crimes*, New York Times (Jan. 6, 2022), https://bit.ly/3mW3Pef.
56. Jonah E. Bromwich, *Manhattan D.A. Sharpens Crime Policies That Led to Weeks of Backlash*, New York Times (Feb. 4, 2022), https://bit.ly/3N4XCqP.
57. Bromwich, *supra* note 54 (statement by Karen Friedman Agnifilo, former deputy prosecutor to Bragg's predecessor, Cyrus Vance).
58. Thorsten Sellig & Marvin E. Wolfgang, THE MEASUREMENT OF DELINQUENCY 131, 140 (1967).
59. See Paul H. Robinson & Robert Kurzban, *Concordance and Conflict in Intuitions of Justice*, 91 MINN. L. REV. 1829, 1855–60 (2007) (listing five additional surveys that come to the same conclusion). Correlations among different demographic groups ranged from 0.71 to 0.94.
60. *Id.* at 1867–72. One way to measure consensus in pairwise ranking is to use Kendall's coefficient of concordance, in which 1.0 shows complete agreement and 0.0 shows no agreement. The participants in the study showed a coefficient of 0.96. By comparison, when readers of a travel magazine were asked to rank eight travel destinations in order of terrorism risk, the coefficient of their pairwise rankings was only 0.52. *Id.* at 1872.
61. *Id.* at 1862–65.
62. Paul H. Robinson, *Criminal Law's Core Principles*, 14 WASH. U. JURIS. REV. 153, 161 (2021).
63. *Id.* at 161–62, notes 20–23; 172, notes 81–82 (citing Judith Smetana, *Preschool Children's Conceptions of Moral and Social Rules*, 52 CHILD DEV. 1333, 1335–36 [1981]; Jerome Kagan, INTRODUCTION, IN THE EMERGENCY OF MORALITY IN YOUNG CHILDREN [Jerome Kagan & Sharon Lamb eds., 1987]; John M. Darley & Thomas R. Shultz, *Moral Rules: Their Content and Acquisition*, 41 ANN. REV. PSYCHOL. 525, 552 [1990]; Elliott Turiel, THE DEVELOPMENT OF SOCIAL KNOWLEDGE: MORALITY AND CONVENTION 91 [1983]).

64. Id. at 168, notes 51–57 (citing Hudson K. Reeve, *Queen Activation of Lazy Workers in Colonies of the Eusocial Naked Mole-Rat*, 358 NATURE 147, 148 [1992]; Peter O. Dunn et al., *Fairy-Wren Helpers Often Care for Young to Which They Are Unrelated* 259 PROCEEDINGS: BIOLOGICAL SCI. 339, 341–42 [1995]; Raoul A. Mulder & Naomi E. Langmore, *Dominant Males Punish Helpers for Temporary Defection in Superb Fairy-wrens*, 45 ANIM. BEHAV. 830, 832 [1993]; Marc Bekoff, *Wild Justice, Cooperation, and Fair Play*, 19 BIOLOGY & PHIL. 489, 493 [2004]; Paul H. Robinson, INSTITUTIONS OF JUSTICE AND THE UTILITY OF DESERT 42 [2013]; Frans B. M. De Waal, GOOD NATURED: THE ORIGINS OF RGHT [SIC] AND WRONG IN HUMANS AND OTHER ANIMALS 157–58 [1996]). Examples include deer attacking young male deer who attempt to mate with females being guarded by adult males, and wolves exiling other wolves who cause injury to others during play-fighting.
65. People v. Grinberg, 4 Misc. 3d 670, 673 (Crim. Ct. 2004) (noting that the first drunk driving law was passed by the New York legislature in 1910); see History, *Mothers Against Drunk Driving*, https://madd.org/our-history/.
66. Mary Pat Treuhart, *Lowering the Bar: Rethinking Underage Drinking*, 9 N.Y.U. J. LEGIS. & PUB. POL'Y 303, 308–09 (2006).
67. Elizabeth Pleck, *Criminal Approaches to Family Violence, 1940–1980*, 11 CRIME AND JUST. 19, 29 (1989) (noting that, other than a statute passed by the Pilgrims, America's first public criminal law against wife-beating was enacted in 1850).
68. Id. at 51.
69. Robert Ellickson, ORDER WITHOUT LAW: HOW NEIGHBORS SETTLE DISPUTES, vii–viii (1994).
70. Id. at 131.
71. Id. at 142.
72. Id. at 251 (quoting James M. Acheson, THE LOBSTER GANGS OF MAINE 75 [1984]). Professor Nils Christie has gone a step further and argued that the entire public criminal justice system is illegitimate because interpersonal conflicts are the property of the individuals involved in the conflict, and the state has improperly confiscated that property (Nils Christie, *Conflicts as Property*, 17 BRIT. J. CRIMINOLOGY 1, 2 [1977]).
73. The goal of rehabilitation has become increasingly absent from modern-day criminal justice policy relative to its position as the dominant theory in the nineteenth and early twentieth centuries. See Edward L. Rubin, *The Inevitability of Rehabilitation*, 19 LAW & INEQ. 343, 343–44 (2001) ("Very quickly, rehabilitation became a dirty word in American corrections."); Francis A. Allen, THE DECLINE OF THE REHABILITATIVE IDEAL: PENAL POLICY AND SOCIAL PURPOSE (1981) (a general consideration); Nora V. Demleitner et al., SENTENCING LAW AND POLICY: CASES, STATUTES, AND GUIDELINES 6 (2004) ("Commentators and others have tended to overstate the prior dominance of rehabilitation, as well as the modern failings of rehabilitative efforts and the general decline of the role of rehabilitation in sentencing."). However, the decline of rehabilitation's role in modern sentencing has not resulted in a complete abandonment of the rehabilitative ideal in the formulation of current sentencing policy. See John Kaplan et al., CRIMINAL LAW: CASES AND MATERIALS 37 (5th ed. 2004) ("Today, we tend to think of rehabilitation as an ancillary goal of penal incarceration, involving educational or therapeutic 'programs' in prison."); see also 18 U.S.C. § 3553(a)(2)(D) (2000) ("The court, in determining the particular sentence to be imposed, shall consider ... the need for the sentence imposed ... to provide the defendant with needed educational or vocational training, medical care, or other correctional treatment in the most effective manner.").
74. There are other, less prevalent, theories for justifying the enforcement of the criminal law. For example, the "curial view" emphasizes the need to "call ... suspected offenders to account in criminal trials," and places a high value on the criminal trial itself, where defendants tell their story and a judgment is rendered. The "communitarian view" states that the criminal law is "a

way of ensuring that the community gets what it is owed from wrongdoers"; it is similar to the retributive view but focuses on healing the wrongs done to society rather than punishing the immoral actions of the perpetrator. See James Edwards, Theories of Criminal Law, *in* THE STANFORD ENCYCLOPEDIA OF PHILOSOPHY (Edward N. Zalta ed., 2021), https://bit.ly/3osCYqn. Similarly, the "reconstructivist view" states that the purpose of the criminal law is to communicate the moral norms of society. In committing a crime, the criminal has attacked these norms and effectively tried to establish a new moral order, where violence is acceptable or private property rights do not exist. In punishing the criminal, society is reestablishing the moral order and formally rejecting the improper norms that the criminal was following. Although this theory is grounded in morality, it is different from retributivism because it focuses not on the moral desert of the defendant but on communicating and reestablishing a moral order in all of society. See Joshua Kleinfeld, *Reconstructivism: The Place of Criminal Law in Ethical Life*, 129 HARV. L. REV. 1485 (2016).

75. I say a utilitarian would "generally" choose this option because the true utilitarian would also be concerned with the resource cost of each option – if prison time were far more expensive than rehabilitation, a utilitarian may choose to invest in rehabilitation even if it was somewhat less effective in preventing future crimes.

76. Most Americans Favor the Death Penalty Despite Concerns About Its Administration, *Pew Research Center*, https://bit.ly/41V1TBm.

77. Note that this shift from punishing defendants in the 1980s and 1990s for using cocaine and heroin to offering treatment to defendants in the 2010s and 2020s for using opioids coincided with the fact that the former defendants tended to be people of color, while the latter defendants tended to be white. People are apparently more likely to seek retribution against those who can be classified as an "other." In addition, individuals who became addicted to cocaine and heroin in the 1980s and 1990s were engaging in criminal activity as soon as they started using drugs, and so could be stereotyped as "criminals" by the general population, while individuals who became addicted to opioids decades later were seen more sympathetically because most of them were initially prescribed these drugs through legitimate medical avenues.

78. Law 196, THE CODE OF HAMMURABI (L. W. King trans., 2010), https://avalon.law.yale.edu/ancient/hamframe.asp.

79. Deuteronomy 19:21 (King James).

80. Stearns, *supra* note 9, at 223.

81. *Id.* at 225.

82. *Id.* at 226–27.

83. See Growth in Mass Incarceration, *supra* note 35.

84. See Juleyka Lantigua-Williams, Are Prosecutors the Key to Justice Reform?, *Atlantic* (May 18, 2016) (citing the work of Professor John Pfaff of Fordham Law School).

85. See, e.g., Joshua Dressler, *The Wisdom and Morality of Present-Day Criminal Sentencing*, 38 AKRON L. REV. 853, 856–59 (2005). Professor Dressler argues that federal and state sentencing laws result in "defendants [being] punished more than they deserve under any decent retributive system, and [punished] far more ... than is necessary for utilitarian purposes." Examples of overly punitive sentences imposed under both state and federal mandatory sentencing laws abound. For instance, under California's Three Strikes law, a defendant received a sentence of twenty-five years to life for stealing a magazine (People v. Romero, 122 Cal. Rptr. 2d 399, 404 [Ct. App. 2002]). His prior convictions were for burglary, hit-and-run, battery on a peace officer, obstructing a peace officer, and lewd conduct with a child (*id.* at 403–04). In an example of an overly punitive sentence under federal sentencing law, one defendant, with no prior record, was sentenced to fifty-five years in prison for three counts of

carrying – not brandishing or using – a firearm in connection with a drug offense (United States v. Angelos, 345 F. Supp. 2d 1227, 1230, 1263 [D. Utah 2004]). According to the district court, federal law mandated a five-year sentence for the first offense and twenty-five years for each subsequent offense of possession of a firearm in connection with a drug offense, on top of the sentence for dealing marijuana (*id.* at 1232). The court imposed the sentence even though it found that the penalty was irrational and unjust because the court believed its hands were tied (*id.* at 1261, 1265). In an effort to show the unjust nature of the sentence, the district court pointed out that those who hijacked an aircraft or committed second-degree murder or rape would receive lighter sentences under the sentencing regime (*id.* at 1230). For information on the average sentences for different crimes, see Matthew R. Durose & Patrick A. Langan, Bureau of Justice Statistics, US Department of Justice, Felony Sentences in State Courts, 2002, 3–4 (2004), https://bjs.ojp.gov/content/pub/pdf/fssc02.pdf; Gerard Rainville & Brian A. Reaves, Bureau of Justice Statistics, US Department of Justice, Felony Defendants in Large Urban Counties, 2000, 32–34 (2003), www.ojp.usdoj.gov/bjs/pub/pdf/fdluc00.pdf.

86. See Growth in Mass Incarceration, *supra* note 35 (quoting the National Resource Council: "Because recidivism rates decline markedly with age, lengthy prison sentences, unless they specifically target very high-rate or extremely dangerous offenders, are an inefficient approach to preventing crime by incapacitation.").
87. See Federal Bureau of Investigations, US Department of Justice, 2016 Crime in the United States: Uniform Crime Reports, table 20 (2016), https://tinyurl.com/fn9adh45 (showing that individuals over the age of forty account for only 18 percent of the murders, 25 percent of the rapes, and 12 percent of the robberies that are committed).
88. Daniel S. Nagin, *Deterrence in the Twenty-First Century*, 42 Crime and Just. 199 (2013).
89. See George Antunes & A. Lee Hunt, *The Impact of Certainty and Severity of Punishment on Levels of Crime in American States: An Extended Analysis*, 64 J. Crim. L. & Criminology 486 (1973); Daniel S. Nagin, *Deterrence in the Twenty-First Century*, 42 Crime and Just. 199, 241 (2013).
90. See Voters Want Big Changes in Federal Sentencing, Prison System, *Pew* (Feb. 12, 2016), https://bit.ly/3mXmnuu (finding that "nearly 80 percent favor ending mandatory minimum sentences for drug offenses and that more than three-quarters support eliminating federal mandatory minimums in all cases," and that "more than 8 in 10 favor permitting federal prisoners to cut their time behind bars by up to 30 percent by participating in drug treatment and job training programs that are shown to reduce recidivism"). Even among those who have been victims of crimes, only a small minority prefer long prison sentences (Sawyer & Wagner, *supra* note 37).
91. See, e.g., People v. Hackler, 13 Cal. App. 5th 1049 (1993); United States v. Gementara, 379 F.3d 596 (9th Cir. 2004).
92. Beth Avery & Han Lu, Ban the Box: U.S. Cities, Counties, and States Adopt Fair Hiring Policies, *National Employment Law Project*, https://bit.ly/3Ln4zCv.
93. Margaret Colgate Love, Collateral Consequences Research Center, The Many Roads from Reentry to Reintegration (2022), bit.ly/41VtMJs.

2 A BRIEF HISTORY OF CRIME

1. James F. Pastor, The Privatization of Police in America: An Analysis and Case Study 34 (2003).
2. *Id.*
3. *Id.*

4. *Id.* at 34–35.
5. Paul Rock, Law, Order and Power in Late Seventeenth- and Early Eighteenth-Century England, *in* SOCIAL CONTROL AND THE STATE: HISTORICAL AND COMPARATIVE ESSAYS 191, 196 (Stanley Cohen & Andrew Scull eds., 1983).
6. See Pastor, *supra* note 1, at 35.
7. David Sklansky, *The Private Police*, 46 UCLA L. REV. 1165, 1198 (1999).
8. *Id.* at 1197–98.
9. David R. Johnson, AMERICAN LAW ENFORCEMENT: A HISTORY 31–32 (1981).
10. See Elizabeth E. Joh, *Conceptualizing the Private Police*, 2005 UTAH L. REV. 573, 582 (2005).
11. Pastor, *supra* note 1, at 36; Sklansky, *supra* note 7, at 1197, 1199.
12. T. A. Critchley, A HISTORY OF POLICE IN ENGLAND AND WALES 900–1966 47–57 (1967); Sklansky, *supra* note 7, at 1165, 1207.
13. Jill Lepore, The Invention of the Police, *New Yorker* (July 13, 2020), https://bit.ly/41QsyPG.
14. Sklansky, *supra* note 7, at 1208–09.
15. Connie Hassett-Walker, *How You Start Is How You Finish? The Slave Patrol and Jim Crow Origins of Policing*, 46 ABA HUM. RTS. MAG. (2021), https://bit.ly/3n39GhO.
16. Seth W. Stoughton, *The Blurred Blue Line: Reform in an Era of Public and Private Policing*, 44 AM. J. CRIM. L. 117, 126 (2017).
17. Sklansky, *supra* note 7, at 1210–17.
18. The agent in charge of this operation – and who personally accompanied the president-elect on his journey to the Capitol – was Kate Warne, thought to be the first female private investigator in the United States. She worked on a number of sensitive assignments for the Pinkerton Agency from 1856 until her death, at the age of 35, in 1868 (Erin Blakemore, The Woman Who Stopped an Early Attempt on President Lincoln's Life, *Time* (Mar. 3, 2017), https://time.com/4689230/first-female-detective/).
19. Gina Robertiello, THE USE AND ABUSE OF POLICE POWER IN AMERICA: HISTORICAL MILESTONES AND CURRENT CONTROVERSIES 20–22 (2017).
20. Sklansky, *supra* note 7, at 1216–17.
21. Sklansky, *supra* note 7, at 1202, 1206–19.
22. Paul Robinson & Sarah Robinson, SHADOW VIGILANTES: HOW DISTRUST IN THE JUSTICE SYSTEM BREEDS A NEW KIND OF LAWLESSNESS 37–39 (2018).
23. *Id.* at 43–45.
24. Beverly A. Smith & Frank T. Morn, The History of Privatization in Criminal Justice, *in* PRIVATIZATION IN CRIMINAL JUSTICE: PAST, PRESENT, AND FUTURE 3, 6–7 (David Shichor & Michael J. Gilbert eds., 2001).
25. Bruce L. Benson, TO SERVE AND PROTECT: PRIVATIZATION AND COMMUNITY IN CRIMINAL JUSTICE 94 (1998).
26. *Id.* at 95 (citing Juan Cardenas, *The Crime Victim in the Prosecutorial Process*, 9 HARV. J. L. & PUB. POL'Y 357 [1986]).
27. Benson, *supra* note 25, at 96.
28. Benson, *supra* note 25.
29. *Id.* at 106; Smith & Morn, *supra* note 24, at 10.
30. Benson, *supra* note 25, at 107.
31. *Id.* at 108.
32. *Id.* The number of arrestees who were discharged includes two for whom no decision was recorded but who were "apparently discharged."

33. *Id.* at 108–9. A similar committee formed five years later in San Francisco, again in response to rising crime rates, and operated for three months.
34. William E. Burrows, VIGILANTE! 20 (1976). Professor Burrows lists the prominent members of society that led or supported vigilante movements on the frontier: President Andrew Jackson; Theodore Roosevelt (before he was president); senators and governors from Missouri, Idaho, Louisiana, New Mexico, and California; and "scores of state legislators, city councilmen, mayors, and other local functionaries."
35. Richard Maxwell Brown, *Legal and Behavioral Perspectives on American Vigilantism, in* PERSPECTIVES IN AMERICAN HISTORY vol. 5 138 (1971).
36. Burrows, *supra* note 34, at 22.
37. *Id.* at 39–40. These quotes come from a manifesto allegedly written by the vigilante's leader, William Lynch. Most historians agree that this set of rules, which came to be known as "Lynch's Law," is the origin of the term "lynching."
38. *Id.* at 37–38. The reports of these "regulators" came from Elizabethtown, New Jersey, in 1752. This vigilante group would dress themselves in women's clothes, "paint their faces," and then force their way into the homes where men were known to beat their wives. They would then "strip him, turn him up his Posteriors, and flog him with Rods most severely, crying all the Time, 'Wo to the Men that beat their Wives.'" One woman reported that, ever since her husband was visited by the regulators, her husband "has entirely left off whipping me, and promises faithfully that he will never begin again," and that "there are some [other men] that are afraid of whipping their Wives, for fear of dancing the same Jigg . . ." (*id.* at 38).
39. *Id.* at 19.
40. *Id.* at 247–69.
41. Robinson & Robinson, *supra* note 22, at 117–26.
42. *Id.* at 16.
43. The United States Marshals were founded at the every beginning of the country, in 1789, but, as noted above, they were court officers who were primarily concerned with courtroom administration and serving warrants.
44. Michael Parker Banton, Police: Law Enforcement, The History of Policing in the West, *Encyclopaedia Britannica*, https://bit.ly/41YnIjM.
45. Number of Full-Time Law Enforcement Officers in the United States from 2004 to 2020, *Statista*, https://bit.ly/44ouRSg.
46. Bureau of Justice Statistics, US Department of Justice, HISTORICAL CORRECTIONS STATISTICS IN THE UNITED STATES, 1850–1984, 34 tables 3–6 (1986), https://bjs.ojp.gov/content/pub/pdf/hcsus5084.pdf.
47. Wendy Sawyer & Peter Wagner, Mass Incarceration: The Whole Pie 2020, *Prison Policy Initiative* (Mar. 24, 2022), www.prisonpolicy.org/reports/pie2020.html.
48. Tara O'Neill Hayes, The Economic Costs of the U.S. Criminal Justice System, *American Action Forum* (July 16, 2020), https://bit.ly/3L8HDFC. $142.5 billion are spent on policing, $88.5 billion are spent on jails and prisons, and $64.7 billion are spent on the court system.
49. *Statista, supra* note 45.
50. Sawyer & Wagner, *supra* note 47.

3 PUBLIC FAILINGS, PRIVATE OPPORTUNITIES

1. Jack B. Weinstein, Opinion: Drugs, Crime and Punishment; The War on Drugs Is Self-Defeating, *New York Times* (July 8, 1993), at A19.

2. Alan Feuer, This Judge Defends "Unredeemables" Even as He Sends Them to Prison, *New York Times* (Dec. 8, 2017), https://perma.cc/96JG-AUGU.
3. John Pfaff, Locked In 72–73 (2017).
4. *Id.* at 56. The median number of days served in prison as of 2010 for these crimes is as follows: armed robbery, 844; aggravated assault, 557; burglary, 427; petty larceny, 511; drug trafficking, between 313 and 455; and weapons charges, 546.
5. See Allegra M. McLeod, *Prison Aboliton and Grounded Justice*, 62 UCLA L. Rev. 1156 (2015); Prison Abolition, *The Marshall Project*, www.themarshallproject.org/records/4766-prison-abolition (last visited Oct. 23, 2022).
6. Bureau of Justice Statistics, US Department of Justice, Pretrial Release of Felony Defendants in State Courts 2 (2007), https://bjs.ojp.gov/content/pub/pdf/prfdsc.pdf; George E. Browne & Suzanne M. Strong, Bureau of Justice Statistics, US Department of Justice, Pretrial Release and Misconduct in Federal District Courts, Fiscal Years 2011–2018, NCJ 252837 (2022), https://bjs.ojp.gov/content/pub/pdf/prmfdcfy1118.pdf.
7. Malcolm M. Feely, The Process Is the Punishment: Handling Cases in a Lower Criminal Court (1992).
8. Carissa Byrne Hessick, Punishment Without Trial 107–29 (2021).
9. See, e.g., Gerald T. Hotaling & Eve S. Buzawa, Vicim Satisfaction with Criminal Justice Case Processing in a Model Court Setting (2003), www.ojp.gov/pdffiles1/nij/grants/195668.pdf.
10. In 1993, the number of violent crime victimizations was 79.8 per 1,000 people aged twelve and over in the United States. By 2021, that ratio had dropped dramatically to 16.5 per 1,000 people (Bureau of Justice Statistics, US Department of Justice, Criminal Victimization, 2021 [2022], https://bjs.ojp.gov/content/pub/pdf/cv21.pdf). However, violent crime rates in the United States tend to outpace violent crime rates in many other countries. For instance, in 2018, the number of homicides per 100,000 people in the United States was 5.01, compared with fewer than 2 per 100,000 in Australia, Canada, Japan, Italy, Germany, France, and the United Kingdom, among others (Victims of Intentional Homicide, *U.N. Office on Drugs and Crime*, https://dataunodc.un.org/dp-intentional-homicide-victims [last visited Oct. 23, 2022]).
11. This number is down from a high value of 48 percent in 1982, but is still higher than in 1965, when it was 34 percent.
12. Crime, *Gallup*, https://news.gallup.com/poll/1603/Crime.aspx (last visited Oct. 23, 2022).
13. Bruce L. Benson, To Serve and Protect: Privatization and Community in Criminal Justice 69 (1998).
14. One observer described the process over thirty years ago: waiting "tedious, unconscionably long intervals of time in dingy courthouse corridors," being "ignored by busy officials," and returning time and again for criminal cases that keep getting adjourned without explanation – although each trip to the courthouse still could instill "tension and terror" at the thought of having to testify in open court against the defendant (Michael Ash, *On Witnesses: A Radical Critique of Criminal Court Procedures*, 48 Notre Dame L. Rev. 386, 390 [1972]). "In sum, the experience is dreary, time-wasting, depressing, exhausting, confusing, frustrating, numbing and seemingly endless" (*id.*). See also Benson, *supra* note 13, at 54. Benson notes that after having already suffered at the hands of the criminal, the victim must pay for transportation and related costs for the multiple trips to meet with the prosecutor and lost wages for the days spent preparing the case or at trial, in addition to the emotional and psychological costs of the process (*id.*). See, e.g., Paul G. Cassell, *Balancing the Scales of Justice: The Case For and the Effects of Utah's Victims' Rights Amendment*, 1994 Utah L. Rev. 1373, 1402–05 (1994) (describing a sexual molestation case

involving numerous children that lasted nearly nine months from arrest to plea, including over ten different court appearances). The victim–witness coordinator on the case stated: "The delays were a nightmare [for the children involved]. Every time the counselors for the children would call and say we are back to step one. The frustration level was unbelievable" (*id.* at 1405; quoting interview with Betty Mueller, victim–witness coordinator, in Weber County, Utah [Oct. 6, 1993]).

15. The limited role of victims in criminal prosecutions has been one of the primary complaints of the victims' rights movement. See, e.g., Josephine Gittler, *Expanding the Role of the Victim in a Criminal Action: An Overview of Issues and Problems*, 11 PEPP. L. REV. 117, 123 (1984): "Increasingly, demands are being made not only for better treatment of victims as witnesses, but also for expansion of the role of the victim beyond that of a witness." As a result of the victims' rights movement, most victims have the right to be notified of the proceedings and to speak at sentencing.
16. President's Task Force on Victims of Crime, *Final Report* ii (1982), https://bit.ly/3L3t1Yd. See also *Office for Victims of Crime*, https://ovc.ojp.gov (last visited Oct. 28, 2022).
17. Sarah Brown Hammond, National Conference of State Legislatures, VICTIMS' RIGHTS LAWS IN THE STATES 19, 25 (2006), www.ojp.gov/pdffiles1/Digitization/218944NCJRS.pdf.
18. Cortney Fisher, WHAT MATTERS: AN ANALYSIS OF VICTIM SATISFACTION IN A PROCEDURAL JUSTICE FRAMEWORK 73 (2014), https://bit.ly/3n01jDL (on a scale of 1 (not at all satisfied) to 4 (very satisfied), survey respondents mean score regarding satisfaction with the criminal justice system was 2.37); Robert C. Davis et al., NO MORE RIGHTS WITHOUT REMEDIES: AN IMPACT EVALUATION OF THE NATIONAL CRIME VICTIM LAW INSTITUTE'S VICTIMS' RIGHTS CLINICS 41 (2014), https://bit.ly/3LtxDIv (among victims who *did not* have a National Crime Victim Law Institute victims' rights clinic attorney – essentially the general, control population for the purposes of this study – the mean satisfaction with the criminal justice process was 2.43 on a scale of 1 [strongly agree] to 5 [strongly disagree]).
19. Hotaling & Buzawa, *supra* note 9.
20. Hammond, *supra* note 17, at 25–26.
21. See After Weeks of Protest, a Look at Policy Changes in U.S. Policing, *Vera Institute* (July 22, 2020), www.vera.org/policy-changes-in-us-policing (hereinafter *Vera Institute*).
22. *Id.*
23. Sam Levin, These US Cities Defunded Police: "We're Transferring Money to the Community," *Guardian* (Mar. 11, 2020), https://bit.ly/44oDNqJ. Some advocates noted that $840 million in cuts is a small percentage of the approximately $100 billion that the nation spends on police every year, but it reverses the trend of police spending having increased by 300 percent over the last four decades.
24. Fola Akinnibi et al., Cities Say They Want to Defund the Police. Their Budgets Say Otherwise, *Bloomberg: CityLab* (Jan. 12, 2021), www.bloomberg.com/graphics/2021-city-budget-police-funding/.
25. See Zusha Elinson et al., Cities Reverse Defunding the Police Amid Rising Crime, *Wall Street Journal* (May 26, 2021), https://bit.ly/41EpUNv (noting that, in response to higher rates of homicide and other serious crimes, "[i]n the nation's 20 largest local law-enforcement agencies, city and county leaders want funding increases for nine of the 12 departments where next year's budgets already have been proposed."); J. D. Capelouto, Atlanta Almost Withheld $73M in Police Funding Last Year. What's Changed Since Then?, *Atlanta Journal-Constitution* (June 21, 2021), https://bit.ly/40FkdNR (noting that, in 2020, the Atlanta City Council came within one vote of cutting the police budget by $73 million and, in 2021, this same council unanimously increased the budget by $15 million in response to higher rates of violent crime); As Violent Crime Leaps,

Liberal Cities Rethink Cutting Police Budgets, *Economist* (Jan. 15, 2022), https://bit.ly/3Hf6Flu (noting that, although the mayor of Los Angeles called for a cut of up to $150 million to the police budget in 2020, the Los Angeles Police Department will get a 12 percent increase in funding in 2022).
26. *Vera Institute*, *supra* note 21. Some might argue that the presence of armed police officers actually decreases the chance that arrestees will turn violent; thus, if a lower percentage of interactions involved armed police officers, the number of violent encounters could increase. This is possible, although it seems equally feasible that the presence of armed officers could be increasing the incidence of violence; it may mean that police officers are less likely to de-escalate a situation, and it may lead to a more confrontational response by the suspect.
27. See, e.g., Colin Kaepernick (ed.), ABOLITION FOR THE PEOPLE: THE MOVEMENT FOR A FUTURE WITHOUT POLICING & PRISONS (2021); Alex S. Vitale, THE END OF POLICING 47 (2017); Alec Karakatsanis, Why "Crime" Isn't the Question and Police Are Not the Answer, *Current Affairs* (Aug. 10, 2020), https://bit.ly/3n3qMMq; Derecka Purnell, How I Became a Police Abolitionist, *Atlantic* (July 20, 2020), https://bit.ly/3HesDFh.
28. Sharon Kwon, It's Time to Defund the Police and Start Funding Social Workers, *HuffPost* (June 15, 2020), https://bit.ly/41XgTi5.
29. The city of Camden, New Jersey, is occasionally used as a model for how a municipality will function after defunding of the police, as it disbanded its police department in the early 2010s. See Chris Megerian, Disband the Police? Camden Already Did That, *Los Angeles Times* (June 10, 2020), https://bit.ly/4212LEv. However, the disbanding of the Camden police department led to more officers being hired to patrol the city under county control. Improvements in police practices and police–community relations came about later as a result of pressure from city activists. See Stephen Danley, Camden Police Reboot Is Being Misused in the Debate over Police Reform, *Washington Post* (June 16, 2020), https://bit.ly/40EKb4b; but see also Thin Lei Win, Defunding the Police: Does Europe Offer Lessons for the U.S.?, *Thomson Reuters Foundation* (June 18, 2020), https://news.trust.org/item/20200618160416-wqfm8/ (discussing European policing models that partially or fully reflect some elements of the previously mentioned reforms).
30. See, e.g., Stephen Rushin & Roger Michalski, *Police Funding*, 72 FLA. L. REV. 277, 277 (2020).
31. See Shima Baradaran Baughman, *Crime and the Mythology of Police*, 99 WASH. U. L. REV., 65, 101–02 (2021) (arguing that "the vast majority of police time is spent on noncriminal functions such as health, transportation and public order").
32. *Id.* at 102.
33. See Julia Haines, States with the Most Arrests for Marijuana Possession, *U.S. News* (Oct. 17, 2022), https://bit.ly/3Nbj5P5 (noting that state marijuana arrests have rapidly dropped from 226,000 in 2020 to 170,856 in 2021).
34. Danielle Cohen, Here's How a 911 Call Without Police Could Work, *GQ* (June 12, 2020), www.gq.com/story/how-a-911-call-without-police-could-work.
35. *Id.*
36. *Id.* See also Win, *supra* note 29.
37. See CAT-911, https://cat-911.org/.
38. *Id.*
39. See Mathew Desmond et al., *Police Violence and Citizen Crime Reporting in the Black Community*, 81 AM. SOC. REV. 857, 864–70 (2016).
40. See Lawrence Rosenthal, *The Law and Economics of De-Policing*, 33 FED. SENT'G REP., 128, 128, 130 (2020) (citing studies of de-policing conducted by Professor Paul Cassell, which show sharp decreases in *Terry* stops and increases in violent crime in many major

cities following the protests over the killing of George Floyd in 2020, as well as a similar occurrence in Chicago following the killing of Laquan McDonald in 2016).

41. See Erin Duffin, Number of Law Enforcement Officers U.S. 2004–2021, *Statista* (Oct. 11, 2022), https://bit.ly/3NmG4qe (statistical analysis of the number of full-time law enforcement officers in the United States demonstrating a steady rise from 2013 to 2019 followed by a drop in 2020 and 2021).

4 PRIVATE LAW ENFORCEMENT

1. Elizabeth E. Joh, *Conceptualizing the Private Police*, 2005 UTAH L. REV. 573, 584–85 (2005) (hereinafter Joh, *Conceptualizing*).
2. See generally Kevin Cook, KITTY GENOVESE: THE MURDER, THE BYSTANDERS, THE CRIME THAT CHANGED AMERICA (2014).
3. James S. Kakalik & Sorrel Wildhorn, RAND Corporation, PRIVATE POLICE IN THE UNITED STATES: FINDINGS AND RECOMMENDATIONS, 11 (1971), www.rand.org/content/dam/rand/pubs/reports/2006/R869.pdf; James S. Kakalik & Sorrel Wildhorn, RAND Corporation, THE PRIVATE POLICE INDUSTRY: ITS NATURE AND EXTENT 34 (1971), www.rand.org/pubs/reports/R0870.html.
4. James K. Stewart, *Public Safety and Private Police*, 45 PUB. ADMIN. REV., 758, 758 (1985).
5. *Id.* at 760. In 1980, an estimated $22 billion was spent on private security and $14 billion was spent on public law enforcement agencies.
6. Amelia Pollard, The Rise of the Private Police, *The American Prospect* (Mar. 3, 2021), https://prospect.org/justice/rise-of-the-private-police/ (last visited Nov. 19, 2022).
7. See, e.g., Michael Barbaro, Hot Off the Shelves: Shoplifting Gangs Are Retailing's Top Enemy, *New York Times* (Nov. 8, 2005), at C1 (discussing retail security efforts); Michael Leahy, Crimes and Misdemeanors: High School Security Chief Wally Baranyk Says Most of the Wrongdoing in Suburban High Schools Goes on in the Shadows. So How Dark Does It Get?, *Washington Post* (June 4, 2006), at W08; Suzanne Smalley, A Force of Their Own: Neighborhood's Private Guards Help Keep the Peace, *Boston Globe* (May 26, 2006), at B1 (discussing residential security patrols); William Yardley, Does It Work? Campus Security: Finding Safety in Numbers, *New York Times* (Jan. 8, 2006), at A18 (discussing security on college campuses). The casino security establishment dedicates substantial resources to gaming enforcement, which also includes a sustained focus on employee monitoring. See generally Gary L. Powell et al., CASINO SURVEILLANCE AND SECURITY: 150 THINGS YOU SHOULD KNOW (2003) (examining various aspects of casino security).
8. Bruce L. Benson, TO SERVE AND PROTECT: PRIVATIZATION AND COMMUNITY IN CRIMINAL JUSTICE 18 (1998).
9. Seth W. Stoughton, *The Blurred Line: Reform in an Era of Public and Private Policing*, 44 AM. J. CRIM. L. 117, 127–41 (2017).
10. National Retail Federation, 2020 NATIONAL RETAIL SECURITY SURVEY 1 (2020), https://bit.ly/41We2Gg.
11. John Colapinto, Stop, Thief!, *New Yorker* (Aug. 25, 2008), www.newyorker.com/magazine/2008/09/01/stop-thief. Experts estimate that department stores lose between 1 and 2 percent of their annual sales to theft. Target had total sales of just over $100 billion in 2021 (Target Corporation, TARGET CORPORATION REPORTS FOURTH QUARTER AND FULL-YEAR 2021 EARNINGS [2022]).
12. Kaveh Waddell, CSI: Walmart, *The Atlantic* (Apr. 3, 2017), https://bit.ly/441IdoH.

13. Among the many clients of the private police industry are government agencies: Federal, state, and local governments rely on private security firms for a substantial part of their work. However, as noted in the introduction, the mere "contracting out" of criminal justice services to private individuals is not the same as privatization, as the public agency dictates the goals of the private security they hire, in the same way that they dictate the goals of the individual police officers they hire.
14. Mary Anne Perez, BOYLE HEIGHTS: Groups Join Forces to Combat Crime, Los Angeles Times (Oct. 2, 1994), https://bit.ly/3V9m1xA.
15. Id.
16. Joe Barrett, In Chicago, Wealthy Neighborhoods Hire Their Own Private Police as Crime Rises, Wall Street Journal (Apr. 29, 2022), https://bit.ly/3Lbspjl.
17. Clifford D. Shearing & Philip C. Stenning (eds.), PRIVATE POLICING 247–48 (1987).
18. David Sklansky, The Private Police, 46 UCLA L. REV. 1165, 1222 (1999).
19. See, e.g., Joh, Conceptualizing, supra note 1, at 590–91:

> Consider the apprehension of a shoplifter in a department store. Assisting in a formal police investigation represents to the store time and effort deflected from its business, as well as the potential for negative publicity – all of which may be more costly than the initial disruption. If the thief is an employee, public prosecution likely means the loss of the employee's services. Finally, crimes such as shoplifting may constitute a low priority for public police departments; for a private police client, such theft may be its most serious problem.

20. See generally Elizabeth E. Joh, The Paradox of Private Policing, 95 J. CRIM. L. CRIMINOLOGY 49 (2004).
21. Id. at 86.
22. Joh, Conceptualizing, supra note 1, at 587.
23. See Clifford D. Shearing & Philip C. Stenning, Private Security: Implications for Social Control, in UNDERSTANDING POLICING 521, 531–32 (Kevin R. E. McCormick & Lily A. Visano eds., 1992).
24. See About Neighborhood Watch, National Neighborhood Watch, www.nnw.org/about-neighborhood-watch (last visited Nov. 20, 2022).
25. National Crime Prevention Council, ARE WE SAFE? THE 2000 NATIONAL CRIME PREVENTION SURVEY (2001), https://bit.ly/3LvFQMc.
26. Campbell Robertson & John Schwartz, Shooting Focuses Attention on a Program That Seeks to Avoid Guns, New York Times (Mar. 22, 2012), https://bit.ly/3Hfhcgw.
27. Sharon Finegan, Watching the Watchers: The Growing Privatization of Criminal Law Enforcement and the Need for Limits on Neighborhood Watch Associations, 8 U. MASS. L. REV. 88, 103–04 (2013).
28. Id. at 104–05.
29. Vicki Quade, For Neighborhoods, The Payoff Is Safety, 69 A.B.A. J. 1806 (1983).
30. Katy Holloway et al., Campbell Crime and Justice Group, CRIME PREVENTION RESEARCH REVIEW NO. 3: DOES NEIGHBORHOOD WATCH REDUCE CRIME? 6, 8 (2008).
31. Vicki Quade, Our Neighbors' Keepers: Citizens Are Joining with Police to Cut Crime, 69 A. B.A. J. 1805, 1806 (1983).
32. Douglas I. Brandon et al., Self-Help: Extrajudicial Rights, Privileges and Remedies in Contemporary American Society, 37 VAND. L. REV. 845, 895–901 (1984).
33. New York City Mayor Ed Koch originally referred to the Guardian Angels as "vigilantes," while the mayor of Elizabeth, New Jersey, said that they were "contrary to what an American democratic society expects" and that the group was "nothing more than

a sophisticated group of young people banded together to form a street gang" (*id.* at 897, notes 333 and 335).
34. *Id.* at 899, note 345.
35. Josh Kruger, Vigilante Group Guardian Angels Restarts in Philly, Chronicles Targeting "Homeless Addicts," *Philadelphia Weekly* (June 1, 2022), https://bit.ly/3V6yC4q.
36. *Id.*; Bruce Handy, Back to the Eighties: Crime, Yucky Subways, and the Guardian Angels!, *New Yorker* (Oct. 11, 2021), https://bit.ly/3HhxtkV.
37. Wesley G. Skogan & Susan M. Hartnett, Community Policing, Chicago Style 173, 174–78, 223–25, 227, 230 (1997).
38. Dan Kahan, *Reciprocity, Collective Action, and Community Policing*, 90 Cal. L. Rev. 1513, 1515–17 (2002).
39. *Id.* at 1537.
40. *Id.* at 1537–38.
41. Samir Ferdowsi, Inside the Now "Cop-Free" Zone Where George Floyd was Killed, *VICE News* (Mar. 12, 2021), https://bit.ly/3mYhu4B. The ability of this police-free zone to maintain security is mixed at best; the George Floyd Square occupied protest had its share of violence in and around the police-free zone. See Mohamed Ibrahim, Officer's trial could reopen intersection where Floyd died, *AP News* (Mar. 6, 2021), https://bit.ly/3oOYtBO (fatal shooting of Dameon Chambers); Paul Walsh, 2nd murder count for death of prematurely born girl whose mother was shot in Minneapolis, *Star Tribune* (Aug. 6, 2020), https://bit.ly/40JtkNw (killing of Leneesha and Baby Columbus); David Schuman, Years later, no arrests in Minneapolis carjacking that left victim in wheelchair, *CBS News* (June 10, 2022), https://bit.ly/3LvmwyC (shooting of Ben Schmid); Libor Jany, Minneapolis police announce 2 arrests in George Floyd Square shooting death, *Star Tribune* (Mar. 11, 2021), https://bit.ly/41I6Iyk (fatal shooting of Imez Wright).
42. Rosette Royale, Seattle's Autonomous Zone Is Not What You've Been Told, *Rolling Stone* (June 19, 2020), https://bit.ly/3ndje9U.
43. Brendan Kiley et al., Seattle Police Clear CHOP Protest Zone, *Seattle Times* (July 1, 2020), https://bit.ly/3L6uoXv. The actual level of violence in CHOP is still a matter of dispute; the Seattle police chief claimed that "This order [to reclaim CHOP], and our police response, comes after weeks of violence in and around the Capitol Hill Occupied Protests Zone, including four shootings, resulting in multiple injuries and the deaths of two teenagers." Many local residents supported CHOP, although some residents (including some of the area's homeless population) left the area because of growing violence within the area. Many business owners inside CHOP pointed to vandalism of their property, threats, and a sense of lawlessness that made it impossible to do business.
44. Meredith Hoffman, Whatever Happened to Arizona's Minutemen? *Vice* (Mar. 22, 2016), https://bit.ly/41YjUPh. The Minutemen were controversial – they were denounced as "vigilantes" by then-President Bush but found support from then-Governor Schwarzenegger. See Peter Nicholas & Robert Salladay, Gov. Praises "Minuteman" Campaign, *Los Angeles Times* (Apr. 29, 2005), https://bit.ly/3LbJeL7.
45. Lorenzo Franceschi-Bicchierai, Meet the Vigilantes Who Hack Millions in Crypto to Save It from Thieves, *Vice: Motherboard* (June 6, 2022), https://tinyurl.com/3jdub9tu.
46. Elizabeth Joh, A Gig Surveillance Economy 5 (2021) (hereinafter Joh, Gig Economy).
47. See, e.g., 3DK9, www.3dk9detection.com/ (last visited Nov. 20, 2022).
48. Drew Harwell, License Plate Scanners Were Supposed to Bring Peace of Mind. Instead They Tore the Neighborhood Apart, *Washington Post* (Oct. 22, 2021), https://tinyurl.com/mskdvw8e. Most of the neighborhoods that install Flock's cameras have a median household income of $60,000 a year. *Id.*

49. John Herrman, All the Crime, All the Time: How Citizen Works, *New York Times* (Mar. 17, 2019), https://tinyurl.com/4nttghte.
50. Amazon originally allowed police to request footage from Ring cameras directly from the user; it recently changed its app so that police must make a public request (Christopher Smith, Neighborhood Watch Goes Rogue: The Trouble with Nextdoor and Citizen, *PC Mag* [July 8, 2021], https://tinyurl.com/2xw99nv6).
51. Brian Stelter, Considering Next Steps for "Wanted," *New York Times* (May 17, 2011), https://tinyurl.com/y2pynr8p.
52. Wayne A. Logan, *Crowdsourcing Crime Control*, 99 TEX. L. REV. 137, 146–47 (2020).
53. RBI: Reddit Bureau of Investigation, *Reddit*, www.reddit.com/r/RBI/ (last visited Nov. 20, 2022).
54. Logan, *supra* note 51, at 147–48.
55. *Id.* at 152–53.
56. Joh, GIG ECONOMY, *supra* note 45, at 6–7. As Professor Joh notes, "None of these gig jobs require special investigatory skills; all can be outsourced cheaply. In this way, these focused surveillance gig jobs share only a surface similarity to traditional private investigation. Moreover, in the arm's-length transactions of the gig economy, individual surveillance gig workers may have no idea for whom or for what purpose they are collecting the information" (*id.* at 7).
57. Smith, *supra* note 49. Professor Logan also points out that crowdsourcing led to misidentifications after the violent actions related to the Charlottesville, Virginia, demonstrations. Logan, *supra* note 51, at 148.
58. Logan, *supra* note 51, at 149.
59. See Rani Molla, The Rise of Fear-Based Social Media Like Nextdoor, Citizen, and Now Amazon's Neighbors, *Vox* (May 7, 2019), https://tinyurl.com/2ndr98tj.
60. Team Nextdoor, Nextdoor Removes "Forward to Police" Feature, *Nextdoor: nBlog* (June 18, 2020), https://tinyurl.com/5n73hm42. The Nextdoor CEO stated that she wanted to "draw... a firm line against racist behavior, racial bias, and racial profiling...." See also Smith, *supra* note 49.
61. See Finegan, *supra* note 26, at 105–06: "[P]erhaps the most troubling problem associated with neighborhood watch programs are their tendency to impinge upon the civil liberties of those living within the community."
62. See Sklansky, *supra* note 17, at 1184.
63. Cal. Penal Code § 490.5(f)(4) (West) (permitting "a limited and reasonable search" of packages, bags, and personal property possessed by the suspect, but not clothing).
64. See Lynn M. Gagel, *Comment, Stealthy Encroachments Upon the Fourth Amendment: Constitutional Constraints and Their Applicability to the Long Arm of Ohio's Private Security Forces*, 63 U. CIN. L. REV. 1807, 1837 (1995).
65. Jonathan Drimmer, *When Man Hunts Man: The Rights and Duties of Bounty Hunters in the American Criminal Justice System*, 33 HOUS. L. REV. 731, 763 (1996).
66. See Skinner v. Railway Labor Executives' Ass'n, 489 U.S. 602, 614 (1989).
67. United States v. Lima, 424 A.2d 113, 121 (D.C. 1980).
68. Barrows v. J.C. Penney Co., 753 A.2d 404, 405–06 (Conn. App. Ct. 2000).
69. See, e.g., John M. Burkoff, *Not So Private Searches and the Constitution*, 66 CORNELL L. REV. 627, 627 (1981); Erwin Chemerinsky, *Rethinking State Action*, 80 NW. U. L. REV. 503, 504–05 (1985). However, see Sklansky, *supra* note 17, at 1270–73 (arguing that to "jettison the state action doctrine altogether in criminal procedure" would be "the wrong response").
70. Daniel S. Nagin, *Deterrence in the Twenty-First Century, in* CRIME AND JUSTICE IN AMERICA: 1975–2025 241 (Michael Tonry ed., 2013). Professor Nagin also uses the term

"capable guardian" to describe these sentinels, a term he borrows from Lawrence E. Cohem and Marcus Felson (Lawrence E. Cohen & Marcus Felson, *Social Change and Crime Rate Trends: A Routine Activity Approach*, 44 AM. SOCIOL. REV. 588 (1979).
71. Sklansky, *supra* note 17, at 1191–92.
72. See Koo Hui-Wen, *Private Security: Deterrent or Diversion?*, 14 INT'L REV. L. & ECON. 87 (1994).
73. See Finegan, *supra* note 26, at 105: "Despite their prevalence and popularity, these programs are rife with challenges. Lack of training, poor organization, tendencies to target certain demographic groups, and overzealous interactions with suspects are common complaints regarding neighborhood watch programs."

5 PRIVATE CRIMINAL SETTLEMENTS AS PLEA BARGAINS

1. See, e.g., Erik Luna, *The Overcriminalization Phenomenon*, 54 AM. U. L. REV. 703, 727 (2005): "Mistrusting citizens are less likely to assist law enforcement and to obey legal commands, which undermines the efforts of police and prosecutors and, paradoxically, renders the law counterproductive."
2. Under the doctrine of collateral estoppel, a criminal conviction is admissible in a subsequent civil case and usually precludes the defendant from challenging the issue of liability. See, e.g., Am. Fam. Mut. Ins. Co. v. Savickas, 739 N.E.2d 445, 449–50 (Ill. 2000).
3. See, e.g., Mike Hepworth, BLACKMAIL: PUBLICITY AND SECRECY IN EVERYDAY LIFE 73–77 (1975); Mitchell N. Berman, *The Evidentiary Theory of Blackmail: Taking Motives Seriously*, 65 U. CHI. L. REV. 795, 860 (1998); Jennifer Gerarda Brown, *Blackmail as Private Justice*, 141 U. PA. L. REV. 1935, 1935–36 (1993); William M. Landes & Richard A. Posner, *Private Enforcement of Law*, 4 J. LEGAL STUD. 1, 42–44 (1975).
4. See, e.g., 18 U.S.C. § 873 (2006); see also Cal. Penal Code §§ 518, 519 (West 2010) (describing extortion as "fear" induced by a threat to expose a secret or crime); N.Y. Penal Law § 135.60(4) (McKinney 2020) (describing the offense of "coercion in the third degree" as a class A misdemeanor); Ohio Rev. Code Ann. § 2921.22(A)(1) (LexisNexis 2010).
5. For a discussion of bargaining theory, see generally Robert J. Condlin, *"Every Day and in Every Way We Are All Becoming Meta and Meta," or How Communitarian Bargaining Theory Conquered the World (of Bargaining Theory)*, 23 OHIO ST. J. ON DISP. RESOL. 231 (2008).
6. See, e.g., Oren Bar-Gill & Omri Ben-Shahar, *The Prisoners' (Plea Bargain) Dilemma*, 1 J. LEGAL ANALYSIS 737, 748–50 (2009) (listing factors that affect potential trial outcome).
7. Malcom M. Feeley, THE PROCESS IS THE PUNISHMENT: HANDLING CASES IN A LOWER CRIMINAL COURT 30–31 (1979).
8. See Ariz. Rev. Stat. Ann. § 12–691 (LexisNexis 2016); Ark. Code Ann. § 16–122-102 (LexisNexis 2016); N.C. Gen. Stat. Ann. § 1–538.2 (LexisNexis 2015); W. Va. Code Ann. § 61-3A-3 (LexisNexis 2014); 11 R.I. Gen. Laws Ann. § 11–41-28 (LexisNexis 2020 Supp.).
9. See Bruce Mohl, Retailers' Message to Shoplifters: Pay Up or Risk Prosecution, Boston Globe (Dec. 11, 2005), at C1.
10. John Rappaport, *Criminal Justice, Inc.*, 118 COL. L. REV. 2251, 2272–76 (2018). The CEC was founded in 2010 and its clients included Walmart, Bloomingdale's, DSW, Abercrombie & Fitch, Burlington Coat Factory, Whole Foods, American Apparel, Goodwill Industries, Sport Chalet, Kroger, Sportsman's Warehouse, and H&M. *Id.* at 2272–73.

11. *Id.* at 2273.
12. *Id.* at 2273–74.
13. *Id.* at 2274.
14. *Id.* at 2273.
15. *Id.* at 2274.
16. *Id.* at 2273, note 132. Approximately 3–4 percent of those who enrolled got a scholarship, which usually covered at least half of the fee.
17. *Id.* at 2274–75.
18. See e.g., *Weekend Edition Saturday: Social Media Posts Warn People Not to Call 988: Here's What You Need to Know* (NPR radio broadcast, Aug. 11, 2022), describing widespread online concern that using the United States' newly activated "988" mental health hotline would invite unwanted involvement from law enforcement, particularly among communities of color and LGBTQ communities; Abimbola Johnson, My Black Friends Fear Calling the Police. That's Why I'm Taking On Racism in the Force, *Guardian* (Oct. 25, 2021), https://tinyurl.com/mu96paf4 (British opinion piece discussing a common fear of calling the police within communities of color); University of South Florida, New Study Reveals Racial Disparities in Fear of Police Brutality, *Phys.org* (June 15, 2020) (citing a study showing increased fear of police brutality among people of color).
19. See e.g., David A. Sklansky, *The Nature and Function of Prosecutorial Power*, 106 CRIM. L. & CRIMINOLOGY 473, 480–81 (2016) (characterizing prosecutors as limitless, absolute rulers in the criminal justice context and citing another's description of their power as "the 'overriding evil' of American criminal justice") (citations omitted).
20. John Gramlich, Only 2% of Federal Criminal Defendants Go to Trial, and Most Who Do Are Found Guilty, *Pew Research Center* (June 11, 2019), https://tinyurl.com/yuu2t33c (noting that, of the 80,000 federal criminal defendants in 2018, 2 percent went to trial, 90 percent pleaded guilty, and 8 percent had their cases dismissed); Lindsey Devers, CSR, Incorporated, PLEA AND CHARGE BARGAINING: RESEARCH SUMMARY 1 (2011), https://tinyurl.com/mrxz22x7 (noting that guilty pleas comprised 95 percent of federal cases disposed of by trial or plea deal in 2003, and citing scholars in the 1990s and 2000s claiming that between 90 and 95 percent of both federal and state court cases were resolved through plea bargaining).
21. One of the most passionate critics of the plea-bargaining process is Professor Albert Alschuler. See, e.g., Albert W. Alschuler, *The Trial Judge's Role in Plea Bargaining, Part I*, 76 COLUM. L. REV. 1059, 1141–42 (1976) (hereinafter Alschuler, *Trial Judge's Role*) (characterizing plea bargaining as a "deliberate mislabeling of offenses"). Professor Alschuler has written at least seven articles attacking the process of plea bargaining; for a summary of his critiques, see Albert W. Alschuler, *Implementing the Criminal Defendant's Right to Trial: Alternatives to the Plea Bargaining System*, 50 U. CHI. L. REV. 931, 931–34 (1983) (hereinafter Alschuler, *Right to Trial*). He concludes that "an effort to describe comprehensively the evils that plea bargaining has wrought requires an extensive tour of the criminal justice system." *Id.* at 934; see also John H. Langbein, *Torture and Plea Bargaining*, 46 U. CHI. L. REV. 3, 18 (1978) (analogizing plea bargaining to medieval torture); Stephen J. Schulhofer, *Is Plea Bargaining Inevitable?*, 97 HARV. L. REV. 1037, 1106 (1984) (arguing that plea bargaining short-circuits the adversarial system); Carissa Byrne Hessick, PUNISHMENT WITHOUT TRIAL: WHY PLEA BARGAINING IS A BAD DEAL (2021) (arguing that the criminal justice system is now designed around plea bargains rather than trials, which leads to a lot of unintended – and socially undesirable – consequences).

22. See, e.g., Gerard E. Lynch, *Our Administrative System of Criminal Justice*, 66 FORDHAM L. REV. 2117, 2136–41 (1998) (arguing that plea bargaining allows prosecutors to exercise necessary discretion); Robert E. Scott & William J. Stuntz, *Plea Bargaining as Contract*, 101 YALE L.J. 1909, 1915 (1992) (arguing that if defendants truly have the right to a jury and other procedural trial rights, they should have the ability to trade these rights away in exchange for the consideration of a lower sentence); Frank H. Easterbrook, *Criminal Procedure as a Market System*, 12 J. LEGAL STUD. 289, 297 (1983) (noting that both parties save resources by agreeing to a plea bargain).
23. See Thea Johnson, *Fictional Pleas*, 94 IND. L. J. 855 (2019).
24. See Alschuler, *Trial Judge's Role*, supra note 21, at 1141–42; Brown, supra note 3, at 1974.
25. *Id.* at 1974.
26. See Alschuler, *Trial Judge's Role*, supra note 21, at 1142. Professor Alschuler also notes that mislabeling can make it difficult for a court or a defendant to determine whether a defendant has been convicted of a crime that has later been found to be unconstitutional, and that mislabeling the crimes "may encourage a belief in the hypocrisy of the guilty plea system" (*id.* at 1141–42).
27. See Johnson, supra note 23, at 898: "The 'downstream actors' – whether a future judge, district attorney, or probation officer, reviewing the rap sheet of a defendant – will not ask themselves if the conviction was or was not the result of a particular type of bargain, but will accept the conviction as fact."
28. See Brown, supra note 3, at 1974: "[Incriminatory blackmail] involves no public review of the facts or interpretation of the law. It transfers an otherwise public process to a private venue where records are sealed and results are inaccessible."
29. See, e.g., Lynch, supra note 22, at 2123 (noting that poorer defendants may end up with less favorable plea bargains, but also arguing that income disparity results in inequality for cases that go to trial).
30. Professor Steven Shavell made a similar point when discussing the possibility of allowing police officers to profit from collecting what he calls "privately arranged bounties" when making arrests (Steven Shavell, *An Economic Analysis of Threats and Their Illegality: Blackmail, Extortion, and Robbery*, 141 U. PA. L. REV. 1877, 1901 [1993]). He criticized this idea because the police would spend a disproportionate amount of resources on investigating wealthy suspects; thus, "a poor murderer would not be sought after since he could not pay much, whereas a wealthy man who got involved in a brawl would be a prime target." This problem could be avoided by forbidding police officers from engaging in private criminal settlements; as police officers have a duty to report (and act on) criminal activity, they should not be permitted to engage in private criminal settlements under any circumstances.
31. See, e.g., Albert W. Alschuler, *The Changing Plea Bargaining Debate*, 69 CALIF. L. REV. 652, 713–16 (1981); Douglas G. Gifford, *Meaningful Reform of Plea Bargaining: The Control of Prosecutorial Discretion*, 1983 U. ILL. L. REV. 37, 58–61 (1983); Kenneth Kipnis, *Criminal Justice and the Negotiated Plea*, 86 ETHICS 93, 97–99 (1976); Scott & Stuntz, supra note 22, at 1948.
32. *Id.* at 1948 (footnote omitted):

> Innocent defendants are probably highly risk averse relative to guilty defendants. . . . In other words, due in part to adjudication costs, the risk from going to trial is likely to be substantial, not because the probabilities of conviction are altered, but because the impact of conviction is so great. Risk averse defendants, meaning in part innocent ones, might well avoid that risk even at the cost of accepting a deal that treats them as if they were certain to be convicted at trial.

33. Oren Gazal-Ayal, *Partial Ban on Plea Bargains*, 27 CARDOZO L. REV. 2295, 2304–05 (2006) (footnotes omitted).
34. See, e.g., Thomas W. Church, Jr., *In Defense of "Bargain Justice,"* 13 LAW & SOC'Y REV. 509, 523 (1979); Stephanos Bibas, *Plea Bargaining Outside the Shadow of Trial*, 117 HARV. L. REV. 2464, 2467–68 (2004) (hereinafter Bibas, *Plea Bargaining*).
35. See, e.g., Stephen J. Schulhofer, *Criminal Justice Discretion as a Regulatory System*, 17 J. LEGAL STUD. 43, 49–60 (1988).
36. See Easterbrook, *supra* note 22, at 289 (arguing that plea bargaining is an element "of a well-functioning market system"); Frank H. Easterbrook, *Plea Bargaining as Compromise*, 101 YALE L.J. 1969, 1972 (1992); see also Church, *supra* note 34; William M. Landes, *An Economic Analysis of the Courts*, 14 J.L. & ECON. 61, 61 (1971); Scott & Stuntz, *supra* note 22, at 1910–11 (arguing that plea bargaining is generally a fair outcome for trials but suggesting certain reforms to prevent the conviction of innocent defendants).
37. See Albert W. Alschuler, *The Prosecutor's Role in Plea Bargaining*, 36 U. CHI. L. REV. 50, 54–55 (1968) (hereinafter Alschuler, *Prosecutor's Role*) (discussing the volume of indictments in Cook County Circuit Court and the pressure put on prosecutors to move cases quickly); Bibas, *Plea Bargaining*, *supra* note 34, at 2477 (discussing attorneys' inconsistent incentives at plea bargaining depending on how the attorney is being compensated); Darryl K. Brown, *Rationing Criminal Defense Entitlements: An Argument from Institutional Design*, 104 COLUM. L. REV. 801, 812 (2004) (pointing out that courts and lawyers have incentives to dispose of cases as expeditiously as possible).
38. See Alschuler, *Prosecutor's Role*, *supra* note 37, at 53–55.
39. See Brown, *supra* note 37, at 812.
40. See Bibas, *Plea Bargaining*, *supra* note 34, at 2477.
41. *Id.* at 2465, 2496–519, 2528.
42. *Id.* at 2528–45.
43. See Tom R. Tyler, *Lecture, Legitimacy and Criminal Justice: The Benefits of Self-Regulation*, 7 OHIO ST. J. CRIM. L. 307, 319–20 (2009) (describing studies of procedural justice); Tom R. Tyler, WHY PEOPLE OBEY THE LAW 74 (1990). Citing six separate psychological studies, Professor Tyler notes that (*id.*, citations omitted):

> Recent research confirms that people evaluate their experience in procedural terms. Such procedural effects have been found in trials as well as in other procedures used to resolve disputes, including plea bargaining, mediation, and decision making by police officers. ... Wherever procedural issues have been studied they have emerged as an important concern to those affected by the decisions.

> As Professor Tyler explains, there are two potential reasons for this focus on process rather than on substance. First, in a complex society, individuals receive a diverse variety of benefits (from monetary benefits to clean and safe streets) and pay a similarly diverse variety of costs (from paying taxes to having liberty restricted to a certain degree). As it is impossible for any individual to keep track of all the benefits received and all the costs paid, the individual finds it easier to focus on the procedure itself and evaluate its fairness. If procedures are generally fair, the individual will conclude that, in the long run, they will pay and receive a just distribution of costs and benefits. The second possible explanation is that, in a diverse society, individuals may disagree on what constitutes a just distribution of substantive benefits and costs, but they can generally agree on what constitutes a fair procedure (*id.* at 109).

As will be shown, the preference for a fair and meaningful process over any specific substantive result has been confirmed in the restorative justice context. As one restorative justice proponent has noted: "Several studies have consistently found that the restitution agreement is less important to crime victims than the opportunity to talk directly with the offender about their feelings regarding the crime." (Mark S. Umbreit, Restorative Justice Through Victim-Offender Mediation: A Multi-Site Assessment, 1 W. CRIMINOLOGY REV., [1998], https://tinyurl.com/mrxkwmaw [citations omitted].)

44. Tom R. Tyler, *Social Justice: Outcome and Procedure*, 35 INT'L J. PSYCH. 117, 121–22 (2000); see also E. Allan Lind et al., *Voice, Control, and Procedural Justice: Instrumental and Noninstrumental Concerns in Fairness Judgments*, 59 J. PERSONALITY & SOC. PSYCH. 952, 952–59 (1990); Anne M. Heinz & Wayne A. Kerstetter, *Pretrial Settlement Conference: Evaluation of a Reform in Plea Bargaining*, 13 LAW & SOC'Y REV. 349, 364 (1979); Tom R. Tyler & E. Allan Lind, *A Relational Model of Authority in Groups*, 25 ADVANCES IN EXPERIMENTAL SOC. PSYCH. 115, 153–58 (Mark P. Zanna ed., 1992) (explaining the preconditions for the effective functioning of authorities).

45. Michael M. O'Hear, *Plea Bargaining and Procedural Justice*, 42 GA. L. REV. 407, 415 (2008).

46. *Id.* at 416.

47. *Id.* at 417.

48. *Id.* at 417–18.

49. *Id.* at 417.

50. *Id.* at 427.

51. *Id.* at 431. O'Hear offers five protocols that could enhance the procedural justice of plea bargaining:

> (1) before starting plea negotiations, ensure that defendants have had a meaningful opportunity to tell their side of the story, either through police officers during pre-charge processing or through counsel after charging; (2) develop objective criteria to guide plea negotiations; (3) explain positions taken in negotiations; (4) expressly acknowledge arguments for more lenient treatment; and (5) refrain from pressure tactics like exploding offers and charging threats.

> O'Hear also suggests that prosecutors "take care to use the appropriate honorific when referring to the defendant (e.g., Mr. Smith, Ms. Jones) and discourage unnecessary handcuffing and other forms of rough treatment" (*id.* at 430).

52. Alschuler, *Right to Trial*, *supra* note 21, at 933.

53. See, e.g., H. Richard Uviller, *The Neutral Prosecutor: The Obligation of Dispassion in a Passionate Pursuit*, 68 FORDHAM L. REV. 1695, 1713–18 (2000).

54. See, e.g., Lynch, *supra* note 22, at 2124–36.

55. Landes & Posner, *supra* note 3, at 38–41. Landes and Posner write that the broad laws passed by legislatures could potentially lead to over-inclusion – that is, criminal laws being enforced against the innocent. Discretionary nonenforcement is the most efficient way to reduce the costs of over-inclusion, without increasing the dangers of under-inclusion (which would occur if legislatures tried to craft their criminal laws more narrowly).

56. John Pfaff, LOCKED IN 72–73 (2017). Prosecutors also influence the law at the legislative stage by lobbying for or against legislation. A recent survey revealed that prosecutors are most successful when lobbying in favor of bills that promote criminal justice reform. Carissa Byrne Hessick, Ronald F. Wright & Jessica Pishko, *The Prosecutor Lobby*, WASH. & LEE L. REV. (forthcoming).

6 PRIVATE CRIMINAL SETTLEMENTS AS BLACKMAIL

1. Lee Romney, Firm that Teaches "Life Skills" to Suspected Shoplifters Extorts Them, Suit Alleges, Los Angeles Times (Nov. 24, 2015), https://tinyurl.com/4fdcsxb9 (last visited Jan. 5, 2022).
2. Id.
3. City Attorney of San Francisco, Court Rules That "Corrective Education" Scheme Is Extortion (Aug. 15, 2017), https://tinyurl.com/5n7dc25u (last visited Jan. 5, 2022). See also People by & through Herrera v. Corrective Educ. Co., No. A149195, 2017 WL 1366020 (Cal. Ct. App., Apr. 13, 2017) for more details of the CEC's methods and the subsequent legal case against the company.
4. Compl. for Pro. Negl., Corrective Educ. Co., et al. v. Best Best & Krieger LLP, et al., No. 18STCV01229 (Cal. Super. Ct. filed Oct. 15, 2018).
5. 18 U.S.C. § 873; see also Cal. Penal Code §§ 518, 519 (West 2010) (describing extortion as "fear" induced by a threat to expose a secret or crime); N.Y. Penal Law § 135.60(4) (McKinney 2020) (describing the offense of "coercion in the third degree" as a class A misdemeanor); Ohio Rev. Code Ann. § 2921.22(A)(1) (LexisNexis 2010). Some statutes have specific defenses and/or exceptions; we will consider these later in the chapter.
6. There is a vast amount of literature on this subject, but the most relevant articles to our discussion are: Jennifer Gerarda Brown, Blackmail as Private Justice, 141 U. Pa. L. Rev. 1935 (1993); William M. Landes & Richard A. Posner, The Private Enforcement of Law, 4 J. Legal Stud. 42–44 (1975); Richard A. Posner, Blackmail, Privacy, and Freedom of Contract, 141 U. Pa. L. Rev. 1817 (1993); and Steven Shavell, An Economic Analysis of Threats and Their Illegality: Blackmail, Extortion, and Robbery, 141 U. Pa. L. Rev. 1877 (1993). For general background on the blackmail debate, see generally Mitchell N. Berman, The Evidentiary Theory of Blackmail: Taking Motives Seriously, 65 U. Chi. L. Rev. 795 (1998); Walter Block & Gary M. Anderson, Blackmail, Extortion, and Exchange, 44 N.Y.L. Sch. L. Rev. 541 (2001); Russell J. Christopher, Meta-Blackmail, 94 Geo. L.J. 739 (2006); Richard A. Epstein, Blackmail, Inc., 50 U. Chi. L. Rev. 553 (1983); James Lindgren, Unraveling the Paradox of Blackmail, 84 Colum. L. Rev. 670 (1984); Henry E. Smith, The Harm in Blackmail, 92 Nw. U. L. Rev. 861 (1998).
7. See, e.g., Berman, supra note 6, at 796.
8. See, e.g., Joseph Isenbergh, Blackmail from A to C, 141 U. Pa. L. Rev. 1905, 1907–08, 1925–32 (1993) (arguing from a law and economics perspective that the social cost to criminalizing blackmail outweighs the social benefit); but see Ronald H. Coase, The 1987 McCorkle Lecture: Blackmail, 74 Va. L. Rev. 655, 674 (1988): "It would be better if this [ultimately suppressed] information were not collected and the resources were used to produce something of value."
9. Douglas H. Ginsburg & Paul Shechtman, Blackmail: An Economic Analysis of the Law, 141 U. Pa. L. Rev. 1849, 1860 (1993); see also Shavell, supra note 6, at 1897–99 (discussing the costs of blackmail to both the blackmailer and the subject of the blackmail).
10. See Block & Anderson, supra note 6, at 546: "There are lots of idle, time wasting, 'sterile' activities which, presumably, no one would wish to make into a criminal offense: watching soap operas, reading poetry, listening to non-baroque music, gardening and camping."
11. Some commentators have argued that blackmail is not actually voluntary, as it involves an implied threat: Pay me money or I will reveal unpleasant information about you. See, e.g., Posner, supra note 6, at 1819 (stating that blackmail is similar to duress because "both involve threats"). However, most economists reject this characterization, arguing that the

blackmail transaction – as it does not involve a threat of violence – is no more "coercive" than any other free-market exchange. See, e.g., Block & Anderson, *supra* note 6, at 545: "Every voluntary interaction can be couched in the form of a threat."

12. See Landes & Posner, *supra* note 6, at 42.
13. See Landes & Posner, *supra* note 6, at 42; Brown, *supra* note 6, at 1941–50; Shavell, *supra* note 6, at 1899.
14. See Brown, *supra* note 6, at 1954–55.
15. *Id.* at 1954.
16. See, Epstein, *supra* note 6.
17. See, e.g., 18 U.S.C. § 3: "Whoever, knowing that an offense against the United States has been committed, receives, relieves, comforts or assists the offender in order to hinder or prevent his apprehension, trial or punishment, is an accessory after the fact." See also N. C. Gen. Stat. § 14-7 (2009) (criminalizing accessory after the fact).
18. The Model Penal Code makes this crime a third-degree felony if the defendant is assisting in covering up a first- or second-degree felony, but the crime is only a misdemeanor if the defendant is assisting in covering up any other kind of crime (Model Penal Code § 242.3 [Am. L. Inst. 1962]). Blackmail is "theft by extortion." See Model Penal Code § 223.4: "A person is guilty of theft if he purposely obtains property of another by threatening to ... accuse anyone of a criminal offense ... ." Under section 223.1(2)(a), the Model Penal Code punishes theft as a third-degree felony if the amount demanded exceeds $500. Thus, if blackmail were legalized, it would make sense to increase the crime level for concealing evidence to a third-degree felony in all cases, thus providing the necessary amount of deterrence to those blackmailers who are tempted to provide criminal assistance to those whom they are blackmailing.
19. Utilitarians offer a number of other justifications for criminalizing blackmail, but none of them is able to justify the breadth of the blackmail prohibition – in particular, they would not serve to justify criminalizing incriminating blackmail. For example, one commentator argues that legalizing blackmail would create an incentive for individuals to invade each other's privacy in the search for potentially valuable information. See, e.g., Jeffrie G. Murphy, *Blackmail: A Preliminary Inquiry*, 63 MONIST 156, 165 (1980). If the potential blackmailers were in fact only looking for evidence of a crime, the cost of the invasion of privacy would usually be outweighed by the benefit of exposing more criminal conduct (unless the privacy intrusion was particularly egregious and the severity of the crime being investigated was relatively minor). Of course, if the invasion of privacy went so far as to constitute an independent crime – a trespass, perhaps, or a theft of private property – the potential blackmailer would be criminally liable without the need for a blackmail prohibition.
20. Berman, *supra* note 6, at 820.
21. See Epstein, *supra* note 6, at 555–57 (distinguishing illegal threats of physical violence from nonviolent, legal threats); Posner, *supra* note 6, at 1818–19 (noting that blackmail "is often grouped" with contracts made under duress, such as when a gun-wielding assailant says, "Your money or your life").
22. See Joel Feinberg, THE MORAL LIMITS OF THE CRIMINAL LAW: HARMLESS WRONGDOING, 4 240–58 (1988). One problem with this narrow definition of blackmail is that it would decriminalize most acts of extortion – acts which many people consider should be criminal – such as threatening to disclose adultery or sexual orientation. *See* Berman, *supra* note 6, at 821–22 (calling this narrow definition "startling").
23. See Gabriel D. M. Ciociola, *Misprision of Felony and Its Progeny*, 41 BRANDEIS L.J. 697, 699 (2003).

24. Daniel B. Yeager, *A Radical Community of Aid: A Rejoinder to Opponents of Affirmative Duties to Help Strangers*, 71 WASH. U. L.Q. 1, 39 (1993); see also Ciociola, *supra* note 23, at 702: "In England, before the seventeenth century, primary responsibility for law enforcement was not delegated to paid, full-time professionals; the community as a whole was obliged to combat crime."
25. Ciociola, *supra* note 23, at 726. See Ohio Rev. Code Ann. § 2921.22 (LexisNexis 2010) ("[N]o person, knowing that a felony has been or is being committed, shall knowingly fail to report such information to law enforcement authorities.") and S.D. Codified Laws § 22-11-12 (2006) ("Any person who, having knowledge, which is not privileged, of the commission of a felony, conceals the felony, or does not immediately disclose the felony, including the name of the perpetrator, if known, and all of the other relevant known facts, to the proper authorities, is guilty of misprision of a felony."). Both statutes apply only to felonies and are subject to certain exceptions (§ 2921.22, § 22-11-12). Both statutes make an exception if the information about the crime is privileged (§ 2921.22, § 22-11-12). Ohio's law also exempts "information that would tend to incriminate a member of the actor's immediate family" (§ 2921.22(G)(2)). No other state has such a broad prohibition on failure to report a crime. See Model Penal Code § 242.5 cmt. (Am. L. Inst. 1980) ("The Model Code accords with the vast majority of jurisdictions in assigning no penalty to simple failure to inform authorities of criminal conduct.").
26. See 18 U.S.C. § 4:

    > Whoever, having knowledge of the actual commission of a felony cognizable by a court of the United States, conceals and does not as soon as possible make known the same to some judge or other person in civil or military authority under the United States, shall be fined under this title or imprisoned not more than three years, or both.

    See also Stuart P. Green, *Uncovering the Cover-up Crimes*, 42 AM. CRIM. L. REV. 9, 23 (2005). Professor Green notes (footnotes omitted):

    > As interpreted by the courts, passive failure to report a crime does not constitute "concealment"; a defendant must engage in some affirmative act, such as making a false statement to an investigator, seeking to divert the attention of the police, harboring a felon, or retrieving and secreting proceeds of evidence of a crime. Indeed, the affirmative act requirement is so important that one court concluded that a defendant's truthful but incomplete disclosure of what he knew about an alleged counterfeiting operation did not constitute misprision, since it did not result in any greater concealment than would have occurred if the defendant had remained silent.

27. For an excellent discussion of this issue, see generally Joshua Dressler, *Some Brief Thoughts (Mostly Negative) About "Bad Samaritan" Laws*, 40 SANTA CLARA L. REV. 971 (2000) (stating the general rule that omissions are not criminal, explaining the reasons for this rule, and noting the exceptions and justifications for the general rule).
28. See Ciociola, *supra* note 23, at 730–31. Many states have so-called mandated reporting laws requiring certain professionals (such as social workers, school personnel, health-care workers, mental health professionals, and childcare providers) to report any signs of child abuse to the authorities. See, e.g., Cal. Penal Code §§ 11165.7, 11166 (West Supp. 2011) (defining who is included as a "mandated reporter" and requiring mandated reporters who have knowledge of or observe a child who is the victim of abuse and neglect to report such abuse or neglect).

29. Ciociola, *supra* note 23, at 730–42. Three states (Massachusetts, Rhode Island, and Washington) require reporting of violent felonies, although, as of 2003, no prosecutions have been reported under any of these laws (*id.* at 730–35); three states (Vermont, Minnesota, and Rhode Island) require assistance to those in peril (*id.* at 735–38); and Florida and Rhode Island have laws specifically requiring that the police be contacted if one witnesses a sexual assault (*id.* at 740–42).
30. Lindgren, *supra* note 6, at 702.
31. *Id.* at 714–15.
32. See Berman, *supra* note 6, at 823–24 (criticizing Lindgren's argument and citing other critics).
33. There is also the more existential question of whether this kind of information can even be "owned" by any specific person.
34. Professor Brown also sets forth a version of this argument, noting that there is not necessarily a "disjunction" between the interests of the state and the interests of the blackmailer. See Brown, *supra* note 6, at 1963–65. Brown argues that "the blackmailer 'appropriates' the state's leverage but also creates some deterrence value that inures to the benefit of the general public . . . . [I]n the absence of a reporting requirement, the public might benefit more from incriminating information if blackmail is allowed" (*id.* at 1965).
35. Berman *supra* note 6, at 836. Berman actually creates an entire scheme for deciding what conduct should be criminalized in a liberal society, and creates three separate criteria for criminalization. He argues that conduct should be made criminal if:

> (1) it is likely in the aggregate to yield net adverse social consequences (taking into account the costs imposed by the criminal ban itself); (2) it (a) tends to cause or threaten identifiable harm and (b) is morally wrongful in itself; or (3) it tends both (a) to cause or threaten identifiable harm, and (b) to be undertaken by a morally blameworthy actor.

Since Berman believes that consequentialist arguments against blackmail fail, and because there is no way to prove the act is morally wrongful in itself, he rejects (1) and (2) as justifications for its criminalization (*id.* at 837).
36. *Id.* at 848. See also *id.* at 843–44.
37. *Id.* at 860–62 (stating that the "crime exposure blackmail" case fits within his evidentiary theory and concluding that "crime exposure blackmail" should be a crime, and one that is more serious than misprision of felony).
38. *Id.* at 872 (quoting Wayne R. LeFave & Austin W. Scott, Jr., CRIMINAL LAW 227 [2nd ed. 1986]).
39. *Id.* at 872–73 and note 249.
40. Currently, only ten states provide for a euthanasia defense to homicide (States with Legal Physician-Assisted Suicide, *ProCon.org*, at https://tinyurl.com/mrsev6uu [last visited Jan. 7, 2023]).
41. Berman, *supra* note 6, at 873.
42. Model Penal Code § 242.5 (Am. L. Inst. 1985):

> A person commits a misdemeanor if he accepts or agrees to accept any pecuniary benefit in consideration of refraining from reporting to law enforcement authorities the commission or suspected commission of any offense or information relating to an offense. It is an affirmative defense to prosecution under this Section that the pecuniary benefit did not exceed an amount which the actor believed to be due as restitution or indemnification for harm caused by the offense.

43. Ohio Rev. Code Ann. § 2905.12(C) (West 2006).
44. Berman, *supra* note 6, at 861.
45. *Id.* at 863.
46. *Id.* at 839.
47. *Id.* at 865.
48. Some would argue that the investigator's actions are morally superior to a pure commercial research blackmailer because the investigator is remaining silent with the knowledge and consent – indeed, at the request – of the victim. However, as we saw when we discussed the second retributive justification, the victim's knowledge and consent cannot be relevant, because the party that truly "deserves" the information is the state, which has still not been informed of the crime.
49. *See* Berman, *supra* note 6, at 861–62.
50. There is another, related, problem with Berman's theory. He argues that blackmail should be criminalized because it tends to both (1) "cause or threaten identifiable harm" and (2) "be undertaken by a morally blameworthy actor" (*id.* at 836). He then assumes that crime exposure blackmail causes harm because "[i]t hampers efforts to punish and deter crime, and ... can be a but for cause of the criminal's future crimes" (*id.* at 861). However, as we saw when we discussed the utilitarian justifications, the blackmailer may in fact be serving the public interest by achieving some level of punishment and deterrence at no cost to the state. Thus, on balance, the blackmailer may not be causing or threatening any identifiable harm.

7 PRIVATE ADJUDICATIONS

1. Jane McManus, If Not the Player, Ray Rice Asks You to Forgive the Man, *ESPN* (Apr. 26, 2017), https://tinyurl.com/3y6hkbh3 (last visited Jan. 7, 2023).
2. Don Van Natta, Jr. & Kevin Van Valkenburg, Rice Case: Purposeful Misdirection by Team, Scant Investigation by NFL, *ESPN* (Sept. 19, 2014), https://tinyurl.com/yckw3x42 (last visited Jan. 7, 2023).
3. Nick Canedo, Outrage over Ray Rice's Two-Game Suspension: "It's an Upside Down NFL World," *Syracuse.com* (July 29, 2014) (citing commentators from the *Dallas Morning News* and the *Huffington Post*; the three senators were Richard Blumenthal (D-Conn.), Tammy Baldwin (D-Wis.), and Chris Murphy (D-Conn.)). See also Matt Fitzgerald, Ray Rice Suspended 2 Games: Latest Details and Reaction, *Bleacher Report* (July 24, 2014), https://tinyurl.com/yc3pw3td (last visited Jan. 7, 2023).
4. Canedo, *supra* note 3.
5. Fitzgerald, *supra* note 3.
6. Van Natta & Van Valkenburg, *supra* note 2.
7. ESPN, Ray Rice: If Signed, 2016 Salary Would Go to Domestic Violence Programs, *ESPN* (July 21, 2016), https://tinyurl.com/29jzuczc.
8. Stanley Wilson in 1985, 1987, and 1989: two one-season suspensions, then a lifetime ban. Jim Owczarski, Bengals 50: Stanley Wilson and the Super Bowl Relapse, *Cincinnati Enquirer* (July 14, 2017), https://tinyurl.com/ctpazrrh (last visited Jan. 7, 2023).
9. Michael Vick in 2007: a suspension of over two years. Vick also served jail time. Larry Fine, New Michael Vick Emerges After Dogfighting Jail Term, *Reuters* (Nov. 30, 2010), https://tinyurl.com/597kcjb2.
10. Donte Stallworth in 2009: a one-season suspension. Sam Farmer, Donte Stallworth of Cleveland Browns Is Suspended for 2009 Season, *Los Angeles Times* (Aug. 14, 2009), https://tinyurl.com/bdd5jhue (last visited Jan. 7, 2023).

11. Adrian Peterson in 2014: a suspension for the rest of the season and was also given probation. ESPN, Peterson's Season Over After Ruling, *ESPN* (Nov. 18, 2014), www.espn.com/nfl/story/_/id/11899414 (last visited Jan. 7, 2023); BBC, NFL Star Adrian Peterson Admits Reckless Assault on Son, *BBC News* (Nov. 4, 2014), www.bbc.com/news/world-us-canada-29908856 (last visited Jan. 7, 2023).
12. Odell Thurman in 2006: a two-year suspension. Bengals' Odell Thurman Reinstated After Two Year Ban, *Reuters* (Apr. 21, 2008), www.reuters.com/article/us-nfl-thurman-idUSL217505820080421 (last visited Jan. 7, 2023).
13. Ray Lewis in 2000: a $250,000 fine. Dave Goldberg, NFL Fines Ray Lewis $250,000, *ABC News* (Aug. 18, 2000), https://abcnews.go.com/Sports/story?id=100761&page=1 (last visited Jan. 7, 2023).
14. Jeff Zillgitt & AJ Neuharth-Keusch, O.J. Mayo Dismissed and Disqualified from NBA for Violation of Drug Policy, *USA Today* (July 1, 2016), https://tinyurl.com/49k37pwc (last visited Jan. 7, 2023) (NBA: drug use); NHL Public Relations, Voynov Suspended for 2019-20 Season and Stanley Cup Playoffs for Unacceptable Conduct, *NHL* (Apr. 9, 2019), https://media.nhl.com/public/news/13101 (last visited Jan. 7, 2023) (National Hockey League: domestic violence); Billy Witz, Catcher Derek Norris Suspended for Season under Domestic Violence Policy, *New York Times* (Sept. 1, 2017), https://tinyurl.com/ycy77vjn (last visited Jan. 7, 2023) (MLB: domestic violence).
15. Van Natta & Van Valkenburg, *supra* note 2.
16. John Barr & Don Van Natta Jr., Program Ray Rice in Is Rarely Granted, *ESPN* (Sept. 12, 2014), https://tinyurl.com/2s3nmvhz (last visited Jan. 7, 2023) (investigative journalism noting that, at the time, New Jersey's program website indicated that "PTI is used in criminal cases that don't involve 'violence' and for 'victimless crimes,'" and that, of the 3,508 assault-related domestic violence cases processed in New Jersey in 2013, only 30 ended in pretrial intervention).
17. Canedo, *supra* note 3.
18. Christopher Robbins, Spurned By Columbia, Student Says NYPD Mistreated Her While Reporting Rape, *Gothamist* (May 19, 2014), https://tinyurl.com/29cmpub3 (last visited Jan. 7, 2023).
19. Malcolm M. Feeley, *Private Alternatives to Criminal Courts: The Future Is All Around Us*, 119 COLUM. L. REV. ONLINE 38 (2019). Professor Feeley argues that private criminal adjudication results from either segmentation or "stratification," which occurs "when the victimized party is so strong vis-à-vis the perpetrator that she can dominate the process and take matters into her own hands, thus bypassing the criminal process" or when the victim's status is so low that they cannot gain support from the public authorities when a crime occurs. Professor Feeley argues that private criminal adjudication cannot exist unless either segmentation or stratification exists, but in defending this assertion he ends up stretching the definition of his terms. For example, he argues that a department store is "a type of segmented and closed community," in which shoppers are "something like invited 'guests.'" However, the shopper and the store are not really part of the same segmented closed community that has its own form of social control; instead, the accused shoplifter and the store are able to agree that they will both be better off outside the public criminal justice system; thus, this article places those types of agreements in a different category, one that uses the public criminal justice incentive for the accused to participate.
20. Ken Belson & Jenny Vrentas, An Arbitrator Left Deshaun Watson's Fate to the N.F.L. Commissioner, *New York Times* (Aug. 2, 2022), https://tinyurl.com/3ekztfr9.
21. *Id.* For example, first offenders who committed violent crimes faced a minimum suspension of six games.

22. *Id.* See also Jenny Vrentas & Ken Belson, Watson Suspended 11 Games and Fined $5 Million in Sexual Misconduct Case, *New York Times* (Aug. 18, 2022), https://tinyurl.com/yftb2tf4. Watson faced charges in the public criminal justice system, but a grand jury refused to indict him in March 2022. As with the Ray Rice case, the failure of the public criminal justice system to hold Watson accountable received almost no media attention, while the NFL's response was widely criticized.
23. Running back Mark Ingram was suspended for four games for using performance-enhancing drugs in 2018. Herbie Teope, Saints RB Mark Ingram Suspended Four Games for PEDs, *NFL* (May 8, 2018), https://tinyurl.com/245j8cnj (last visited Jan. 7, 2023).
24. Safety Don Jones of the Miami Dolphins was fined and suspended for tweeting "Horrible" after another NFL team drafted an openly gay player in 2014. Dan Hanzus, Report: Don Jones Reinstated After Michael Sam Tweets, *NFL* (May 19, 2014), https://tinyurl.com/y77dc2jw (last visited Jan. 7, 2023).
25. Adam Schefter, Sources: Jaguars Assured Calvin Ridley Will Be Ready upon Return, *ESPN* (Nov. 6, 2022), https://tinyurl.com/jma4f96t (describing a one-year suspension for a player who bet on NFL games); Kris Rhim & Ken Belson, Here Are the Longest N.F.L. Player Suspensions, *New York Times* (Aug. 18, 2022), www.nytimes.com/article/nfl-suspensions.html.
26. Rhim & Belson, *supra* note 25.
27. Hanna Kozlowska, Why Cruise Ships Have a Sexual-Assault Problem, *Quartz* (July 6, 2017), https://tinyurl.com/5n7nrpre.
28. Feeley, *supra* note 19.
29. *Id.*
30. Feeley, *supra* note 19.
31. John Jay College of Criminal Justice, THE NATURE AND SCOPE OF SEXUAL ABUSE OF MINORS BY CATHOLIC PRIESTS AND DEACONS IN THE UNITED STATES 1950–2002, 4 (2004) (hereinafter John Jay Report). At the request of the US Conference of Catholic Bishops, the John Jay College of Criminal Justice conducted a comprehensive study of the Catholic Church sex-abuse crisis in the United States between 1950 and 2002. The study noted that "a total of 10,667 individuals made allegations of child sexual abuse by priests. Of those who alleged abuse, the file contained information that 17.2% of them had siblings who were also allegedly abused." *Id.*
32. See, e.g., CBS, Predator Priests Shuffled Around the Globe, *CBS News* (Apr. 14, 2010), www.cbsnews.com/news/predator-priests-shuffled-around-globe/.
33. See Laurie Goodstein, Early Alarm for Church on Abusers in the Clergy, *New York Times* (Apr. 2, 2009), www.nytimes.com/2009/04/03/us/03church.html?_r=1&hpw (last visited Jan. 7, 2023) (highlighting the letters written by Father Gerald Fitzgerald, founder of a Catholic ministry dedicated to serving priests dealing with alcoholism and substance abuse, to Catholic leadership urging them to not allow sexually abusive priests to return to the ministry because "they could not be cured").
34. See Joshua J. McElwee, Francis Summons World's Bishop Presidents to Rome for Meeting on Clergy Abuse, *National Catholic Reporter* (Sept. 12, 2018), https://tinyurl.com/42bmcak4 (last visited Jan. 7, 2023); Nicole Winfield, A Global Look at the Catholic Church's Sex Abuse Problem, *Associated Press* (Feb. 21, 2019), https://apnews.com/article/8cb4daf509464bad8c13ef35d44a0fc5 (last visited Jan. 7, 2023).
35. In 2020 – about two decades after the scope of the scandals came to light – the Vatican released new guidelines instructing its bishops to report clergy sex crimes to the police. See Associated Press, Vatican Now Says Bishops Should Report Sex Abuse to Police

Whether Bound by Law or Not, *Los Angeles Times* (July 16, 2020), https://tinyurl.com/5n6j2cbj (last visited Jan. 7, 2023). In addition, many states have implemented mandated reporter laws that require anyone who hears about child sex abuse to report the accusation to the authorities.

36. Sarah Fowler, "A Nightmare." Man Tells All, Says He Was Abused by Mississippi Priest More than 75 Times, *Clarion Ledger* (Jan. 22, 2019), https://tinyurl.com/366x922j.
37. *Id.*
38. See Tatyana Bellamy-Walker, et al., Bernard Haddican, *ProPublica: Credibly Accused* (Jan. 28, 2020), https://tinyurl.com/3kwyn3kt.
39. The argument that the Catholic hierarchy was attempting to redeem Haddican is not especially strong in this particular case; unlike in other cases in which the church made some attempts to reform abusive priests, there is no record here that the vicar took any action toward redemption.
40. In 1985, as now, Mississippi did not have a statute of limitations for sexual assault against minors. See National District Attorneys Association, STATUTES OF LIMITATIONS FOR PROSECUTION OF OFFENSES AGAINST CHILDREN (2012), https://tinyurl.com/4dfhhuuy.
41. See John Jay Report, *supra* note 31, at 4. Often, by the time the victim decided to report the crime to the police, the statute of limitations had run out or the priest had died – the average age at which victims decide to report to someone outside the Catholic Church is 52 years. *Id.*
42. Feeley, *supra* note 19.
43. See Ohio Wesleyan University, OHIO WESLEYAN UNIVERSITY STUDENT HANDBOOK 2007–08, 29, 35–39 (2007).
44. See Ohio Wesleyan University, OHIO WESLEYAN UNIVERSITY CODE OF STUDENT CONDUCT 2007–08, 29–33 (2007).
45. Janet Napolitano, *"Only Yes Means Yes": An Essay on University Policies Regarding Sexual Violence and Sexual Assault*, 33 YALE L. & POL'Y REV. 387, 400 (2015).
46. Only a quarter of all reported rapes lead to an arrest, and only 20 percent lead to prosecution. Of those, only half result in felony convictions. Why Schools Handle Sexual Violence Reports, *Know Your IX*, https://tinyurl.com/j76vsc45.
47. *Id.*
48. Matthews v. Eldridge, 424 U.S. 319 (1976).
49. *Id.* at 335.
50. Goss v. Lopez, 419 U.S. 565 (1975).
51. *Id.* at 584.
52. See Sara O'Toole Note, *Campus Sexual Assault Adjudication, Student Due Process, and a Bar on Direct Cross-Examination*, 79 U. PITT. L. REV. 511, 533–36 (2018).
53. Fellheimer v. Middlebury Coll., 869 F. Supp. 238 (D. Vt. 1994).
54. *Id.* at 245.
55. *Id.* at 241.
56. The operative language of Title IX is "no person in the United States shall, on the basis of sex, be excluded from participation in, be denied the benefits of, or be subjected to discrimination under any education program or activity receiving federal financial assistance." See 20 U.S.C. § 1681.
57. See US Department of Education, Dear Colleague Letter (Apr. 2, 2011), https://tinyurl.com/55f9tahk (rescinded).
58. *Betsy DeVos Scraps Obama-Era Guidance on Campus Sexual Assault*, CBS NEWS, Sept. 22, 2017, https://www.cbsnews.com/news/betsy-devos-scraps-obama-era-guidance-on-campus-sexual-assault/ (last visited Jan. 7, 2023).

59. Tyler Kingkade, *Biden Admin Proposes Sweeping Changes to Title IX to Undo Trump-Era Rules*, NBC NEWS (June 23, 2022), https://www.nbcnews.com/politics/biden-admin-proposes-sweeping-changes-title-ix-undo-trump-era-rules-rcna34915 (last visited Jan. 7, 2023).
60. As restorative justice theorists are quick to point out, however, the theory of restorative justice is anything but new. Signs of restorative justice have, for example, been detected in the practices of "ancient Arab, Greek, and Roman civilizations," of the "Germanic peoples who swept across Europe," not to mention "Indian Hindus as ancient as the Vedic civilization . . . and ancient Buddhist, Taoist, and Confucian traditions." Likewise, restorative justice has been discovered in the practices of the "Aboriginals, the Inuit, and the native Indians of North and South America" (Stephen P. Garvey, *Restorative Justice, Punishment, and Atonement*, 2003 UTAH L. REV. 303, 304, 306–07 [2003]).
61. Some restorative justice programs also attempt to restore the community to its pre-crime condition. See Lawrence W. Sherman, *Domestic Violence and Restorative Justice: Answering Key Questions*, 8 VA. J. SOC. POL'Y & L. 263, 268–69 (2000) (describing broad participation by victims' family members and other community members in restorative justice processes).
62. Howard Zehr, THE LITTLE BOOK OF RESTORATIVE JUSTICE 37 (2002).
63. John Braithwaite, RESTORATIVE JUSTICE AND RESPONSIVE REGULATION 11 (2002).
64. Mark S. Umbreit et al., *Restorative Justice in the Twenty-First Century: A Social Movement Full of Opportunities and Pitfalls*, 89 MARQ. L. REV. 251, 254 (2005).
65. Zehr, *supra* note 62, at 21.
66. See Gordon Bazemore & Mark Umbreit, US Department of Justice, A COMPARISON OF FOUR RESTORATIVE CONFERENCING MODELS 2 (2001), www.ojp.gov/pdffiles1/ojjdp/184738.pdf.
67. See Mark S. Umbreit, MEDIATING INTERPERSONAL CONFLICTS: A PATHWAY TO PEACE 140–45 (1995).
68. See Sherman, *supra* note 61, at 268: "Certain kinds of harm are clearly irreparable, and beyond any meaningful exchange of value. This may even be more true of emotional harm than of physical harm." Professor Sherman gives the example of a husband who hits his wife; the defendant can pay for medical treatment to heal the physical injuries, but "there can never be the same level of trust and security that there was prior to that first assault."
69. See Richard Delgado, *Goodbye to Hammurabi: Analyzing the Atavistic Appeal of Restorative Justice*, 52 STAN. L. REV. 751, 755 (2000).
70. See, e.g., Umbreit et al., *supra* note 64, at 254: "Most contemporary criminal justice systems focus on law violation, the need to hold offenders accountable and punish them, and other state interests. Actual crime victims are quite subsidiary to the process and generally have no legal standing in the proceedings."
71. See Sara Sun Beale, *The News Media's Influence on Criminal Justice Policy: How Market-Driven News Promotes Punitiveness*, 48 WM. & MARY L. REV. 397, 400 (2006); Mark S. Umbreit, *Restorative Justice Through Victim-Offender Mediation: A Multi-Site Assessment*, 1998 W. CRIMINOLOGY REV. 1 (1998).
72. Heather Strang & Lawrence W. Sherman, *The Practice of Restorative Justice: Repairing the Harm: Victims and Restorative Justice*, 2003 UTAH L. REV. 15, 27 (2003).
73. See Tom R. Tyler, WHY PEOPLE OBEY THE LAW 122 (1990).
74. See Umbreit et al., *supra* note 64, at 256.
75. See Strang & Sherman, *supra* note 72, at 18.
76. John Braithwaite, *Restorative Justice: Assessing Optimistic and Pessimistic Accounts, in* 25 CRIME AND JUSTICE: A REVIEW OF RESEARCH 1 (Michael Tonry ed., 1999). A 1997 survey of

victims who participated in the Polk County, Iowa, victim offender reconciliation program found that 96 percent of victims stated they would choose the program again and would recommend it to other victims (Frederick W. Gay, *Restorative Justice and the Prosecutor*, 27 FORDHAM URB. L.J. 1651, 1654 [2000]).

77. Braithwaite, *supra* note 76, at 20–28.
78. Strang & Sherman, *supra* note 72, at 18 (citations omitted).
79. Thalia González, *The State of Restorative Justice in American Criminal Law*, 2020 WIS. L. REV. 1147, 1197 note 342 (2020) (hereinafter González, *State*). See also Thalia González, *The Legalization of Restorative Justice: A Fifty-State Empirical Analysis*, 2019 UTAH L. REV. 1027, 1039–41 (2019).
80. See Latanae Parker, *Penal Reform and the Necessity for Therapeutic Jurisprudence*, 20 GEO. J. LEGAL ETHICS 863, 866 (2007).
81. See Umbreit et al., *supra* note 64, at 284–89 (citing numerous meta-analyses that show reduced recidivism rates for restorative justice procedures); see also Heather Strang, Lawrence W. Sherman, Evan Mayo-Wilson, Daniel Woods & Baraj Arieil, *Restorative Justice Conferencing (Rjc) Using Face-to-Face Meetings of Offenders and Victims: Effects on Offender Recidivism and Victim Satisfaction. A Systemic Review*, 12 CAMPBELL SYST. REV. 47–49 (2013) (showing a lower level of recidivism as long as both the defendant and the victim consent to the process).
82. It is important not to overstate this argument, however. The public criminal justice system does occasionally result in restitution for a victim or community service in the neighborhood where the defendant committed the crime. Defendants in the public criminal justice system – especially first-time offenders – are frequently given a chance at rehabilitation through drug treatment programs, anger treatment programs, or other mandatory counseling sessions. More fundamentally, there are no doubt plenty of victims who feel "restored" by seeing the defendant severely punished. Indeed, whether punishment is able to restore victims is the question that lies at the core of the debate over restorative justice. See Umbreit et al., *supra* note 64, at 257 (citations omitted):

> Retributive theory holds that the imposition of some form of pain will vindicate, most frequently deprivation of liberty and even loss of life in some cases. Restorative theory argues that "what truly vindicates is acknowledgement of victims' harms and needs, combined with an active effort to encourage offenders to take responsibility, make right the wrongs, and address the causes of their behavior."

However, this debate merely reinforces the argument that the traditional criminal justice system cannot do all things for all victims. By expanding restorative justice programs – or by privatizing the adjudication process using restorative justice programs as a guide – we can increase the options available to victims and defendants. Those victims who prefer the punitive and retributive model will always have the option of using the traditional criminal courts.

83. See Umbreit et al., *supra* note 64, at 255; see also John Braithwaite, *A Future Where Punishment Is Marginalized: Realistic or Utopian?*, 46 UCLA L. REV. 1727, 1730–31 (1999); Strang & Sherman, *supra* note 72, at 16–17.
84. Josephine Gittler, *Expanding the Role of the Victim in a Criminal Action: An Overview of Issues and Problems*, 11 PEPP. L. REV. 117, 125–26 (1984).
85. John H. Langbein, THE ORIGINS OF ADVERSARY CRIMINAL TRIAL 11 (2003).
86. Gittler, *supra* note 84, at 125–32 (describing the historical development of the public prosecutor in the American colonies). Prior to the development of a public prosecutor, certain public officials were sometimes involved in criminal prosecution in England. For

example, the attorney general would prosecute cases of treason, although such cases "occurred quite rarely" (Langbein, *supra* note 85, at 12–13). Under the Marian statutes of 1555, justices of the peace were given certain prosecutor-like duties to "reinforce citizen prosecution" (*id.* at 40). The justices of the peace could issue search warrants and arrest warrants, and examine those suspected of committing crimes, frequently resulting in confessions (*id.* at 40–43).
87. See Mark S. Umbreit & Jean Greenwood, Office for Victims of Crime, US Department of Justice, NATIONAL SURVEY OF VICTIM-OFFENDER MEDIATION PROGRAMS IN THE UNITED STATES 8–9 (2000).
88. Aside from restorative justice programs, there is another form of criminal mediation that has attracted some scholarly attention: "case-management mediation." See generally Maureen E. Laflin, *Remarks on Case-Management Criminal Mediation*, 40 IDAHO L. REV. 571 (2004). Unlike restorative justice, case-management mediation does not seek to repair the harms done or lead the perpetrator toward atonement. Instead, case-management mediation is essentially assisted plea bargaining, in which the trial judge calls the attorneys and the defendant into chambers and tries to broker a settlement (*id.* at 586–87). This type of mediation is not really a step toward privatization (as formal charges are already filed and both the judge and the prosecutor are involved in the procedure); it is really only another method of public plea bargaining.
89. Umbreit et al., *supra* note 64, at 269–70.
90. *Id.* at 269.
91. See Patrick Glen Drake, *Comment, Victim-Offender Mediation in Texas: When "Eye for Eye" Becomes "Eye to Eye,"* 47 S. TEX. L. REV. 647, 665 (2006).
92. *Id.*
93. As one scholar has noted, "[s]ince the mid-2000s, there has been rapid expansion of restorative justice laws, developing what can now be appropriately characterized as a restorative justice scheme" (González, *State, supra* note 79, at 1149).
94. *Id.* at 1156–57.
95. This tailoring of the criminal process and outcome to the values of smaller groups over those of the public is an extension of the general principles of subsidiarity that undergirds the US justice system. While the federal government seeks to establish some level of uniformity in process (and perhaps disposition) in state criminal proceedings, state political organs are permitted to establish the parameters of justice within their jurisdiction according to their people's common values. Likewise, localities are permitted regulatory powers over low-level code violations according to their smaller communities' values. While not a perfect analogy, private adjudications do highlight the same subsidiary interests present in these first two categories – especially when the specific violation's impact is highly concentrated on a small number of people, rather than society as a whole.

8 PRIVATE DISPOSITIONS

1. Vigilante, *Merriam-Webster*, www.merriam-webster.com/dictionary/vigilante (last visited Jan. 9, 2023).
2. William E. Burrows, VIGILANTE! xi (1976).
3. *Id.* at 6–7.
4. *Id.* at xiii.
5. Paul Robinson & Sarah Robinson. SHADOW VIGILANTES: HOW DISTRUST IN THE JUSTICE SYSTEM BREEDS A NEW KIND OF LAWLESSNESS (2018).

6. *Id.* at 97, 100–04. The full list of rules is as follows:
    (1) Don't act unless there is a serious failure of justice.
    (2) Don't cause more harm than is necessary and just, and avoid injury to innocent bystanders.
    (3) Don't act unless there is no lawful way to solve the problem.
    (4) Don't act alone.
    (5) Before acting, be sure of the facts, and take full account of all relevant mitigations and excuses.
    (6) Show restraint and temperance, not arrogance or vindictiveness.
    (7) Warn the government that it is in breach of its social contract with its citizens, and give it an opportunity to fix the problem, unless it is clear that such a warning would be useless.
    (8) Publicly report afterward what you have done and why.
    (9) Respect the full society's norms of what is condemnable conduct.
    (10) If it becomes clear that the problem cannot be fixed through vigilante action, then withdraw from further action.
7. *Id.* at 13.
8. *Id.*
9. *Id.* at 14.
10. *Id.* at 15.
11. *Id.* at 31.
12. For an excellent application of the Robinsons' criteria for moral vigilantism, see Stephen E. Henderson, *Daredevil: Legal (and Moral?) Vigilante*, 15 Ohio St. J. Crim. L. 133 (2017).
13. Robinson & Robinson, *supra* note 5, at 109.
14. See Rick Seltzer & Grace M. Lopes, *The Ku Klux Klan: Reasons for Support or Opposition Among White Respondents*, 17 J. of Black Stud. 91, 95 (1986).
15. Nathaniel Sheppard Jr., *Abortion Doctor and Wife Are Freed*, New York Times (Aug. 21, 1982), § 1 at 7, https://tinyurl.com/ytajzu6m.
16. Michael Griffin, *Murderer of Pensacola Abortion Doctor David Gunn, Is Denied Parole*, Pensacola News Journal (Nov. 1, 2017), https://tinyurl.com/k33vaps8.
17. Emily Crockett, *Poll: Most Americans Think Attacks on Abortion Clinics Are "Domestic Terrorism,"* Vox (Dec. 2, 2015), https://tinyurl.com/yrf4hxyt (citing a poll that found that 54 percent of Republicans considered attacks on abortion clinics to be terrorist actions and that over 70 percent of Republicans believed that the FBI should investigate such attacks).
18. See Douglas I. Brandon, Melinda L. Cooper, Jeremy H. Greshin, Alvin L. Harris & James M. Head Jr., *Self-Help: Extrajudicial Rights, Privileges and Remedies in Contemporary American Society*, 37 Vand. L. Rev. 845, 876 (1984): "The persistence of self-help perhaps is attributable to public frustration with and contempt for the American criminal justice system, which many people perceive as inadequate or ineffective." Rabbi Meir Kahane, the founder of the paramilitary Jewish Defense League, explained the motivation behind founding his group in similar terms: "When we have seen, over weeks and months and years, that, for whatever reason given, the police have proven themselves inadequate to enforce the basic duties of the state, it is criminal *not* to act." (Meir Kahane, Never Again! 278 [1971].) One dictionary defines vigilante committees as "a portion of the citizens of a place, who, *assuming the regular magistrates are unable or unwilling to execute the laws*, undertake to watch over its safety, and punish criminals" (Burrows, *supra* note 2, at 6 [emphasis added], quoting John Russell Bartlett's Dictionary of Americanisms). Professor Burrows writes that "the men who form a vigilance committee do so, they tell one another, only because robbers and murderers are breaking the law – municipal, territorial, or state statutes, which were written to protect them but which they think aren't being enforced by the authorities" (Burrows, *supra* note 2, at 13).
19. Robinson & Robinson, *supra* note 5, at 22–23.

20. Beverly A. Smith & Frank T. Morn, *The History of Privatization in Criminal Justice*, in PRIVATIZATION IN CRIMINAL JUSTICE: PAST, PRESENT, AND FUTURE 3, 6–7, 8 (David Shichor & Michael J. Gilbert eds., 2001).
21. Owen Wister, THE VIRGINIAN 435–36 (1902).
22. Burrows, *supra* note 2, at 17.
23. State v. Puryear, 30 N.C. App. 719, 729 (1976).
24. Johnston v. Harris, 387 Mich. 569, 576–577 (1972) (Brennan, J., dissenting):

    The intrusion of private industry into the business of public safety has been one of the most unfortunate phenomena of the 1960's [sic] and the 1970's [sic]. Already, there are subdivisions which operate their own patrol cars; private police and private guards are multiplying; vigilante forces of private citizens roam the streets with walkie-talkies; store owners and apartment managers arm themselves and set traps for burglars . . .

25. The state's monopoly on force has been a mainstay of liberal political thought for centuries. As the prominent sociologist Max Weber noted: "The modern state is a compulsory association which organizes domination. It has been successful in seeking to monopolize the legitimate use of physical force as a means of domination within a territory" (Max Weber, ESSAYS IN SOCIOLOGY 78 [Hans H. Gerth & C. Wright Mills trans., 1958]). See also Robert Nozick, ANARCHY, STATE, AND UTOPIA, 26, 138–39 (1974); and Clifford J. Rosky, *Force Inc.: The Privatization of Punishment, Policing, and Military Force in Liberal States*, 36 CONN. L. REV. 879, 889–96 (2004). Rosky adapts Weber's concept of a "monopoly of force" and applies it to the private law enforcement context, noting that, in the twentieth century, "the West fought two world wars and developed a massive network of military, policing, and punishment institutions, which were characterized by unprecedented levels of specialization, professionalism, bureaucratization, and strength" (*id.* at 896 [citations omitted]).
26. Indeed, many minor crimes are resolved in the public criminal justice system without resorting to incarceration. See, e.g., Jeff Bleich, *The Politics of Prison Crowding*, 77 CAL L. REV. 1125, 1168–69 (1989). In practice, the small but growing movement toward private resolution of criminal law cases has shown that resolving criminal cases need not involve the use of force or incarceration against the accused. Some advocates of reform movements such as restorative justice believe that traditional coercive punishments are almost never appropriate for criminal defendants, regardless of the severity of the crime. John Braithwaite, *A Future Where Punishment Is Marginalized: Realistic or Utopian?*, 46 UCLA L. REV. 1727, 1735–42 (1999) (arguing that restorative justice is an alternative that can and should marginalize the use of punishment). Our expanded definition of vigilantes would include any private individual who seeks to resolve a criminal dispute without resorting to the court system, perhaps through a mediation with the alleged perpetrator to achieve restitution for the victim.
27. See Elizabeth Joh, *Conceptualizing the Private Police*, 2005 UTAH L. REV. 573, 589–91.
28. See, e.g., David R. Karp & Todd R. Clear, *Community Justice: A Conceptual Framework*, in 2 CRIMINAL JUSTICE 2000: BOUNDARY CHANGES IN CRIMINAL JUSTICE ORGANIZATIONS 323, 355–56 (Charles M. Friel ed., 2000).
29. Farhang Heydari, *The Private Role in Public Safety*, 90 GEO. WASH. L. REV. 696, 709 (2022).
30. See Frequently Asked Questions, *Perverted Justice*, www.perverted-justice.com/index.php?pg=faq.

31. Jessica Contrera, How Vigilante "Predator Catchers" Are Infiltrating the Criminal Justice System, *Washington Post* (Sept. 22, 2022), https://tinyurl.com/mwwc9sa8; Hanna Kozlowska, There's a Global Movement of Facebook Vigilantes Who Hunt Pedophiles, *Quartz* (July 24, 2019), https://tinyurl.com/3a2umn2t.
32. Ross Anderson, *Why Information Security Is Hard – An Economic Perspective*, in 17TH ANNUAL COMPUTER SECURITY APPLICATIONS CONFERENCE 5 (2001).
33. Neal Katyal, *Community Self-Help*, 1 J. L. ECON. & POL'Y 33, 50 (2005).
34. Winn Schwartau, Cyber-Vigilantes Hunt Down Hackers, *CNN* (Jan. 12, 1999), www.cnn.com/TECH/computing/9901/12/cybervigilantes.idg/.
35. Jay B. Kesan & Ruperto Majuca, *Optimal Hackback*, 84 CHI. KENT L. REV. 831, 834 (2010).
36. Schwartau, *supra* note 34. Schwartau describes one especially enthusiastic online security manager who claims that his company responded with physical, not just virtual, actions:

> "We have actually gotten on a plane and visited the physical location where the attacks began. We've broken in, stolen the computers and left a note: 'See how it feels?'" On one occasion, he says: "We had to resort to baseball bats. That's what these punks will understand. Then word gets around, and we're left alone. That's all we want, to be left alone."

37. Katyal, *supra* note 33, at 60–62.
38. In some cases, the private party inflicting the punishment may explicitly explain that fact to the perpetrator, for example: "Either I call the police right now, or you stay here for a couple of hours while I process these papers and have you sign a confession." In these cases, premeditated punishments become an implicit type of private criminal settlement.
39. Brandon et. al., *supra* note 18, at 887.
40. Sometimes the victim of a sexual assault will impose a private punishment on the perpetrator if the perpetrator returns to threaten the victim again; in such cases, the victim-turned-vigilante will have a plausible self-defense claim. See Crumpton v. Confederation Life Ins. Co., 672 F.2d 1248, 1250 (5th Cir. 1982) (an alleged rapist returned to the victim at her home and approached her, at which point she shot him; the rapist had threatened to kill her children if she went to the police).
41. Paige Williams, Kyle Rittenhouse, American Vigilante, *New Yorker* (June 28, 2021), https://tinyurl.com/yk2n6fbk.
42. Erin Ailworth, Julie Wernau & Akane Otani, Wisconsin Identifies Officer Who Shot Jacob Blake, *Wall Street Journal* (Aug. 27, 2020), https://tinyurl.com/3n63smk7; Kenosha Police Shooting Updates: Fires Blazing in Several Kenosha Locations, Protests Continue in Madison, *Milwaukee Journal Sentinel* (Aug. 25, 2020) https://tinyurl.com/yxknfpxf; Mark Guarino, et al., 17-Year-Old Charged with Homicide After Shooting During Kenosha Protests, Authorities Say, *Washington Post* (Aug. 26, 2020), https://tinyurl.com/2nrnfwpd.
43. Williams, *supra* note 41.
44. *Id.*; Michael Tarm, Scott Bauer & Amy Forliti, Shooting Victim Says He Was Pointing His Gun at Rittenhouse, *AP News* (Nov. 8, 2021), https://tinyurl.com/yck2bhvd.
45. Campbell Robertson & John Schwartz, Shooting Focuses Attention on a Program That Seeks to Avoid Guns, *New York Times* (Mar. 22, 2012), https://tinyurl.com/4bwuwr6v.
46. Lizette Alvarez & Michael Cooper, Prosecutor Files Charge of 2nd-Degree Murder in Shooting of Martin, *New York Times* (Apr. 11, 2012), https://tinyurl.com/bd8dn9ka.
47. Renee Stutzman, Several George Zimmerman witnesses change their accounts, *Orlando Sentinel* (May 22, 2012).
48. Russ Bynum, 3 Men Charged in Ahmaud Arbery's Death Convicted of Murder, *AP News* (Nov. 21, 2021), https://tinyurl.com/y9ffr75j.

49. Ralph Blumenthal, Shootings Test Limits of New Self-Defense Law, *New York Times* (Dec. 13, 2007), www.nytimes.com/2007/12/13/us/13texas.html?_r=1&oref=slogin.
50. Sharon Finegan *Watching the Watchers: The Growing Privatization of Criminal Law Enforcement and the Need for Limits on Neighborhood Watch Associations*, 8 U. MASS. L. REV. 88, 123 (2013).
51. Noah Feldman, Noah Feldman: Think the Kenosha Shooting Case Is Simple? It Isn't, Because of the Gun Kyle Rittenhouse Brought with Him, *Tulsa World* (Oct. 17, 2021), https://tinyurl.com/4fm44jme.
52. *Id.*
53. Cynthia Lee, *Firearms and Initial Aggressors*, 101 N.C. L. REV. 1, 21–31 (2023). Professor Lee also cites a third category of initial aggressors: those who agree to engage in mutual combat. This is a rare occurrence and it is not relevant to discussions about private enforcers or private dispositions.
54. Kimberly Kessler Ferzan, *Provocateurs*, 7 CRIM. L. & PHIL. 597, 598 (2013).
55. Lee, *supra* note 53, at 24.
56. *Id.* at 25–27.
57. *Id.* at 27–28.
58. See, e.g., People v. Dunlap, 734 N.E.2d 973, 981 (Ill. App. Ct. 2000).
59. See, e.g., United States v. Peterson, 483 F.2d 1222, (D.C. Cir. 1973).
60. See, e.g., State v. Jones, 128 A.3d 431, 452 (Conn. 2015).
61. Lee, *supra* note 52, at 24–25.
62. The courts do not seem to be willing to go down this road; Professor Lee does not provide any specific examples in which the mere displaying of a firearm led a defendant to be deemed an initial aggressor.
63. John Shattuck & Mathias Risse, REIMAGINING RIGHTS & RESPONSIBILITIES IN THE UNITED STATES: GUN RIGHTS AND PUBLIC SAFETY 3 (2021); Percentage of Population in the United States Owning at Least One Gun in 2022, By Political Affiliation, *Statista* (Nov. 2022), https://tinyurl.com/tev6xxpb.
64. See, e.g., N.Y. State Rifle & Pistol Ass'n v. Bruen, 142 S. Ct. 2111, 2122, 2156 (2022) (affirming the right to carry a handgun outside the home).
65. Michael Mannheimer, Trayvon Martin and the Initial Aggressor Issue, *PrawfsBlawg* (Mar. 26, 2012), https://tinyurl.com/57tyt5pe. As Mannheimer notes, the term "provokes" remains ambiguous in self-defense law:

> "Provokes" might imply that some intent to precipitate violence is necessary. On the other hand, "provokes" can be read more broadly as simply triggering a violent response without intent that it occur, as when, in the classic voluntary manslaughter example, a wife "provokes" a fatal attack by her husband when he catches her in the arms of her lover, even if she did not expect to be discovered. The problem with this broad a reading is that one could be said to be the initial aggressor even by engaging in behavior that is entirely innocent, such as by asking a passerby for a handout, or even constitutionally protected, such as by telling the passerby that he practices a false religion and will burn in hell for it.

> See also, Cynthia V. Ward, *"Stand Your Ground" and Self-Defense*, 42 AM. J. CRIM. L. 89, 115 (2015) (arguing that a person is not a provocateur under self-defense law unless they "make the first move" to assault someone).

66. Alafair Burke, What You May Not Know About the Zimmerman Verdict: The Evolution of a Jury Instruction, *HuffPost* (Sept. 14, 2013), https://tinyurl.com/mr2pjdm3. See also

Jeffrey A. Fagan, *The Zimmerman Verdict and the Initial Aggressor Exception*, *Columbia Law School* (Dec. 10, 2013), https://tinyurl.com/yc6nmwsu.
67. Lee, *supra* note 53, at 44.
68. See, e.g., Ira P. Robbins, *Citizen's Arrest and Race*, 20 Oh St. J. Crim. L. 133, 149–50 (2023) (citing examples of whites confronting Blacks and attempting to make "citizen's arrests" over trivial minor traffic infractions or minor crimes).
69. See Lee, *supra* note 53, at 10–12. Professor Lee, who has written extensively about this particularly harmful version of implicit bias, cites dozens of studies supporting this proposition. See, e.g., Birt L. Duncan, *Differential Social Perception and Attribution of Intergroup Violence: Testing the Lower Limits of Stereotyping of Blacks*, 34 J. Personality & Soc. Psych. 590, 595 (1976) (finding that 75 percent of individuals observing a Black person shoving a white person thought the shove constituted "violent" behavior, while only 17 percent of individuals observing a white person shoving a Black person characterized the shove as "violent" and 42 percent characterized the shove as "playing around"). Lee, *supra* note 53, at 10.
70. However, see Finegan, *supra* note 50, at 124–25. Professor Finegan refers to the many programs that have attempted to reduce the level of implicit bias and racially disproportionate treatment among the public police and concedes that, even though the effectiveness of these programs is "a matter of debate," the state is at least making efforts to reform the implicit bias and discriminatory efforts of the public police. No such effort is being made for private police – and, given the decentralization of the private criminal justice system, it is unlikely that any such effort will ever occur.

9 REGULATING PRIVATE CRIMINAL JUSTICE

1. James F. Peltz, *How the Nation's Largest Security-Guard Firm Adapts to Changing Threats*, *Los Angeles Times* (Aug. 4, 2016), https://tinyurl.com/yc5mh2hn (last visited Jan. 28, 2023).
2. See generally Brian A. Reaves, Bureau of Justice Statistics, US Department of Justice, *State and Local Law Enforcement Training Academies, 2013*, 249784 NCJ Bull. (2016), https://bjs.ojp.gov/content/pub/pdf/slleta13.pdf.
3. See, e.g., Mich. Comp. Laws § 338.1069 (2001) (stating that private security guard uniforms may not "deceive or confuse the public or be identical with that of a law enforcement officer"); Tenn. Code Ann. §§ 62-35-127 to 128 (1997) (prohibiting the use of the word "police" anywhere on a private security officer's badge).
4. See David A. Sklansky, *The Private Police*, 46 UCLA L. Rev. 1165, 1177 (1999).
5. See Ohio Rev. Code Ann. § 4749.06 (West 2009 Supp.); Ariz. Rev. Stat. Ann. § 32-2624 (2022 Supp.).
6. See Neb. Rev. Stat. Ann. § 71–3202 (LexisNexis 2014); Md. Code Ann., Bus. Occ. & Prof. § 13-301 (LexisNexis 2010).
7. Farhang Heydari, *The Private Role in Public Safety*, 90 Geo. Wash. L. Rev. 696, 740 (2022) (citations omitted).
8. See, e.g., Heidi Boghosian, *Applying Restraints to Private Police*, 70 Mo. L. Rev. 177, 177 (2005): "It is not surprising that security personnel frequently find themselves in court accused of using excessive force and violating the constitutional rights of others." A review of case law shows that "the discretion afforded private security guards has resulted in a spate of legal cases, ranging from excessive force claims to claims of 'consumer racism' against minority shoppers by private security guards in retail stores" (*id.* at 189).

9. Sharon Finegan *Watching the Watchers: The Growing Privatization of Criminal Law Enforcement and the Need for Limits on Neighborhood Watch Associations*, 8 U. MASS. L. REV. 88, 128 (2013).
10. *Id.* at 131. Professor Finegan also has other suggestions for applying constitutional protections to non-state actors. We will consider those later in this section.
11. See, e.g., McDonald v. City of Chicago, Ill., 561 U.S. 742 (2010) (holding that the individual right to bear arms precludes cities and states from banning firearm possession).
12. The manifestation of police immunity most often comes in the form of traditional sovereign immunity statutes attributed to public officers of the relevant state. See, e.g., Ga. Code Ann. § 50-21-25 (2006); Ohio Rev. Code Ann. § 9.86 (Supp. 2006). However, some statutes do address specific immunities of police in the exercise of their statutory duties, such as immunity from false arrest claims for recovery of a suspect detained by a private individual through citizen's arrest (see, e.g., Cal. Penal Code § 847[b] [2006]) or even broad immunity for exercising arrest authority in certain contexts (see, e.g., Miss. Code Ann. § 93-21-27 [2004]; Or. Rev. Stat. § 133.315 [2005]). Likewise, private citizens acting upon command for assistance by a public police officer are most often afforded explicit civil and criminal immunity. See, e.g., Colo. Rev. Stat. § 16-3-202 (2006); Ga. Code Ann. § 16-3-22 (2007).
13. There are some reasons why a state may extend some kind of immunity to private police. For example, lawmakers might want to incentivize private law enforcement because the state itself is unable to meet the demand for public law enforcement. This is not a particularly convincing argument, as private police lack the two major justifications for qualified immunity: the principles of general state sovereign immunity and the special duties of public police to intervene and uphold the law.
14. This is not to say that private police are limited in their powers. Ordinary citizens, of course including traditional private police, enjoy what is generically referred to as the right of citizen's arrest. In most states, this authority extends to arrests for felonies, and sometimes to misdemeanors, that are committed in the individual's presence or of which the citizen possesses some other requisite knowledge. See, e.g., 725 Ill. Comp. Stat. Ann. 5/107-3 (2006); Ky. Rev. Stat. Ann. § 431.005(6) (1999); Ohio Rev. Code Ann. §§ 2935.04 and 2935.06 (2006). Private citizens – and private police – are also allowed to search a suspect if given consent and to interrogate a suspect in order to obtain a confession. Private police are more aware of these powers than average civilians and therefore use them more often and more aggressively. See Lynn M. Gagel, *Comment, Stealthy Encroachments Upon the Fourth Amendment: Constitutional Constraints and Their Applicability to the Long Arm of Ohio's Private Security Forces*, 63 U. CIN. L. REV. 1807, 1837 (1995). Some private police, such as bounty hunters, have the same powers of search and arrest as police do. Jonathan Drimmer, *When Man Hunts Man: The Rights and Duties of Bounty Hunters in the American Criminal Justice System*, 33 HOUS. L. REV. 731, 763 (1996). And, of course, all private police are free from the constitutional restrictions that limit the powers of the public police. See *infra* notes 16–29 and accompanying text.
15. Sklansky, *supra* note 4, at 1183. In one case, a woman brought a civil action against J.C. Penney for false imprisonment after two security guards accused her of shoplifting, brought her back inside the store, and held her in a room for twenty-one minutes. A jury awarded her $2,000 (Barrows v. J.C. Penney Co., 58 Conn. App. 225, 227, 228 [2000]).
16. See, e.g., Heydari, *supra* note 7, at 752 (seeking something close to "parity" between private police and public police); Finegan, *supra* note 9, at 132 (arguing that applying constitutional protections and the exclusionary rule to private searches would "better protect due process guarantees"); John M. Burkoff, *Not So Private Searches and the Constitution*, 66 CORNELL L. REV. 627, 627–28 (1981) ("[T]he traditional treatment of all private searches as

a separate and distinct activity untainted by 'state involvement' is more an exercise in semantics than a sound application of precedent, and it does not adequately account for contemporary policing practices"); Wayne A. Logan, *Crowdsourcing Crime Control*, 99 Tex. L. Rev. 137, 162 (2020) (arguing that applying the exclusionary rule to private parties would avoid abuses of "crowdsourcing," whereby the police rely on a vast number of volunteer citizens to gather clues and information about criminal activity).
17. See Edmondson v. Leesville Concrete Co., 500 U.S. 614, 621–22 (1991).
18. See Elizabeth E. Joh, *Criminal Law: The Paradox of Private Policing*, 95 J. Crim L. & Criminology 49, 83–86 (2004).
19. See Sklansky, *supra* note 4, at 1258–59.
20. See Burkoff, *supra* note 16, at 666.
21. See Sklansky, *supra* note 4, at 1247–69.
22. *Id.* at 1252.
23. *Id.* at 1259–60.
24. *Id.* at 1263–64.
25. Indeed, the state action doctrine in this area is so muddled that some commentators have argued that it should be abolished entirely, so that every actor, public or private, must abide by the same rules. See, e.g., Erwin Chemerinsky, *Rethinking State Action*, 80 Nw. Univ. L. Rev. 503, 555 (1985). However, see Sklansky, *supra* note 4, at 1270–73 (arguing that to "jettison the state action doctrine altogether in criminal procedure" would be "the wrong response"). This would, of course, mean that private police would be subject to the same constitutional limitations as their public counterparts.
26. It may be that scholars must do more work to help the courts in understanding this new phenomenon before courts are able to address the problem more rationally. The current lack of theory surrounding private law enforcement has certainly hobbled the courts, so that "when courts talk about private policing, they make unstated and sometimes erroneous assumptions" (Elizabeth E. Joh, *Conceptualizing the Private Police*, 2005 Utah L. Rev. 573, 575 [2005]).
27. See, e.g., Tex. Code Crim. Proc. Ann. art. 38.23 (West 1987).
28. Compare People v. Zelinski, 594 P.2d 1000 (1972), with Initiative Measure (Prop. 8), approved June 8, 1982 (California Proposition 8 [1982]).
29. See 18 U.S.C. 2515–2518 (codification of the Wiretap Act).
30. Nearly every state in the country designates certain professions as mandated reporters, such as teachers, health-care workers, and social workers. See Child Welfare Information Gateway, US Child. Bureau, Mandatory Reporters of Child Abuse and Neglect (2019), www.childwelfare.gov/pubPDFs/manda.pdf.
31. See, e.g., Ohio Rev. Code Ann. § 2921.22(A)(1) (LexisNexis 2010). Ohio's law provides for an exception for all privileged information and exempts individuals from reporting family members (§2921.22[G]).
32. See Wayne A. Logan, *Citizen Searches and the Duty to Report*, 83 Oh. St. L. J. 939, 941–45 (2022).
33. *Id.*
34. *Id.* (citations omitted).
35. There is an argument for at least equivalency between private and public "spying" on this point, particularly if the newly legalized blackmailers coalesced into large, private entities with control over large portions of people's lives. Much of the harm of the surveillance state is not necessarily its efficient capture of criminal activity, but its collateral capture of legal, but personal/controversial, activity. To this point, there may not be much of a difference between the FBI keeping a list of political "subversives" and monitoring

their activities, and the blackmail division of some large corporation seeking out such information to blackmail such individuals with threats to their careers or reputations.
36. Logan, *supra* note 32.
37. Matthews v. Eldridge, 424 U.S. 319, 335 (1976).
38. Stuart M. Widman, *The Protections and Limits of Confidentiality in Mediation*, 24 ALT. TO THE HIGH COST OF LITIG. 161, 161 (2006); see also In re Teligent, Inc., 640 F.3d 53, 57–58 (2d Cir. 2011).
39. See Fed. R. Evid. 408, 410 (the most significant exception is that criminal defendants are not barred from admitting statements made during plea bargaining).
40. Widman, *supra* note 38, at 162.
41. Malcolm Feeley, *Private Alternatives to Criminal Courts: The Future Is All Around Us*, 119 COLUM. L. REV. ONLINE 38, 77 (2019) (citations omitted).
42. The American Arbitration Association resolves hundreds of cases a year through arbitration and mediation. See *American Arbitration Association* (2023), www.adr.org/. There are a number of other national alternative dispute resolution organizations and hundreds of such organizations on the state level.
43. Paul H. Robinson & Sarah M. Robinson, SHADOW VIGILANTES: HOW DISTRUST IN THE SYSTEM BREEDS A NEW KIND OF LAWLESSNESS 15–16 (2018).
44. *Id.* at 127–28.
45. *Id.* at 97.
46. Jay B. Kesan & Ruperto Majuca, *Optimal Hackback*, 84 CHI.-KENT L. REV. 831, 838 (2010).
47. *Id.* at 834.
48. *Id.* at 838.
49. Cynthia Lee, *Firearms and Initial Aggressors*, 101 N.C. L. REV. 1, 52–53 (2023). Lee also notes that gun possession is already quite common in the United States, and recent Supreme Court cases have strengthened the right to possess guns. See N.Y. State Rifle & Pistol Ass'n, Inc. v. Bruen, 142 S. Ct. 2111 (2022). Lee argues that "with the rules on carrying guns in public – what one might call 'front end' laws – becoming less restrictive, it becomes increasingly important to strengthen what one might call 'back end' laws or laws that seek to deal with the significant harms caused by gun use" (Lee, *supra* note 49, at 16).
50. Lee, *supra* note 49, at 58–59 (emphasis added).
51. Lee notes that the burden of proving the intent of the defendant would be determined by the state's already-existing laws for a self-defense claim. Some states already require a defendant to prove the elements of a self-defense claim; others require the prosecutors to disprove one of the elements once the defendant has raised a credible self-defense claim. The Supreme Court has stated that either method is constitutionally permissible (*id.* at 71–72); see also Martin v. Ohio, 480 U.S. 228, 235–36 (1987).
52. Of course, the "castle doctrine" – which allows for a more liberal use of deadly force against someone who has invaded the perpetrator's home – would still need to be preserved as an aspect of the self-defense instruction.

10 THE VERDICT ON PRIVATE CRIMINAL JUSTICE

1. See, e.g., Stephen P. Garvey, *Restorative Justice, Punishment, and Atonement*, 2003 UTAH L. REV. 303, 306–07 (2003) (distinguishing between "harms," which are torts in which an individual suffers material loss or bodily injury, and "wrongs," which contain an element of

moral injury because of the intentional or reckless infliction of the harm by the perpetrator onto the victim, such that "all crimes do wrong, and some crimes also cause harm").

2. *Id.* Garvey cites, as an example, conduct that causes a risk of harm to another, but no actual harm, such as reckless endangerment. Other so-called victimless crimes might fit into this category – narcotics offenses, prostitution, gambling, etc. – in which the perpetrator is not harming any specific victim (at least not directly) but is committing a "wrong" because they are showing "contempt, not so much for anyone in particular, but for the law itself, which forbids such conduct. While the rest of us play by the rules, the offender behaves as if he is above them, free to do as he wishes" (*id.* at 307).

3. See Mark S. Umbreit et al., *Restorative Justice in the Twenty-First Century: A Social Movement Full of Opportunities and Pitfalls*, 89 MARQ. L. REV. 251, 269–70 (2005) (noting that in at least two types of restorative justice programs – group conferencing and circles – community representatives participate).

4. See, e.g., Gretchen Ulrich, *Widening the Circle: Adapting Traditional Indian Dispute Resolution Methods to Implement Alternative Dispute Resolution and Restorative Justice in Modern Communities*, 20 HAMLINE J. PUB. L. & POL'Y 419, 439–40 (1999) (explaining that in one type of restorative justice program in Minnesota – sentencing circles – a judge must approve the sentence recommended by the circle).

5. See Randy E. Barnett, *Restitution: A New Paradigm of Criminal Justice*, 87 ETHICS 279, 287 (1977); Randy E. Barnett, *The Justice of Restitution*, 25 AM. J. JURIS. 117, 117 (1980).

6. Many criminal defendants have little or no money, so a tort case against them would not be worth the time or expense. Josephine Gittler, *Expanding the Role of the Victim in a Criminal Action: An Overview of Issues and Problems*, 11 PEPP. L. REV. 117, 139 (1984). In contrast, a private criminal system using a mediation process similar to what is currently used in restorative justice programs could help the victim and defendant craft a flexible resolution, even if the defendant were judgment-proof.

7. *Id.*: "[V]ictims, who have already been through a criminal proceeding, may not have the energy and stamina required to become involved in yet another proceeding."

8. *Id.* at 118.

9. *Id.* at 119.

10. See generally John C. Coffee Jr., *Does "Unlawful" Mean "Criminal"?: Reflections on the Disappearing Tort/Crime Distinction in American Law*, 71 B. U. L. REV. 193 (1991).

11. See, e.g., John H. Langbein, *The Criminal Trial Before the Lawyers*, 45 U. CHI. L. REV. 263, 282–83 (1978) (noting that there was usually no prosecuting attorney for most felony trials in England until the late 1700s); Allen Steinberg, *From Private Prosecution to Plea Bargaining: Criminal Prosecution, the District Attorney, and American Legal History*, 30 CRIME & DELINQ. 568, 571–73 (1984) (describing private prosecutions in America before the revolution).

12. See, e.g., Carolyn B. Ramsey, *The Discretionary Power of "Public" Prosecutors in Historical Perspective*, 39 AM. CRIM. L. REV. 1309, 1316–17 (2002): "Relatively few commentators want to return to the ... early nineteenth century, when crime victims in New York and Philadelphia often settled their cases out of court." Most commentators have condemned the traditional system of private prosecution. See, e.g., John D. Bessler, *The Public Interest and the Unconstitutionality of Private Prosecutors*, 47 ARK. L. REV. 511, 569 (1994); Ahmed A. White, *Victims' Rights, Rule of Law, and the Threat to Liberal Jurisprudence*, 87 KY. L. J. 357, 413–14 (1999).

13. See David Garland, THE CULTURE OF CONTROL: CRIME AND SOCIAL ORDER IN CONTEMPORARY SOCIETY 145 (2001).

14. See Farhang Heydari, *The Private Role in Public Safety*, 90 GEO. WASH. L. REV. 696, 729–31 (2022) (citations omitted): "Most prosecutors and sheriffs run unopposed and without term limits, remaining in power for a generation. Their elections hardly function as a check against abuse of power, particularly for the politically powerless. In fact, the electoral process can give outsized influence to the wealthy and powerful."
15. See, e.g., William J. Stuntz, *The Pathological Politics of Criminal Law*, 100 MICH. L. REV. 505, 513–14 (2001) (describing the reform of the state's penal code in 1961 due to the Model Penal Code project).
16. Garland, *supra* note 13, at 152–65.
17. Stuntz, *supra* note 15, at 528–29.
18. *Id.* at 530.
19. *Id.* at 510. See generally John Pfaff, LOCKED IN (2017).
20. See, e.g., Jennifer Gerarda Brown, *The Use of Mediation to Resolve Criminal Cases: A Procedural Critique*, 43 EMORY L. J. 1247, 1293–95 (1994).
21. See James A. Strazzella, American Bar Association, THE FEDERALIZATION OF CRIMINAL LAW 7 (1998): "[T]he trend to federalize crime has continued dramatically, covering more conduct formerly left to state prosecution." Even though most criminal law is still enforced and adjudicated by the states, "[c]rime's politics have become increasingly nationalized" (Stuntz, *supra* note 15, at 533).
22. Kenworthey Bilz & John M. Darley, *Law and Psychology: What's Wrong with Harmless Theories of Punishment*, 79 CHI. KENT L. REV. 1215, 1251 (2004).
23. Heather Strang & Lawrence W. Sherman, *Repairing the Harm: Victims and Restorative Justice*, 2003 UTAH L. REV. 15, 125 (2003) (arguing that victims must be "stakeholders equal to offenders and the community").
24. Zvi D. Gabbay, *Justifying Restorative Justice: A Theoretical Justification for the Use of Restorative Justice Practices*, 2005 J. DISP. RESOL. 349, 362: "[R]estorative justice provides crime victims with a process that answers their most important needs: for participation, involvement and acknowledgement."
25. This check on power is, of course, less relevant for judges who have lifetime appointments, but even some of those judges (at least those who aspire to a higher bench) must keep public opinion in mind when they make their decisions.
26. The prosecutor or judge may consult with the victim before seeking or imposing a specific sentence, and many states have victim's rights laws that give the victim a right to be heard, but the victim does not have any substantive right to approve or reject the ultimate sentence. Likewise, the defendant in the public criminal justice system has the right to accept a given plea deal or go to trial, but they do not have the same influence that they would have in a mediation context.
27. This intervention will rarely be necessary if a resolution treats the defendant too harshly; such a resolution would probably not be accepted by the defendant in the first place and, even if it were, the prosecutor would lack the power to lessen the burden on the defendant. Furthermore, as we have seen, restorative justice programs tend to be much more lenient toward defendants than the traditional criminal justice system has been.
28. Micheal Barbaro, *Some Leeway for the Small Shoplifter*, New York Times (July 13, 2006), www.nytimes.com/2006/07/13/business/13walmart.html.
29. *Id.*
30. See Heydari, *supra* note 14, at 735–36.
31. *Id.* at 731. Nonetheless, Heydari is wary of the privatization of the criminal justice system; while he is clear-eyed about the problems of the public criminal justice system, he is

concerned about the lack of legal accountability and the perverse economic incentives of private actors (*id.* at 736–45).

32. See Jill Richey Rayburn, *Neighborhood Justice Centers: Community Use of ADR – Does It Really Work?*, 26 U. MEM. L. REV. 1197, 1200 (1996).
33. See generally Timothy Hedeen, *Institutionalizing Community Mediation: Can Dispute Resolution "of, by, and for the People" Long Endure?*, 108 PENN. ST. L. REV. 265, 269 (2003).
34. Rayburn, *supra* note 32, at 1206. Although the victim can initiate the process, the Community Boards also take referrals from courts. See *Community Boards*, https://communityboards.org/.
35. *Id.* at 1208.
36. *Id.* at 1206, 1208, 1211.
37. Both men and women commit domestic violence crimes, but the majority of cases involve violence of men against women. Callie Marie Rennison, US Department of Justice, INTIMATE PARTNER VIOLENCE, 1993–2001 1 (2003), https://bjs.ojp.gov/content/pub/pdf/ipv01.pdf (stating that "85% of victimizations by intimate partners in 2001 were against women").
38. Many jurisdictions now have mandatory arrest policies for domestic violence cases. See Linda G. Mills, *Killing Her Softly: Intimate Abuse and the Violence of State Intervention*, 113 HARV. L. REV. 550, 558 and note 32 (1999) (listing jurisdictions with mandatory or limited-discretion arrest policies for domestic violence).
39. See Deborah Epstein, *Procedural Justice: Tempering the State's Response to Domestic Violence*, 43 WM. & MARY L. REV. 1843, 1866, 1868, 1882 (2002); Mills, *supra* note 38, at 589–91; Marion Wanless, *Mandatory Arrest: A Step Toward Eradicating Domestic Violence, But Is It Enough?*, 1996 U. ILL. L. REV. 533, 534–43 (1996).
40. See Robert C. Davis et al., *Increasing Convictions in Domestic Violence Cases: A Field Test in Milwaukee*, 22 JUST. SYS. J. 61, 61, 69 (2001); see also Richard R. Peterson & Jo Dixon, *Court Oversight and Conviction Under Mandatory and Nonmandatory Domestic Violence Case Filing Policies*, 4 CRIMINOLOGY & PUB. POL'Y 535, 539–40 (2005).
41. See Angela R. Gover et al., *Combating Domestic Violence: Findings from an Evaluation of a Local Domestic Violence Court*, 3 CRIMINOLOGY & PUB. POL'Y 109, 113 (2003); see also Epstein, *supra* note 39, at 1857.
42. See Molly Butler Bailey, *Improving the Sentencing of Domestic Violence Offenders in Maine: A Proposal to Prohibit Anger Management Therapy*, 21 ME. BAR J. 140, 144 (2006).
43. See Mills, *supra* note 38, at 604, 606–09; Brenda V. Smith, *Battering, Forgiveness, and Redemption*, 11 AM. U. J. GENDER SOC. POL'Y & L. 921, 935 (2003). Cf. Epstein, *supra* note 39, at 1899–1900 (discussing how negotiation and alternative dispute resolution can improve results in civil cases as well).
44. See C. Quince Hopkins et al., *Applying Restorative Justice to Ongoing Intimate Violence: Problems and Possibilities*, 23 ST. LOUIS U. PUB. L. REV. 289 (2004); Smith, *supra* note 43, at 937–38 (discussing the use of restorative justice for domestic violence cases).
45. Aya Gruber, *#MeToo and Mass Incarceration*, 17 OHIO ST. J. CRIM. L. 275, 290 (2020). Unsurprisingly, other scholars disagree, arguing that the sanctions imposed outside the public criminal justice system are insufficient and that the solution is to fix the public criminal justice system. See, e.g., Janet Napolitano, *"Only Yes Means Yes": An Essay on University Policies Regarding Sexual Violence and Sexual Assault*, 33 YALE L. & POL'Y REV. 387, 401–02 (2015):

> Survivors are choosing not to report to law enforcement because of their lack of faith and confidence in the criminal justice system. If that is the case, it can be argued that rather than pushing institutions to become surrogates for the criminal justice

system, more work should be done to improve that system's handling and prosecution of sexual assault cases. Law enforcement has the tools to effectively investigate these crimes. The criminal justice process has the authority to impose serious punishments on offenders, including incarceration. The most serious sanction that a college can impose is dismissal, which is wholly inadequate where a crime has been committed.

46. See Gruber, *supra* note 45, at 288–90.
47. See, e.g., Bruce J. Winick, *Therapeutic Jurisprudence and Problem Solving Courts*, 30 FORDHAM URB. L. J. 1055, 1060 (2003).
48. See, e.g., Heidi Boghosian, *Applying Restraints to Private Police*, 70 MO. L. REV. 177, 177–183 (2005); Elizabeth E. Joh, *The Paradox of Private Policing*, 95 J. CRIM. L. & CRIMINOLOGY 49, 86 (2004); Elizabeth E. Joh, *Conceptualizing the Private Police*, 2005 UTAH L. REV. 573 (2005); David A. Sklansky, *The Private Police*, 46 UCLA L. REV. 1165, 1177 (1999); Clifford J. Rosky, *Force Inc.: The Privatization of Punishment, Policing, and Military Force in Liberal States*, 36 CONN. L. REV. 879 (2004).
49. See Brown, *supra* note 20, at 1288–89; Andre R. Imbrogno, *Using ADR to Address Issues of Public Concern: Can ADR Become an Instrument for Social Oppression?*, 14 OHIO ST. J. ON DISP. RESOL. 855, 858–60 (1999).
50. See Carissa Byrne Hessick, PUNISHMENT WITHOUT TRIAL: WHY PLEA BARGAINING IS A BAD DEAL 20 (2021).
51. See Albert W. Alschuler, *Implementing the Criminal Defendant's Right to Trial: Alternatives to the Plea Bargaining System*, 50 U. CHI. L. REV. 931, 971–72 (1983).
52. See, e.g., Albert W. Alschuler, *The Prosecutor's Role in Plea Bargaining*, 36 U. CHI. L. REV. 50, 52 (1968); Raymond I. Parnas & Riley J. Atkins, *Abolishing Plea Bargaining: A Proposal*, 14 CRIM. L. BULL. 101, 101 (1978); Stephen J. Shulhofer, *Plea Bargaining as Disaster*, 101 YALE L. J. 1979, 1979 (1992); Hessick, *supra* note 50.
53. See, e.g., Brown, *supra* note 20, at 1266. Professor Brown also considers there to be "coercion" in some existing restorative justice programs, arguing that an offender's refusal to mediate or rejection of an offer during mediation can be used against them in the subsequent public adjudication (*id.* at 1269–70). A court is likely to take this into account only if the case has been referred to mediation from the public court system, with a public entity represented in the process; in a true private system, a defendant's refusal to participate would not be counted against them in any subsequent public adjudication because the refusal would take place before the state was ever involved in the case.
54. *Id.* at 1270–71. Professor Brown also points out that, in many existing restorative justice programs, the defendant is a first-time offender or a juvenile, while the victim may be a repeat player or a large savvy institution (*id.* at 1271–72).
55. This is not always the case, however. Many smaller jurisdictions do not assign defendants attorneys for minor cases and allow the defendant to waive his right to counsel and plead guilty at arraignments without ever consulting an attorney.
56. Heather Strang & Lawrence W. Sherman, *Repairing the Harm: Victims and Restorative Justice*, 2003 UTAH L. REV. 15, 18 (2003).
57. See Boghosian, *supra* note 48.
58. *Id.* at 180–82.
59. See Sklansky, *supra* note 48, at 1189–90.
60. See, e.g., Akhil Reed Amar, *Fourth Amendment First Principles*, 107 HARV. L. REV. 757, 811–16 (1994).
61. Hudson v. Michigan, 547 U.S. 586, 558 (2006).

62. See Marc L. Miller & Ronald F. Wright, *Secret Police and the Mysterious Case of the Missing Tort Claims*, 52 BUFF. L. REV. 757, 762–66 (2004).
63. *Id.* at 766–70. The website FiveThirtyEight in partnership with The Marshall Project obtained public records on the payments that thirty-one of the largest fifty cities in the United States made to pay out claims against police officers. They found that these thirty-one cities have paid out $3 billion over the last ten years. Twenty-seven of the cities each paid at least $1 million over that time period (Amelia Thomson-DeVeaux, Laura Bronner & Damini Sharma, Cities Spend Millions on Police Misconduct Every Year. Here's Why it's so Difficult to Hold Departments Accountable, *FiveThirtyEight* [Feb. 22, 2021], https://tinyurl.com/bdf9eu9a).
64. Miller & Wright, *supra* note 62, at 762, 781–82. Miller and Wright point out that very little is known about what entity actually pays these damages and settlements. However, they do conclude that:

> [T]he monetary cost of judgments against police are not always fully or directly born [sic] by police departments or by individual officers. Civil judgments come out of city or county funds, or perhaps from insurance policies that the local government purchases–i.e., from taxpayers ... It is city council members, county boards, and city and county administrators who bear the financial and political cost [of these lawsuits].

65. Thanks to Professor Noah Smith-Drelich of Chicago-Kent College of Law for this analogy.
66. Brown, *supra* note 20, at 1970.
67. See, e.g., Brian P. Marron, *Promoting Racial Equality Through Equal Educational Opportunity: The Case for Progressive School-Choice*, 2002 BYU EDUC. & L. J. 53, 106, note 234 (2002) (documenting numerous instances in which members of Congress argued against privatization of the school system by use of vouchers because such a system would drain public schools of scarce and necessary funding); Kimberly McLarin, Ohio Paying Some Tuition for Religious School Students, *New York Times* (Aug. 28, 1996), https://tinyurl.com/24rvpchv (reporting on the beliefs of those opposed to privatizing schools through the use of vouchers: "Voucher opponents say the program, which will cost $5.2 million over two years, will drain badly needed money.").
68. See, e.g., Johanna E. Bond, *International Intersectionality: A Theoretical and Pragmatic Exploration of Women's International Human Rights Violations*, 52 EMORY L. J. 71, 128 (2003) ("In the United States, poor women of color experience barriers in accessing health care due to increased privatization of the health care industry."); Dorothy E. Roberts, *Privatization and Punishment in the New Age of Reprogenetics*, 54 EMORY L. J. 1343, 1349 (2005) ("The ownership society and the privatization philosophy it reflects demand that individuals rely on their own wealth to meet their needs and discourage government aid for poor mothers who face systemic hardships in caring for their children.").
69. Jack Weinstein explained the argument in the context of alternative dispute resolution in the following way (Jack B. Weinstein, *Some Benefits and Risks of Privatization of Justice Through ADR*, 11 OHIO ST. J. ON DISP. RESOL. 241, 261–62 [1996] [citations omitted]):

> There is the risk ... that as the rich move out of the courts to private dispute resolution forums, only criminals and the poor will be left in the courts, thus, reducing the effective power of these institutions over all society. A recent news report confirms the immediacy of the threat that increased resort to ADR will result in creation of "a two

tier system of justice." According to the report, California's "three strikes law" is forcing diversion of civil judges to criminal trials to handle the increased caseload. With the public resources to handle civil cases shrinking, some are predicting that one day only the rich will have recourse to civil litigation–by hiring private judges as provided for under California law. We can imagine without much difficulty a future "in which wealthy litigants will use private ADR while the poor and powerless will be consigned to public courts which government will have little incentive to fund because their constituents lack political clout." This would create a situation analogous to what has happened to public education in some of our central cities because of the middle class exodus to private schools and the suburbs.

70. See Gerald E. Frug, *City Services*, 73 N.Y.U. L. REV. 23, 75 (1998): "Low-crime and high-crime areas within any metropolitan region can be located on a map, and, usually, the most privileged suburbs are low-crime areas while poor suburban and central city neighborhoods are high-crime areas."

71. For instance, those with an annual family income of $7,500 or less suffer a robbery victimization rate of 5.6 per 1,000 individuals in that category, while those with an annual family income of $75,000 or more suffer a robbery victimization rate less than half that, at 2.1 per 1,000 individuals in that category (Bureau of Justice Statistics, US Department of Justice, CRIMINAL VICTIMIZATION IN THE UNITED STATES, 2005 STATISTICAL TABLES 27, table 14 [2006]). Likewise, those with an annual family income of $7,500 or less suffer an assault victimization rate of 29.9 per 1,000 individuals in that category, compared with a rate of 13.7 per 1,000 individuals in the category of those making more than $75,000 a year (*id.*). The rate of victimization tends to decrease as income increases (see *id.*).

72. In 1973, the National Advisory Commission on Criminal Justice Standards and Goals recommended the following maximum caseload: 150 felonies per attorney per year or 400 misdemeanors per attorney per year (American Bar Association, GIDEON'S BROKEN PROMISE: AMERICA'S CONTINUING QUEST FOR EQUAL JUSTICE 17 [2004], www.in.gov/pub licdefender/files/ABAGideonsBrokenPromise.pdf). However, examples abound of caseloads far exceeding this recommendation. For example, in Rhode Island, public defender felony caseloads exceed the recommended number by 35 to 40 percent, and misdemeanor caseloads exceed it by 150 percent (*id.*). In Baltimore, public defenders were handling 80 to 100 serious felonies at any given time, typically exceeding the recommended 150 per year (*id.* at 18). See also Joshua Dressler & Alan C. Michaels, UNDERSTANDING CRIMINAL PROCEDURE vol. 2, 56, note 68 (4th ed. 2006) (noting that most states pay court-appointed defense counsel between $40 and $70 per hour for non-capital cases and that many states have an overall cap for any given case, which is usually around $3,000 but could be as low as $445). As Dressler and Michaels point out, "[i]n New York, a defendant facing a life sentence may get a lawyer who spends as few as 20 hours on the case; the lawyer may get as little as $693 for the work, a figure less than the average cost for a real estate closing" (*id.*).

73. In 2009, 38 percent of felony defendants in the seventy-five largest counties were unable to make bail and stayed in jail until their case was resolved (Bureau of Justice Statistics, US Department of Justice, FELONY DEFENDANTS IN LARGE URBAN COUNTIES, 2009 17, table 12 [2009], https://bjs.ojp.gov/content/pub/pdf/fdluc09.pdf). More than half of those with a bail amount had it set at $10,000 or more (*id.*). The mean average bail set for drug offenses was $34,200, for property offenses was $33,200, and for violent offenses was $115,000 (*id.* at 19, table 16).

74. See Joseph L. Lester, *Presumed Innocent, Feared Dangerous: The Eighth Amendment's Right to Bail*, 32 N. KY. L. REV. 1, 51 (2005). Lester argues that a free defendant can assist in finding witnesses, has fuller access to their attorney, and does not suffer from the pressure to accept or initiate a guilty plea. Furthermore, a free defendant's case often proceeds at a slower pace. The longer a case goes without being tried, the more difficult the government's case becomes due to witnesses' memory losses and destruction of evidence (see *id.* at 51 and note 434). A detained defendant does not have these advantages.
75. *Id.* at 50: "If pretrial detention is ordered, or if bail is set at a level that the defendant cannot afford, and the defendant is detained as a result, then the likelihood that the defendant will accept a plea bargain increases." Whether by guilty plea or conviction at trial, defendants detained until disposition have a conviction rate of 81 percent, compared with a conviction rate of 60 percent for defendants released until disposition (Bureau of Justice Statistics, US Department of Justice, FELONY DEFENDANTS IN LARGE URBAN COUNTIES, 2002, 24, table 24 [2006]). Defendants detained pending disposition not only have higher overall conviction rates, but are more likely to be convicted of a felony rather than a misdemeanor (see *id.*, showing that defendants detained pending disposition are convicted of felonies in 72 percent of cases, compared with a felony conviction rate of only 48 percent for defendants released pending disposition).
76. Stephanos Bibas summarized this reality as follows (Stephanos Bibas, *Plea Bargaining Outside the Shadow of Trial*, 117 HARV. L. REV. 2463, 2491–93 [2003] [citations omitted]):

> Most criminal cases ... involve misdemeanors or minor felonies, such as petty theft, that usually carry short sentences. Though many defendants make bail for these offenses, some do not have enough money or are detained without bail. One empirical study found that roughly four times as many defendants charged with misdemeanors or lesser felonies are imprisoned before trial as are after conviction. The pretrial detention can approach or even exceed the punishment that a court would impose after trial. So even an acquittal at trial can be a hollow victory, as there is no way to restore the days already spent in jail. The defendant's best-case scenario becomes not zero days in jail, but the length of time already served.

77. Robert G. Lawson, *Difficult Times in Kentucky Corrections – Aftershocks of a "Tough on Crime" Philosophy*, 93 KY. L. J. 305, 368–69 (2004): "'Research has yet to reveal the precise effects of incarceration on future employment, although several studies show that former inmates have more difficulty than other people finding and keeping a job.' ... Most inmates [are] handicapped ... by the fact that they search for work as persons who served time in prison ('ex-convicts')." (quoting Marta Nelson & Jennifer Trone, STATE SENTENCING AND CORRECTIONS PROGRAM: WHY PLANNING FOR RELEASE MATTERS 2 [2000]).
78. See generally John Hagan & Ronit Dinovitzer, *Collateral Consequences of Imprisonment for Children, Communities, and Prisoners*, 26 CRIME & JUST.: REV. RES. 121, 131–48 (1999).
79. Studies demonstrate a reduction in recidivism rates for participants of restorative justice programs (Gabbay, *supra* note 24, at 385). Some restorative justice supporters explain this effectiveness with the reintegrative shaming theory (*id.* at 384). This theory uses family and community conferencing to emphasize the disapproval of the act while refraining from negatively stigmatizing and humiliating the offender. This allows the offender to acknowledge their crime without being cast out of the community, thereby effectively rehabilitating or reintegrating the offender into society (*id.*).
80. See Margo D. Beller, Shoplifting Study Finds the Rich Steal More, CNBC (July 18, 2011), https://tinyurl.com/uyesnnza (noting that those with an annual income of over $70,000 shoplift 30 percent more than those with an income of under $20,000). An older study

showed that 71 percent of those who shoplifted were from the middle or upper classes (Who the Shoplifters Are, *Washington Post* [Oct. 2, 1986], https://tinyurl.com/24pftz4w).

81. Malcolm Feeley, *Private Alternatives to Criminal Courts: The Future Is All Around Us*, 119 COLUM. L. REV. ONLINE 38, 69 (2019) (citations omitted). There is an interesting law and economics argument against monetizing the penalty for criminal activity and allowing the victim to receive compensation. From a law and economics perspective, the moral transgression on the part of the defendant would require a significant sanction against the defendant in order to deter the behavior, particularly because many perpetrators are not caught. If monetized, this sanction would almost certainly be more than the victim would deserve for the harm they suffered; it would also frequently be more than the defendant could pay. Under this theory, it instead makes sense for the state to intervene in order to impose heavier sanctions, either through a fine or community service (which gives back to the "community" that suffered as a result of the moral transgression) or through incarceration (which does not unduly enrich the victim, but [theoretically] provides the optimal amount of deterrence to would-be perpetrators). See generally Richard A. Posner, ECONOMIC ANALYSIS OF LAW 215–19 (6th ed. 2003). This argument is mitigated somewhat by the fact that a broadening of the private criminal justice system would ensure that more perpetrators were caught, so a lesser monetary punishment would still achieve the same level of deterrence as the higher penalties in today's system.
82. Willie Sutton, *FBI*, www.fbi.gov/history/famous-cases/willie-sutton.
83. Wayne Logan, *Crowdsourcing Crime Control*, 99 TEX. L. REV. 137, 152–3 (2020). Professor Logan concedes that the public law enforcement system is "far from perfect," but argues that "as the historic evolution of crime control itself highlights, organized, trained, and sworn public law enforcement officers, in theory at least democratically accountable and subject to constitutional regulation, are preferable to privatized justice and mob rule (by 'netizens' or others)" (*id.* at 153 [citations omitted]).
84. Feeley, *supra* note 81, at 80–84.
85. William M. Landes & Richard A. Posner, *The Private Enforcement of Law*, 4 J. LEGAL STUD. 1 (1975).
86. *Id.*
87. See, e.g., Douglas I. Brandon, et al., *Self-Help: Extrajudicial Rights, Privileges and Remedies in Contemporary American Society*, 37 VAND. L. REV. 845, 875, 876 (1984): "Self-help in many cases, unfortunately, is antithetical to order and peace because it allows individuals to disregard legal rules and determine for themselves what is law."
88. Kelly D. Hine, *Vigilantism Revisited: An Economic Analysis of the Law of Extra-Judicial Self-Help or Why Can't Dick Shoot Henry for Stealing Jane's Truck?*, 47 AM. U. L. REV. 1221, 1244–48 (1998).
89. *Id.* at 1252–53: "Punishing a citizen for providing a benefit to society is simply nonsensical. It lowers total social wealth by wasting scarce judicial resources and by creating perverse incentives to avoid socially beneficial behavior."

Index

Alschuler, Albert, 85
Amazon Ring, 65, 66
America's Most Wanted, 65
Aquinas, Thomas, 13
Arbery, Ahmaud, 148, 153
Arizona Border Recon, 64

Baughman, Shima Baradaran, 49
Belenchia, Mark, 123, 124
Berman, Mitchell, 111, 112, 113, 114, 115
Bibas, Stephanos, 90, 91
Biden, Joseph, 127
Black Lives Matter, 23, 64, 147
Black October, 36
Bragg, Alvin, 19
Bryan, William, 148, 152, 153
Burke, Alafair, 152
Burrows, William, 135, 136, 139

Capitol Hill Organized Protest (CHOP), 63
Catholic Church, 123, 124
Chicago Alternative Policing Strategy (CAPS), 62, 67
Citizen app, 65, 66
civil demand letters, 79
Clinton, Bill, 38
CODE OF HAMMURABI, 25
commercial research blackmail, 104, 106, 107, 108, 114
Community Alternatives to 911 (CAT-911), 51
Community Boards, 181
contract model of plea bargaining, 90, 91, 92
Corrective Education Company (CEC), 2, 80, 81, 101, 102
Crime Victims' Rights Act of 2004, 47
cruise ships, 122
Cyberangels, 142

Deacons for Defense and Justice, 33, 140
defunding police, 48, 49
due process clause, 126

early policing, 30
Easterbrook, Frank, 89
Ellickson, Robert, 21
evidentiary theory of blackmail, 111, 112

Federal Rules of Evidence, 164
Feeley, Malcolm, 45, 78, 121, 189
Feldman, Noah, 150
Fellheimer v. Middlebury College, 126
Fifth Amendment, 68, 160
Finegan, Sharon, 158, 159
Flock corporation, 65
Floyd, George, 63
Fourth Amendment, 68, 160

Garland, David, 173
Genovese, Kitty, 55
gig surveillance economy, 66
Gillibrand, Kirsten, 120
González, Thalia, 130
Goodell, Roger, 117
Goss v. Lopez, 126
Gruber, Aya, 182
Guardian Angels, 2, 32, 61, 64, 71, 156

hack-backs, 144
Haddican, Bernard, 123, 124
Henry I, 29, 131, 172
Henry II, 29
Heritage Foundation, 17
Herrick, Carissa, 45
Heydari, Farhang, 158, 180
Hine, Kelly, 191
Horn, Joe, 149, 151, 153

Index

245

Joh, Elizabeth, 54, 59, 60, 66
Johnson, Lyndon, 15

Kahan, Dan, 62, 63
Kesan, Jay, 166
Ku Klux Klan, 32, 36, 136, 137

Landes, William, 97, 105, 191
Langbein, John, 131
Lavender Panthers, 33, 140
Lee, Cynthia, 150, 151, 152, 167
Leider, Robert, 18
license plate readers, 65, 66, 189
Locke, John, 14
Logan, Wayne, 66, 67, 162, 190
Lynch, William, 36

Majuca, Ruperto, 166
mandated reporter laws, 162
Mannheimer, Michael, 152
Martin, Trayvon, 148
mass incarceration, 5, 6, 16, 24, 26, 27, 38, 42, 43, 81, 98, 182, 193
Matthews v. Eldridge, 126, 164
McMichael, Gregory, 148, 152, 153
McMichael, Travis, 148, 152, 153
merchant codes, 145
merchant's privilege laws, 67
#MeToo movement, 127
Minutemen, 2, 32, 63, 64, 72
Model Penal Code, 15, 113, 173
Model Standards of Conduct for Mediators, 164
Mothers Against Drunk Driving (MADD), 20

Nagin, Daniel, 69
natural law, 10, 13, 14, 16, 23
neighborhood watch, 2, 7, 32, 60, 61, 64, 66, 67, 71, 72, 81, 82, 142, 146, 148, 150, 156, 157, 158, 159
Nextdoor app, 65, 67
night watchmen, 30
Nunsegger, Paul, 120, 121

O'Hear, Michael, 95, 96
Olympic neighborhood Business Watch, 57
opportunistic blackmail, 104, 105, 106
over-criminalization, 17, 18, 28, 190, 191

pedophile hunters, 143, 144
Perverted Justice, 143
Pfaff, John, 43
Pinkerton, 31, 32, 38, 140
Plymouth colony, 25
Posner, Richard, 97, 105, 191
Private Enforcement of Law, The, 191

private enforcers, 146, 152
procedural justice, 92, 94, 95, 96, 100, 116, 129, 130
Process Is the Punishment, 45
progressive prosecutors, 8, 16, 19, 26, 52

racism in the criminal justice system, 40, 67, 154, 155, 193
Reagan, Ronald, 47
restitutive theory of criminal justice, 172
restorative justice, 2, 12, 48, 52, 80, 120, 127, 128, 129, 130, 131, 132, 170, 171, 172, 174, 175, 183, 184, 188, 192
retributive, 22, 23, 24, 108, 109, 111, 114, 115, 132, 143, 161, 184
Rice, Ray, 117, 118, 119, 121
Rittenhouse, Kyle, 12, 136, 147, 148, 149, 150, 152, 153, 167
Robinson, Paul, 20, 35, 135, 136, 139, 153, 165, 166
Robinson, Sarah, 35, 135, 136, 139, 153, 165, 166
Roosevelt, Theodore, 37

San Francisco vigilante committee, 34
SHADOW VIGILANTES, 35, 135, 165
shaming punishments, 27, 142, 192
Shapiro, Richard, 61
Shasta County study, 21
Shearing, Clifford, 57
Sklansky, David, 58, 70, 160
slave patrols, 31
stand-your-ground laws, 150
Statute of Winchester, 30
Stenning, Phillip, 57
Stoughton, Seth, 31
Stuntz, William, 174
Sulkowicz, Emma, 120, 121, 125

Target forensic lab, 56
Theodore Roosevelt, 37
Title IX, 127
To Catch a Predator, 143
Trump, Donald, 127

university disciplinary proceedings, 4, 48, 124, 125, 126, 133, 165
utilitarian, 16, 22, 23, 24, 26, 46, 72, 103, 104, 106, 107, 108, 111, 115, 143, 161, 172

Victim–Offender Mediation, 132
victims' rights movement, 47
vigilante, 2, 3, 8, 12, 32, 34, 35, 36, 38, 42, 61, 72, 74, 118, 133, 134, 135, 136, 137, 139, 140, 141, 142, 143, 144, 153, 165, 166, 192
moral, 137, 166

vigilante (cont.)
  on the frontier, 35
  regulators, 35
  shadow, 135, 153

Wackenhut prisons, 6
Walmart, 178, 179

Watson, Deshaun, 122
Weinstein, Jack, 43, 44
white hat hacking, 64

Zehr, Howard, 128
Zimmerman, George, 12, 136, 141, 148, 149, 150, 152, 153, 167

Printed in the United States
by Baker & Taylor Publisher Services